MARKETING
PRINCIPLES AND PRACTICE

Dennis Adcock, Ray Bradfield,
Al Halborg and Caroline Ross

Coventry Business School, Coventry University

PITMAN
PUBLISHING

PITMAN PUBLISHING
128 Long Acre, London WC2E 9AN

A Division of Longman Group UK Limited

First published in Great Britain 1993
Reprinted 1993 (twice)

British Library Cataloguing in Publication Data
A catalogue entry for this book is available
from the British Library.

ISBN 0-273-60146-6

Printed in England by Clays Ltd, St Ives plc
Typeset in Palatino by 📐 Tek-Art, Addiscombe,
Croydon, Surrey.

MARKETING
PRINCIPLES AND PRACTICE

CONTENTS

PREFACE

This book was inspired by the increasing numbers of students from all backgrounds choosing to take a course in marketing as part of their university studies.

The choices open to engineers, designers, lawyers and many others have been widened by the move to modular programmes in many colleges and universities, although courses with a marketing input are being developed in other ways. Perhaps the reasons for this interest lies with the subject itself, but equally it could be a reflection of the increasing awareness of how marketing touches all our lives, and how important good marketing can be to commercial and personal success.

Whatever the reasons, the authors, who are all practitioners currently teaching the subject, saw a need for an introductory course at a level suitable for undergraduates coming to the subject for the first time. The book is also suitable for post-experience students who are not only studying the subject, but also, by virtue of their jobs are what are now being called part-time marketers: that is, anyone whether meeting the final customer or not, whose efforts contribute to the success of an organisation. That is, *everyone!*

The book is structured to be used in a single academic year, but it can, of course, be used in other ways. The five main sections start with the environment and how customers behave, moving through information and research, to the marketing offering, promotion of that offering, and finally some of the key issues of marketing in action. The emphasis on practical examples in the text is deliberate, and these are supported by short case studies and questions for testing.

The aim is to provide readers with a concise and reasonably comprehensive view of marketing, in a form that is readily accessible, both to those who only tackle one course in the subject, and to those who then wish to take their studies further. A Lecturer's Guide containing teaching notes on the case studies and questions, and also comments on the chapters in this book, is available from the publishers.

There are many people who have helped make this book a reality. Our thanks to the students at Coventry who made helpful suggestions on the first drafts; to our colleagues, both full-time lecturers and part-timers who used the early material and cases and provided constructive feedback; and to our publishers for their patience. The most important thanks, however, go to Marie Hooper who typed and amended the text with supreme efficiency and great patience, and to Jean, Gail and Elsie who had their workload increased while Marie typed the book. Our thanks also to Danny O'Meara of the Coventry University Teaching Resources Unit for his diagrams and artwork. And last, but by no means least, thanks to our families, who put up with the stresses as deadlines approached and writing took over.

Dennis Adcock, Al Halborg
Caroline Ross and Ray Bradfield
March 1993

1

WHAT IS MARKETING?

Marketing involves everyone

Marketing is a subject that touches all our lives. In the western world we have now realised a position where there are many products available and we continually have to choose which ones to buy. Perhaps you chose Frosties to eat for breakfast when there are many cereals available; or you purchased a pair of jeans in Top Shop rather than from some other store. There are many other similar decisions each of us make every day. If you were asked why you made that particular purchase you would probably have a very good reason such as Frosties taste better, or Top Shop had a sale on and the jeans were good value.

What other factors may have influenced your choice? Clearly the Frosties had to be available in your local supermarket at a price that was not too outrageous. There is, however, the more basic choice of eating cereal for breakfast rather than having a can of Coke and a doughnut. Of course, if you were a doughnut manufacturer you would perhaps be wondering if you could change peoples' habits so that they bought doughnuts rather than Frosties for breakfast. You would also be looking at the cost of such a programme and how you might get the best return for your efforts.

The purpose of marketing

In order to prosper all business organisations have continuously to encourage their potential customers to buy their products, and they must achieve this as efficiently as possible. This is the purpose of *marketing*. It is thus not confined to advertising and selling, but covers everything related to what was once described as providing,

'The right product, in the right place, at the right price, and at the right time'.

What is right? From the marketing viewpoint it is right if it gets the desired response from the potential customer, efficiently and ethically. As customers we expect to have a choice when we spend our money, and we can also choose not to spend any money at all by choosing not to buy a product. When we do decide to buy, then an exchange takes place. Money is exchanged for the chosen product and hopefully both parties will feel happy with their side of the bargain. Usually, in addition to the actual money spent, it is necessary to invest time to study a catalogue or to visit the shop or other selling outlet, and at times deciding what to buy can involve discussion with family or friends.

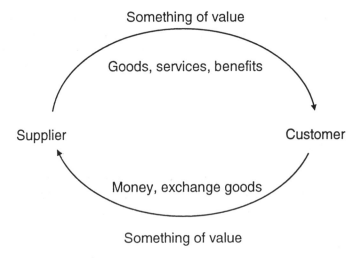

Fig 1.1 A simple exchange process

A specific purchase also means the sacrifice of not being able to buy something else with the money spent (the opportunity cost of the purchase).

Marketing definitions

A supplier of a product or service has to make it available to their customers when and where those customers want it. This involves many aspects of business, but it also leads us towards a definition of marketing. One of the most basic comes from the American author of marketing textbooks, Philip Kotler.

> **Marketing is the human activity directed at satisfying needs and wants through an exchange process.**   (Kotler, 1980)

Since 1980 Kotler's definition has become longer.

> **Marketing is a social and managerial process by which individuals and groups obtain what they want and need through creating, offering, and exchanging products of value with others.**   (Kotler, 1991)

The major addition is the phrase *'of value'* and this will be explored as the subject develops.

There are many other useful and equally acceptable definitions. The one preferred by Chartered Institute of Marketing (CIM) is:

> **Marketing is the Management process responsible for identifying, anticipating and satisfying customers' requirements profitably.**

You can see these definitions are applicable to either the purchase of jeans or the buying of a breakfast cereal. Both Kotler and CIM focus on the 'profitable' exchange with the supplier. In this context 'profitable' is not used in the accounting sense, but as a wider measure to show that both parties feel they have benefited from the exchange.

As in other specialist subjects, certain terms are used in marketing which have acquired specific meanings. This specialist terminology includes words such as 'needs' and 'wants', and phrases such as 'management process'. These then become useful as concepts necessary to the proper understanding of the subject. You will find, particularly in articles on the subject, other terms which have become part of the jargon associated with the subject. The use of these terms will be as far as possible avoided in this text.

The exchange process

Economic prosperity and progress is only possible when individuals and societies have developed ways by which products can be exchanged. At the simplest level this would be restricted to exchanges with near neighbours. Unfortunately they were often producing the same things as you any way. To increase the variety of products available meant establishing a meeting place where people with things to exchange could gather and offer them. This is only sufficient providing the variety of available products is matched by the demands of those present. It would not be suitable for the person who has a pig and wants some wheat unless he is able to find someone with wheat who wants a pig.

Economic progress is thus restricted until a means of exchange can be established. This could be a valued product such as salt (paid to Roman soldiers and from which the word salary is derived), tea, precious stones or something made out of precious metal . . . or the tokens of value that we accept as money. The use of money allows the person to sell the pig on a day when there is someone wanting to buy a pig and buy the wheat on another day when there is someone wanting to sell wheat. It also allows a very precise relative value to be placed on different products depending upon size, availability and demand. Thus if there are few pigs available the person with the pig may find that what he receives in exchange for it will buy several bags of wheat. Alternatively the person could find that to buy one bag of wheat it will be necessary to sell two pigs.

The demand and availability for some products such as wheat, or other seasonal products such as vegetables, may well depend upon the weather, with the result that the price may vary significantly from month to month. Other products will not be affected in this way, which means that an accepted price for these products can become known by both sellers and buyers. This makes it unnecessary for the buyer to visit the market, allowing goods to be purchased through intermediaries or dealers.

An increase in the numbers of markets and availability of a convertible currency provides individuals with the possibility of buying from many more potential suppliers. It also provides the suppliers with the possibility of selling to many more potential customers. But it means that suppliers and customers become increasingly separated: not only by physical distance and time, but also by culture and attitude. Marketing, by focusing on the exchange process, ensures these links are both effective and efficient.

What is a market?

Essentially a market could be considered to be a meeting place for making exchanges and where it is accepted that the relative value of different products is established. In practice, to be effective a market needs to have rules and a procedure for their enforcement. This is the basis for the definition used by economists.

The word market is also often used to mean the individuals or organisations who are or could be purchasers of a particular product. Very often this can cause confusion. For instance, the UK car market could mean the 12 million car users or more usually the 1.5 million or so new cars which are purchased in any one year. It is important always to use the word carefully so its meaning is clear and ensure that you understand how it is being used when you come across it in your reading.

The origins of marketing

The technical developments of the first decades of this century provided great opportunities for businesses, since the demand for the new products available exceeded supply. These products included the equipment needed to supply electricity to every house, as well as appliances such as vacuum cleaners, refrigerators and washing machines, radio receivers, and of course, motor vehicles. This demand provided business for companies manufacturing the tools and equipment needed to make these products, and in turn employment opportunities for the workforce. The resulting economic growth was interrupted in Europe by World War I (1914–1918) but continued unabated in the USA.

The result was expansion of production, and by the mid-1920s production was beginning to exceed demand. For the first time customers began to find they were being offered a real choice by different manufacturers. Suppliers responded by increasing their selling efforts. The benefits offered to the customer by the products began to be emphasised. Business had moved from the *production era*, when businesses needed to focus on increasing production, to the *selling era*, when businesses needed to focus on increasing their sales relative to their competitors. Unfortunately, in the USA production continued to exceed sales in many markets, and this was one of the many factors which led to the crash of 1929 and the Great Depression that followed it.

The subsequent recovery was followed by World War II (1939–1945), which again changed the balance, with demand again exceeding supply until the mid 1950s. Then as manufacturing grew worldwide it began to be realised by the managements of the most effective, mature companies in the USA that the selling approach was not the answer to moving larger amounts of products. They saw that in order to succeed in an increasingly competitive environment it was important to understand and respond to the needs of customers. As a result these companies began to move into the *marketing era*. To do this they began to apply the various concepts of marketing which had been developed at the University of Wisconsin and the Harvard Business School since the early 1900s. These ideas were to become an integral part of what became known as modern management training.

By the early 1960s it was clear that business in the UK was becoming increasingly uncompetitive by world standards. One of the reasons was believed to be the shortage of trained managers. The remedy was seen to be the introduction of formal management training courses like those which had been developed in the USA. Marketing was thus initially taught as part of these courses.

Subsequently, the competitive situation for businesses in the UK has become increasingly like that of the USA. As markets have become global, marketing has become even more important. Because of this the subject is increasingly being included in courses for engineers, designers and many others who are not training to be marketing specialists.

Marketing as a business philosophy

The word 'marketing' has two distinct meanings in terms of modern management practice. These are:

(a) the specific specialist *functions* of marketing carried out within many organisations.

(b) an approach or *concept* which can be used as the guiding philosophy for all the activities of an organisation.

This concept is one area where marketing touches every part of an organisation. Peter Drucker once wrote 'There is only one valid definition of business purpose: to create a customer'. At its simplest if you do not have any customers for the product or service your organisation offers, then there is no reason for continuing existence.

As far back as 1776, Adam Smith, the father of modern economics wrote:

Consumption is the sole end and purpose of all production and the interests of the product ought to be attended to only so far as it may be necessary for promoting those of the customer.

Everyone in an organisation should be required to understand the final customer for their efforts, and thus to have a *customer focus* in their job. A marvellous article by N W (Red) Pope entitled 'Mickey Mouse Marketing' looked at the success of the Walt Disney organisation. Disney have a very positive attitude and their own terminology.

At Disney if your job has you interfacing with public (customers) in any way whatsoever, you're 'on stage'. If your work is not public interfacing you're 'backstage'. One is not better than the other. That is emphasised. No little insignificant 'jobs'. It takes many people, doing many types of jobs to 'put on the show'.

Disney know the way to successful shows is centred on satisfying the paying public. The recent launch and initial results for EuroDisney could show that the organisation has forgotten some of the lessons known to the late Walt Disney. However, it will be interesting to watch the changes made to EuroDisney to see how they respond to the correct problems and improve the benefits to the paying public.

While Adam Smith was concentrating on manufactured products, in the case of the Disney organisation the 'product' is less tangible: perhaps it is the enjoyable experience when visiting Disneyland. The marketing concept can be extended further into all kinds of 'products'. For instance a charity such as 'Save the Children Fund' also markets itself. The 'product' is the feeling you have after making a donation, so that even in this situation a real exchange is taking place between the giver and the charity.

The foregoing example illustrates the relevance of a Marketing approach to activities and sectors that are far-removed from the stereotype 'cornflake' market ... the marketing concept may have been spawned in the fmcg (fast moving consumer goods) field, but it has in recent years gained currency in both the industrial and service field, the public sector and the voluntary sector.

If 'customers' are those that use, consume, buy or recommend a product or service, then clearly most organisations will need to maintain customer relationships, often with a variety of different customers. Table 1.1 demonstrates that customers come in many different guises and may be described differently by organisations in different fields. The broad common factor is that they require special treatment from the provider. A customer-orientated approach can therefore apply equally to a food manufacturer or a public sector organisation.

Table1.1
Who is the Customer

BUYER	SPONSOR	PATIENT
CUSTOMER	PATRON	PUPIL
CONSUMER	SUBSCRIBER	PARENT
USER	SUPPORTER	MOTORIST
RECIPIENT	MEMBER	PASSENGER
ADVISER	COLLEAGUE	GUEST
CLIENT	CO-WORKER	DELEGATE
ACCOUNTANT	VIEWER	TOURIST
CONTRACTOR	READER	SHOPPER
DISTRIBUTOR	LISTENER	HOUSEHOLD
AGENT	LENDER	TAXPAYER
RETAILER	BANKER	RESIDENT
STOCKIST	APPLICANT	RATEPAYER
FACTOR	PROSPECT	VOTER

The implications of marketing

There are two implications of the marketing concept as a focus for an organisation. First, it encourages organisations to ask the right questions, and second, it assists the integration of company activities.

An organisation will initially ask the basic questions:

- Where are we now?
- Where do we want to get to?
- How do we get there?

Obviously the analysis of current position is vital, but it is important to consider such issues for the future and not be obsessed with the past. A marketer will ask questions specifically aimed at the future, and place them firmly from the customers' perspective. The questions asked by a marketer will therefore be :

Who are our existing/potential customers?
What are their current and future needs?
How can we satisfy these needs?
- Can we offer a product/service the customer would value ?
- Can we communicate with customers ?
- Can we deliver a competitive product or service ?
Why should customers buy from us?

It is the responsibility of marketing management to find answers to these questions, and thereby develop solutions to market needs, within the constraints of the organisation's resources and policies. Especially important is the final question, which recognises customers in most markets have many products from which to choose.

To answer this question we need first to understand the environments in which all organisations operate (*see* Chapters 3 and 4). We also need to develop a basic knowledge of how people behave when making buying decisions (Chapter 5).

Applying the marketing concept

Organisations applying the marketing concept will be committed to:

- a customer orientation;
- co-ordinated efforts by all parts of the organisation; and
- profitability, rather than sales volume.

Customer orientation has already been touched on – everyone in the organisation must aim to serve the customer whether directly or indirectly. This is customer sovereignty: it places the customer effectively at the top of the organisation chart. The substance and credibility of this customer-centredness will daily be put to the test in all sorts of ways (e.g. how long to answer the telephone, promptness of delivery, product quality). The performance and integration of all these activities requires management and training. They cannot be left to chance.

Co-ordination of efforts will itself relate directly to management and the commitment of the organisation to marketing. Marketing management is really all about the co-ordination of customer-directed activities. Particularly, good practice and competitive pressure should ensure that a customer focus prevails throughout the organisation. It must be present during each and every activity, **rather** than fall casualty to the sectional interests and biases of individuals or functional groups. For resource reasons, too, marketing activities should be tightly and smoothly scheduled, without undue delays, cost-overruns or other problems that would affect profitability and competitiveness.

The acid-test of marketing orientation will be how consistently *over time* the organisation manages to abide by these conditions ... good marketing requires a stable or improving relationship with customers over a period of time. Marketing is therefore future-orientated and dependant on performance, rather than on promises or former achievements. The issues of good marketing practice can be summarised as:

- choosing and targeting appropriate customers;
- positioning your offering;
- interacting with those customers;
- controlling the marketing effort; and
- continuity of performance;

The marketing concept requires commitment to customer satisfaction, and a flexibility to respond to customer requirements and changes in the commercial environment. In turn this may require following policies that are guided by key principles consistent with good marketing.

While marketing is probably too new to have developed a 'general theory', and in any case markets are too dynamic and diverse to support formula approaches, many writers have commented on the key principles underlying successful marketing. As an example, John Howard, an American marketer, proposes that a structured approach rests on six 'pillars' of good practice, which are outlined in Table 1.2. (*Note*: Most of Howard's 'pillars' or key principles have been mentioned already, though the term 'market segmentation' may be unfamiliar – basically, it involves dividing a market into 'segments' or sub-markets, for targeting and planning purposes. It will be discussed in detail in Chapter 6.)

Table 1.2
Howard's pillars of the marketing concept

The marketing concept

1 Generic Product Definition
2 Customer Orientation
3 Marketing Information
4 Market Segmentation
5 Integrated Marketing
6 Long -Term Viewpoint

(Source: Adapted from J Howard, Marketing
Management, Analysis and Planning, Irwin, 1963.)

An alternative, though compatible, set of key principles is offered by Hugh Davidson, a British writer, who argues that successful marketing requires the application of POISE. That is, marketing should be:

P – Profitable
O – Offensive (rather than defensive)
I – Integrated
S – Strategic (= future-orientated)
E – Effective (it gets **results**)

The common thread in these observations, and those of other writers, is the recognition that marketing has to be consciously planned and integrated. Organisationally, marketing involves a set of activities that has to be managed. The management process involved might be generalised as the following sequence:

1 Research and Information	NB	
2 Analysis	}	Informed
3 Plans and forecasts		decisions
4 Organisation & co-ordination	}	Integration
5 Implementation		
6 Control	}	Responsiveness
7 Review		Results – orientation

The process might be viewed as a continuous cycle of managed activities, guided by key principles such as those presented by Howard and Davidson. The management tasks involved would be broadly the same for all functions within marketing: good planning and management are seen as critical ingredients for success throughout.

Functions within marketing

Marketing is a broad functional area that encompasses a number of sub-functions. These sub-functions will range from more familiar activities such as sales and advertising, to specialist fields such as merchandising, research, product development, distribution, and customer service.

In practice these specialist activities will be planned and integrated within an organisation's marketing programme. The exact mix of activities will vary according to the demands of the target market and will be the subject of major strategic decisions by marketing management.

There is a debate between the merits of *product* management and *market* management. In the former a product champion works to maximise objectives through the controllable variables available to his organisation. The latter focuses on a specific market or market segment and aims to offer the best mix of products to meet the requirement of this group. The merits of these different approaches will be discussed in more detail later, with respect to marketing organisation. There are also organisations with no formal marketing department but to succeed in a dynamic market the key functions are performed either by specialists or by managers who intuitively understand market requirements. Also, everyone in an organisation needs to be aware of the importance of the customers of the organisation, which leads to the concept of part-time marketers, discussed in the next chapter.

Conclusion

You will already be able to grasp the basic concept behind marketing. While there are many complex techniques and models used by sophisticated exponents the basic concept is really very simple. It focuses on customers, and involves interacting with those customers and controlling and developing profitable exchanges over time. Tom Peters put profit into perspective:

> **Long-term profit equals revenue from continuously happy customer relationships minus cost.**

Marketing is therefore much more than selling, although some aspects of persuasion and influence to encourage the chosen customers to demand your product is inevitably present. Satisfying customer needs over time, but not at any cost, is an ideal but this requires that they are customers of your organisation, not your competitors. The obvious problem is that profit is required in an exchange, or, at least, a situation where income from all sources exceeds expenditure even for so called not-for-profit organisations. In addition there are wider ethical and moral issues discussed in Chapter 23. Advertising is a powerful persuader and the large range of tools available to skilled marketers make them adept at creating environments which favour their offerings. But business today is not sales at any cost. A prominent US businessman once suggested:

> **There is a new bottom line for business – social approval. Without it, economic victory be pyrrhic indeed.**

You might like to consider whether this is the true goal of a marketing-led organisation.

References

Davidson, J H, *Offensive Marketing*, Cassell, 1972.

Drucker, P, *The Practice of Management,* Pan, 1968.

Howard, J, *Marketing Management, Analysis and Planning*, Irwin, 1963.

Kotler, P, *Marketing Management, Analysis, Planning Implementation and Control 7th Edn*, Prentice-Hall, 1991.

Kotler, P, *Marketing Management 4th Edn,* Prentice-Hall, 1980.

Peters, T, *Thriving on Chaos*, MacMillan, 1988.

Pope, N W (Red), *Mickey Mouse Marketing, American Banker,* 25 July 1979.

Smith, Adam, *The Wealth of Nations,* 1776.

Case study: the Cola wars

The per capita consumption of colas in the UK is reported to have reached 30 litres per year in 1990. This makes it a market worth £1.7 billion and accounts for over 40 per cent of all carbonated soft drinks. This is high in a European context though low compared to the USA, but a very significant market notwithstanding.

Currently Coca-Cola outsells Pepsi Cola by more than two to one, and a similar dominance is shown by Diet Coke over Diet Pepsi, with Diet products contributing 40 per cent of the Cola volume in both companies.

Advertising in main media in 1990 was:

Coke + Diet Coke	£9.7 mn
Pepsi + Diet Peps	£6.3 mn

If the 'Pepsi Challenge' is to be believed, consumers actually prefer the taste of Pepsi, but the sales figures dramatically favour Coke. But Pepsi have a 1p a can advantage on their 1992 list price to support their product.

The problem for Pepsi is therefore: why does Coke continue to do so well? Is it the heavy advertising spend or is it something else?

Both products are well marketed in a highly competitive market. In order to answer the question above it would be good to start collecting as much comparative data as possible about the two products. This market is well researched and regular reports are published so it should not be too difficult. But as you will see, facts alone will not answer the question. However, in debating the issues you should be able to look at the role of marketing in the financial success of both cola products.

2

PRODUCTS, SERVICES
AND BENEFITS

Introduction

The times shown on this timetable are not the times when the trains will leave: rather they are the times before which the trains will not leave.

INDIAN TRAIN TIMETABLE.

In the introduction to this book, marketing was described in terms of a profitable exchange between a buyer and a supplier. Both must be satisfied otherwise there will not only be little chance of further sales (repeat business) but there will also be a good chance that the dissatisfied buyer will tell friends, family or other contacts. This publicity could affect other people, who would decide not to buy our product/service. In fact 'word of mouth' comment from someone you respect or trust is one of the most powerful influences on attitudes. Positive comments are much more important than millions of pounds spent on TV commercials, negative ones can undo a lot of what you are trying to build in support of your product. This will be discussed further in the chapter on promotional planning (Chapter 17).

The opening quotation is an excellent example of not offering benefits that cannot be achieved. Train services in the UK are provided by British Rail who on 3 May, 1992 introduced a passenger's charter. This is a statement of BR's commitment to provide a high quality service for all customers. They offer :

- A safe, punctual and reliable train service.
- Clean stations and clean trains.
- Friendly and efficient service.
- Clear and up-to-date information.
- A fair and satisfactory response when things go wrong.

It would be interesting to discuss the benefits offered by British Rail and compare them to the expectations of a train passenger in India. This can then be extended into the operations and resources necessary for BR to avoid creating dissatisfied customers.

It is important that any product or service offered satisfies its customers by fulfilling the needs of those customers. However, it is equally important that there is no confusion on the benefit offered. The Indian train service may not fulfil all needs of train passengers in India. But, more importantly, it is very clear what is not being offered, so customers do not have hopes raised unrealistically. All the promotion in the world rarely sells a bad product *twice*. There is a logical progression from people's needs for travel, into wanting to travel by train. The individual product or service, such as *the 9.10 from Euston to Birmingham* is just one 'product' offered to try to satisfy a potential demand.

Products and services

You will have already realised from these comments that this book is about suppliers trying to *market* their products or services successfully to customers. The products we shall consider will include existing products already on sale, where the requirement is to develop sales and keep the product up to date, as well as new products and how to develop and launch these successfully. In fact there are three stages of marketing.

1 Pre-consumption, when the goal is to create or manage expectations.
2 During consumption, with an aim of producing customer satisfaction.
3 After consumption, where the aim is to maintain or develop the relationship with customers, to ensure good reports and future repeat sales.

(*Note*: 'product' is a general term used to cover any output from the capabilities of a supplier. Products and services will be treated as interchangeable because a service is only a product without a tangible core. We do not want to stray too far into jargon so the difference between products and services is best illustrated by the following example from one of the authors.)

I own a car. This obviously is a product, very tangible; I can touch it, polish it, put petrol into it and I am very happy if it is reliable.

I use it to get to work and of course it is important that I get to work on time.

One day I could not start my car so I took a taxi to work. This made use of a service. I know I could also touch the taxi but it is not the same as my own car. There is no tangible 'product' for me and yet I derived the same benefit – getting to work on time – albeit that in this case the service was rather more expensive.

Of course there are many reasons for owning a car but I do not own it to leave it sitting on the drive for my neighbours to see. I own it to enable me to travel easily to work, to see friends, to do the shopping and many other things. Some people do not own cars but they have the same needs. They probably do not use taxis on a regular basis – although I know one old lady who does. Most use other means of transport, buses, trains, bicycles, even walking. So when I drive my own car we have:

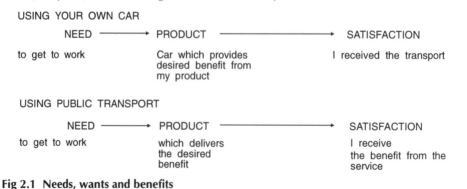

Fig 2.1 **Needs, wants and benefits**

This example should illustrate that the only difference between a product and a service could lie in the ownership. It does not occur in respect to the benefit people receive, only in the way it is satisfied. One of the key roles of marketing is to identify customer needs and express these needs in terms of both the benefits to customers and the product/service provided by the suppliers.

Marketing myopia

In a famous article in 1960 Theodore Levitt then a lecturer at the Harvard Business School, asked the key question that all organisations must answer, 'What business are we really in?'

Levitt gave examples of organisations that had failed to understand the benefits their customers derived from the product offered. In the case of the American railroads, for example, he argued:

> The railroads did not stop growing because the needs for passengers and freight transportation declined. That grew. The railroads are in trouble today, not because the need was filled by others (cars, trucks, airplanes, even telephones), but because it was not filled by the railroads themselves. They let others take customers away from them because they assumed themselves to be in the railroad business rather than in the transportation business. The reason they defined their industry incorrectly was because they were *railroad-orientated*; they were product-orientated not *customer-orientated*.

Later we will take this orientation further, from customer to total market orientation. Levitt's achievement was to get individual businesses to look at themselves from the customer's viewpoint and assess their offerings in terms of customer benefits. This includes not only the basic product but the added features and service which make up the **total product** which is effective in satisfying customers (*see* Fig 2.3).

	Ineffective	Effective
Inefficient	Die quickly	Survive
Efficient	Die slowly	Thrive

Fig 2.2 The contrast between efficiency and effectiveness

(Adapted from R. Brown, 'Marketing – a function and philosophy', *Quarterly Review of Marketing*, Spring 1987.)

Effectiveness comes from meeting customer needs with a total product offering. Even a relatively inefficient company which is effective at creating and keeping customers will survive. Companies who fail to satisfy customers are classed, ineffective, and they will die over time.

Total products

Even if we are able to answer Levitt's question, and understand that airlines are substitutes for trains, and trains or taxis for private cars, we still have not fully understood everything that makes up a *total product*. Again it may best to start with an example.

> A Mars Bar is a good example of a product widely accepted and as popular now as it ever was. The ingredients panel states that it contains[1]
>
> > MILK CHOCOLATE, GLUCOSE SYRUP, SUGAR, SKIMMED MILK POWDER, HYDROGENATED VEGETABLE FAT, FAT-REDUCED COCOA POWDER, MILK FAT, MALT EXTRACT, WHEY POWDER, SALT, EGG WHITE, HYDROLYSED MILK PROTEIN, and FLAVOURING.
>
> These are the ingredients we consume when we eat a Mars Bar. We are not told the actual proportion of chocolate to milk fat but a clever food scientist could make an acceptable analysis, and further could probably make a good copy of a Mars Bar. The copy would offer a similar degree of enjoyment to anyone eating it.
>
> Some 20 years ago a rival confectionary firm (Cadbury's) did in fact develop a product called 'Aztec', which marketing research showed to be comparable to Mars in many ways. The product was launched, and as Cadbury's is a large company with wide resources it was easily able to persuade retail shops to buy the product. The trouble was that not enough consumers (members of the public) bought it from the retailers to make it financially viable. You have probably never heard of Aztec because Cadbury's stopped making it after only a short time. Now why did Aztec fail against Mars in what is after all a very large market?
>
> It was not the basic product – they were very similar. Nor the price, nor the availability. It was the other features: brand name, packaging styling, quality and most important *image*. We don't know if Mars helps you 'work, rest and play' but there are certainly some psychological features which are part of a Mars bar.
>
> [1] As this book was being completed Mars announced it was relaunching the MARS BAR with a revised recipe, the best ever chocolate, and a smoother centre. The ingredients above are from the new product. The Managing Director of MARS said 'we want to make the MARS BAR more appealing to existing consumers, particularly young adults and teenagers, and to bring lapsed users back into the fold.' The long running slogan 'Mars a day helps you work, rest and play' has also been dropped. The new advertising has yet to be broadcast.

It is also possible to go one stage further because in offering a product the supplier hopes customers will buy it in preference to other products.

The most obvious difference between products is sometimes thought, naively, to be price. But there are many examples of product which succeed in spite of higher prices. A few examples are set out opposite.

1 Fruit and vegetables in Sainsbury's supermarket are more expensive than my local market. Is it convenience of location that people pay extra for?
2 People hire televisions from Radio Rentals when it is 'cheaper' to buy. Is it the convenient way of spreading expenditure or the after sales service they value?
3 Company car purchasers buy from the Ford Motor Co and pay extra for Fordsure cover. Why do they pay the extra? Is it peace of mind they purchase with the extra warranty, or perhaps the warranty is an additional product which 'adds value' to the basic product?
4 A local carpet supplier is not the cheapest but offers free fittings. Is this the reason they get customers?

Perhaps you can think of other examples.

What is happening here is that products are being 'augmented' by additional features which are of value to some customers. In this book we call the different levels of additions the 'real product' and the 'total product'. It makes the product different and attractive and therefore the total product rather than just the price becomes relevant to the decision to buy. Chapter 12 will explore product issues in greater detail.

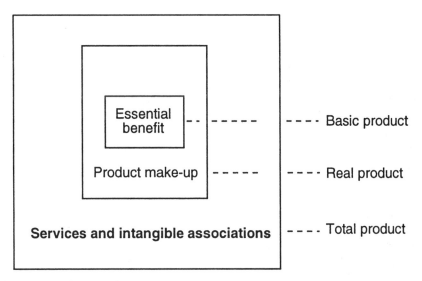

Fig 2.3 Three facets of the product

Exercise

Go into your local supermarket and find a product that is offered both as a manufacturers brand (e.g. Kelloggs, Maxwell House, Chum) and as a store's 'own label' product. Compare the product in every detail, design, pack size, price, value for money.

It is possible the 'own label' product offers a more cost efficient option. But both products sell regularly or they would not be given shelf space. Why do you think there are still customers who buy 'branded' shelf products?

What characteristics do you think describes
1 purchases of 'own label'
2 purchases of 'branded' products?

Think benefits

It is really important for marketers to be able to think like customers. The marketing function is the interface between organisations and their customers. Marketers reflect customers needs inwardly to others within their organisation as well as reflecting the company and its products outwardly to potential customers.

You could say the latter is the task of a salesperson, and of course you would be right, but marketing encompasses not only the direct sales push but also advertising, PR, packaging, and many other areas related to developing the right product at the right price, in the right place at the right time.

It is important to understand the difference between a product-orientated company, a sales-orientated company and a market orientated-company. A product orientation comes from organisations that 'know' their product is right. They work on their product in the belief that it is good enough to ensure somebody will buy it. They may be lucky but consider the example of Sir Clive Sinclair and his C5.

The Sinclair C5 Development

Sir Clive Sinclair is an electronics genius who has achieved a number of 'world firsts' including the executive pocket calculator (1972), and the microvision pocket TV (1977). In 1979 his main involvement was designing and developing a range of personal computers (including the very successful ZX Spectrum). Sir Clive is a world class inventor but he is very weak when it comes to marketing. He openly admits he does not believe in market research. He thinks a product should be developed and then a market created for it. This goes against the principles of marketing, which say that consumers' needs and wants should be determined, and then a product developed that will immediately fulfil them. This was one reason for his most notable marketing disaster, the C5. However, in 1992 he was back in the news launching an electric bicycle.

The development of the C5 electric car can be traced back to 1973 when various ideas for electric vehicles were considered. However, in 1979 preliminary investigations were started into the opportunity for a personal electric vehicle as a result of the energy crises which made the world more energy-conscious. In developing the C5, Sinclair failed to define any groups of potential customers. He did not determine whether there was a market opportunity, deciding instead to develop the product on his own convictions.

In relating the experience of the C5 to the procedure in new product development at the idea-generation stage, Sinclair failed to utilise external ideas . He preferred to have development kept very internal to the company, and this was a fundamental error. Also, the amount of emphasis on the different stages of development was peculiar. There seemed to be a huge emphasis on product development, but very small emphasis on idea generation, screening, concept development and testing. More time and effort should have been spent in these area. Test marketing was totally ignored, even though it may have been useful in sorting out problems that occurred after the national launch – in particular, problems of distribution. Results of test marketing may have induced changes that could have saved the vehicle. Specific areas of criticism in the C5 case can be listed as being:

- Actual development
- Badly-defined market
- Safety and performance aspects
- General marketing
- Lack of quantitative and qualitative research

For future products to be successful, Sinclair must pay more attention to the marketing orientation of his business. If he fails to do so, future developments may be subject to a great risk and possible failure. It may be too soon to pass judgement on the 1992 electric bicycle!

Orientation of a business

Businesses are often defined as *production*-orientated, *sales*-orientated or *marketing*-orientated. These are considered as stages along a progression from production through sales to marketing.

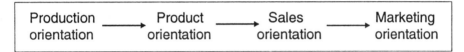

Fig 2.4 Business orientations

At the left hand end we have companies that concentrate on producing what they think customers want, like Sinclair. It is happening in many parts of the USSR today with companies that have no competition. If there is little choice for customers then those customers might purchase a product that is not quite what they require but is better than nothing at all. Certainly this attitude was prevalent in the UK nationalised industries and even now the local power and water monopolies leave us little choice for domestic supplies. You might take the view that the product is not too bad, but it is interesting to see the changes in the services offered by British Telecom now they are competing with Mercury for both business and domestic custom. You can now get itemised bills, credit card services with no surcharge, cheaper international calls, although you could counter this with having to pay for directory enquiries, a source that has historically been free. British Telecom is aware of customers and knows they have a choice in some matters. Here they have reacted to give customers what they seem to want. In other parts of the business, such as enquiries, British Telecom realise it is a need but one for which there are few alternatives. You could go to a library and look up in the directory, but that takes time and effort. It is easier to dial enquiries from your own phone and for this convenience BT charge. Interestingly, they do not yet charge for enquiry calls from public pay phones. The charge for enquiries does not make us warm to BT as a customer orientated, company but there have been significant changes in other services since competition was introduced.

It would be unfair to leave this section without some reference to successful product orientated companies. You will notice there is a difference between production and product orientation.

A company with a similar attitude to Sinclair is Sony of Japan. The founder, Masaru Ibuka, is also a brilliant inventor and he has said, 'Merchandising and marketing people cannot envisage a market that does not exist'. But where both he, and his commercially aware partner, Akio Morita, differ from Sir Clive Sinclair is that they purposely get out to meet potential consumers. They both deliberately visit places where people gather. They talk about benefits. It might be unusual for company chairmen of major international companies to do market research, but that is exactly how Morita found there was a need for a personal and portable tape player. He recognised a need, and in spite of scepticism from his marketing people proceeded to design the 'Walkman'. This success is well known.

However there will be many ideas developed by people who do not have the marketing vision of the Sony Chairman. Also some observers are speculating whether Sony will be able to maintain the momentum when the current chairman retires. Companies such as Polaroid and ICI have shown that success can breed marketing apathy.

Production orientation

We produce excellent, well-designed, quality products which are great value for money. Customers are sure to want our products.

With many companies the movement from production orientation occurs only when customers stop buying their products. A good, rigorous sales campaign is often seen as the answer, and hence the company adopts a sales orientation.

Sales orientation of the business accepts that we must promote our product aggressively, but usually the product already exists and it is the responsibility of the sales staff to identify suitable customers who might buy it. This does not mean salespeople are customer orientated, as that would involve starting with customer needs and not the product.

Sales orientation

We have a good product. However, in this competitive market we must push it hard to achieve our sales goals.

All the authors have extensive experience of selling and do not want to be unfair to the thousands of *good* salespeople throughout industry. Good sales staff understand the benefits their products offer and use these 'selling points' to convince customers. They also understand competition, as they are at the 'sharp end' of business and often their pay includes an element of commission on actual sales.

The case study on p 19 is reprinted from the Association of Graduates Career Advisory service booklet on selling as a career.

Selling is well described in this case study, emphasising the task involved. It is a logical development of the product orientation.

Selling orientation can emphasise one of two directions – a competitor focus or a customer focus. It may be enough to beat the competition. There are no prizes for being second in a sales negotiation. But if you win the contract, make the sale and see the sales graph rise there is satisfaction as described above. Kenichi Ohmae introduced the concept of a competitive triangle. This considers that a customer can choose between a number of different, maybe even dissimilar, products or services. Each customer will choose the one that best meets his/her needs and reject the others. If this is accepted it is enough that we

Job case study

Gary, a Plant Science Graduate working for a major pharmaceutical company as a Medical Representative, got his job through a specialist agency. He describes his work thus:

Within my own territory I have sole responsibility. I get a quarterly allowance for entertainment/meetings – how I spend this is up to me, but I am expected to get value for money.

I have large quantities of prescription only samples and free promotional material, which are also my responsibility. I also have a company car, film equipment, company stationery, etc. I work alone for most of the time. At the other times I am being field trained, attending sales meetings or being assisted by a colleague at a large promotional meeting.

My working hours are not defined, but on average I leave the house at 7.30–8.00 am (later if working near home) and get back about 5.00–6.00 pm. I have an hour for lunch, flexible, but usually 1.00 till 2.00 pm. I work a five-day week, but may do meetings or attend exhibitions in the evenings or Saturdays, for which I get extra pay.

I do not have to keep records of hours worked, it doesn't affect salary anyway. I spend Thursday evenings doing administration to be posted on Friday to my manager.

The job is not a calling – we do it for the money. It is not a doddle, so there is a high drop-out rate. We are expected to be very smart at all times. Promotion is limitless – our managing director started as a rep – but it must be earned by success, and not time served.

You need to get on with people, especially self-important ones, and to work on your own initiative. The ability to read minds is the most important asset possible. Being able to speak in public is essential, but it comes with practice anyway. You must be able to drive, and must have a clean licence when you start.

Major satisfaction is rare, and only once for me so far, when a doctor came up and thanked me for telling him about a drug because he saved someone's life with it. Most satisfaction comes from nice sales graphs with steep climbing lines on them, and therefore a healthier bank balance.

offer a better match than our competitors. (*see* Chapter 4 for more on the competitive triangle.)

However, customers' needs will change over time, whether for industrial or consumer products. Maybe we have persuaded a customer to buy our product because it offered the best price or because of some high pressure selling. Then, as soon as a product that is a better match for the customer's requirements is introduced they might drop us in favour of the new product. We have not earned much customer loyalty. If we have worked hard to develop our product to reflect customers' needs then they may not switch so readily. It is up to our company to be both competitor- and customer-orientated. This is called a marketing orientation. To return to the words of Kenichi Ohmae:

Competitive realities are only what you test possible strategies against. You define what you want to do in terms of customers.

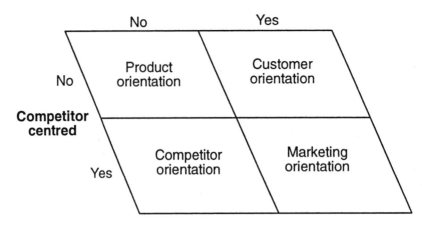

Fig 2.5 Market orientations

Question

Which of these statements best describes a marketing orientation?

- I *make* what I can *sell*
- I *sell* what I can *make*

The part-time marketer

We now should begin to understand the importance of a marketing orientation and the crucial need to start with the customer in defining the business we are in. However, it is very much more difficult to implant a marketing orientation in a company than it might seem. Marketing orientation does not occur because a company has a marketing department or because the Managing Director says so. It occurs when the customer notices the difference. It only happens when all people in an organisation measure themselves in terms of the benefits offered to customers. It does not matter whether you are on-stage or back-stage (Disney World) or, in marketing jargon, whether you are directly interfacing with a customer or not.

In most organisations a whole range of people have contact with customers. This would include the telephone operator, delivery driver, repair mechanic, or invoice clerk as well as the usual sales and marketing contacts. There is a humorous training film entitled 'Who lost the sale?' which shows among other events a delivery truck with a company logo being driven badly and affecting a buyer who deals with that company.

Many organisations are now running customer care programmes which include *all* members of staff. Those who are not directly involved in the marketing function can be called part-time marketers because they also have a key customer support role. Some organisations such as the 'Body Shop' do not have any specific marketing staff yet this company has been incredibly successful. Everyone is involved with customers and Anita Roddick, the founder, spends much of her time ensuring her products are right for her customers.

Customer relationships are particularly important if you are in a service organisation. We have already seen that one of the differences between a service and a product is the ownership of the core product. Another is that the production of the services takes place at the time of delivery. This was true with the taxi example. The taxi driver is not a marketer, but a taxi driver. In Coventry there are three or four major taxi firms, but because in the earlier example one particular firm gave prompt, efficient and cheerful service, when a taxi is next needed this will be remembered and that firm will get repeat business. This is a good example of a part-time marketer at work. A *marketing-orientated* organisation will be full of part-time marketers.

Conclusion

In this chapter we have studied the differences between products and services. There are three levels of products. First, the basic core, which is not present in a service. Then the tangible features of package and brand name; it is the role of marketing to make the basic core into a desirable product. This can be augmented by other features which add value to it and differentiate it from competitors.

In defining customer needs we must be aware of the benefits the customer receives from our product and our competitors' products. One famous quote by Theodore Levitt emphasised that:

Purchasing agents don't buy ¼-inch drills; they buy ¼-inch holes.

We don't know how many ways there are of making ¼-inch holes, but it is reasonable to suppose drills are not the only way. So we should define our market in terms of customer benefits.

We can take this further into the way we think about our products, as illustrated by Charles Revson of Revlon Cosmetics.

In the factory we make cosmetics; in the store we sell hope.

Marketing is about finding out what customers want, then producing it and packaging and promoting it. If we do this successfully it will be easier (although never easy) to sell the product.

Questions

1 Revson said 'In the store we sell hope' (*see above*). Compile a list of the factors that might be important to a customer for cosmetics.

2 Select an advertisement which describes benefits rather than product features and comment on its effectiveness.

3 Brand names are shorthand for products and their benefits. What might the following brand names convey to their customers:

- Mars
- Marlboro
- Federal Express
- Polaroid

4 In what ways is it difficult to convey the benefits of a service compared to those from a product?

References

British Rail Passengers' Charter, May 1992.
Brown, R, 'Marketing – a function and a philosophy', *Quarterly Review of Marketing*, Spring 1987.
Kotler, P and Armstrong, G, *Principles of Marketing*, 4th Edn, Prentice-Hall, 1989.
Levitt, T, 'Marketing myopia', *Harvard Business Review*, 1960.
Marks, A, 'Sinclair', *European Journal of Marketing*, January 1989.
Martin, P, 'How to succeed in business by really trying', *Sunday Times Magazine*, 5 November 1989.
Morita, A, *Made in Japan*, Dutton, 1986.
Ohmae Kenichi, *The Mind of the Strategist*, Pan, 1983.
Slater, A and Kolizeras, K, *Graduate Careers Information Book – Sales Careers Services Trust*, 1988.

Case study: what went wrong?

Chamberlain Drop Forgings Plc

Chamberlain's was founded one hundred years ago and in that time has established an international reputation for high quality drop forgings. They proudly claim to have the ability to supply any type of forging in any quality and any quantity, although much of their output is high-volume runs for Midland automotive and engineering companies.

Business has been becoming increasingly difficult for several years, and the increasing availability of Far East forgings at prices up to 50per cent below Chamberlains has reduced both margins and volume. However, the company has responded by installing the latest technology and by using computer techniques to speed up diemaking which is done in-house.

Nevertheless, Chamberlains are keen enough to respond to every new enquiry from any source. Early last year they were approached by Barry Barnes Engineering, a small recently established company in Yorkshire.

A Chamberlain sales representative called on Mr Barnes the following week to discuss requirements, specifications and, most important, price. In spite of the newness of the customer, Mr Barnes suggested he would require up to 10, 000 forgings in a full year. He also asked for normal credit terms, which were granted after the usual bank references proved acceptable. An immediate trial order of 500 was telephoned through and Chamberlains were pleased to offer this new customer expedited delivery within 14 days.

The problems started when it came to deliver the order. Chamberlain's driver arrived at 12.30 on Friday to find Barnes's warehouse closed, for lunch according to the notice. In fact the staff returned around 3.00 pm, having been celebrating the birthday of one of the employees. They were not very helpful and after a lot of argument the delivery driver unloaded the order, discovering the signature on the delivery notes was signed 'Mick the Mouse'.

No further orders were received for three months and to make things worse nor was any payment. When the sales representative contacted him, Mr Barnes apologised for the accounting problems of his company and immediately sent a cheque for the drop forgings, although he did not add on the delivery charge which is made on all orders under 1000. He wrote on the invoice that his total orders would exceed that, so he was not paying it. He also sent in another order for 500 forgings.

This order came at a time when Chamberlains were very busy with a major order for a European auto assembler. The sales representative telephoned Mr Barnes, who was away, but his secretary said she was sure it would be fine to deliver the order in four weeks' time. It was only a fortnight later that Mr Barnes was on the telephone wanting to know where his order was. He also complained that the price quoted on the confirmation of the order was higher than last time, and had the cheek to ask if distribution costs had been added on to the unit prices.

The sales representative explained the telephone call to Mr Barnes' secretary, agreeing four weeks for the order, and pointed out that the rate quoted on the earlier order was on the basis of 10, 000 units per year. He said current orders were nowhere near that level but offered a retrospective discount if they did indeed reach the figures discussed in the first meeting. He also told Mr Barnes that as a gesture of goodwill Chamberlains would write off the delivery charge for the first order but in future orders less than 1000 would be subject to a charge. He reiterated delivery would be possible in another two weeks' time.

Production of the Barnes order went to schedule, but when the distribution manager rang to arrange delivery a Barnes employee said they did not need them yet as there had been a hold up from one of their customers, so could they be stored for a couple of months until Mr Barnes got in touch. Things got a little heated in this call with a deal of bad language before the customer's employee put the phone down. When the sales representatives called to speak to Mr Barnes it was discovered he was abroad for three weeks. However, promptly at 8.00 am on the day Mr Barnes returned to his office the sales rep called and spoke about the order. He explained the deal he thought was agreed in the telephone call some five weeks earlier, agreeing delivery and other details. Obviously very upset, he was flabbergasted when Mr Barnes said if that was his attitude then Barnes did not want the order, anyway they had found a cheaper and more reliable source.

In spite of many subsequent attempts no further progress has been made and Mr Barnes refuses to answer any call from Chamberlains.

3

THE MARKETING ENVIRONMENT

Introduction

The marketing environment consists of a complex set of interacting forces and influences, outside the organisation, that can significantly affect the success of marketing activities and indeed can determine the future of the whole organisation. These interacting influences – whether economic, political, social or technological – are best viewed as forces beyond the direct control of the firm or organisation, and are thus often referred to as uncontrollable variables. They are to be contrasted with so-called controllable variables, which for marketing purposes are the policy decisions of a company with respect to issues within its own domain, such as price, product management, promotion, etc.

The significance of this distinction between controllable and uncontrollable variables is that marketing practitioners should concentrate on those matters that they can influence, but they need to understand the wider environment in order to deploy their marketing resources in the most cost-effective manner. The distinction is not complete or watertight, however, since it is necessary to stress that the controllable variables themselves are at least indirectly affected by the uncontrollable elements of the marketing environment. Simply stated, marketers should ensure that the controllable elements within their marketing plans reflect the realities of the uncontrollable variables within the marketing environment. Figure 3.1 illustrates this necessary relationship.

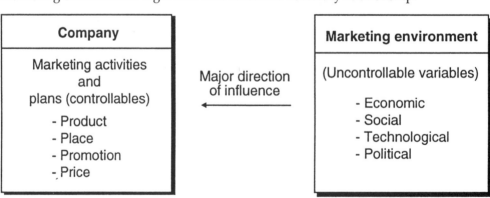

(*Note*: Controllables are partly influenced or controlled by the uncontrollables of the environment.)

Fig 3.1 Environmental influence

In this requirement to reflect and respond to environmental influences, a company's marketing activities are no different to company activities in other functional areas, such as production or finance. In practice all company activities should be guided by a sensitivity to the wider environment: no company is an island.

The marketer and the environment

Marketing as a function is basically all about matching the offerings of the organisation to the outside world, in particular, the marketplace. Not surprisingly, many functions within marketing, such as selling, product development and market research, concern themselves with issues, problems and opportunities outside the organisation, and focus on responding to outside events and circumstances. Indeed, Kotler identifies in this external role the need for marketers to develop an outside–in perspective, an ability to work on external cues and stimuli to the profit of the whole organisation. Another marketing writer of note, John Howard, emphasises the strategic role of marketing as 'the function by which the firm responds to changes in its environment.'

Response and sensitivity to the environment remains one of the acid-test indicators of success or failure in business in general, and in marketing in particular. The annals of business history and new product development are littered with instances of companies that have lost touch with their markets, misinterpreted or ignored tell-tale signs of change, or become blinded by previous successes and guided by some corporate inertia. Theodore Levitt's example of the US railroads, and the case of the ill-fated C5 electric car, have already been instanced in Chapter 2. While other examples will be developed later in the text, readers might find it instructive to examine a company report, or columnist commentaries on company results, and consider the significant influence on company performance that environmental issues may wield.

At first sight it may seem difficult to see how companies cannot but spot the environmental issues that affect their performance. After all, the environment is all about us, literally staring us in the face! Unfortunately, companies all too often become preoccupied with their day-to-day problems, and hard-pressed managers become engrossed in priorities and deadlines more squarely within their responsibility than perhaps marginal changes outside. This is possibly one of the key difficulties with the external environment: it is outside the hubbub of today's business problems, and, excepting the rare instances of sudden change, it tends to present an all too comforting picture of at best *gradual change*; sudden changes *are* exceptional and, in any case, cannot be missed! The norm is generally a picture of incremental change over an extended period of time. It is this 'norm' that can prove deceptively dangerous, as the following commentary by Charlotte Villiers demonstrates:

> To look at British industry today is to be reminded of one simple, if rather brutal, analogy that top managers should take to heart: if you put a frog into a pan of cold water and turn on the heat, the frog will happily sit there without noticing the water is getting hot. The result, inevitably, is one boiled, dead frog. But if you drop a frog into some warm water, the frog realises immediately that it is too hot and jumps straight back and out again.
>
> The moral of this tale is simply that people do not notice incremental change going on around them until it is too late. Like the doomed frog, many businesses fail to notice what is happening in their environment until their fate is sealed.

The dimensions of the environment

In examining the environment in more detail, a basic model will be presented of different dimensions or levels of the environment, each more complex, distant and all-embracing than the previous one. A useful analogy would be to view the marketing environment as a series of sub-set within sets, within an ultimate or universal set – the inner sub-sets are more accessible and familiar to the marketer, the outer sets more indistinct and vague, like a distant landscape. Figure 3.2 illustrates this multi-dimensional view.

Level 1	Level 2	Level 3	Level 4	
The company	Company markets	Company stakeholder system	Economic Social Technological Political	The wider environment

Fig 3.2 Four levels of the marketing environment

Predictably, it is the more distant and complex dimensions of the wider environment (Level 4 in Fig 3.2) that occasion most concern and problems among marketers, and therefore warrant more detailed coverage.

However, the nearer reaches of the marketing environment, Levels 1–3 in Fig 3.2, are important elements of the everyday setting of Marketing – Kotler refers to these collectively as the company's *microenvironment*. They are subject to many of the same external factors and the next chapter says some more about this aspect of marketing.

The Company Setting (Level 1)

Whether organised as a separate department or not, the marketing function operates within an organisational context, and is most effective when well-managed, planned and resourced. Within marketing itself, sub-functions such as sales, advertising, research and promotion need to be co-ordinated to produce effective results. The marketing function must integrate with other functions such as production, engineering, purchasing, accounting and personnel. Close working relationships between marketing and functions such as R&D and production will be critical to key ventures such as new product innovation, and will generally affect everyday performance indicators such as customer service. Within this 'inner environment', therefore, a wider role for marketing will be to communicate company-wide the market's requirements and their implications – an aspect of internal marketing. Marketers should be able to assess the organisation's strengths and limitations in major functional specialisms, since important policy issues such as product development and competitive strategy will depend heavily on the commercial exploitation of comparative advantage. Such internal 'audits' of relative strengths and weaknesses will often be routinely made in problem-solving and planning, and will commonly be combined with information on the external situation, trends and events.

Company Markets (Level 2)

Many companies begin operations within one clearly-defined market and develop, through market penetration, by servicing the market more efficiently and knowledgeably. Later growth, however, may depend on finding or developing *new* markets, and learning to service new types of customer with differing requirements. For other companies, multi-market operations may be entered into from the outset, as a conscious policy decision. Figure 3.3 presents a simplified view of the types of market that a company might choose to service.

Consumer markets Industrial markets Intermediary markets Institutional markets	Products	Domestic
	Services	International

Fig 3.3 A typology of markets

Although most of the terms used are self-explanatory, it is important to note that requirements may differ greatly between the market types, e.g. consumer markets usually involve many more customers, buying for various personal requirements, while industrial markets will involve a smaller number of professional buyers, sourcing for commercial reasons. Intermediary markets involve reseller organisations such as retailers, wholesalers and brokers, selling on to other buyers *at a profit*. The term, institutional markets, denotes buyers within institutions such as schools, hospitals, dedicated associations and organisations (e.g. the Church), local authorities and central government. Buyers in such markets may operate through strict rules and procedures and by well-documented plans.

Clearly, the market environment within which a company chooses to operate will vary greatly according to market type. Even if specialising in one market, the company would need to conduct regular research and feedback exercises in order to monitor market changes and turning-points.

Last but not least, the competitors a company faces will vary according to the choice of market, or even the corner or sector of the market that it services – competitors are as much part of the market environment as customers.

The Stakeholder System (Level 3)

As the term implies, a company operates within the context of a network of interest groups, each of which has a particular relationship with the organisation, and often conflicting interests and motivations. Figure 3.4 illustrates the stakeholder system for a hypothetical company operating within the prescription medicines field.

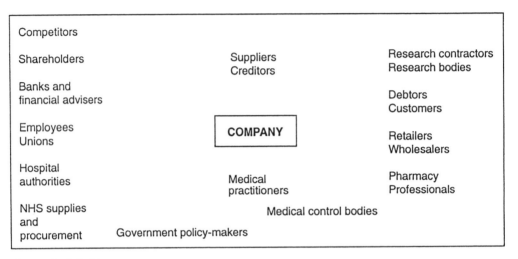

Fig 3.4 Stakeholders

Certainly part of this stakeholder system will be the participants in the company's *value chain*. The concept of the value chain, originated by Harvard Professor Michael Porter, models the vertical supply-market system within which a company seeks to fine-tune its performance in the interest of adding customer value and furthering corporate objectives. More detailed comment will be made on value chain analysis.

It should be stressed that the stakeholder system is a negotiated environment in which company relationships with different parties have to be carefully cultivated and managed. The company effectively has a series of publics – customers, shareholders, suppliers, employers, community bodies, etc. – with which it must maintain contact and ensure mutually productive relations. The marketing significance of this is that the state of these relationships can exert a powerful influence on success criteria such as brand image, product, acceptability, customer service, trade relations and company reputation.

The Wider Environment (Level 4)

In the wider environment, sometimes termed the macroenvironment, the company is faced by a complex set of uncontrollable variables that collectively shape its markets, its resources and the competitive climate, and that pose challenges and opportunities that may determine the success or failure of the company as a whole.

Figure 3.5 presents a simplified matrix of the four major sets of influence normally identified within the macroenvironment: social, technological, economic and political

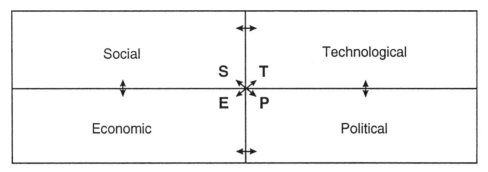

Fig 3.5 Macro-environmental factors

influences. These four broad categories are conventionally used as generalised headings, each of which encompasses a wide variety of variables, e.g. the social category includes factors at work in society in general, such as demographic and cultural influences. Further, the variables involved may work at different levels of aggregation – sectoral, regional, national and international – and they are likely to be interrelated across the four quadrants, e.g. changes in economic factors like investment may affect technological issues such as innovation (hence the arrows linking the quadrants). The letters denoting the four quadrants form the simple mnemonic STEP, often employed as a basic structure for STEP-analysis in outlining environmental forces relevant to business problems. A more detailed examination will now be made of these four sets of environmental influences.

Social and cultural influences

Though sometimes difficult to pinpoint, these constitute, literally, the society-wide influences and changes that can affect the marketing environment. For convenience, they will be divided into two broad areas: demographic factors and cultural factors.

Demographic factors

These concern the population aggregates and patterns within a society - population size and make-up. While these factors change only slowly, and are statistically predictable, they nevertheless exert powerful effects on the volume and nature of demand for most products and services. Furthermore, they are the building-blocks of the patterns of lifestyle within a society, and constitute the circumstances in which consumers enact their commercial and social roles. Figure 3.6 presents a summary of the demographic variables of interest to marketers.

Some of these factors will have obvious influences on companies and services in particular markets: for example, the demand for baby-clothes, cots, nursery products, maternity and ante-natal services will be directly correlated with birth-rate statistics. Not surprisingly, birth-rate will influence, with a time-lag, the demand for kindergarten facilities, primary education, toys and playthings, pre-school clothes, and paediatric medicine. In like manner, an ageing population – a common phenomenon in industrial-ised countries – results in increased demand for age-related products and services such as sheltered accommodation, mobility aids, large-print books, pre-retirement counselling and geriatric nursing.

Data trends and projections	Population:		
	Size Growth rate	Age structure Birth/death - rates	Sex distribution Life expectancy
	Density	Location	Geographical / regional shifts
	Household size Family size	Single/non-family households Marriage/divorce statistics	
	Income and wealth distribution	Working population	Educational participation
	Socio - economic groups	Occupation groups	Ethnic composition

Fig 3.6 Demographic influences on markets

Other factors will exert influences that are less obvious and may vary geographically, or across social groups: especially over time, demographic factors will exhibit multiple influences that may present marketers with either opportunities or threats. An example of such temporal changes is given in Fig 3.7, which shows the changes in UK beer and cider consumption over a 10 year period.

Exercise

Identify the major changes shown in Fig 3.7 and comment on their likely or possible causes

General demographic trends? Certainly in the UK and other industrial countries, recent years have witnessed major movements within the demographic landscape. It is worth noting that, though such changes appear general, and even international, they may not yet be described as irreversible. Some of the common factors in these demographic movements are highlighted below:

1 **Population age distribution** – many countries have experienced in recent times a slowing in the birth-rate, after a period of high birth statistics in the 1950s and 1960s (the 'baby-boom' post-World War II period). This, combined with an extension of life

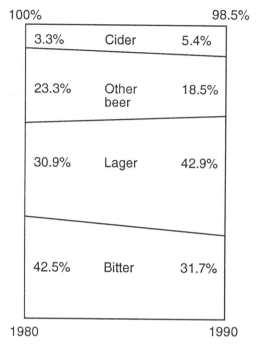

Fig 3.7 Changes in UK beer/cider consumption

expectancy related to medical, dietary and economic improvements, results in a right
ward shift in the population profile – the classic symptoms of an ageing population.
Some of these changes have far-reaching economic implications of interest to policy-
makers e.g. the increasing burden of the retired sector (even the 'super-old': 80 years
and above) on social services, and the problems of the projected decline in the
workforce pool – French government economic planners now view policy on this
issue as a major priority.

2 **Household/family composition** – In many countries there have been major changes in
household and family size and make-up. Social and economic changes have led to later
marriages, with fewer children. Workforce participation among married women has
increased significantly, and many married women nowadays succeed in managing a
return to work and career development after maternity breaks.

Career couples, with no children, are now quite commonplace – indeed, they have
been labelled by advertisers as 'Dinkies' ('dual income, no kids'), an advertising target
group of some apparent interest!

Alongside these changes, the number of non-family households has increased
substantially. Some of these households are made up of young careerist adults, or
adults choosing bachelorhood, while others represent adults that are divorced or
widowed. If note is taken also of the growing number of single-parent families, it is
hardly surprising that a researcher definition of 'head of household' is far from the
straightforward matter it might have been thirty years ago. Significantly, these house
hold changes have had a major effect on the pattern of demand for a wide range of
everyday goods and services.

3 Geographical shifts – Many 'post-industrial' societies, such as the UK and the US, have witnessed in recent years a major decline in traditional industrial regions and a parallel growth in 'new territory' regions based on service industries, e.g. the US Sunbelt and Silicon Valley phenomenon. Other countries are experiencing similar movements of people and investment associated with rural depopulation and accelerated urbanisation and industrialisation. Though these phenomena are different, and may even co-exist across regions within any one country, their economic and commercial impact may present common symptoms and problems. The marketer must reflect on the medium-term effects of such changes and consider how company development and investment plans are affected by them.

Cultural factors

Culture within any society is the complex of elements that reflect the society's beliefs and values, perceptions, preferences and behavioural norms. These elements of culture express themselves in people's attitudes and behaviour, in their general lifestyle and in their working lives. Culture is therefore all-embracing and multi-dimensional, such that neat and exact definitions are difficult and elusive, and better left to specialists such as sociologists and anthropologists.

For the marketer, however, it is necessary to understand that culture will vary within and between societies, so that cultural norms may vary between countries, regions and culture groups or sub-cultures.

Within a society, culture may be most distinguishable by the prevalent *core* beliefs and values that people hold, which express themselves in family and friendship relations, in social conventions and rites, in social institutions and the social order itself. Such longstanding facets of culture change very slowly, as they are the product of family upbringing, the education system, national history and political development, religion, and a multiple of other influences such as aesthetic developments, communications and the media.

Below these prevailing core values may be identified a variety of secondary beliefs and values, which tend to be less durable, less universal and more situational. These may be tied in some way to core beliefs, but reflect the development of individual or group choices and feelings, e.g. a belief in education may be rooted in core values, whereas attitudes for or against private education will be an expression of secondary values and beliefs.

These secondary-level beliefs and values are therefore more likely to vary within society, to change over time, and be open to change and persuasion. Furthermore, they may be recognisable within the development of sub-cultures within a society. Sub-cultures develop in many ways and for different reasons, though they usually entail a grouping of people with common interests, experiences or motivations. Sub-cultures may therefore be associated with age groupings (the 'youth culture'), regional affiliations (Lancashire v Yorkshire), religious or ethnic associations, or even situational facets of lifestyle (working mothers, single parents, students).

Secondary beliefs and values may sometimes exhibit society-wide changes over time, affecting a gradual change in the society's general orientation, e.g. in attitudes to work and leisure, an increased interest in self-development and choice, a growth in voluntary sector participation, ecological concern, consumerism, etc.

Environmental awareness is an interesting reflection of how society-wide concerns have delivered a powerful message to governments and business leaders. While the 'greening' of consumers has achieved comparable progress across a spread of international markets, the acceptance of 'green' consumerism in the UK was perhaps most notably marked by the 1988 publication of *The Green Consumer Guide* (Victor Gollancz), which recorded bestseller status and earned for its authors, John Elkington and Julia Hailes, a place in the United Nation's Environmental Programme Global 500 Roll of Honour, announced on World Environment Day in June 1989. That the book market has sustained multiple reprints and a much-welcomed follow-up title, *The Green Consumer's Supermarket Shopping Guide*, testifies to the growing interest in 'green' products among the general public and, equally gratifying, among consumer goods manufacturers and retailing groups. Social responsibility and ethics in marketing is discussed further in Chapter 23.

Exercise

In June 1989 a MORI poll conducted in the UK showed that more than 18 million people – almost half the adult population – had within the survey period made at least one product purchase decision on the basis of environmental selection criteria.

1 As an individual consumer, note the most recent purchase you have made of an environment-friendly product, answer the following questions and be prepared to discuss your purchase in–class:
- Where did you buy the product?
- What competing products were on display, and how did they compare on ecology-friendly terms?
- Did 'going-green' involve a price premium?
- To what extent do you choose green products as a matter of principle?

2 As a student group, devise a simple checklist (say 12 headings) by which to assess the 'green policy' of supermarkets. Between the group, visit five leading supermarket stores and apply the checklist you have developed. Analyse and present your group results in class.

Technological influences

Technology is the touchstone of economic progress, a leading source of competitive advantage commercially, and an indispensable part of everyday lifestyle for the modern consumer. 'Technology' as a term is perhaps misleadingly general, as the 'technologies' encompassed are highly disparate and may vary from the most apparently obscure improvement or technique to the substantive breakthroughs associated with quantum leaps in science and engineering. What cannot be denied is that technology is a major driving force for change, everywhere. Furthermore, technological change appears to be multiplicative, so that the rate of change increases. A simple illustration of this would be to consider the major changes that have taken place in the last twenty or more years – within the lifetime of the average business studies student – through innovations in the fields of information technology, biotechnology, fibre optics, aerospace and materials science. Though developments in these fields have followed different, sometimes faltering, paths, they have in some way combined to produce major changes and challenges, and to raise the commercial stakes of success and failure.

An earlier commentary on the commercial realities of technology was provided by Schumpeter, an American economist, who styled technology as a force for 'creative destruction', sweeping aside old products and their providers and replacing them with new competitors and technologies – a dynamic process that has been more recently expounded in the 5-Forces model of Michael Porter, another economist.

An everyday marketing perspective on the effects of technology would be the growing consensus that product life cycles are becoming ever shorter – agreement on exact figures varies, though most marketers would reckon that as many as 80 per cent of products on today's market will have altogether disappeared within ten years. The corollary of this is that companies' sales and profits are becoming increasingly dependent on a *managed* succession of new product introductions. This, in turn, will hinge on success in the costly and speculative process of R&D and innovation.

While developments in leading-edge technologies and 'super science' may be associated with high expenditure efforts in pure research, these high visibility cases are by no means the standard route by which technology advances. Technology may often move incrementally and diagonally, through a chain process of linking developments, often 'authored' by competitor organisations that jostle for possession of the baton. (Sometimes final leadership position will be the result of a long and costly rivalry between competing 'systems' – witness the confusing period of contention between Sony and Philips in the video-recorder market.) Furthermore, while commitment and investment is required in programmed research, even high-spending researcher companies (some pharmaceutical multinationals devote over 25 per cent of turnover to R&D) have found that high budgets alone are not the key to success. In managerial terms, research efforts need to be programmed, monitored for cost-effectiveness and directed towards market needs.

Market needs represent the link between invention and innovation. While successful R&D outcomes might prove themselves in a new formulation, a product or process development, real success will not be achieved until users in the marketplace have adopted the new development. Technological progress therefore ultimately depends on a process of *technology transfer* and *innovation*, both of which involve commercialisation through an understanding of market needs. Here, then, is a critical role for marketing, to direct development efforts and facilitate their commercialisation.

Logically, market needs will be identified by research among customers – the market. Interestingly, this research does *not* have to be wholly esoteric or technical, as what is sought is an insight into the *customer's* problems and interests, rather than those of the technologist. Perhaps the most telling illustration of this principle was provided by the Sony Corporation in developing the Walkman. In terms of technology sophistication, the Walkman formula was apparently basic and unexciting – the key element of its success was that it met a latent market need for a cheap, portable cassette-player, at the right moment in time. While Sony sales records doubtless catalogue the real success of the product, the hundreds of copycat versions that have been marketed worldwide are proof enough. Equally, follow-up Sony successes through the Watchman and the Discman are testimony to the market lead developed by the original product.

Market needs in other fields may be signalled by resource shortages, environmental problems and hazards, or the drive to reduce waste. Certainly in the past, technology itself has presented environmental problems such as pollution and blighted landscapes, that now require technological solutions. Given the recent awakening of international concern about the natural environment, it would be no exaggeration to assert that all organisations should consciously review their stance and performance in this regard.

Technology, then, is a major force for change for *all* organisations. Far-removed from the regulated atmosphere of the research laboratory, even the everyday High Street service firm must consider technology in the following terms.

- How will technological change affect our physical plant, equipment, work routines?
- How will it affect these issues for our customers, and what will this imply for *our* operations and offerings?
- How can we harness technology, or even take a lead role, in developing technology-based competitive advantage?

Exercise

Select one of the following service organisations and consider how technology (a) has affected the way the organisation operates, and (b) offers scope for future competitive advantage:
- Solicitors' partnership
- Doctors' practice
- Travel agency
- Estate agency

The economic environment

The economy is a total system within which material and energy inputs are processed and converted to finished goods and services for distribution and final use. As in economic accounting terms all companies and organisations are part of the system they have a direct interest in monitoring economic developments and guiding their policy decisions accordingly. Most performance-centred companies nowadays incorporate economic data analysis into their business plans and marketing programmes, generating and inputting the relevant information as part of a formal Marketing Information System (MKIS).

The logic of this is that the current and projected events and trends in the economy – so-called *macroeconomic* variables – will likely affect the overall level of demand for goods and services, and related aggregates such as stock levels, prices, capacity utilisation and the like. In other markets, often tied to primary resource supplies and distribution, e.g. petroleum, companies make a practice of studying the *microeconomic* variables within their immediate market or sector.

While microeconomic factors will obviously vary for companies in different sectors, macroeconomic aggregates will present a common backcloth for all companies. Furthermore, as international communications and trade links develop, it is becoming more necessary to talk of the world economy – many Head Offices of large multinationals now operate around the clock, controlling operations across a spread of markets. While economic globalisation is being advanced through international and investment trade links, at the intermediate level regional trade blocs such as the EC, EFTA (European Free Trade Area), ASEAN, have superimposed a marked zoning influence within the trade statistics of many member countries. In the UK, for example, EC trade links now account for almost 60 per cent of overseas trade compared with a 30 per cent share in 1971. The prospect of 1992 and after provides a topical illustration of the realities of the economic environment for companies within both the UK and the wider European Community, since the free movement of goods, services and people is likely to pose major changes within national markets formerly assured as 'home territory'.

The economic environment is therefore a complex network of international, domestic and regional influences and dependencies that shape the market *potential* facing companies. Company performance itself will depend critically on the quality of preparation and decision-making that is brought to bear on this potential.

Table 3.1
A typical databank reportage of major economic variables, showing a comparison between recent UK economic performance and that of selected competitors countries

	France	Germany	Italy	Japan	UK	US
% change* GDP	+2.2	+1.1	+1.4	+1.6	−0.6	−1.6
% Retail price increases	2.6	3.6	5.1	1.7	3.7	3.0
% Earnings rise*	3.8	5.4	4.8	2.5	5.7	2.3
% Rate unemployed	9.8	6.3	10.4	2.2	8.8	6.8
% prime lending rate	9.85	11.0	17.0	4.25	9.0	6.0
Trade balance ($ bn)*	+4.0	+20.4	−12.3	+124.9	−21.8	−74.0

Note: *Figures for 12 month period to latest official statistics published.
Some figures rounded for simplification. Compiled end October 1992.

While cross-sectional data such as that shown in Table 3.1 may give a clue to current economic events, a firmer appraisal to underpin major decisions such as plant investment or international expansion, would require methodical analysis of relevant indices, showing turning-points, trends and projections, with accompanying commentary and qualifications. Larger companies will retain in-house economists and planners for such purposes, or enlist the services of outsiders such as economic consultants, merchant bankers or venture capitalist organisations.

The significance of the economic data in Table 3.1 is that over time they will indicate major economic developments of direct interest to marketers and business people generally. Such 'economy-watching' may enable the vigilant company to respond in time to scenarios such as the following:

- **Recession** – a downturn in economic activity of variable intensity. The diagnosis may range from a Chancellor's dismissive 'blip' or setback, to a world recession. Usual indicators will be a fall or levelling in GNP (and GDP), industrial output, household income, consumer spending and investment expenditure, order-books and notified vacancies. Rises will be recorded in measures such as stocks, unemployment, company bankruptcies.

As spending will be affected, market conditions become thin and more competitive. Though sales for some products and within certain income groups may be little affected, the general picture will be more difficult, while companies in some sectors (e.g. industrial components, machine tools, construction) may suffer heavier reversals through order cancellations, project postponements and stock depletion.

- **Recovery** – the opposite of the above, again varying in intensity and time. Terms like boom, upturn, reflation will be used by economists. Marketers in some sectors will benefit from an early upturn in sales (their sales patterns may provide 'early indicators' of economic activity useful to forecasters, while other sectors, by contrast) may recover late ('lagging indicators'). Major upturns in economic activity may result in 'overheating', with higher costs and prices, import surges, bottlenecks and shortages, failures through overtrading. Indicators such as investment and stock-levels may vary by sector and according to the 'investment climate'.

- **Inflation** – rising prices may be associated with buoyant conditions, demand growth and shortages. Athough perverse combinations such as 'stagflation' (inflation *and* recession) are not unknown, severe inflation (hyperinflation, strato-inflation) may rock economic foundations and demand drastic policy remedies such as depreciation, tariffs and IMF visitations.

The scenarios above are rather simplistic and generalised, and by no means illustrate the real complexities to be met with in practice (the student is referred to an economics text for more authoritative detail). What these pictures do illustrate, though, is the way the economic 'isobars' may change and steepen, domestically and internationally. An added complication for the marketer will be the effect of government policy measures designed to stimulate or manage the economy. While these measures will vary by political preference and according to economic circumstance, they will usually entail manipulation of key instruments such as taxation and expenditure (fiscal policy), interest rates and credit (monetary policy), that will have obvious effects on markets. Furthermore, some industries may be subject to microeconomic measures, e.g. in respect of merger control or competition policy, investment or locational incentives. Companies engaged in international marketing will also need to respond to similar economic controls within their overseas markets. Finally, economic policies are likely in future to be more directly influenced by multilateral agencies and agreements (UN, GATT (General Agreement on Tariffs and Trade), etc.) and the expansion of common market blocs such as the EC.

The political and legal environment

The economic policies cited in the previous section are but one aspect of the political environment, which comprises the controls and checks instituted by central and local government, government agencies and quasi-official bodies. Also of relevance will be the growing influence of international laws and agreements, and at a more local level the activities of various professional and trade bodies, pressure groups and voluntary associations.

Although such a regulatory environment may appear to change only slowly, and clear frameworks of rights and representations will usually exist, it is still necessary for marketers to be aware of the policy interpretations of the *status quo*, and to be attuned to the likely direction and nature of changes to the system. As company stakeholders may sometimes pursue particular interests and grievances through the 'political' system, it is in the interests of companies to frame policies that minimise stakeholder grievances and generally support a record of commercial good practice and social responsibility. In short, companies should seek to demonstrate good corporate citizenship by upholding the letter and the spirit of the law, and generally behaving in a responsible and responsive manner.

The marketing interpretation of such a stance would squarely equate with marketing excellence, and in practical terms might relate directly to a corporate mission statement that guides company activity from higher strategic issues, such as market choice, to everyday performance standards in respect of quality, service levels, customer protocol and the like.

While such autonomous standards of performance are to be commended, some markets and trades have developed general voluntary codes of conduct and control, supported and monitored by a central membership body. Practice within established professions such as medicine and accountancy has long been controlled by strict codes of professional behaviour – professionals within the Chartered Institute of Marketing now have to abide by the new Code of Practice drawn up to support the recent vesting of Charter status.

Self-regulation aside, most governments have developed a body of legislation and enforcement frameworks in respect of industry and trade. In particular, the following areas of control are of direct concern to business:

1 **Legislation in respect of monopoly and competition standards.** In the UK enforcement powers have in recent years been channelled particularly through the Office of Fair Trading and the Monopolies and Mergers Commission, both vested with wide competition reference powers. Statutory provisions in these matters derive from legislation such as the Fair Trading Act 1973, the Competition Act 1979, the Restrictive Practices Act 1976 and the Resale Prices Act 1977. As a full EC-member, the UK is also subject to Community provisions in respect of these issues: in particular, Article 85 of the Treaty of Rome concerns practices hindering competition, and Article 86 of the Treaty addresses abuses of a dominant market position. Significantly, widening Treaty powers in this field are being proposed within Directives currently progressing through the Brussels chambers.

2 **Measures to protect consumers**, whether as groups (e.g. children, patients), individuals, as users of certain products and services (e.g. cigarettes, alcohol, gambling, food, drugs and medicines), or particularly as targets for business activities (mailshots, sales, promotion, etc). In the UK the original provisions in consumer protection, founded in the law of contract and equity amendments to common law, have been supplemented significantly through legislation that is at least in part attributable to the growth of consumerism. Relevant legislation has included the Trades Descriptions Act 1973, the Consumer Credit Act 1974, the Supply of Goods (Implied Terms) Act 1973 and the Unfair Contract Terms Act 1977. A number of these statutes enhanced or introduced measures directly relating to marketing practices such as pricing claims, warranties, consumer information, product quality, and credit terms. Additionally, a welter of other measures relate to specific issues as diverse as branding (Trade Marks Act 1938), weights and measures (various Acts), food safety (Food and Drugs Act 1955 and revisions), product origin (Imported Goods Act 1972), promotional competitions (Lotteries and Amusements Act 1976), and inertia selling (Unsolicited Goods and Services Acts 1971 and 1975).

Additional to these provisions, government bodies exist with statutory and discretionary powers to control the business community in respect of a variety of other issues, from environmental protection and planning restrictions to commercial disclosure and public standards of decency. Figure 3.8 presents a collage of recent newspaper cuttings that illustrate the scope of such controls.

N Korea unveils law on foreign investment

By John Burton in Seoul

NORTH KOREA yesterday appeared to take its first step along the "capitalist road" by announcing a new foreign investment law.

The communist state said it would allow foreign companies to set up wholly-owned facilities in special economic zones.

It also provided details on the operation of foreign con-

joint ventures is estimated at $100m.

No western company has invested in North Korea since it defaulted on international loans in the 1970s.

The move by North Korea to attract foreign investment is meant to revive its ailing economy which contracted by 5.2 per cent in 1991 due to a shortage of oil and foreign currency following the deterioration of trade relations with the former Soviet bloc.

China, Pyongyang's closest ally, has tried to convince the North Koreans that the adoption of Beijing's market measures, including economic zones, will help them avoid the fate of their former socialist

It also guarantees property rights, and promises compensation in the case of "unavoidable" nationalisation.

Foreign companies can lease land for up to 50 years in zones and they will be exempt from tariffs on imported goods except those designated by North Korea.

However, western companies are likely to remain wary of the liberal terms since they are still millions of dollars for goods delivered to North Korea decades ago.

North Korea has one of the worst credit ratings in the world due to defaults.

Although it announced the controlled cost-

Machine tool industry decimated by embargoes

By Richard Donkin

BRITAIN's machine tool industry has been decimated by the loss of business resulting from embargoes on Iraq.

In 1986 the UK machine tool industry had no exports to Iraq. This was before the

were enjoying sales of £31.4m, promoting Iraq to number three after the US and West Germany in the table of Britain's machine tool export markets.

Most of Britain's machine tool makers had exports to Iraq at the time. Many of the exports were being used for the

end of the industry can be counted on one hand.

Matrix Churchill, the company with the biggest Iraqi orders, is in receivership. Wickman Bennett, of Coventry has also ceased production. It agreed a fine with Customs and Excise over exports to Iraq.

Mr David Phillips, an industrialist, said much of

Ofwat warns on efficiency

By Bronwen Maddox,
Environment Correspondent

WATER COMPANIES which are inefficient will face tighter price controls in future, the industry regulator Ofwat said yesterday.

Ofwat's consultation paper said it would look favourably on water companies which controlled cost-

level of water and sewerage bills."

The water companies' 10-year modernisation programme to bring water standards in England and Wales into line with European Community directives could even cost £45bn.

Ofwat said the rate of increases "must bear relationship to the costs of the relationship and a mechanical one. If increases are shown to be justified it will be set against charges.

Ofwat added that without charge-

to make a "reasonable" return on capital and that it would not try to "claw back" retrospectively any savings companies have made above the efficiency targets initially assumed.

Mr David Luffman, finance director of Thames Water, said: "There are a number of positive things such as being able to retain efficiency gains, one stage in a periodic review when the review comes round and that assum-

Japanese to keep foreign rice ban

By Robert Thomson in Tokyo

JAPAN's agriculture ministry insisted yesterday that the rice market would remain closed to imports regardless of EC-US negotiations on farm products trade.

Tokyo has watched the apparent progress in US-EC talks anxiously, as the present factional struggles within the ruling Liberal Democratic party (LDP) have distracted party leaders from the politically-sensitive issue of rice imports.

The agriculture ministry said the ban would not be relaxed, even if the EC and US reach a formal and final agreement as part of Gatt's Uruguay Round.

Mr Frans Andriessen, EC external relations commissioner, has said multilateral farm talks could resume soon. His comment followed a weekend meeting with trade ministers from the US, Japan and Canada, at which negotiators were said to be on the verge of making progress on the outstanding issues of farm subsidies and oil seeds.

An understanding exists among senior LDP officials that rice imports must eventually be allowed, if only in limited amounts. But last week's resignation of Mr Shin Kanemaru, the party's power-broker, reduced any prospects for liberalisation.

Mr Kanemaru was one of few Japanese politicians with the prestige needed to deal with an issue as complex as rice. He is known to have accepted that opening the rice market was inevitable.

But before opening the market, the LDP would have to begin talks with the influential farm lobby. Few LDP politicians want to be the first to risk the change of policy on rice which the farm groups say has sacred role in Japanese life.

Mr Koichi Kato, chief cabinet secretary, said yesterday that the Japanese government was watching the progress of talks between the US and and would "cautiously consider future events".

Compulsory local tendering to widen

By Andrew Adonis and John Willman

THE GOVERNMENT intends to press ahead with plans to extend compulsory competitive tendering of local-authority services to the white-collar sector, but the procedure will be more flexible than previously announced.

Mr Michael Howard, environment secretary, said his department estimated that tendering had generated cost savings of about 6 per cent for blue-collar services "while standards have in general been maintained or improved".

He told the annual conference of the Association of County Councils at Winchester, Hampshire: "It is vital that we do not underestimate what can be achieved in the white-collar services."

However, three changes are to be made to the proposals set out consultation

ing and property management services, 25 per cent for – the proportion of council spending to be subject to tendering will be reduced per cent to 90 per cent.

"For all services "double envelope" under which contractors will be obliged to submit threshold and the contracts on price be made voluntary.

Mr Howard said authorities will be in place their own for making judgments on the trade-off between and cost. We do not lay down from on detailed rules under a framework. We want with local government other interested parties developing a system that can work well."

For services not relating to construction, the proportion of spending to be subject to tendering will be as laid in consultation paper

Taiwan tightens investment rules for foreigners

TAIWAN is tightening its screening of foreign investment applications and bids for infrastructure contracts to block projects by companies with large mainland Chinese shareholdings, officials said yesterday, Reuter reports from Taipei.

"We are screening foreign investment applications prudently to prevent Communist Chinese capital from slipping through," said Mr Chen Ming-pang, secretary-general of the government's investment Com-

nese shareholdings. Companies with big investments will be blocked from bidding contracts under Taiwan's $300bn (£193.5bn) development plan, economics ministry officials said.

Taiwan has curbed contacts with China end of the civil war. Under a law companies with mainland Chinese shareholders are barred than 20 per cent from investing. Local new Chinese restriction be

Litigation threat to auditors outlined

By Andrew Jack in Washington

LEGAL action against auditors is the most serious threat facing the accounting profession, the World Congress of Accountants in Washington heard yesterday.

Mr David Smithers, president of the Institute of Chartered Accountants in Australia, said: "Unless we solve the problem of liability there will not be another World Congress."

Mr Smithers was discussing the recent A$1.1bn claim against KPMG Peat Marwick as auditors to Tricontinental, the merchant banking subsidiary of the State Bank of Australia. Total outstanding claims in the country now exceed A$2.5bn (£1.1bn).

That case was overshadowed this month by the £88m claim against Ernst & Whinney and Price Waterhouse in London for their role as auditors to the collapsed Bank of Credit and Commerce International.

Speakers said an important role in controlling litigation could be played by auditors using more sophisticated risk management in their choice and retention of clients. Mr Smithers said nearly half of litigation was driven by poor risk management.

Mr Richard Murray, chairman of Minet Global Professional Services, the indemnity insurer, stressed that auditors did not cause financial losses, but were finding themselves held responsible for them when a collapse took place.

He said insurers were at the point of refusing to provide professional indemnity cover for accountants, and that there might be a need for governments to step in.

Antiques trade association launches code of practice

By John Thornhill

THE antiques industry has launched a code of practice in an attempt to improve consumer confidence in a sector where some dealers have gained a reputation for sharp practice.

The London and Provincial Antique Dealers' Association, which has 700 members throughout the UK, has drawn up an Antique Buyers' Charter, outlining dealers' responsibilities and shoppers' rights.

It has been approved by the Office of Fair Trading. Shoppers will be able to take

complaints to the association, which will consult antiques experts for arbitration, scrutinised by an independent adjudicator. Statutory legal rights will not be affected by the process.

Lord Derwent, association chairman, said: "Antiques is an unusual business in that it relies on expert opinions which sometimes genuinely differ. If you buy a refrigerator and it does not work that it is pretty clear-cut. But what happens if you buy some Meissen and do not believe it is Meissen?"

Member companies will display the charter in their shops and give detailed

information about an article's price, date of manufacture, material and maker's name, and state whether it has been subject to restoration or reproduction.

Members found to have broken the code will be required to resign.

The number of antique dealers in the UK is not known but the association estimate that it represents about quarter of the industry.

Shoppers' charters are becoming increasingly common in service industries – the Office of Fair Trading working with about 30 trade associations to draw up codes

Fig 3.8 Collage of news articles

Exercise

After studying the cuttings in Fig 3.8, consult recent editions of the business press and collect a number of comparable photocopy stories. Prepare a brief presentation for discussion in class.

You may carry out the exercise as a group or individually – if as a group, more extensive reporting will be required, and evidence of group work.

Aside from direct action by government and regulatory bodies, companies have in the last 20 or more years had to recognise the increasingly strident concerns of consumerists and related environmental pressure groups and lobbyists. Consumer groups in particular have posed new challenges to marketers, especially through the publication of independent product quality and test information – in the UK, the Consumers' Association, publishers of *Which?*, now claims 7 million members. Through affiliation to BEUC (Bureau Européen des Unions de Consummateurs) it is connected with groups of similar strength in countries such as France and Germany.

Conclusion

The marketing environment comprises the playing-field upon which competitive marketing must take place. While some of the 'rules' of the playing-field may be common knowledge to all players, most 'game-plans' cannot be inspired wholly by mechanistic guidelines. The game is dynamic, and most moves are finally umpired by buyer preferences. Companies need to monitor and decide rational responses to changes in the environment in order to win their colours. The environment will almost invariably wield greater strength than a company can muster, so that pragmatic responses are generally more sensible than Canute-like gestures of defiance. Competitive management can benefit, *within* the rules, by good intelligence and planning *and* flexible execution – analysis and monitoring alone are not enough. This is perhaps best summarised by the old adage:

There are three types of companies. Those who make things happen. Those who watch things happen. Those who wonder what happened.

Questions

1 Taking any established product market, consider the various environmental changes that have influenced it over the last 15–20 years.

2 Develop a stakeholder map for a typical airline company, and comment on the conflicting interests that the various stakeholders might have in respect of the airline.

3 Consider the extent to which demographic changes are likely to influence the commercial success of *(a)* a supermarket chain, *(b)* a car manufacturer.

4 Many writers have proposed that the world is rapidly becoming a 'smaller place', as globalisation gathers pace. Consider how such a globalisation process will affect a company's market environment.

References

Kotler, P, *Marketing Management: Analysis, Planning Implementation and Control,* Prentice-Hall, 1991.
Howard, John, *Marketing Management,* Irwin Dorsey, 1976.
Villiers, Charlotte, 'Boiled Frog Syndrome', *Management Today,* March 1989.

Case study: duty-free sales environment

'We stand to lose £55 million worth of duty free sales ... and even more if Norway and Sweden join the EC'. In such a way did Barry Gibson, Commercial Director of Heathrow Airport, describe the scale of business threatened by the EC plan to abolish duty-free and tax-free retailing for intro-EC travellers in the next decade. The abolition of duty-free shopping is a logical extension of the harmonisation of EC into a single market. However, the effect on the British Airports Authority, where 70 per cent of profits come from duty-free sales, is severe. As a commercial organisation, Heathrow Airport will have to act now if the consequences are to be mitigated.

Gibson was reported as saying, 'I can see us abandoning tobacco and almost becoming a non player in liquor'. However, he does foresee a wide range of niche operations, up-market concessions selling 'the best international brands'.

Pointing to the growth in duty-paid retailing at Heathrow over the past five years, he suggests it is possible 'to sell a wide range of goods provided they are targeted properly'. In particular an industry observer has added, 'Business people rarely have the time to compare prices. They are more interested in buying the right thing as quickly and easily as possible, than in getting a bargain'. However, it must be remembered that business travellers are not the only users of Heathrow.

In view of these impending changes, suggest what Barry Gibson should do now to prepare for the loss of the duty-free sales.

(Quotes are from 'Devising Gains without Frontiers', *Marketing Week,* 8 November 1991.)

4

THE COMPETITIVE ENVIRONMENT

Introduction

A few years ago there was an article in *Business Week* entitled 'Forget satisfying the consumer – Just outfox the other guy'. This is some people's view of marketing. There are no rewards in telling your sales manager. 'I came second in the bid for a particular contract'; if you did not get the business it does not matter if you come second or twenty second. The 1970s saw an emphasis on a strong customer focus within marketing organisations. In 1980 Michael Porter of the Harvard Business School published his key book, entitled *Competitive Strategy*, which was quickly followed by Kenichi Ohmae's *The Mind of the Strategist*. Both books are wider than marketing, but both look at the importance of a competitor orientation for any organisation. They make the point that if you forget the competitive environment in which you operate,you could lose your business. This carries through private companies into the public services in the UK,where government legislation has introduced compulsory competitive tendering (CCT) for many local authority contracts.

Philip Kotler, a most prolific marketing author, also wrote about competition when he jointly authored an article with Ravi Singh entitled 'Marketing Warfare in 1980s'. Interest in the parallels between military strategy and business has been fascinating writers for a long time. Kotler and Singh suggested various attack and defense strategies which could help win a marketing war. These include several alternatives to the direct attack, since a direct assault rarely achieves victory – a view supported by a study of military history. There are differences between war and business, however, and the Chairman of Electrolux was once reported to have said 'Unlike the Military, Industry is always at war. If there is peace, they call it a cartel, and, as everyone knows, those are not allowed'.

The early 1980s also saw the publication of Peters and Waterman's book, *In Search of Excellence*. This focused on a survey of a number of then highly successful companies. Although this book says little on beating the competition, it does re-emphasise 'closeness to customers', and building stronger relationships, as one of the key principles of success. However, within this section they do suggest the art of 'nichemanship': 'Finding a particular niche where you are better at something than anybody else'. This encapsulates winning over the competitors. In their survey Peters and Waterman found that 'a very large share of the companies looked at are superb at dividing their customer base into numerous segments so they can provide tailored products and services'. The issues of how customers make buying decisions will be discussed in Chapter 5, and segmentation in Chapter 6. What this survey shows is that it may not be possible to win the competitive battle for all your potential customers, but it is possible to be the preferred product/service for a particular segment of the customer population.

'*In Search of Excellence*' dismisses the move to a more competitive focus, stating: 'The competitor issue is easily put to rest. The excellent companies clearly do more and better competitor analysis than the rest'. It is this ability to understand competitors and predict their actions which is vitally important to all marketing-orientated organisations.

Tom Peters redressed the lack of competitive emphasis in his later book, '*Thriving on Chaos*' albeit in a chapter on 'Creative Swiping'. Here he advocates becoming obsessed with competitors. Not just the major obvious competitors but all potential competitors. He suggests three tasks:

1 collect data on competitors;
2 update it regularly; and
3 share it widely within the firm.

Industry structure

The performance of an organisation will be influenced by the structure of the industry in which it operates because this will affect the level of competition in that market. Porter (1982) suggested that in addition to analysing what he calls 'Jockeying for position' by obvious competitors, there are four other forces which affect the level of competition. These are:

- the bargaining power of suppliers;
- the bargaining power of customers;
- the threat of new entrants; and
- the threat of substitute products or services.

If either there is only a small number of key suppliers, perhaps controlling a key ingredient, or a small number of customers, then they can use this to squeeze profitability in an industry. There are other sources of power but the factors which give rise to this power will change over time, so it is important to continually reassess this situation. As an example, some years ago Tesco supermarkets took over a small regional group called Hillards. The concentration of food retailers who are customers of food manufacturers thus increased. Companies who supplied Hillards but not Tesco were considered as potential suppliers to the wider group. However, since the Hillards stores were changed to Tesco layout, the predominant change was not in their favour. Certainly this was one example of a change in bargaining power for the food manufacturing industry in relation to its direct customers, the food retailers.

We could also look at a related industry, food retailing. The customers here are families, students, housewives, and anyone who purchases food. While there are millions of customers they each spend only a small amount in relation to the turnover of a single large supermarket, let alone a company like Sainsbury or Tesco with total turnovers in excess of £6.5 billion.

An individual customer for Hillards might not like the Tesco store which replaced it. However, while all customers have a choice to purchase food wherever they like, the bargaining power of an individual is small and unlikely to affect Tesco's policy. In many cases the choice of supermarket is determined by location and not by the range of items on sale in a particular outlet. Therefore many customers who used the former Hillards store now use it in its 'Tesco' style. In defence of Tesco, it has to be said that during the 1980s Tesco has very successfully changed its stores which now attract increasing numbers of customers. However, for food manufacturers the problem is the bargaining power of the large retail groups, which encouraged *Marketing Magazine* to publish an article in 1987 entitled 'The Five people who decide what we eat'. This referred to the buyers from the five largest grocery supermarkets who are extremely powerful when choosing which products to stock.

The threat of new entrants can also be studied in the context of food retailing. The 1990's have seen the large German retailer, Aldi, move into the UK, with a plan to open 80 stores in the Midlands and North West. These new stores, with a distinct format, are already attracting customers, and since total food consumption is relatively static they must be winning customers from existing food retailers. Perhaps no obvious substitutes exist in food retailing, but in many industries new ways of applying benefits can be a significant threat. The subject of benefits and 'marketing myopia' were discussed in chapter 2. From this you will already appreciate how a substitute way of delivering a customer benefit could alter the competitive environment in a dramatic way.

The competitive environment

The competitive environment is likely to be of more immediate importance to marketers than the other environments discussed in Chapter 3. The different types of competitive environment can affect the way an organisation markets its products. At one level there is what economists call perfect competition. Here we have many small firms which are all too small to have an individual impact on price or performance norms. Usually it is easy to enter or leave such an industry, but the rewards are small due to the intense competition. In this market all firms have similar technologies and costs, and the product or service offered is impossible to distinguish from others. This is a very difficult marketplace as there is no obvious reason why any buyer should choose any particular supplier.

At the other extreme is a monopoly where only one supplier exists. The only decision faced by customers is to buy or not to buy the product. However, most markets lie somewhere in between these two extremes.

In creating reasons for customers to prefer one product over another some form of competitive advantage is necessary. The study of competitors and the comparison of the strengths and weaknesses of competitor operations is very important in developing successful marketing plans. Marketing plans are also influenced by the stages of industrial development. In newly emergent industries such as video games, or new forms of entertainment, the emphasis is on developing customer awareness, as many will be first-time buyers. Growth markets still offer rewards for all competitors, but here the 'jockeying' for a favourable position really begins. As markets mature we find that:

- competition focuses on 'market share' and not market growth; and that
- customers are usually experienced repeat-buyers who understand the product benefits and know something about the different offerings.

In this market the emphasis is also on modified (improved) products, added value or operational efficiency. This becomes more intense as industries decline when excess production capacity is apparent and profits are falling. The concept of industry or demand life cycles can be linked to product life cycles, discussed in Chapter 12.

Identifying competitors

In order to develop competitive marketing strategies it is vital that we decide who are our competitors. The most obvious competitors are other organisations which offer identical products or services to the same customers as our organisation. However, the subject of substitute products and services highlights the indirect competitors, who also must be analysed. Perhaps it is helpful to define five levels of competitors.

1 Direct competition.
2 Close competition.
3 Products of a similar nature.
4 Substitute products.
5 Indirect competition.

Direct competitors

Perhaps we could see Pepsi Cola as a direct competitor to Coca-Cola. Both products offer similar products to the same general market. In this case the production methods employed are also very similar, although the actual formula for the basic cola essence is different and a closely guarded secret in both companies. With the Cola companies it is a tough, high profile marketing battle to gain business. Pepsi, with its famous 'taste test' challenge, did try to suggest differences between the products and a preference for Pepsi, but basically these products are in direct competition.

Close competition

Is Pepsi also a competitor to Tango orange drink? Both products offer similar benefits to similar consumers. The difference between orange and cola flavour is easier to recognise than the difference between Coca-Cola and Pepsi, but basically the products are substitutes for each other. In any analysis of drinks all fizzy drinks need to be considered. Of course it could be argued that other fizzy drinks include Perrier sparkling mineral water and champagne. Here we are moving away from close competition.

Products of a similar nature

Perrier is a naturally sparkling mineral water from Southern France. The water comes up through a field of natural gas, hence the claim to naturally sparkling as opposed to added carbon dioxide, in Pepsi or even other sparkling waters. However, it is the marketing decision to target Perrier at an adult market rather than the younger age targeted by Pepsi that makes Perrier less of a close competitor. Champagne also has an alternative way of producing the fizz. 'Methode Champenoise' is a secondary fermentation of the wine after it has been bottled. But again, it is not the different way of producing the bubbles, rather than positioning of the product, which makes it less relevant when considering competitors.

Substitute products

Is an ice cream a substitute for a fizzy drink? In some situations this is a reasonable choice. Marketers need to consider those products which can substitute in this way. The study of buyer behaviour is critical in deciding how wide such a study should go.

Indirect competition

Sometimes it is impossible to guess where competition is coming from. Any product that competes for the same customer income could be considered a competitor. If we consider a student surviving on a limited grant, could there sometimes be a choice between a Pepsi Cola and a newspaper? Perhaps here both are low value items and the distinction is easily made. An article about the American motor cycle company, Harley Davidson, quoted a dealer as saying, 'We're competing against conservatories and swimming pools, not other (customised) bikes' (*Sunday Times*, 23 September 1990).

Another example was a decision by Boots The Chemist to reorganise its stores. The managing director of a company supplying dog biscuits to Boots was told his product would be discontinued although it was selling well in the stores. The reason was an increase in the space allocated to audio and photographic products and other areas. Pet foods were not contributing enough profit per square foot of store and were being completely phased out. This type of competition is almost impossible to assess although it could be said that the dog biscuit company really knew very little about the objectives and needs of the customer. Boots required profit from its shops and not dog biscuits to sell to its customers!

Exercise

The following products could be seen as competitors. Which level of competition is involved and what attention do you think a marketing manager should give to analysing the competitive threat?

(a) A manufacturer of vinyl records when looking at vinyl records versus compact discs.
(b) British Rail when considering the threat posed by coach travel.
(c) A flower shop considering the shop next door which sells fancy chocolate products.
(d) A Chinese restaurant looking at the range of pre-prepared chinese meals available in a local supermarket.
(e) A large brewery company when considering home-brew kits.

You could also list other direct or indirect competitors for each of the examples above.

Competitor analysis

The above section should demonstrate that it is not always easy to identify who is your competitor for the purpose of understanding their strategies. Nevertheless Tom Peters is right when suggesting 'excellent companies do better competitor analysis'. The task is to understand the constraints restricting competitors and to predict competitor moves. The objective of this analysis is to find 'points of leverage' which can be used at minimum cost against competitors. It is not appropriate to collect data for its own sake, rather the analysis should focus on essentials which can help take decisions on how to win in the market-place.

It is not necessary at this stage to list the type of data collected in a competitor analysis. The need is specific to any particular set of competitors. It is, however, wider than the obvious marketing issues, and will include issues such as financial strength, operational efficiency and production capability, which could affect a competitor's market performance.

A typical evaluation process could follow the sequence below:

1 Evaluation of competitor objectives.
2 Evaluation of competitor's strategy.
3 Evaluation of competitor's success to date.
4 Evaluation of competitor's strengths and weaknesses.
5 Prediction of future competitor behaviour.

It is the future responses that are important for a marketer. However, many firms will behave in a consistent manner, so study of past actions can help to predict how your competitors might react in the future, and this is of course vital when formulating your organisational plans.

Information on competitors will come from both formal research and informal information channels. The latter includes dialogue with customers, often conveyed in reports from sales staff, but also obtainable from suppliers or other third parties. Although unnecessary data is to be discouraged, an efficient marketing information system is appropriate. The assessment of information needs to be made by a marketing-orientated employee who understands the dynamics of the particular market.

The competitive triangle

Figure 4.1 is inspired by the work of Kenichi Ohmae. It is an excellent way of remembering that customers have choices. From the apex of the triangle customers can assess the different offerings of all companies and their competitors.

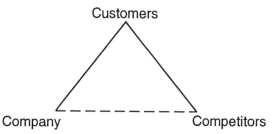

Fig 4.1 The strategic triangle

Obviously, customers will choose to do business with that company which best matches requirements. Of course, the workings of customers' decision processes are not simple. These are discussed in the following chapter. Nevertheless the match between the various offerings and particular customers, or groups of customers, should not happen by chance. The role of marketers is to try to influence factors in such a way that their organisations are chosen.

The object of this is to try to gain a sustainable advantage over competitors. Writing in the *Harvard Business Review* on this subject, Pankaj Ghemawat stated, 'For outstanding performance, a company has to beat the competition. The trouble is that the competition has heard the same message'. He summarises three areas of potential advantage from cross-industry findings:

1 Product innovation. Competitors secure detailed information on 70 per cent of all new products within a year of their development. Patenting usually fails to deter imitation. On average, imitation costs a third less than innovation and is a third quicker.
2 Production. New processes are even harder to protect than new products. Incremental improvements to old processes are vulnerable too. If consultants are to be believed, 60 per cent to 90 per cent of all 'learning' ultimately diffuses to competitors. Production often blurs competitive advantage: recent studies show that unionised workers pocket two-thirds of the potential profits in US manufacturing.
3 Marketing. Non-price instruments are usually ascribed more potency than price changes, partly because they are harder to match. Rivals often react to a particular move, however, by adjusting their entire marketing mix. Such reactions tend to be intense; limited data on advertising suggest that the moves and countermoves frequently cancel out.

Nevertheless, Peters still suggests that the goal should be uniqueness. He advises, 'Uniqueness most often comes not from a breakthrough idea, but from the accumulation of thousands of tiny enhancements'.

In the early days of marketing it was suggested that organisations looked for the one Unique Selling Point (USP). In fact, as Peters points out, it is much more complex. Therefore, to achieve competitive advantage a marketer needs to be involved with the total offering, both inside and outside the organisation.

Mega-marketing

Kotler suggested that competitive advantage could be gained by altering the external environment. This is undoubtedly possible, as exemplified by Pepsi bringing about the exclusion of Coca-Cola from India for more than a decade. The voluntary agreement limiting car imports from Japan to the UK is another example of reducing competition. However, the role of the EC Commissioner for Competition is specifically aimed at ensuring that no unfair competitive situations develop. Therefore, most organisations are open to the full power of competition and they have only the internal variables, controlled within their organisation, with which to achieve competitive advantage as seen by customers outside the organisation.

Conclusion

The competitive environment is the most dynamic environment in which an organisation will operate. Other organisations both obvious and remote are planning to offer their products or services and are aware that success comes from improving on the existing offers. It is in this ever changing arena that organisations have to strive for ongoing survival.

Companies can decide to try to lead developments and move faster than their rivals into new areas. This requires investment in Research and Development and a clear vision of the future. Other organisations will follow fast when new products or services are launched, hoping to improve on an idea with the benefit of seeing customers' reactions. However, laggard companies which react too late find that the market has already moved on.

The study of competitors activities is vital. But is must be linked to a study of potential buyers and how those buyers behave now and how they are likely to behave in the future. This is the subject of the next chapter. It completes the study of the competitive triangle discussed here. It is necessary for marketers to study both customers and competitors. One alone is not enough, it leaves the triangle incomplete. If it is a failure to appreciate the ever changing competition then the words of warning at the end of Chapter 3 will be even more relevant: 'There are those companies who wonder what happened'.

Questions

1 In a market of your choice, select two leading companies or brands and identify the means by which they compete with each other.

2 Do you think a marketer should take the advice
   "Never mind the customer just outfox the competition'.

3 Why do customers still buy branded food products in supermarkets when the retailers own label is often of similar quality and cheaper?

4 To what extent might competition come from unrelated markets in the form of a substitute product?

References

Brown, P B, Buell, B, Davis, J E, and Dreytack, K, 'Forget satisfying the customer', *Business Week,* 7 November 1985.
Ghemawhat, P, 'Sustainable advantage', *Harvard Business Review,* September/October 1986.
Kotler, P, 'Mega marketing', *Harvard Business Review,* 1986.
Kotler, P, '*Marketing management*', 7th Edn, Prentice-Hall, 1991.
Kotler, P and Singh, R, 'Marketing warfare', *Journal of Business Strategy,* Winter 1981.
Ohmae, K, *The Mind of the Strategist,* Penguin, 1983.
Peters, T, *Thriving on Chaos,* Macmillan, 1988.
Porter, M E, *Competitive Strategy,* The Free Press, 1980.

Case study: Wearport Docks Board

John Sampson has just been appointed to the newly created post of General Commercial Manager at the Wearport Docks Board. Working alongside the Board's General Operations Manager, he has been given a brief to halt and reverse the decline in traffic and profits that the port has been suffering in recent years.

In its heyday the busiest coal-port in the North East of England, Wearport is nowadays the typical example of a township suffering the problems of past dependence on basic industry. With the decline in output from the local coalfield, and a fall-off in employment and business in the ship-repairing and engineering industries, the port's performance in recent years has mirrored the fortunes of the borough itself. The figures published by the Docks Board for 1990 are testimony to the very difficulties that have ushered in John Sampson's new post. While the port had long been a casualty to regional decline, the recent recession has served to present new problems: in 1988 the bankruptcy of a major local customer, a steel stockholder, spelled the loss of 20 per cent in port traffic.

General changes in trade patterns since EC membership have led to a steady shift southwards in UK port shipments, while major shipowner's have responded to cost pressures by concentrating operations at the more efficient container ports.

Wearport Docks (Revenue Account – 1990 figures)

Traffic (m.tonnes)	Revenue (£m)	Profit/Loss (£m)	Total Workforce
0.95	3.8	(1.3)	160

John Sampson has spent his first few weeks in office familiarising himself with the current position of the docks. Although the coal trade has been declining for some time, coal exports still account for some 40 per cent of the port's traffic volume. The balance is represented by a mix of general cargo business such as timber, grain, and animal feedstuff imports; and exports of scrap iron, chemicals, refractories and light machinery. Most traffic is on coastal or near-water routes to Holland, Germany, Scandinavia and Eastern Europe.

The port has two serviceable basins, given over to coal-handling and general cargo work respectively. A third dock, now disused through heavy silting, has at various times been the subject of abortive development plans by the Local Authority.

On pacing the weed-choked marshalling yard one evening, Sampson is struck by the picture of despair and disrepair that is evoked by the rusting crane derricks and corrugated store-sheds. He nevertheless feels that the port could better realise the potential left to it, given a more systematic and commercial approach to the management of its marketing efforts. In three weeks' time he has to present to the Board a situation report and a preliminary analysis of market opportunities, as a first input to the preparation of a formal Business Plan.

Present your proposals on the investigations, analyses and preparations that John Sampson should treat as priorities during the next three weeks.

5

BUYER BEHAVIOUR

Introduction

It should be clear from the points made throughout the first four chapters, and especially in Chapter 2, that effective marketing involves focusing organisational activity on the needs of the potential customer. This requires understanding what determines these needs and how customers respond to them. Indeed an appreciation of the factors which are most relevant in a decision to buy a particular product is likely to be crucial to the effectiveness of many if not all marketing decisions. This aspect of marketing comes within the scope of what is termed 'buyer behaviour'. This chapter provides an introduction to this important specialist marketing subject and will provide the reader with the fundamentals needed to properly understand the basic principles of marketing covered in the remaining chapters of the book.

The simple buying decision process model

The decision to buy a product, whether it be a soft drink or the shop selling soft drinks, involves responding to a stimulus. The decision to buy a soft drink may be as a result of being thirsty on a hot day or to be sociable having volunteered to be 'driver' for a night out with friends at a country pub.

One approach to studying the buying decision process is to develop a model of it. The simplest way of doing this is to consider only the stimuli received by the person making the decision and the result – the person does or does not buy. This is a simple version of the classic stimulus–response model of behaviour which assumes that people will generally respond in some predictable way to a stimulus. The person making the decision is thus treated as a 'Black Box' which is a type of model generally accepted as useful for investigating complex systems which cannot be observed directly, such as the a decision-making process of a buyer (*see* Fig 5.1). It provides a framework which focuses on the inputs, the stimuli and the outcomes, of the decision, but offers no insight as to why a decision was made.

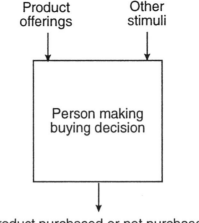

Fig 5.1 The simple 'Black Box' model of buying behaviour

The economic factors affecting buying decisions

From elementary economics it might be expected that buying decisions would be made by logically comparing the available choices in terms of cost and value using criteria such as:

- economy of purchase or use;
- convenience;
- efficiency in operation or use;
- dependability in use; or
- improvement in earnings (e.g. factory equipment).

A review of our own personal buying habits will show that in practice these factors are seldom considered and rarely of paramount importance when we make buying decisions.

Exercise

Think of a product you have purchased within the last week or so. Consider carefully why you chose that product. Write down as many reasons as you can to justify your purchase decision. When you have done this, list as many possible alternatives to the product purchased as you can. Remember not to purchase anything is often an option.

Are you able to justify your choice against each of the alternatives you have listed solely in terms of the economic factors listed? Are there any other explanations? Refer back to your list of reasons as you read the rest of this chapter to see whether there might be a better explanation for your decision. Repeat the exercise for someone very different from yourself who might also have purchased the same product, and consider whether they might have different reasons for their purchase decision.

There are many reasons why economic criteria are ignored when making purchase decisions. Often the person making the decision does not have the necessary information or it is difficult to compare the different products on this basis alone.

The principal buying decision variables

While it is not difficult to establish that buying decisions are not generally made on the basis of logical economic criteria it is considerably more difficult to identify the factors or variables which affect buying decisions. One reason is that many of these are dependant upon the person making the decision so are referred to as personal buying decision variables. These personal buying decision variables can be grouped under the following three categories:

1 the psychological variables;
2 the social influences variables; and
3 the demographic variables.

In addition the influence of the purchase situation needs to be recognised; internal stimuli such as thirst or fatigue – the physiological variables – need to be separated from external stimuli such as the aroma of freshly brewed coffee, and the decision process separated from the variables. The basic relationships between these elements are summarised in Fig 5.2

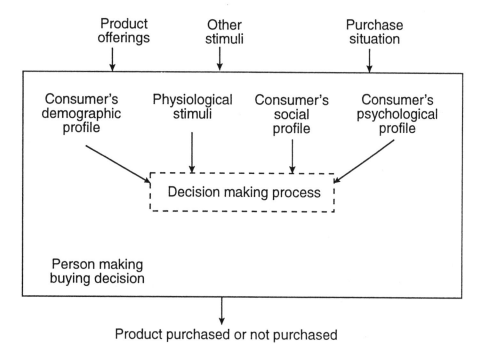

Fig 5.2 The basic elements of a buyer behaviour model

The buying decision process

The person who recognises a need effectively becomes a potential customer. It is the recognition of a need that creates a want. A person may be thirsty so be in need of a drink but this may be expressed as wanting a glass of champagne. The creation of a want involves a decision process which can involve some or all of the following seven stages:

1 Recognition of the need – this is a prerequisite of further action.
2 Choice of involvement level – how much time and effort does the need/want justify?
3 Identification of alternatives.
4 Evaluation of alternatives.
5 Decision – choice made.
6 Action.
7 Post purchase behaviour – need to resolve anxieties about choice made.

Most day-to-day purchases involve little or no risk in terms of being dissatisfied with the decision so justify little time or effort. The choice is made on the basis of the immediately available information.

Complex buying behaviour

For very high risk purchases buyers are likely to go through each stage of the decision-making process. This is termed 'complex buying behaviour' and is seldom adopted because of the time and trouble involved.

An example where this approach might be justified could be the purchase of a wedding present for someone overseas – in New Zealand perhaps. Stage one comes with the engagement announcement. Because it is so far away the need to take extra time and trouble could well be accepted with little thought, whereas stage three might involve finding out how long parcel post takes by sea and air and the relative costs; whether the electrical supplies are the same as in the UK and, whether a present list is being circulated around other friends and family in the UK. Possible alternatives might then be chosen on the basis of the amount of money available for the present. Stage five, the selection could be made on the basis of ease of shipment and availability. Then, after the present has been purchased, stage seven might occur when it is being packed since if this is difficult the choice made may well seem less suitable than an alternative which could have been packed and shipped by the supplier.

Information search

The third stage of the process – information search – may involve starting from scratch such as when the product is entirely new or is totally unfamiliar to the buyer. Obvious examples might be skis being purchased by the first-time skier or a hang glider by someone who has only tried the sport. This is however relatively uncommon. Most products are by their nature in some way associated with other products. Thus someone considering buying a new television is likely to consider the brand of their existing television favourably if it has been reliable: unfavourably otherwise. Perhaps the brand of their radio, music centre, CD player or other similar product would then be at least initially considered.

The evoked set

Those brands which initially come to mind when considering a purchase are referred to as the 'evoked set'. Clearly any brands which most people bring to mind in relation to certain types of product have a distinct advantage compared with other brands. It is the brands which are regularly within the evoked set of potential purchasers which set the standard that alternative products have to better if they are to be selected.

The concept of the Evoked set was developed by Howard and Sheth as a result of their work on the development of a comprehensive buyer behaviour model.

Exercise

Most people considering buying a personal computer would include IBM as one of the possible brands. They might not actually evaluate this option believing the IBM products would be too expensive but the brand would be known. What other brands would you initially think of relative to personal computers? Repeat the exercise for another fairly specific product, for example a small inexpensive new car, breakfast cereal, or a soft drink. Compare your list with others considering the same products.

Evaluation of alternatives

Stage four (evaluation of alternatives) is another important part of the process since it will inevitably depend upon making a comparison of only a few specific potential differences between the products. These are known as the salient attributes. Other differences are known as the non-salient attributes. Examples relevant to the choice of a motor vehicle might be the availability of fuel injection, a sun roof or electric windows. Other factors such as more secure door-locking systems or low-level access to the boot, have until recently been considered non-salient attributes by most buyers. This is in spite of these features having significantly greater potential for saving inconvenience or injury than any of the attributes usually considered salient.

Studies have shown that there are many different evaluation procedures which are used when making buying decisions. This work has also shown that these tend to be complex since they involve comparing attributes within the context of brand beliefs and attitudes.

Beliefs and attitudes

Other factors significant in the context of evaluating alternatives are the beliefs or attitudes held about the brands. Beliefs are perceptions of a brand which are based on explicit information. Attitudes are firmly held ideas which are often neither confirmed nor explicitly shown to be wrong by available information.

Returning to the personal computer example, users often take the view that IBM products are expensive. This view could be as a result of comparing the price of a range of similar machines. It could then be classed as a belief since it would be a descriptive thought based on the assessment of available data. Such beliefs may be modified by new information. It could, however, just as easily be based on prejudice rather than a rational assessment of available data. It would then be classed as a brand attitude. These tend to be enduring evaluations which are resistant to new information. It is quite likely that brand selection will also be significantly influenced by the buyer's understanding of the brand beliefs and attitudes of others, particularly close family.

The purchase decision

Even when a decision to buy a particular product has been made the purchase decision can be affected by unanticipated situational factors such as the cancellation of overtime working or because of the numerous other decisions often directly associated with the purchase: the vendor, the quantity, when and how to pay.

The quantity decision can often involve associated items such as batteries, film for cameras, tape for recording machines,etc., rather than the main item being purchased. Very often the supplier or the vendor removes the need to make these decisions by either including the essentials in the form of a pre-packaged kit or by providing these as a discount on the price. The provision of the associated items as a kit can be considered a marketing strategy whereas if they are provided as a form of discount, this would be a selling strategy.

The timing decision is often linked to the payment decision and the acceptance of credit cards has to a large extent reduced the importance of these decisions for many purchasers.

Post-purchase behaviour

The final stage of the complex buying process is post-purchase behaviour. Since it is seldom possible to make a fully rational purchase decision, it is hardly surprising that purchasers often doubt the wisdom of their choice when, finally, the purchase has been made. This leads to minor faults being found with the product itself or its features.

Recognising this, manufacturers have found it beneficial to aim some of their advertising directly at new owners to reassure them that they have made a wise decision. This approach is often used by motor vehicle and copier manufacturers: they have appreciated how important an influence existing users can be on potential customers. The provision of free telephone help-lines, call-out services and 'no quibble' return policies such as those adopted by Marks and Spencer, are aimed specifically at overcoming this problem. It was also within this context that an increasing number of suppliers have recognised the importance of having good instruction manuals.

The utilisation of complex buying behaviour

It would be logical to assume that complex buying behaviour is generally used for important purchases. Suppliers who believe this applies to their products tend to promote them on the basis of the features and benefits that are the result of the efforts and capabilities of their designers. This approach used to be seen in automobile catalogues which always included pictures of the engine and details of the technical features of the vehicle.

However, research showed that very few buyers have the knowledge necessary to appreciate the relative importance of this type of information and instead simply assume that competitive products are equivalent with regard to these features. This improved understanding of buyer behaviour can be seen in contemporary catalogues which seldom refer to these features. Instead, choice is focused specifically on acceptability for purpose (e.g. how many seats) and often to an even greater extent on the perceived prestige of the product. Promotion has also been increasingly focused on this aspect of the product. For example, 'Peugeot 205 – the choice when you are ready for four wheels'.

Dissonance-reducing buying behaviour

When buyers perceive commonplace products as being complex they are likely to compensate for this by adopting a less involved style of buying behaviour. Usually this reduces the scope of any information search which means the buying decision is often made from only small range of the available products. The decision is made with the objective of limiting the possibility of being disappointed with the product. This is called 'dissonance reducing buying behaviour'. It usually involves selecting a product on the basis of a few obvious, often new features rather than on the basis of the features actually required.

Domestic cookers are a very good example of a product for which this style of buying behaviour is typical. As a result, easily identified features such as automatic timers and light units are emphasised rather than basic performance or ease of use. Because of this even comparatively low-cost, though useful features such as thermostatically controlled hobs failed to gain general acceptance. Even more remarkable has been ready acceptance in the UK of 'built in' ovens which lack the separate grill which was an essential feature of the traditional British cooker. This is clear evidence that when purchased little or no consideration was given to the way the existing cooker was used.

Since the purchase choice is likely to be made from a limited range of products it is essential for sellers to promote their brands to ensure they are considered by as many people as possible. This is achieved by emphasising and promoting recognisable brand names. It also means that products that are subject to dissonance reducing buying behaviour are likely to become increasingly standardised. This is because manufacturers will tend to focus their competitive effort on the features of the product which have the largest market share, rather than on those having the highest performance or most innovative features.

Habitual buying behaviour

For most day-to-day purchases the process is even less involved since there is a whole range of products which are bought mainly as a result of habit. Newspapers, magazines, beverages, petrol, and most food products are examples of products which are very often purchased on the basis of habitual buying behaviour.

Variety-seeking buying behaviour

As an alternative to habitual buying behaviour most people adopt a less predictable approach to buying, at least for some of these low-value products. Usually these are products for which there is no clear preference either by the individual making the purchase or, more particularly, by the users of the product, e.g. the family. A typical example of a product in this category is breakfast cereal. Very often this is selected on the basis of buying an alternative to what was purchased on the previous occasion. Another example is the choice of magazine prior to an occasional train journey. Both of these are examples of variety seeking buying behaviour.

This type of buying behaviour does not apply to high-value items except where the wealth of the individual is such that this would be a trivial purchase. Thus the ordinary car user who changes brand with every purchase is more likely to be an example of dissonance reducing buying behaviour in which brand is of little importance than an example of variety seeking buying behaviour.

The psychological factors affecting buying decisions

Buying decisions which are made by individuals will inevitably, to at least some degree, be determined by the personality and experience of that individual. Within the context of buying behaviour the areas of specific interest are those concerned with Motivation, Perception, Learning, Personality and Attitudes.

Individual human behaviour has been studied since ancient times and systematically by psychologists, sociologists and other behavioural scientists for at least the past 100 years. Within the context of this work theories have been developed to explain the behaviour of individuals and groups in specific situations such as the workplace. All of those listed as relevant to buyer behaviour are also likely to be studied within the context of human resource management and are therefore likely to be familiar to many readers.

Motivation

In contrast to much of the early work on motivation which was concerned with deviant behaviour, Maslow's approach was to consider the factors concerned with the ultimate goal of 'self-actualisation' in terms of a hierarchy. He initially proposed that the individual would endeavour to meet the needs within each level sequentially. However, he recognised that in reality individuals would often be trying to meet the needs within different levels simultaneously. From the view point of buyer behaviour the essential point of the theory is the realisation that there are different classes of need and the main focus of individuals will depend upon their individual circumstances.

The theory recognises that individuals have limited needs for existence. Thus at the most basic level, human needs are physiological and concerned with sustenance (food and drink), recuperation (sleep) and procreation (sex). The theory then proposes that individuals who are able to satisfy these physiological needs will seek to make their situation more secure by trying to satisfy their 'safety' needs which involve physical protection, ensuring continuity of supply of the basic physiological needs, and the physical well-being of health and fitness.

Individuals who have satisfied these second level 'safety' needs will then tend to focus upon satisfying what are defined as the 'social' needs – love, friendship, status and esteem. Again, once these seem to be satisfied the focus moves to what have been defined as the 'personal' needs – achievement, self-esteem, fun, freedom.

The fifth level represents self-actualisation. Maslow saw this as a goal which, for most people, was easily abandoned due to social pressures and other priorities. It provides a link with other self-actualisation theories but is considered of little relevance to buyer behaviour so is usually omitted in this context. The hierarchy of needs defined by Maslow is usually summarised in what is known as the Maslow triangle (*see* Fig 5.3.)

The different values attributed to the levels can be used when selecting product benefits. In particular it has been found that effective advertising messages are often those which appeal to the most appropriate need level. For example, Procter & Gamble found the appeal 'Keeps your baby dry and happy' was more effective than 'Saves you time and trouble' during the initial promotion of their Pampers disposable nappies. In terms of the Maslow theory this can be explained on the basis that the first message appeals at a higher level (the social needs of the mother) than the second which appeals at the physiological level (the need for rest).

Fig 5.3 The Maslow hierarchy of needs

Exercise 5.3

Take any newspaper colour supplement and see how many of the advertisements can be rated in terms of the Maslow need level to which they are designed to appeal. Clearly some cannot be graded on this basis since they are designed to provide information rather than draw attention to a need or want.

Since one of the main functions of marketing is to ensure that product offerings meet the needs of potential customers it is clearly essential that great care is taken to understand as fully as possible what these needs are likely to be. Maslow's theory of Motivation not only provides a framework which sometimes can be useful for doing this, but also shows that whereas needs can be defined relatively simply they are likely to be expressed as very much more complex and diverse wants.

Consider someone who is thirsty. If that person is climbing in the Pyrenees the need for a drink might be completely met by spring water drunk from cupped hands. To meet the same need while at the Ascot races the same person is likely to want to drink champagne from a crystal glass. The basic need is the same, but in the second case the want recognises the additional needs of meeting the expectations resulting from being part of a social group and perhaps the self-esteem that comes from doing the 'right' thing. The late Rajiv Gandhi earned great respect from the people of India by recognising that his need was the same as every villager and always drank the local water when travelling in rural areas.

The Maslow and other theories of motivation (such as Alderfer's ERG theory, (Existence Relatedness and Growth Needs) which is an alternative to Maslow but one which accepts a hierarchy might not exist, or Herzberg's two-factor theory) are well known and considered relevant in the context of both human resource management and marketing. They are useful for identifying categories and patterns of human needs yet can easily be used to justify the conclusion that 'everyone is different'. Indeed, this is the view taken in Schein's model of 'Complex man' which asserts that:

> Human needs fall into many categories and vary according to the stage of development and total life situation. These needs and motives will assume varying degrees of importance to each person creating some sort of hierarchy but this hierarchy is itself variable from person to person, from situation to situation and from one time to another.

While in itself, of little help to someone trying to solve a specific marketing problem, this does provide a framework for analysing individual buyer behaviour.

Demographic factors

Buying decisions often depend upon a person's demographic profile. Within this any of the following variables can be relevant to an individual buying decision.

1 Age: There are many needs which are age-dependent, for instance baby food for the very young, mobility aids for the very elderly.
2 Stage in life cycle: Furniture purchases are likely to be more dependent upon stage in life cycle than age.
3 Occupation: More formal clothing is probably purchased by white collar workers.
4 Economic circumstances: Many products are dependant upon perceived discretionary income, e.g records, theatre tickets, books.
5 Lifestyle: This may increase the need for minor luxuries such as champagne as an alternative to, for instance, car ownership.
6 Personality/Self concept: This can affect willingness to try new products.
7 Perception/Learning: Choice is subject to knowledge of alternatives resulting from selective exposure, selective distortion and selective retention.

The social influence variables

The following social factors will also affect buying decisions made by individuals:

1 Family background: Political views, how education is valued, etc.
2 Reference groups: For example, primary, secondary, aspirational and dissociative reference groups
3 Roles and status: Relative to the product being considered.

The significance and the relevance of reference groups to buying behaviour varies widely according to the type of product being purchased; in particular, whether the product is a necessity or a luxury and whether the product is consumed in private or in public. Primary reference groups are those groups to which the person is considered to be a full member. Of these the most important is likely to be the immediate family, groups of close friends and co-workers. Primary reference groups are of particular importance with respect to purchases which directly affect the other members of the group – for example, holidays.

Secondary reference groups are those within which contact is more formal and less continuous such as those resulting from membership of professional associations, trades unions, religious organisations or as a result of where you live or work. Status within such groups is not necessarily automatic so purchases which may imply status within this type of group are likely to be affected by the expected attitude to the product selected. Menswear could, in general, be considered in this category.

Aspirational groups are those of which the purchaser would like to be considered a member. There is an implied association, however unrealistic, in owning the same brand of tennis racket as a favourite tennis star. The importance of this can be judged, at least in part by the keenness with which manufacturers wish to sponsor these public heroes.

Dissociative groups are those with which one would prefer not to be associated. As a result there are probably many people who refuse to use a Filofax not because it would not be useful but because they do not want to be thought of as 'Yuppies'.

In addition to the factors already mentioned the impact of reference groups on an individual buying decision will depend to some extent on the degree of risk perceived in the purchase decision. This factor is also likely to affect the way by which the buying decision is reached.

Within the context of the family, as might be expected, the degree to which a buying decision is made by either a husband or wife as individuals or shared between the partners has been shown to depend upon the type of product involved. Research undertaken by Davis and Rigaux in Belgium suggested that of the decision-making roles husbands and wives could be classified in Fig 5.4.

Organisational buying behaviour

In the last section the effect of reference groups on purchase behaviour was discussed in the context of different types of product. The particular interaction between husband and wife with regard to family purchases was also considered. Clearly other people have a major effect on even everyday buying decisions. This effect is likely to become increasingly important and formalised when purchase decisions are being made for an organisation.

This is a major aspect of marketing since the production and supply of goods and services involves many stages and organisations. Each of these involves the purchase of supplies and equipment from other organisations. Thus the volume of inter-organisational trade is in total many times greater than that for consumer trade. It is, however, subject to different and generally more formalised buying processes. These are categorised under the general heading of organisational buying behaviour. This applies to:

1 Industrial manufacturers.
2 Service providers including government.
3 Resellers.

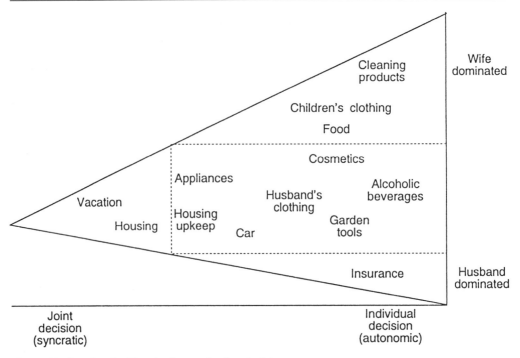

Fig 5.4 Husband and wife roles in purchasing decisions

Industrial manufacturers vary in size from multinational oil companies to individuals making Christmas crackers in their front room. Service providers vary from the National Health Service, possibly the largest employer in Western Europe, to the busker on the street corner. Likewise, resellers will vary from national chains such as Sainsbury to the individual newspaper vendor.

Organisational buying behaviour as a process is not specifically determined by the product. Toilet paper is a product which is purchased not only by individuals and families but by every type of organisation. Some products, such as cocoa beans, may only be used by organisations yet the buying decisions are normally entrusted to an individual specialist bidding at an auction. Even buying decisions involving items such as industrial plant may be made by individuals such as a company owner or a farmer. These exceptions show that although organisational buying is often referred to as industrial buying it needs to be defined in terms of the responsibility for the buying decision or the characteristics of the buying situation rather than the product.

Exercise 5.4

Consider a product such as a personal computer and list the people who might have an influence on your decision as to which brand you would buy. Then consider the same purchase but for use by a club, society or other organisation of which you are a member. Who would be the other people who would expect to be consulted? How might this explain the claim that 'No one was ever fired for buying IBM'?

The characteristics of organisational buying

The main characteristics of the organisational buying situation are:

1 Specific objectives: organisations buy to achieve defined objectives in terms of production output of goods or services. Their demand is thus derived from the demand of their customers and decisions made within budget and profit constraints.
2 The process is formal and involves many individuals, including specialists and professional buyers: the buying centre concept or decision-making unit (see below)
3 Decisions are often technically complex.

The contributors to organisational buying decisions.

It has been found helpful to view organisational buying decisions as being made by a group which has the required authority. These groups are referred to as either 'buying centres' or 'decision-making units'. Generally these groups include both formal and informal members and the individuals involved are likely to assume specific roles. These would be:

1 Users: these are the individuals who will be responsible for using the item being purchased.
2 Influencers: this group should provide the technical expertise necessary to make a rational decision. It is, however, possible within this context for an outsider, such as a relation of a high-status member of the decision-making unit, to have a deciding though unseen influence.
3 Buyers: the individuals who are responsible for actually placing the order. This group often have limited power for promoting a choice, but considerable power in limiting choice.
4 Deciders: the actual decision-makers. Their contribution depends upon their level of involvement. This can vary from personally gathering the information needed to make the decision, to simply confirming the selection made by others.
5 Gatekeepers: within most organisations there are individuals such as secretaries and receptionists, who can inhibit the flow of information to and between members of the decision-making unit. Even though this may be unintentional it can have a significant effect on a buying decision. In view of this it is helpful to consider anyone who might influence a decision-making unit in this way as being a gatekeeper and as such a member of the decision-making unit.

Each of these contributors have a specific effect on certain stages of the buying process.

Organisational buying situations

Just as individual buying behaviour varies according to the situation, so does organisational buying behaviour. This is classified according to the four identifiable buying situations:

1 Straight rebuy: this is the equivalent of habitual buying behaviour. Products are ordered as a routine. An essential procedure to ensure efficiency.

2 Modified rebuy: when a product cannot be obtained from the usual supplier or has not proved to be satisfactory an alternative supplier has to be found. Since the requirements are well defined it is difficult to justify the time and effort needed to find the best alternative. In addition, this situation provides an opportunity for the alternative supplier to oversell his product with the result that another poor buying decision is often made.

3 New Task: this is the equivalent of the complex buying behaviour. The decision-making unit (DMU) is likely to be a formally established group with established working procedures. Generally, the greater the risk perceived to the purchasers the larger the number of decision participants, the more information demanded, and the longer decision-making takes.

4 Systems buying: the benefits of buying rather than making a particular component can easily be lost because of the additional administration involved. To reduce this there is an increasing trend for manufacturers to purchase assemblies and sets of parts rather than individual parts. This is usually referred to as systems buying or, for the vendor, systems selling.

Organisational buying influences

Each member of a decision-making unit is likely to be influenced by different factors according to the situation. Of particular importance in the context of organisational buying behaviour are the following:

1 Organisational: the organisational status of the members of the decision-making unit often has more significance than technical expertise. Because of this there is a tendency for technical information to be selected in such a way that it provides justifications for the views of the deciders.

2 Interpersonal: buyers who have day-to-day contact with suppliers often will try to preserve this relationship either because it simplifies their task, or in their view, it is of direct value to their company.

3 Individual: members of a decision-making unit as individuals are likely to be subject to the constraints of individual buying behaviour. As a result factors such as branding can often be of critical importance. In addition, inter-company competition at the individual level can significantly affect the view taken by an individual member of a decision-making unit.

4 Environmental: economic, technical and ecological considerations are likely to be factors in any organisational buying decision. Within this context safety can be seen as being particularly important especially where individual accountability is clearly defined.

Conclusion

Buyer behaviour, whether individual or organisational, provides some valuable insights which can be applied usefully in many marketing situations. It also provides a framework, concepts and a vocabulary which can be used to analyse many marketing issues.

The complexity of the subject, however, is such that it cannot realistically be used prescriptively since it is likely to raise more questions than it answers. There is at least some circumstantial evidence to suggest that attempts have been made to apply these concepts in political campaigns both in the USA and the UK with little apparent success. This should not be seen to devalue the usefulness of the approach, but rather to emphasise the complexity of the marketplace and the need to make marketing decisions on the basis, at best, of an incomplete understanding.

Questions

1 Identify a product which is more appropriate to the 'self-esteem' needs as suggested by Maslow, rather than the more basic needs of a customer.

2 Consider a purchase you have made recently and identify the factors that influenced your decision to buy.

3 What do you consider is the role of consumer magazines such as '*Which?*' or '*What Computer?*' in influencing buyer behaviour.

4 Which employees in an organisation might fulfil the role of

(a) influencer; and
(b) gate keeper with respect to buying decisions?

References

Howard, J and Sheth, N, *Theory of Buyer Behaviour*, Wiley, 1969
Solomon, M R, *Consumer Behaviour*, Allyn & Bacon, 1992
Engel, J F, Blackwell, R D and Miniard, P W, *Consumer Behaviour*, 5th Edn, Holt, Rinehart and Winston, 1986.

Case study: Shell Traveller's Check Petrol Stations

After opening the first of its new-style petrol retailing outlets with the 'Traveller's Check' brand name in 1987, Shell Oil Company Ltd invested heavily to establish the concept countrywide. The main features of these new-style petrol stations were: easily accessed petrol pumps, car wash facilities and a small shop which sells a common range of snack foods, confectionery, gifts and commonly required car parts such as headlight bulbs. To establish these facilities Shell were prepared to close down, often against the advice of their site managers, any other activities which were carried out on the site, such as car repair and servicing, tyre centres and shops which offered DIY, gardening and other miscellaneous products.

The concept of Traveller's Check was the result of a detailed market research programme initiated by the Shell Retail Planning Group and carried out by Cooper Research & Marketing. This found that most motorists considered buying petrol a chore and did not differentiate between the branded outlets. The concept design also involved using specialist new product design consultants Craton, Lodge and Knight. Thus, the offering made by Shell had been both thoroughly researched and expertly implemented. Yet in the 5 April 1990 edition of *Marketing* it was reported that Shell were to phase out their Traveller's Check forecourt shops, would be opening convenience stores at 500 sites to compete directly with BP's Express Shops and were being advised on this new strategy by US petrol retailing consultants Strasburger Enterprises.

Why did the Traveller's Check concept fail to meet expectations in spite of being a well-designed product based on research carried out by specialists? What went wrong? To analyse this problem some basic questions need to be asked:

First, who did Shell consider to be the target customer for their Traveller's Check petrol stations? Was it to be the general motorist or a specialist group such as the economy-minded (traditionally targeted by Jet), or the company car user? Was the product designed to be superior to that offered by other brands? If so, in what respect: the speed of service, the overall standard of the facilities provided, the range of goods offered? Was that aspect of the product likely to appeal to the target group?

It may be worth noting at this point that the first Traveller's Check to be opened had no signs showing passing motorists the price of the petrol. This was intended to be a feature of all Traveller's Check sites but caused so much controversy and media coverage that Shell were, in effect, forced to accept the need to display their prices in the traditional way at these sites.

This case highlights many of the essential difficulties involved with any attempt to understand buying behaviour. Most of the theories, while useful for explaining the way groups such as motorists are known to behave in a particular situation, are inadequate for predicting how a group might behave. In particular it shows that market research cannot always be relied upon to provide answers to these questions since the results not only depend upon asking the appropriate questions, but also in interpreting answers which may well fail to reflect how the individual will actually behave in a given situation which is not within that person's actual experience.

6

SEGMENTATION OF MARKETS

Introduction

In the 1950s the pioneers of mass-marketing, multinational firms such as Procter & Gamble and Coca-Cola, had the power to sell large quantities of standardised goods to a 'homogeneous' mass-market, using the promotional attraction of mass media (national press, and especially television). Even earlier, Henry Ford made his fortune by mass-marketing, offering his Model 'T' car in 'any colour as long as it is black'. Now things have changed in the marketplace. Coca-Cola now offer caffeine-free, diet, cherry and other variants which combine some or all of these attributes. Ford make cars from the Fiesta to the Granada in a host of finishes, colours, and specifications. At a basic level this could be seen just as an increase in the variety of products offered, but of course the cause of this proliferation is to attempt to meet customer needs more precisely.

If marketing is the satisfying of the needs and wants of customers, then those wants must at least be established even if they are found to be different for every single consumer. This fact recognises that customers do not always form a homogeneous group, nor are the demands of two, outwardly similar, people necessarily the same. However, you will remember that marketing really involves 'profitable exchanges', so as part of the marketing decision process there must be a view on which customer groups are to be supplied. If different customers and prospects have different needs then why not offer them different products to meet those needs? And why not market those products in a way that appeals best to each particular group?

The previous chapter suggested the buying decisions of consumers should be linked to relevant characteristics associated with individual buyers, e.g. baby foods are bought by new mothers or business suits are purchased by white collar workers. These examples already illustrate how some specific groups could be more likely to buy a particular product than another group. It is, of course, difficult to identify those people who prefer a red car rather than a black car, but these preferences certainly do exist.

The identifying of the different groups, and so sub-dividing the market into those groups which can be attacked by a specific marketing strategy, is termed segmentation. The use of different marketing strategies for each distinct segment is known as target marketing, or differentiated marketing (*see* Fig 6.1). Target marketing is discussed again later in this book when considering how to market a product. This chapter looks at the identification of segments and the benefits of focusing on these segments. It also covers the criteria necessary for a segment to be useful to a marketer.

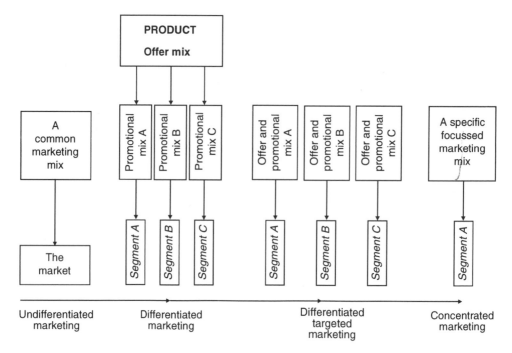

Fig 6.1 Segmentation and strategy

It has already been stressed that marketers should ask themselves: Why should customers buy from us ? Michael Porter, of the Harvard Business School, suggested that if you were not the cost leader (lowest cost producer *not* necessarily the lowest price) then you had two options to succeed in a competitive market place: either differentiate (i.e. offer a different product from that offered by your competitors) and/or focus (i.e. concentrate on a specific group of customers and meet their needs exceptionally well). Porter suggested that confusion of cost leadership with differentiation could be a problem, as these different strategies require very different organisational skills and philosophies of working. He did, however, allow a focuser to determine whether they were pursuing a strategy of cost and focus or differentiated focus.

These different strategies are likely to appeal to very different groups of customers. Consider the type of people who buy food in a delicatessen shop compared to those who regularly shop at a discount food store such as Kwiksave or Aldi. Even if some people use both outlets, the motivations for the visiting of such very different stores will enable those shoppers to be distinguished from those who only visit one of the outlet types mentioned.

There has recently been some debate about the definitions used by Porter and, while these should be noted, his work has nevertheless become a standard from which debate on strategy can follow. In marketing terms it is possible to differentiate either the 'promotional mix' alone, or to make a different 'offer mix' together with a different 'promotional mix' to a particular segment. The first, which could use a different advertising strategy to each different segment, is termed differentiated marketing, the second is target marketing.

Useful segmentation

The basic principle of segmentation is very simple. There is, however, a difference between the process that explores whether distinctive homogeneous subsets exist in a particular market, and the practical use exploiting the existence of such groups for effective marketing strategy. Classification in any of a wide range of ways is fundamental to understanding customers and initiating strategies to influence them. It is only by identifying similar people and placing them together into groups, then describing how the behaviour relevant to our product category varies between those groups, that we can get close to isolating the reasons why the group members react in the way they do. But identifying usable segments is very difficult. Segmentation of markets was described as one of the fastest-growing marketing techniques of the last decade. However, too often the segments are defined in very traditional and static ways. It is easy to recognise a segment such as (a) all men or all women; it is far less easy to communicate with this segment. On the other hand, it is less easy to recognise (b) people who prefers red cars as opposed to black cars.

Here, the marketing problems are both the difficulties of communicating with the segment as well as describing other characteristics of the segment. The first segment is demographic and easily recognisable. The second segment is psychological, difficult to define, and yet it may be more relevant to a particular marketing decision than the first. Most likely, a combination of different types of descriptors will be used to enable a usable segment to be described.

The work of subdividing a market into segments is justified only if it can be used to improve marketing effectiveness. To meet this objective the segment must be both relevant to the purchase decision and able to be reached by both distribution and communications with some measure of precision.

The traditional approach uses variables which can be described as geographic and/or demographic. Much of the data collected by the various UK media owners is quoted in terms of the socio-economic groupings shown in Table 6.1.

Table 6.1
Market segmentation by socio-economic groupings

A	Upper Middle Class	High managerial/administrative/professional e.g. Company Director, or established doctor or solicitor.
B	Middle Class	Intermediate managerial/administrative/ or professional.
C1	Lower Middle Class	Supervisory/clerical/junior managerial.
C2	Skilled Working Class	Skilled manual workers.
D	Working Class	Semi-skilled or unskilled workers.
E	Pensioners, casual workers and others.	

(*Source:* JICTAR)

There are many potential problems when using a scale derived from the occupation of the ' head of the household' to determine how people behave. Anyway the descriptions above are already archaic, using terms such as working class. The classification is also made less easy to use by the changing social order, for instance the move away from the traditional 'husband, wife and 2.4 children' household that dominated when this classification was started. Now most homes contain either one or two people and the traditional family group described above represents a minority of homes.

A longitudinal study by Kirk McNulty looked at the changing face of UK society. He based his categories on the Maslow hierarchy discussed in Chapter 5. The study shows his 'Inner Directed' groups are expanding as a percentage of the population, while other groups decrease. Inner direction covers

1 Social resisters: Caring group; altruistic, green, and likely to join pressure groups.
2 Experimentalists: Fun seekers, materialistic, pro-technology and individualistic.
3 Self explorers: Share social concerns, not materialistic, motivated by self-expression.

All these groups are defined in terms of Maslow's self actualisation category. These groups make their own decisions and can afford to do so. As the size of these groups increase there will be more fragmentation of traditional markets, and more opportunities for '*micro-marketing*' to ever smaller target groups.

Similar groups have been identified in the USA by studies such as the VALS (Values And LifeStyle) research. This classifies consumers on the basis of self-orientation and resources. It is a commercial classification which has proved very popular with major US advertising agencies (*see* Fig 6.2).

Principle orientated	Status orientated	Action orientated	Resources
Fulfilleds	Actualisers	Experiencers	Abundant
Believers	Achievers	Makers	↑
	Strivers		↓
	Strugglers		Minimal

Fig 6.2 Value And Life style categories (VALS) (SRI International)

The problems in finding a usable way of describing a segment does not mean the concept of marketing segmentation is not useful. There are too many examples of successful target marketing which can be found. In fact the industrial product sector is a good example where the organisational characteristics (demographic and geographic, such as type of company, size, industry, etc.) can be successfully linked with personal characteristics of employees who might be: users; influencers; buyers; deciders; or gatekeepers. By identifying how to reach a group of 'deciders' a positive marketing result can be achieved as in the example below.

Example

A campaign to communicate with the financial controllers of companies with large transport fleets was undertaken by a major tyre company. The company realised financial controllers were a key 'advisor' group and in some cases held the 'decider' role. They were primarily interested in the lowest total cost of operation, not just the cheapest tyre. They could be reached directly, and a campaign was directed at them, emphasising areas they considered important rather than issues important to the transport manager. It proved successful in boosting sales levels.

Returning to the consumer market, another useful set of segments is the ACORN grouping (A Classification Of Residential Neighbourhoods). This is a combination of traditional demographic descriptors developed in a way that makes communication with this segment easy. It is sometimes termed geo-demographics, as it links postcodes in Britain to the prime characteristics of the occupants of the households. A total of 38 groupings has been produced, so that a marketing organisation or other user can buy a list of all addresses in a particular category – say all post codes which have a majority of 'private flats with single pensioners' (category K38). A mail shot to this segment offering them a relevant product will have a greater success rate than a more random method of contacting this group. Alternatively, a company could collect all the addresses and postcodes of its customers. By analysing these against the ACORN database the predominant categories can be established and plans laid to communicate with other potential customers in the same categories. This can prove very rewarding, but it does not assume that all people in the same postcode groupings behave in the same way. Compare your family with your own neighbours. However, it does assume, and can demonstrate, that the probability of similarities exist. This is enough to make the database valuable to marketing managers. There are other rival databases such as MOSAIC and PROFILES, offering similar services.

Requirements for a usable segment

There is no limit to the numbers of ways a market may be segmented in particular circumstances, but to be useful a segment must be:

- definable;
- sizeable;
- reachable;
- relevant.

Definable

This means we must be able to describe the market segment and for this the key characteristics of this segment should show a degree of homogeneity. The segment is of course a subset of a heterogeneous total market, because if the total market were homogeneous there would be no need for segmentation. It is also useful to be able to measure the market size and define the boundaries of the segment.

Sizeable

Is the segment large enough and can it produce the required turnover and profit for your organisation? This criterion depends on the particular organisation, as a minimum revenue of £10 m. for a brand sold by a large multinational might be appropriate, while another company might find £0.5 m. acceptable and a major part of turnover. So size is relative, but organisations also need to make profits. Toffler suggests that markets are 'de-massifying' into ever-multiplying, ever-changing sets of mini-markets that demand a continually expanding range of options, models, types, sizes, colours, and customisations. That is the challenge of marketing, but useful segments must be assessed in terms of organisational resources and objectives.

Reachable

There must be a way of reaching the segment both effectively and efficiently. This includes the obvious physical distribution of a product, as well as communicating with customers via media or in a direct way. ACORN meets the communication test, but it is less easy to find a way of communicating with categories such as the 'experimentalists' or 'self-explorers' described by McNulty.

Relevance

This has already been mentioned as the most important test for any described segment. It cannot be considered in isolation from the other criteria as there is no point in describing a relevant segment which cannot be reached.

The message of this section is that, although segmentation can be an effective marketing technique, it should be treated carefully. In the era of de-massification, organisations can easily appeal to segments which are too small to be viable or perhaps too costly to reach. While segmentation can help in the process of understanding customer similarities and differences, careless use could lead to the development of too many product variants, confusion of customers, and the failure to capitalise on real opportunities that such a study of markets and their subsets offers.

Segmentation variables

In order to describe segments there are two different approaches which can be used. The first concentrates on the characteristics of the buyer. Generally these are classified under one or a combination of the three categories:

- demographic;
- geographic; and/or
- psychographic.

However, an alternative but just as powerful, set of variables can be derived which allow a focus on *how* customers behave, and the benefits sought by those customers from a product or service. While benefits do link closely with lifestyles and *psychographics*, they do warrant attention as a separate category for classification. So the other two categories are:

- behaviourial; and
- benefit segmentation.

Demographic segmentation

Demographics are the most widely used method of classification of marketing segments. It is the basis for the collection of many government statistics and the standard system used by the media industry. Pym Cornish of RSL, who is an acknowledged authority on demographics, wrote

> Demographics are often thought of as consisting of no more than the dimensions of sex, age, social grade, region, and a few others that have traditionally been used as a standard market research variable in Britain. But society does not stand still. It has evolved, old generalisations about the family, such as that women look after the house and children while men earn the money, have become less and less true. Yet this does not mean that demographics have become less useful, only that the traditional classifications should be superseded by others that reflect the current structure of society more accurately.

The counter argument by advertising boss, Adam Lury, in an article entitled 'Demographics tell me nothing I want to know' is discussed in Chapter 11. The real point is made by Cornish when he talks of accurately reflecting the *current* structure of society. Maybe he should have indicated that, even if we can reflect the current structure, it is the future which must concern marketers, and the use of segments to predict future behaviour is a problem neither of these authors addresses in their articles.

So, following on from Cornish's article, the traditional demographic bases are: sex, age, marital status, socio-economic classification and occupation. To these we must add descriptors such as family type and size, income levels, ethnic origin, education levels and stage in life cycle. The last factor was described in more detail in Cornish's article.

For industrial products there are equivalent demographic categories which can be used, such as industry type (SIC codes), turnover and/or profit, numbers of employees, and numbers and types of customers.

Such demographic data are relatively easy to obtain. Every ten years in the UK there is a full Census of the Population, so that government statistics can be updated. This does not cover issues like lifestyle in great depth, but it does provide a good basis from which to start. Many organisations use census data as a basis for decisions on market potential. The type of information provided is called secondary data, in that it is collected for one purpose but it is often used for a secondary one. The sources of secondary data are discussed in Chapter 9.

It cannot be stressed too many times that the information collected must be *relevant* to the purchase decision. Far too many companies hoard all sorts of information even after it has ceased to be relevant. The categories which are actually relevant can change, as in the example of Red Stripe lager. This Jamaican lager was originally imported into Britain from the Caribbean. Its price reflected the cost of importing, and it was primarily sold to areas with a high population with Jamaican connections. The brewers, Desnoes and Geddes, then arranged for the product to be brewed under license in the UK. While they were very careful to maintain the distinctive quality of the lager, it was decided that the price could be modified and there were opportunities for appealing to a wider number of drinkers. Hence ethnic origin is no longer such a relevant demographic variable for this product.

However, stage in the life cycle does affect consumption of beers and lagers. As people move through the stages of pre-family, family and post family they change their drinking habits. Also, some people remain single or form a relationship but do not have any children. They, too, show changes in drinking according to life cycle. Life cycle is more powerful than age alone in this analysis, as it is able to include relative levels of disposable income and, equally important, leisure time, which a family with children finds is in short supply. Of course the traditional variables do help in describing segments as, for instance, men drink more beer than women, and there are differences identified by socio-economic groups (*see* Fig 6.3). In order to describe their customers the major brewers use a combination of demographic data with other bases such as lifestyle (as distinct from life cycle) which is covered under *psychographics*.

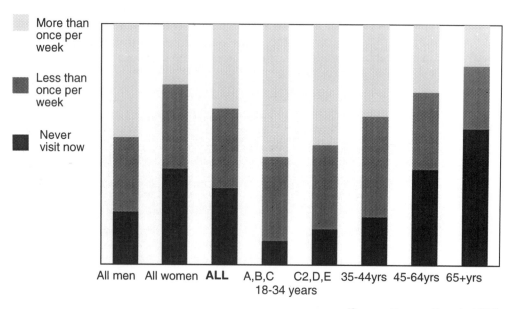

(Source : Brewery Reports 1988)

Fig 6.3 Frequency of pub visiting

One very full database which covers demographic profiles but also other bases is the TGI (Target Group Index), produced by the British Market Research Bureau. BMRB is a commercial organisation which carries out 3000 interviews every month and continually updates information on the several thousand brands and product categories covered. It offers purchasers of the index detailed demographic and lifestyle profiles of consumers. It also covers the media which reach the various segments, and is an invaluable source of information linking consumer product segments to the 'promotional mix'.

Geographic segmentation

This type of classification is often considered as another type of demographic variable. In some ways it is, and the development of geo-demographic bases such as ACORN links it yet tighter. Nevertheless it is an obvious grouping, and geographic variables can be considered separately. Issues, such as rural *vs* urban , warm *vs* cold, north *vs* south, all can be considered where appropriate. The consumption of sweet (sugar based) products is greater in Scotland than in the rest of the UK. Is this perhaps useful information when planning a new product?

There are also opportunities for the commercial market, such as planning new retail outlets. One company might look for a location in the key area bounded by outlets such as Marks and Spencer, Boots, and W H Smith which provides the greatest density of shoppers in many town centres. Another trader might base decisions on the number of suitable customers living within a specific radius or travelling a distance into the centre of a city. Both are dependant on geographic segmentation studies.

It might be appropriate to add a warning regarding large, apparently attractive segments. These naturally attract competitors and may not provide the anticipated level of business. There are many small shops serving a limited geographic area without direct competition and making a reasonable profit. Located in the High Street of a major town, the competition would change the situation. So although the numbers of potential customers is far greater, the actual custom may not be, and with the increased costs involved in running a city-centre outlet the result could be disaster.

Psychographic and lifestyle segmentation

Psychographics seek to classify people according to their personality traits. They are used more in relation to consumer products but there is no reason why corporate interests, such as a measure of levels of social responsibility, could not be used when considering issues relevant to segmenting organisations. There is some debate over whether psycho-graphics should be restricted to issues of sociability, self-reliance, assertiveness and other personality traits, or whether it should be widened to include lifestyles which cover attitudes, interests, and opinions. This book will follow the conclusions of Weinstein in considering psychographics to be a combination of personality traits and lifestyles. The bringing together of these factors from the two areas provides a more useful and robust segmentation base. There are still problems in using personality traits to explain customer behaviour, and so the study of lifestyles and integrating them with other psychographics over the past 20 years has brought a new dimension to the understanding.

The use of lifestyle characteristics is attractive to the marketer for two reasons. First, it provides a simple link to the variables used in behaviourial theory, e.g. attitudes, perception, and social influences. Second, although lifestyles can change over time and over the life cycle of a person, there tends to be a consistency of action in selecting products and services which match the 'persona' of a consumer at a particular period.

To establish psychographic characteristics a series of questions will be developed and respondents are asked to agree or disagree with statements such as: 'I like to do all my car maintenance', 'Traditional home cooking is best', or 'I worry about environmental issues'. Thus scales are developed from a battery of questions, enabling a detailed picture of attitudes and lifestyle to be constructed. A fuller exposition of the market research procedures required to construct these segments can be found in Margaret Crimp's excellent book *The Marketing Research Process*.

The results of a demographic analysis of whisky drinkers might show they are primarily class – AB, sex – male, age – 45 plus. A life style study of this category shows it is not homogeneous, and there are many other spirits consumed by the segment, but it could identify key attitudes of those who drink whisky rather than gin. This can then be applied to positioning the product (*see* Chapter 11) and promoting it (Chapters 17 and 18).

In 1974 an early article on 'The concept and application of lifestyle segmentation' by Plummer identified the following list of subjects on which questions could be posed in lifestyle studies. This list shows the scope of such studies.

Activities	Interests	Options
Work	Family	Themselves
Hobbies	Home	Social Issues
Social Events	Job	Politics
Vacation	Community	Business
Entertainment	Recreation	Economics
Club Membership	Fashion	Education
Community	Food	Products
Shopping	Media	Future
Sports	Achievements	Culture

Behaviourial segmentation

The concept of psychographic segments, which concentrate on life style and attitude, can be extended to study how people behave with respect to purchasing a particular product. The most obvious requirement is to study usage rates and brand loyalty. Questions that can be answered include ones such as: How do heavy users differ from light users?; Can we isolate brand-loyal consumers? If we can identify usage levels and link this to other segment criteria, then differentiated marketing strategies can be adopted for each group. Such groups could be:

- Heavy users (say every day)
- Medium users (maybe once a week)
- Light users (say once a month)
- Occasional users
- Non users – Never used brand
  – Lapsed users of brand.

Inevitably a version of the Pareto effect will apply. Perhaps 80 per cent of a company's sales will go to 20 per cent of its customers (heavy users). The temptation is to concentrate on these people, as they provide the bulk of the profitable sales. In fact, they need a marketing mix that retains and reinforces their custom. This will probably be very different from the message to occasional or light users, who may either purchase competitors' products or alternatively not use the product category very often.

Other behaviouristic criteria include:

- Usage rates
- Loyality levels
- Purchase occasion
- User status
- Readiness status.

Purchase occasion is an obvious discriminator with buying behaviour, and therefore needs to be considered when carrying out a segmentation study.

The behaviour of purchasers buying, say, beer or lager will vary between orders in a public house, occasional purchasing from an off-licence, or regular purchasing as part of a regular shopping trip to a licensed supermarket. The same is true for an ice cream purchased during the interval in a theatre, where prices of up to £1 are commonly paid, and bulk purchase in a freezer centre where the same £1 could buy 4 individual ice creams.

Dickson went further, linking purchase situation with benefits to fill what he termed, 'person-situation: segmentation's missing link'. This work is just one example of linking criteria together to provide usable segmentation to assist marketing decisions.

A direct marketing organisation subdivides its mailing list by what they term the 'customer pyramid' (*see* Fig 6.4).

Fig 6.4 The customer pyramid

The customer pyramid is one form of measure of readiness to buy, where each requires a different approach from the suppliers. Another way of looking at readiness is the AIDA sequence discussed in Chapter 18. Customers need to progress from Awareness through Interest to Desire and Action. This progression could take time, and behaviour will be different for potential customers in different stages of this continuum.

The usual marketing response following a segmentation exercise is to develop a distinct and differentiated marketing mix to match the needs, wants and demands of the customers in a particular segment or group of segments. It is possible to consider customers' existing behaviour and capitalise on it. The power tool company, Black and Decker, see themselves offering a range of tools to Do-it-Yourself enthusiasts and professional craftsmen. The company built its reputation on power drills, but now supply a large range of equipment. There is, of course, a large element of 'life style' in the Black and Decker segment and this has enabled them to effectively extend their range by a series of innovative new products. Their research showed that professional tradesmen started to see Black and Decker products in terms of amateur 'Do-it-Yourselfers' and were rejecting them. Black and Decker's response was to launch the DeWalt range of professional tools sold through trade outlets and, while matching the needs of this segment, capitalise on existing behaviour by the members of the segment. At the same time Black and Decker's standard range is widely available in many outlets.

Benefit segmentation

The idea of segmentation on the basis of the benefit received is wholly consistent with the marketing concept. A motor car purchased as the main or only one for a family will provide a very different benefit from a company car supplied to an employee or a car purchased as a second car for a spouse or for a son/daughter about to go to college. The benefits received are different and thus the actual car bought will be assessed by very different criteria. Benefit segmentation will help to isolate these factors, so that a specific marketing package can be constructed.

Michael Porter gives a good example of a successful cost/focus strategy based on benefit segmentation. He describes the US hotel chain, La Quinta, which offers a specific product for business travellers. La Quinta have above average size rooms and good quality construction to ensure minimum external noise in any room. They provide a fast, efficient check in/out system and certain business facilities required by travelling businesspeople. They are conveniently located on major roads but do not offer restaurants or food service. There is always a 24 hour restaurant nearby if required, but not run by the hotel. La Quinta concentrate on providing a value package for a particular segment who claim to require facilities to do an evening's work after a day of meetings but do not require on-site eating. A restaurant is expensive to run and so why provide it, if the benefits are not required? A similarly focused development in the UK is the development of no frills, cheap, but good value overnight hotels by the Trust House group on sites close by their Little Chef restaurants.

Benefit segmentation depends on causal relationships rather than descriptive criteria of segment members. It is equally applicable to industrial products or services as well as consumer goods. In fact some products span these categories. For instance, a portable calculator could be a consumer item for use by a student, or an industrial product if used in an accounts office. An electrical maintenance service can be offered to a commercial organisation or a private home. A service situation such as this provides the maximum flexibility in target marketing, since each contact between supplier (electrician in this case) and customer is distinct and the delivery of the service is inseparable from the production. Hence the supplier can provide a precise service to match the benefit required.

In other situations the product is not offered to a discrete segment. An aeroplane could contain passengers who have

(a)   bought tickets at full price;
(b)   bought discount tickets in advance (APEX); or
(c)   bought even cheaper standby tickets or maybe 'bucket-shop' offers.

All groups receive the same prime benefit – air travel to their destination. But the problems regarding full-fare business travellers has been tackled by providing 'Club' or 'business' class as distinct from 'economy' class. Nevertheless some passengers buy full economy fares, others are discounted. The difference in benefits such as ability to change times of travel if you hold a full-fare ticket, compared to the possibility of not travelling at all with a standby, illustrate the wider range of benefits which must be explored for the same product offering.

Benefit segmentation was popularised 25 years ago by Russell Haley, who studied the toothpaste market in the USA. He identified four groups (*see* Table 6.2). From such an analysis, it can be seen how different brands can be designed to meet each of the benefit segments identified above.

Table 6.2
An example of benefit segmentation in the toothpaste market

	Benefit required	**Other characteristics**
Sensory segment	flavour + product appearance	usually children
Social segment	sound bright teeth	outgoing and active young (sometimes also smokers)
Worrier segment	decay prevention	heavy users; family
Independent segment	low prices	predominantly male, little loyalty, bought brand on offer

Conclusion

The alternative approaches and scope of marketing segmentation have been described under the separate headings above. There should be no doubt that these bases are dependent on each other. Effective segmentation could make use of all of the categories, and will usually require a combination of more than one type. By combining the way market segments are analysed it is possible to understand them in great detail, and also to follow changes in the dynamics of those segments. The task of constructing a marketing position and an offering and promotional mix to appeal to the segments identified will be considered in Chapter 11 and subsequent chapters.

Questions

1 How might you segment the market for:

   (a) motor cars; and
   (b) holidays?

2 Segmentation leads onto differentiated marketing. How might a company avoid producing too many varieties of a product?

3 Do you think demographics alone are a useful way of segmenting the market for educational courses?

4 What variables do you think organisations should include in a marketing database to aid segmentation studies?

References

Advertising Association, *Advertising Association Pocket Book*, 1992.
Cornish, P, 'Demographics: not standing still', *Admap*, December 1990.
Crimp, M, *The Marketing Research Process,* 2nd Edn, Prentice-Hall, 1985.
Dickson, P R, 'Person–situation: segmentation's missing link' *Journal of Marketing*, 46, 1982.
Haley, R, 'Benefit segmentation: a decision-orientated research tool' *Journal of Marketing* , 32, July 1968.
Lury, A, 'Demographics tell me nothing I want to know', *Admap,* December 1990.
McNulty, W Kirk, *UK Change Through a Wide Angle Lens*, Futures, 1985.
Porter, M E, *Competitive Advantage*, The Free Press, 1984.
Mitchell, A, *The Nine American Lifestyles*, Macmillan, 1983.
Plummer, J T, 'The concept and application of life style segmentation', *Journal of Marketing*, 38, January 1974
Toffler, A, *The Third Wave*, Collins,1980.
Weinstein, A, *Market Segmentation,* Probus Publishing, 1987.

Case study: CROWN SPORTS

Following a takeover, an accountant friend of yours has been made redundant. He has decided to realise his ambition of running a sportswear retail shop. His redundancy payment (£25k) plus a loan guaranteed against his house will raise the £50, 000 needed to purchase the business of CROWN SPORTS. This business, started in 1959 by Charlie King after an undistinguished career as a professional footballer, trades from a 1000 sq ft shop about half a mile from the new Queen's Shopping Centre. Charlie is now 68 years old and is concerned that he is losing customers to the new Olympus shop in the shopping centre. He did, however, achieve a turnover of £150, 000 in 1992 and after his salary of £12k, made a net margin of 2 per cent. Half the current turnover is in footwear with the rest split between equipment and clothes. Charlie has not specialised in any particular sport but rather covers the more popular ones, changing the emphasis depending on the relevant season, i.e. soccer/rugby in winter; cricket/tennis/golf in summer. He does, however, have a wide selection of footwear from such major manufacturers as Nike, Reebok, Dunlop and Hi Tec. There have been some past problems with Adidas who insisted on minimum order quantities which Mr King felt excessive, so currently no Adidas equipment is stocked.

Your friend believes he can improve the financial control of the business. The major trends all seem to indicate sports activities are thriving and in spite of the demographic decline in the teenage market and recent curbs on consumer spending there is every chance of this market continuing to grow ahead of the rate of inflation. There is, however, continuing development of 'high technology' specialist equipment which could involve stocking more expensive items. Also major competition for retail sports equipment is coming from the growth of sports chain stores (e.g. Olympus) and of buying groups (e.g. Inter Sport) who use their buying power to achieve significant deals which they advertise to attract customers.

Before your friend acquires the business he needs to consider how he can develop it. He does not think he can compete on price with the likes of Olympus but might be able to attract customers by specialising on particular parts of the market. Can you advise him on the marketing issues he should consider in this case?

7

THE MARKETING–ENVIRONMENT INTERFACE

Introduction

The introductory section (Chapters 1–6) has attempted to put marketing in the wide context of the dynamic competitive environment and to stress the importance of understanding your customers. The challenge facing marketers is how to take the initiative and how to ensure their products succeed in this hostile world.

It is said that a product is not sold until it has reached the ultimate consumer; in fact we could go further and say it is not sold until it is paid for and used by the final consumer. It is only then that there is any possibility of selling further products to that customer.

Marketing variables

Consumer acceptance of the product is therefore vital for continued sales. However, before actually buying or trying a product, the potential customer must be aware it exists, must know where it is available, and must feel able to afford it. This introduced what we will call the '4 As':

- Awareness
- Availability
- Affordability
- Acceptability.

The Coca-Cola Company have been using the last three – Availability, Affordability and Acceptability – as their test of strategy for many years. Perhaps they already know most of the world is aware of their product. No product or service would be sold without the customer being aware a product exists, that it is available, that it is affordable and considered acceptable. These four factors are relevant to the purchaser of the product. How they can be translated into variables which can be controlled by the supplier is done through the following direct relationships:

- Awareness is developed by Promotion;
- Availability by distribution (sometimes represented by Place);
- Affordability is a function of Price; and
- Acceptability is of course determined by the Total Product or service.

You will notice we now have both '4 As' and '4 Ps'. The '4 Ps' are usually referred to as the marketing mix and will be seen in most marketing texts. The order of these variables can be reversed to put them in the order in which a company would approach them. Consumers do not approach the factors in this order and it is necessary to bear this fact in mind when developing a marketing plan. These variables which a company can control will be the main input in Chapters 12 to 20.

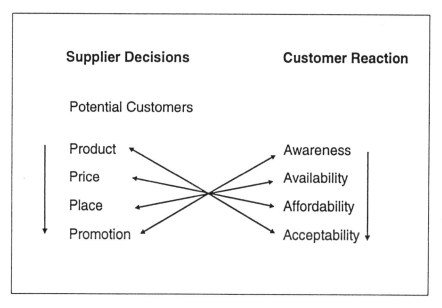

Fig 7.1 Supplier/customer exchanges

The term 'the marketing mix' was first used in a paper by Neil Borden in 1964 when he listed 12 factors which a company can control in the marketing areas (*see* Chapter 11). He appreciated that a cocktail or mix of these factors was necessary and that this mix would vary depending on circumstances. Jerome McCarthy grouped Borden's twelve factors together into the '4 Ps' and this now appears in most marketing books as the *key* areas for marketing action.

Who are our customers?

Before developing the marketing mix for any organisation there is a key question all marketers must answer: *Who are our customers?*

It is very unlikely our product will appeal to everyone, and while any sales are welcome there will be particular segments where it is best suited. These segments become the target which is aimed at by promotion and other marketing efforts. While these issues will be explored in greater depth later, it is sufficient to put the identification of potential customers at the top of our marketing decisions.

It is the customer not the supplier who judges acceptability and affordability for any product and these judgements will be made in the environment those customers find themselves in. This includes the economic and social pressures on the customers as much as the competitive offerings available to them. It is because of these pressures that marketing action must involve an environmental appreciation relevant to the chosen target customers. But the selection of the actual target segment comes first, only then can the related issues be explored to see if our offerings are really able to meet customer needs.

Marketing exchange process

The marketing mix model shows the links between supplier decisions and market (customer) evaluation which is the fundamental basis of marketing. On the left-hand side is our supplier organisation. Here we may have no initial product, just an idea of a need within a particular target group. In this situation decisions need to be taken using the simple set of questions.

WHO are our potential customers?   – already asked
WHAT are their current/future needs?   – product
HOW do they judge value?   – price
WHERE and **WHEN** can we reach these customers? – place & promotion

You will note the last questions covers both 'Place' and 'Promotion' as we need to reach customers with the actual product (Availability), and to communicate with them (Awareness and encouragement to purchase).

An example of a new product idea being spotted was mentioned in Chapter 2. Akio Morita of Sony visited places where young people meet. He found they wanted to listen to music on a very personal basis. Back at his company he gave the engineers a target of developing high quality earphones combined with a simple light-weight tape player. When his marketing people heard of the project they did not think that such a system would sell unless the player also recorded music. The Sony marketing team had their attitudes fixed on past products. Morita overruled them and the Walkman was born.

This example shows how important it is to start with an understanding of *customer needs*, not of *available products*. It does not matter if a product is newly launched or a very familiar existing one, because in all cases the really vital question which marketers should continually ask is: **WHY** will our potential customers buy from us?

Competitive advantage

The earlier chapters describe how people's demands can change, making existing products obsolete. In particular competitors may launch new products which customers find more attractive. Because of this, organisations must update their products or services to keep them relevant to the changing needs of customers.

There are now many tape only players competing with the Walkman, and many are much cheaper. The name Walkman has become a generic term for this type of product just like Thermos or Hoover in other product areas. In spite of there being cheaper alternatives, the Sony Walkman products continue to be the market leader. It was the original product and people aspire to own the real thing. The product has developed since it was first introduced in 1981, both technically and in design and appearance. More recently Sony introduced personal video and CD players creating new customer demand. They also now have a Walkman which records reflecting customer requirements.

It is interesting to reflect on Sony's first pocket-sized product, a transistor radio. When launched in 1955, it was found to be slightly too large for a shirt pocket so Sony started making shirts with large pockets to sell alongside the radio. An interesting solution.

In fact if you are responsible for products already on the market you need to continually ask all these basic questions. Up to a few years ago the Tesco supermarket chain had been developed on the 'pile it high, sell it cheap' philosophy of its founder, Sir Jack Cohen. The new Chairman, Sir Ian McLaurin, reviewed the operation and made many changes. He changed the 'product' by a radical revision of the groceries and provisions stocked. He discontinued 'Green Shield' stamps and changed the pricing policy. He closed down many older stores and developed new larger sites with much improved layout. The advertising featured food quality especially the fresh fruit, vegetables and meats. The new Tesco was aimed specifically at the 25–35 age group seen as a relatively affluent sector of food shoppers. This strategy has succeeded in that Tesco is now considered a supplier of quality food to rival Sainsbury with a very high market share in the target customer group. This has resulted in a dramatic improvement in both sales and profits for the company. Developments such as these are going on all the time and show the importance of the Marketing–Environment interface.

Controllable variables

The variables a supplier can change are the '4 Ps' of the marketing mix. Those they have to monitor are the '4 As' of their customers and the '4 Ps' of their competition. The next three chapters deal with marketing information and the techniques for obtaining this. These techniques are generally referred to as marketing research. This must be a continuous exercise to pick up changes in customer demands which could affect sales of existing products and the development of new product ideas.

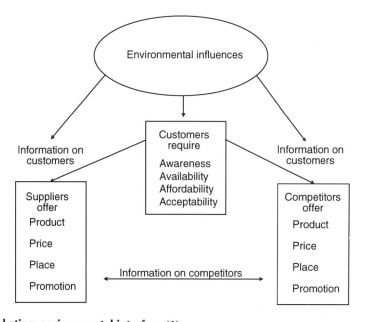

Fig 7.2 Marketing–environmental interface (1)

Competitors have an important influence on how customers respond to the Marketing Mix selected by a supplier. Customers are in the position to decide between competitive offerings and hence the importance of the question: **WHY** should customers buy from us? Newly established competitors often reflect changes in the environment, such as new technologies or new attitudes by offering modified products before existing companies: **WHY** did Body Shop have such a success with environmentally friendly products when major competitors such as Boots failed to see the opportunity? **WHY** were quartz/ electronic watches from companies such as Casio able to take such a large share of the market before the Swiss watch industry fought back with Swatch?

In both examples there was still a continuing customer demand. What was considered acceptable or affordable changed when new alternative products became available and potential customers became aware of these products. It was changes in the controllable offerings which changed the basis of customer evaluation of competitive offerings. David Ogilvy, the Scottish-born founder of one of the world's largest advertising agencies, once said 'Marketers who ignore marketing research are as guilty as generals who ignore intelligence reports during battle'. It is only after studying customers and the ever changing marketplace that decisions about the '4 Ps' can be made.

Stakeholder influences

In order to complete the influences on a marketing company it is necessary to consider the stakeholder groups as discussed in Chapter 3. These groups are interested parties and should include everyone who has an interest in the organisation. A list of such groups would include:

- Customers
- Employees
- Competitors
- Shareholders
- Creditors
- Suppliers
- General Public
- Governments
- Unions
- Local Communities

Each of these stakeholders is involved in some form of exchange process with the organisation. In consequence, the relationship between an organisation and its customers must be considered against the background of other interactions. Some of them can have a major effect on a company's approach to marketing.

Employees may wish to demonstrate their pride in their work as much as to increase their earnings. Owners may be more interested in the standing of their company as a leader in technology than in return on investment. Other shareholders are likely to be more interested in return on investment. Bankers are likely to be interested in the asset value of the organisation. The Government, as a law maker, may wish to protect customers from the harmful effect of products such as cigarettes.

Conclusion

To finish this chapter we will return to our model of the exchange process with a major addition – competitors (*see* Fig 7.2) You will note the similarity to the triangle of Ohmae

(Fig 4.1). The role of the marketer is shown at its most challenging. Being aware of the influences, either via formal or informal information, is necessary. However the key test is whether the customers buy from your company, rather than a competitor, or may be they do not purchase any product in the category offered.

Customers in Western countries are offered far more products and services than they can afford or need. To be successful in such a competitive and dynamic situation requires marketers to understand their environment and continually look for market advantage in the context of all the influences of the supplier–buyer relationship they seek to build.

Questions

1 Consider how a product, such as a Ford Escort car, has changed since its launch. Why do you think this has happened?

2 In a market of your choice suggest changes that might take place over the next five years?

3 How might an organisation identify key changes in its marketing environment?

4 What is the role of a marketing manager in matching a company offering to the marketplace?

8

MARKETING INFORMATION

Introduction

While the overriding theme in this and every book on the subject of marketing is that successful organisations meet the needs of their customers, the point was made in Chapter 7 that organisations also have responsibilities to other groups' or stakeholders. It is clear from those listed on page 86 that at least some of these groups are likely to have conflicting interests. The ability of management to reconcile these interests is likely to depend partially upon the overall efficiency of the organisation. As a result, many of the decisions which managers in organisations have to make involve the efficiency of the methods used by an organisation to meet the needs of its customers. It follows from this that managers are more likely to make good (rather than bad) decisions if they understand the effect that a decision is likely to have on their organisation's customers. They can only do this if they understand who their customers are, and the needs of these customers.

The importance of asking the question, 'who are our customers?' has been mentioned already in previous chapters. Generally, however, it is a much more difficult question to answer with any degree of precision than to ask. To say that the customers of a manufacturer of small cars are 'mostly young people who prefer or can only afford a small car' may be true, but is not very helpful in the marketing context. It might not even be true. To be useful such information needs to classify these customers in more definite terms. This could be with regard to other purchases such as newspapers, magazines or even by occupations. It would also be useful to know how large these groups are and equally, what proportion of the group are already customers. For example, there is little point in modifying a product to suit a customer group only to find that most of the potential customers in this group have already bought your existing product.

The ultimate purpose of all marketing information is to provide the knowledge necessary when making any decisions which will affect an organisation's customers. Unfortunately this knowledge is by its very nature seldom complete. At best it is like a mosaic, where the picture can still be clear, even though a large number of pieces may be missing. Generally, the knowledge provided by marketing information changes over time. Thus, returning to our analogy of a mosaic, the colours of some pieces will fade over time. To revive the pattern pieces must then be removed as new ones become available, since information used for marketing decisions must be up to date. Again, like the pieces used to make a mosaic marketing information has to be obtained from many different sources and sometimes alternative sources can be used.

The objectives of this chapter are to define marketing information and show how it can be relevant to decisions throughout an organisation as well as to those functions which are specifically concerned with marketing. As a specialist management activity the provision of marketing information is generally referred to as marketing research. This involves the collation, analysis and presentation of appropriate, available and required data. There are well-established techniques for doing this as a formal business activity and these are described and discussed in the next two chapters.

Organisational information

Before the essential characteristics of marketing information can be considered it is necessary to define organisational information generally. This is essentially complex. Simply to function, an organisation, by definition, has to exist independently from the individuals who make up the organisation. Thus, for an organisation to exist, there usually has to be some record showing that it has been created and is functioning.

In most organisations there is ample evidence of such information. In the business context it can be seen everywhere – stored in desk drawers, filing cabinets, cardboard boxes in archives, and on computer files. Most of this information can be classified in terms of the different business functions. Hence there will be files containing accounting information, personnel information, production information, design information and so on. It can also be seen, moved and referred to and can, for this reason also be referred to as *tangible information*.

Although impressive in terms of the quantity of information contained in these files, the tangible information represents only a part of the information which is actually needed for an organisation to function. First, it is usual for very little of this tangible information to be required in the course of an organisation's day-to-day activities. Most of it is the stored record of past activities. As will be seen in Table 8.1, much of this information is kept to comply with the legal and other regulations which apply to all organisations.

Table 8.1
Legal limitations for document retention

Title of document	Period of retention (yrs)	Reason
Cheques/remittance advice	6	Statute of limitations
Cash book listing	10	Commercial/Company's Act
Invoice	6	VAT/Company's Act
Shipping documents	3	VAT
Income Tax documentation	6	Taxes Management Act

In addition most organisations and individuals maintain records in order that past successes can be repeated and past mistakes avoided. Information relating to the avoidance of mistakes is often used to establish a procedure within an organisation. This reduces the organisation's reliance on individual members of staff and the likelihood of errors resulting from this. A simple example is the normal practice within all types of organisation for cheques to be signed by more than one person.

Very often a procedure is introduced or changed in order to cope with exceptional or new circumstances. However, since the purpose of a revised or new procedure is to allow the exceptional or new circumstance to be treated as routine, the information used when devising or changing routines is generally difficult to trace. Procedures thus once established continue to be followed because they are seen to work.

The procedures used within an organisation, and the routines which are used to implement these, are an essential part of organisational information. Unlike the files contained in office cabinets or on computer discs there is often no physical evidence of the existence of this information. Within this category of information is also included the personal skill and knowledge of the individuals in the organisation who carry out these procedures and routines. In practice it is only through this *intangible information* within an organisation that any of the files representing an organisation's tangible information are created, maintained and are of value to the organisation.

Some readers will, by this time, have realised that much, if not most, of the information being categorised as intangible, can be made tangible simply by setting out in writing the procedures and routines used within an organisation. Indeed, there are few large organisations which do not have an operations manual in which the procedures and routines used are described. Many of these also include job descriptions for the different members of staff who are required to carry out these routines and procedures, and copies of the forms and schedules used to do this. However, it is important to realise that, as already mentioned, procedures and routines develop from the need to cope with change and exceptional circumstances. As a result, any operations manual can, at best, be nothing more than a record of best practice at the time of writing. Furthermore, while job descriptions can define the skills and abilities required for specific staff functions they cannot define the knowledge, skills and abilities actually used by the individuals doing these jobs.

The combination of tangible and intangible information is thus a fundamental characteristic of organisational information. A second characteristic is no less important in that it allows specific combinations of tangible and intangible information to be classified as being within one of the two categories of organisational information. The first category comprises the information which an organisation needs in order to provide the service or manufacture the product for which purpose the organisation exists. This category of information is clearly essential as without it the organisation cannot fulfil its purpose. This we will call *production information*. Thus, for example, to provide a service to which the owners of sick domestic, or farm animals can turn for advice and help, it is essential to have someone who has, or has access to, a knowledge of veterinary medicine.

The second category of information is that which an organisation needs to ensure the products or services which it manufactures or provides are actually required by sufficient customers or clients to make the organisation viable. This we will call *marketing information*. A simple example might be the information needed by a recently qualified vet in order to set up a practice in a particular location. As will be seen below, this can involve any category of information other than production information.

Production information

Direct production information

To manufacture leather jackets requires an individual or group of people who have the information or knowledge needed not only to design and manufacture leather jackets, but who also have the essential associated knowledge. This includes knowing where to obtain the leather and other materials used to manufacture leather jackets, the price which should be paid for these, and sources for the machinery and equipment needed to carry out the manufacturing process efficiently. Although very different, the production information in this example is clearly directly equivalent to the veterinary science information needed in the earlier example. These are both examples of *direct production information* since they relate directly to the service being provided or the product being manufactured.

Indirect production information

Organisations cannot operate simply by manufacturing a product or providing a service. Each leather jacket manufactured has to be packed and shipped to the person or more usually, in the first instance, the organisation that ordered it. Thus, in addition to actually manufacturing leather jackets, the organisation has to produce delivery notes and invoices. Furthermore, information is required again, usually in the form of procedures and routines, not only to produce these items but also to keep track of them. By these means monthly statements are produced for each customer and measures made of the financial standing of the organisation. Equally, information, again usually in the form of routines and procedures, is needed to process customer orders, to place orders on suppliers, pay their accounts, select staff, pay wages, meet the requirements for collecting VAT, National Insurance contributions and Income Tax, and similar tasks. All of these activities are as essential to the operation of the organisation as those involved directly in producing the product or providing the service so the information needed to carry them out is clearly equally important. Because of this the tangible and intangible information needed to carry out these activities is also considered to be production information.

There is, however, an important difference between this information and direct production information. Unlike direct production it is generally not product- or service-specific. It is likely that an enterprise manufacturing leather jackets and one providing veterinary services will use similar routines for charging their customers and clients, for producing monthly statements, ordering supplies, and other similar tasks. As a result, it is useful to distinguish this type of information as *indirect production information*. The terminology is similar in principle to that used in cost accounting to distinguish between costs which are directly attributed to the production of a product or service and those costs which relate to functions which facilitate these activities.

Marketing information

As mentioned in the introduction to this chapter, marketing as a business activity has developed as a result of recognising that the success of an organisation often depends upon decisions which require knowledge of the organisation's customers and the needs of those customers. In the short term these decisions are likely to be concerned with meeting the needs of customers efficiently. In the longer term they are likely to focus more on the organisation's need to respond to the ever changing expectations of customers and the users of its products and/or services, and what has already been introduced as the marketing environment. Included within the marketing information category is information such as who the organisation expects to have as its customers, estimates of the size of these groups, how many are already customers, how many are customers of the competition, how much they will pay for the product or service and how non-users/customers might learn about the availability of the product or service.

While all of these are examples of marketing information, its scope needs to be much wider than this if it is to fulfil its purpose of providing managers with the information they need to make decisions which affect their organisation's customers. It needs, for instance, to include information relating to the regulations which affect the provision of the service or the manufacture, sale or use of the product being manufactured or supplied. Because of this it is useful to consider marketing information as *any* information which is relevant to the success of an enterprise other than that either directly or indirectly concerned with the provision of the service or the production of the product.

Like production information, marketing information can be either tangible or intangible. Unlike production information, in many organisations there is often little evidence of tangible marketing information. There are several reasons for this. First, the files containing, for instance, catalogues showing the products offered by competitors, are usually minute in comparison with the files needed by the production functions of an organisation. Second, these files are quite likely to be dispersed within an organisation. Some departments such as sales, design or advertising may have formal files, but in addition many managers are likely to have their own file labelled 'Competition' and containing catalogues collected at an exhibition or other similar event. Third, as mentioned in the introduction, marketing information is time-dependent. It is of no value when it is out of date and so can then be discarded since there is no legal requirement to store it.

While it is inevitable that marketing decisions often have to be made on the basis of incomplete marketing information, it is important to recognise that because of the changing nature of most marketplaces there is often no way of knowing the relevance of any information which is not available. As previously mentioned, it is in this respect that marketing information is clearly different from production information, since if this is incomplete any problem which arises is immediately apparent.

Example

If the company manufacturing leather jackets considered in an earlier example received an enquiry from overseas asking them to quote for supplying 300 jackets in mixed sizes, and standard colour, they may well quote their standard price. If the order is received and it is clear that the standard colour in this market is light brown whereas for the manufacturer it is black, the lack of this information could have resulted in a bad marketing decision being made. The wrong price could have been quoted.

For production the problem is different. If an order for light brown jackets is accepted without knowing where to buy suitable light brown leather they cannot produce. For production this information is essential.

It is important that the requirement for adequate marketing information in addition to having the required production information is recognised since this is fundamental to the success of an enterprise. Earlier in this chapter, veterinary science was used as an example of necessary production information. If to pursue this example, the person wishing to set up the service was a recently qualified vet, he or she would have the necessary production information. This would be tangible in the form of the reference books and notes which had been collected during training and intangible in terms of the personal knowledge and skills acquired prior to and since qualifying. Furthermore, if the person had worked in a neighbouring town or area while training, he or she may well have at least some idea of the number of animal owners who could be expected to use the service if it was started. The person may also know the area sufficiently well to be able to choose a suitable location for the practice and know which estate agents to go to for the type of property required. A map of the area, a copy of the telephone directory and any visit notes made while working in the area would, furthermore, be tangible marketing information. The more general information about the area while working there would be the essential intangible marketing knowledge. Clearly this person would have both the production knowledge and the marketing knowledge required to set up a practice in this area with a reasonable expectation of success.

Compare this with the situation of another recently qualified vet who wishes to set up a practice in the town where he or she went to school. The person has the same tangible and intangible production information and by obtaining a map and telephone directory at least a majority of the tangible marketing information. It is also likely that the area would be equally familiar, but not having worked as a vet in the area, this second person is unlikely to know how many vets there were currently practising in the area (the competition), whether there is a large proportion of animal owners, where the best location for the practice might be, and who would be the appropriate agents to visit when looking for suitable premises. To obtain this marketing information would, at the very least, involve visiting and spending time in the area. This would mean investing time and money, for travel and accommodation, or perhaps more money to employ someone locally to obtain the information required. To proceed without this marketing information would make any expectation of success for the venture at best be somewhat unreasonable.

The same proposal could be taken one step further by considering the situation of a person who wishes to start the business by purchasing an expert computer system to provide the required veterinary (production) knowledge. This could be a well-proven system which over many years has been shown to be better at diagnoses than a human vet, even when operated by a technician. The success of the enterprise would then not only depend upon the factors of importance to the recently qualified vets, but also upon other non-production factors such as whether the regulations concerning setting up a veterinary practice would permit one to be run without a qualified vet, whether pet owners in the area concerned would trust the advice provided by a computer, whether they would be willing to pay fees similar to those charged by normal vets, whether local veterinary surgeons would be willing to co-operate with the practice by carrying out any surgical work referred to them, and other associated questions. Any reasonable expectation of success would clearly depend upon having satisfactory answers to these far more difficult questions. Being more difficult questions it is likely that the person wishing to set up the computer based practice would require specialist knowledge or professional help to obtain reliable answers.

It should be evident from these examples that when required marketing information has to be obtained, this will inevitably involve an investment in time, financial capital, or both. This is no different from the acquisition of the production information which for this enterprise, would involve six years' veterinary training or a substantial capital investment in the expert computer system. It is also clear from this example that the marketing information required to provide an enterprise with a reasonable chance of success can depend upon the production knowledge being used. For many organisations there is an equally important opposite relationship in that the viability of many production decisions depends upon having appropriate marketing information.

Consider the problems facing someone wishing to open a restaurant. Their individual skill as a chef or their access to this skill is likely to determine the type of restaurant. If in the intended location there were already clearly too many Chinese restaurants it would be more sensible for a Chinese chef to seek an alternative location rather than attempt to open an Indian restaurant. Apart from that one exception almost all the associated production decisions relating to the restaurant are likely to depend largely upon marketing information. For instance, while the overall size of the restaurant may be determined by the availability of premises in a suitable location, the relative size of the kitchen and dining areas, the equipment needed in the kitchen and the decor of the dining area will depend on the type of restaurant. At the very least, to be successful a high-class restaurant will require a greater investment in the dining area. It is accordingly essential for the owner to establish the likelihood of there being sufficient customers either in the area or willing to travel from adjacent areas who could afford the significantly higher prices which would be expected at a high-class restaurant. If not, it would be preferable to provide simpler fare, cater for many more people each day, and design the restaurant to suit.

The inter-relationship between marketing and production information becomes even more critical when considering product manufacture. This is because the relationships between the rate of production and the cost of production are far more complicated than is usual in service industries. In general, as the rate of production is increased so the cost of production decreases. This is not, however, a straight relationship, but a series of individual relationships each of which represents a difference in the level of investment required to implement the adjacent level of manufacturing capability.

The relationships between production rate and cost have been further complicated by technical developments which not only allow costs to be reduced as the rate of production is increased, but also at the same time, improve the quality of the product and allow variations of the product to be made with minimum effect on production efficiency. This has significantly increased the risk involved in selecting manufacturing processes without reliable marketing information.

Exercise

Consider an enterprise with which you are familiar and itemise the production knowledge likely to be necessary to produce the product or provide the service and the marketing information necessary to implement this production knowledge successfully.

Categories of marketing information

It is useful to classify marketing information in terms of three main categories. These respectively relate to: **1** the clients, customers or users served by an organisation; **2** the product or service being provided; and **3** the environment in which the product or service is produced, provided, supplied and used.

Customer information

Customer information is central to the concept of marketing. Many existing businesses, especially those providing services, have direct contact with the people who use their service. For instance, hairdressers can judge from this direct contact whether their clientele is getting older and more prosperous or older and less prosperous. By consciously recognising such trends, hairdressers can maintain the prosperity of their businesses either by ensuring that the service offered is changed to match the changing needs of the clientele or to attract another category of clientele. Customer information obtained through direct contact although intangible, is likely to be the best available.

The management of larger organisations, even those who essentially provide services such as banks, can easily lose direct contact with their customers. To avoid this, managers need adequate tangible marketing information since without it, they will have no option but to make decisions based on the intangible information they gained prior to becoming managers. As a result, decisions are likely to be made based on out-of-date information. The problem is even worse for the manufacturers of products. Very often these are sold through wholesale and retail intermediaries which means that managers could be making decisions without having any contact with their final customers and users.

Product information

There is often no clear dividing line between what may be defined as product information and what may be defined as production information. In practice this is not actually important. What is important is the appreciation that the success of a product is dependant as much upon the alternatives available to a potential customer as upon the product itself. It is the appreciation of these alternatives and the impact that they are likely to have on the acceptability of a product to the potential customer which often requires specific marketing information.

The development of the Sony Walkman as a new product, which has already been discussed in an earlier chapter, is an interesting example of a product which, at least for a time, affected the market for some apparently unrelated products. One example was the market for good quality pens. Both Walkmans and quality pens were similarly priced gift items for young people and were therefore direct competitors in the gift market.

Perhaps even more significant is the difficulty faced by manufacturers as a result of technological changes, which can effectively remove overnight a manufacturer's competitive advantage. This happened to a market leader in small kitchen appliances. The reputation of Swan brand kettles was, at least in part, due to the production expertise which had been developed for manufacturing aluminium- and chromium-plated products. This could be seen in the quality and value for money offered by the Swan range of products. However, this expertise became effectively irrelevant as a result of the development of plastics which were suitable for manufacturing kettles. Swan was affected in three ways:

First, it allowed new competitors to enter the market with a radical new design – the 'jug-style' kettle; second, it meant that Swan no longer had the production expertise relevant to its main product range; and third, to compete Swan had to master an entirely new technology. It is hardly surprising that Swan is no longer the market leader for this type of product. Indeed, it is unlikely that any company enjoys anything like the share of this market which had been held by Swan prior to the development of the new plastics.

The marketing environment

In earlier chapters the various aspects of the marketing environment have been identified and discussed. Often, events which are likely to have an impact on an enterprise are seen, in the first instance, within one of the following four sectors of the marketing environment.

1 The political environment

Both customers and providers of goods and services are affected by and have to respond to changes in the political climate. For example, the government not only sets its overall policy with regard to the transportation system by investing in aspects of the transportation infrastructure such as road or railways, but also has to respond to the concerns of the public in directly related areas, such as road safety and pollution control. Such trends can directly affect the manufacturers of many different products.

2 The technological environment

Over the past twenty years many manufacturers have been affected by developments in technologies remote from their own. Major sectors of the metal working industry were made obsolete by the development of digital electronics. Weighing machines of all types, typewriters and cash registers are all examples of this. More recently, developments in digital electronics are likely to start affecting specialist sectors of the chemical industry such as those involved with the manufacture of photographic film, papers and processing chemicals. As a result many established manufacturers of these products are likely to need to introduce alternative new products simply to survive.

For many companies these technological changes have been difficult to detect as economic growth has been erratic in most of the developed economies, often hiding the real cause of a reduction in business activity. Developments in digital electronics have not only changed the form of products, but have also changed the way they are designed and manufactured. Computer-aided design not only permits more complicated shapes to be created, but, when linked to computer aided manufacturing technology, allows these to be manufactured without incurring additional cost. As a result, the companies with the capital to invest in these technologies have been able to use them to introduce strikingly different new products quickly. These technologies have, in addition, increased the variety of the products available to the customer. Even a low-cost item such as a plastic patio chair can be bought in twenty or more different styles.

3 The legal environment

Changes in the political and technical environments are generally reflected in the legal environment. Usually there is a time lag in that the legal changes follow technical and political changes, but this is not always the case. The banning of CFCs for use as aerosol propellants in the USA was more a case of legislators trying to do the 'right' thing than as a result of major public pressure. More recently, anti-pollution legislation in the USA has resulted in companies moving production from the USA to Mexico or other countries which are not yet considering such legislation. This may well result in the products manufactured at these plants becoming a new source of competition for the European manufacturers of similar products.

The legal environment includes not only legislation, but also the way consumers and users of products view the law as a means of seeking redress when things go wrong. This again can add to costs in certain markets.

In Europe companies have to meet both the legislation imposed by the individual national governments and by the EC. This adds a further complication especially in view of the high level of trade between member countries.

4 The cultural and social environment

The cultural and social environment is at the heart of what can be best considered local knowledge. Throughout the 1980s the affluent sectors of society in North America increasingly emphasised health and fitness while these declined significantly in the more deprived sectors of the same society. Such trends have allowed the manufacturers of soft drinks to successfully introduce many new products, especially low-calorie or sugar-free variations of their existing brands. Further development included the introduction of caffeine-free versions of the main types of cola soft drinks. The advertising used to launch the new products is quite likely to have highlighted the potential problems associated with caffeine to the drinkers of tea and coffee accelerating the trends towards decaffeinated coffee and soft drinks in general. Thus, developments in the soft drink sector of the beverage market also affected the hot drink sector by encouraging both the existing trend towards decaffeinated coffee and the trend from hot beverages, such as tea or coffee, to cold beverages such as soft drinks and fruit juices.

Exercise

Consider what impact the trend from hot to cold beverages is likely to have in the future. Are there any associated products which are likely to be affected by these changes?

Data collation

In the examples given earlier in the chapter the individuals intending to start a veterinary practice or open a restaurant either had, as a result of recent experience, the marketing information needed or would have had it after they had sought it. The gathering together of required information is data collation.

For small organisations data collation is likely to be essentially informal and is no different from the production information required, for instance, by a chef. Most of the recipes that a chef will use will be known and others will be found easily in books or notes. It is also likely that a list of suppliers for seldom-used special ingredients, or a directory listing these suppliers, would also be available.

As organisations get larger so the need for marketing information to be collated formally increases. Furthermore, as the amount of information collated increases so does the need to keep this information in a prescribed way. As a result, large organisations maintain detailed operations manuals. McDonald's restaurants, for example, specify the ingredients which will be used for each product served and precisely what a 'Crew Member' should call each product when taking an order from a customer. Once developed, these operation manuals have been used by organisations such as McDonald's to expand their business very rapidly by *franchising*. Franchising allows an independent businessperson to open a branch of an organisation and retain any profits which remain after meeting the normal business costs and the franchise fee.

The production information for a manufacturing business is likely to be contained in sets of detailed drawings, standard specifications, lists of suppliers, work schedules and operations sheets. Such information specifically details what has to be done and, usually in less detail, how it should be done. This is because it would be assumed that the information would be used only by someone with the necessary skill and training.

Because, as was mentioned earlier, an organisation cannot function unless the necessary production information is available, the costs involved in producing this information and in keeping it up to date are accepted as normal costs. However, the cost of keeping marketing information up to date is often not seen in this way and, as a result, is often maintained on an individual basis rather than as a normal procedure within the organisation. The provision of marketing information is generally made more complicated in organisations which manufacture variations of a basic product. This is because the information of interest to those having to make marketing decisions is fundamentally different from that needed by production. Let us consider the following, simple example.

Example

As a result of market analysis the marketing department of a major car manufacturer found that they were selling a lower proportion of four-door cars than their competition. Should they wish to investigate this further, they would need to look at the sales of this type of vehicle in terms of the level of trim, e.g. L, GL, GTi, and so on; the size of engine; the type of gearbox and even perhaps by colour. They might also want to know whether there were any regional variations in demand.

Although it might be expected that production would have records from which such information could be easily obtained, in practice their records may not show this. For production purposes the information would be required in a different form. It could well show that of every 100 vehicles built 50 have 1300cc engines, 30 have 1600cc engines and 20 have 1800cc engines, and 50 have two doors, 30 have four doors and 20 are estates with five doors. From these components any combination of vehicle could be built and any minor variations in demand would be allowed for by adjusting the next batch accordingly. There is no reason why any records should be kept of how many four door cars have 1600cc engines against either of the alternatives. Nor is there any reason for knowing whether the overall mix changes according to season or other factor. Thus, to obtain the information wanted by the marketing department would involve either having a separate system designed specifically to provide this information or analysing individual customer orders, invoices or shipping notes, which would inevitably be a tedious and error prone process.

Indeed, it is because such information is so often effectively unobtainable that many marketing decisions have to be made without adequate information and can easily be based on incorrect assumptions. For instance, it maybe logical to assume that since the estate version of the vehicle looks larger than any of the other models, most of estates sold would have the larger engines. Equally, this could be entirely wrong since buyers of the estate model might consider it a utility vehicle and so rate its performance as relatively unimportant.

This example illustrates another important aspect of marketing information: its sheer volume. Most data collection within an organisation involves the collation of information. For example, total shipment values are summarised in terms of individual customer accounts or the turnover of the company as a whole. Marketing information, by its nature, involves the identification of individual transactions often in terms of a very large number of individual criteria. This is further complicated by this information being also time-dependent.

Marketing information systems

One apparently logical approach to the problem caused by large quantities of information is to develop, using computer technology, a data system which stores and provides access to the information needed by those making marketing decisions. The term *marketing information system* or MIS is used to describe such a system. Such systems are generally discussed in the context of marketing information or marketing research. It should be noted that the term MIS is equally used for the somewhat more far reaching 'Management Information System'. While it is essential for organisations to have systems by which marketing information can be stored and accessed, it should be clear from the points made regarding the nature of organisational information in general and marketing information in particular, that such systems have fundamental limitations. At best the system can only handle such tangible and intangible information as is made available to it.

Computer-based systems are particularly useful for handling numerical information, but can provide only limited assistance when handling qualitative information based on descriptions and ideas. The need to address this problem has been recognised and much work has been done to develop 'Decision Support Systems' designed to provide the information needed for marketing decisions. No doubt the number of companies developing and using such systems will increase. However, the benefit of these systems is likely to continue to depend upon the validity of the marketing problem as on the data used to find a solution. Thus, the main benefit offered by such systems is likely to be the facilities they offer for accessing the available information rather than the actual marketing information provided. Because of the volume, complexity and time-dependent nature of marketing information, the provision of marketing information will continue to be the specialist marketing activity of marketing research.

Conclusion

Marketing, no less than other functions, depends for its efficiency on the availability and utilisation of internal and external information. Information internal to the organisation may range far beyond data on marketing activities proper, and will include central and dispersed sources on operational tasks, procedures and routines throughout the company. In particular, information on production processes and stages may be critical to marketing success, as it will guide managers on the quality and capacity limitations of the organisation, product specifications and current commitments. External information sources will be required for giving guidance on customer needs, market trends and general constraints and opportunities within the company's environment.

Questions

1 'Information is power'. Discuss this in relation to the cross-functional information flows necessary for good customer service.

2 Taking as an example any commercial product, consider the information sources that would shed light on changes in its market and economic environment.

3 Outline what you consider to be the characteristics of an effective marketing information system, and consider the means by which it might be designed and maintained.

4 Discuss the relationship between marketing information and marketing planning.

9

RESEARCH FOR MARKETING

Introduction

In the previous chapter marketing information was defined in the context of organisational information, as compared with production information. Its importance to marketing decision-making was discussed. This chapter introduces the formal approach to obtaining marketing information. As a specific business activity this is known as *marketing research.*

Although as a business or organisational activity the term marketing research is universally used, it has no generally accepted definition. This is in spite of many attempts having been made to define it by both the celebrated authors and the respected organisations involved in marketing. One of the most straightforward definitions is the one proposed in 1960 by the American Marketing Association, which defined marketing research as the 'Systematic gathering, recording, and analysing of data about problems relating to the marketing of goods and services'. While satisfactory with regard to the basics, this definition ignored the important problem-solving and reporting aspects of marketing research as a business function. It was for this reason considered unsatisfactory by many authors including Kotler, and in 1987 was replaced by the following definition. 'Marketing research:

> uses information to identify and define marketing opportunities and problems; generate, refine and evaluate marketing actions; monitor marketing performance; and improve understanding of marketing as a process. It communicates findings and their implications.'

This satisfies the main criticisms made of the earlier definition, but ignores the more fundamental point made by Buzzell in 1963. In an article from the *Harvard Business Review*, he suggested that the title 'marketing research' as such was deceptive. In his opinion the function was in reality like military intelligence and the title marketing intelligence would accordingly be more appropriate.

In spite of the logic of this argument the term 'marketing research' continues to survive, and, to confuse the situation further, is used by many authors interchangeably with the term 'market research'. This is unfortunate since, particularly in the UK, the term 'market research' is accepted as the term used to define the specialist activities involved in collecting information directly through the use of questionnaires and other associated techniques. Accordingly it is useful to consider *Market Research* as a specialist activity which is within the scope of the marketing research function rather than an alternative name for it. To emphasise this, market research is treated in this book as a specialist subject in Chapter 10.

Marketing research as a marketing function

As might be expected, it was the adoption of a marketing approach which in many organisations increased the requirement for formal (tangible) marketing information and hence to the development of the marketing research function. Generally, in these organisations marketing was seen as a business philosophy and success was being sought through the application of sound marketing principles if not actual marketing theory. There were, however, other organisations where the development of a marketing research function was in itself considered to be adopting the marketing philosophy. This was fundamentally incorrect as an approach to marketing, and inevitably resulted in significant amounts of information being produced much of which was of little value to the organisation.

It is interesting to note that this approach to marketing research can still be detected in commentaries relating to product success and failure. This is because superficially success can usually be attributed to the foresight and judgement of an organisation's management and a product or business failure to a lack of marketing research. More detailed investigations, however, are likely to be more revealing and show that usually successes are examples of the application of sound marketing principles whether by accident or design, and the failures are examples of these principles having been ignored. Accordingly, the suggestion that failure was due to a lack of market research is misleading since this is unlikely to have prevented the failure unless, by chance, it improved the overall understanding of the market. The following are examples of this.

Example 1

For more than thirty years the Rover Mini has been accepted as an example of the exceptionally innovative design capability of the engineering team led by Sir Alec Issigonis. That the design approach pioneered by this team has been adopted or tried by virtually every major motor vehicle manufacturer in the world is a testament to the quality of their innovation. Yet investigation shows that the product was not a success in terms of meeting the requirements of the market for which it was intended. As a result, the product was never satisfactorily profitable since it had to be sold on price against competitive products which better suited the needs of the target market.

Example 2

The American Automobile manufacturers have also shown this inability to understand the real needs of a significant proportion of their customers. This was not due to any lack of marketing research. Rather their research confirmed that their customers favoured American made luxury vehicles and that luxury meant large. What was not appreciated was that for their customers American made also meant nationwide service and small also meant unreliable. Their apparent preference for large/luxury vehicles was therefore significantly due to these being seen as easily serviced and reliable.

The lack of understanding only became apparent when the demand for small cars became significant after a small, imported car developed a reputation for reliability and the manufacturer/importer developed a strategy to show that service was available in every town throughout the USA.

Example 3

The Sinclair C5 electric vehicle has already been cited in an earlier chapter as an example of a product which was launched without any marketing research having been carried out. It failed. However, it is probably less significant than the fact that the product had been designed without a customer in mind. This is evident from seeing how difficult it is to answer even the most basic questions about the potential customer, for example:

1 Who might want to buy this product?
2 What else could they buy for the same amount of money?
3 Where could the product be stored when not in use?
4 Is the store likely to have electric power?

These are basic customer-orientated marketing questions which, if not seen as important by those responsible for launching this product, were unlikely to have been included within the brief of any marketing research undertaken.

Each of these examples show that the real value of marketing information and the research which provides it depends on the marketing analysis for which it is required. As was explained in Chapter 8, marketing information is not like production information which has to be complete to be of value. The actual value of marketing information to an organisation is thus only its relevance to the marketing criteria about which decisions need to be made. This means that while marketing research can make an essential contribution to the marketing analysis and decision making process, it cannot be considered in any way a substitute for this.

The purpose of marketing research

There have been a number of studies into the extent to which organisations undertake marketing research and the reasons why it is done. These show that most organisations recognise that marketing research is necessary for sales forecasting and that this involves analysis of market size, shares held by market participants and market trends over time. For small and medium sized companies and many serving industrial markets this is often the only tangible marketing research regularly undertaken due to limited resources. Occasionally additional research may be carried to investigate product usage or the market for a new product, but generally managers have to depend on the tangible information produced by the accounting department, the tangible and intangible information they receive from their sales department and such intangible marketing information as they can personally acquire by talking to customers and visiting exhibitions. This, of course, is often all that is required for sound marketing decisions when the manager has, through experience, a good understand of the market.

In larger, more diverse companies, senior managers are unlikely to be able to depend on this approach and must instead either rely on formal marketing information or ensure that marketing decisions are delegated to managers who have the necessary intangible information. This option is not available to very large companies and these should have the resources to justify formal marketing research departments which can undertake or commission from outside specialist organisations a planned research programme. If such a programme is to be of value to the organisation it needs to be determined by a market planning process. In large organisations, as will be seen in Chapter 21, this is increasingly a formal process based on a comprehensive reference document, the preparation of which would be one of the routine functions of the Marketing Research Department.

The marketing research function

In order to fulfil its overall functions of providing the information needed to make informed marketing decisions, solve marketing problems, and recognise marketing opportunities, the following five responsibilities could be justified as coming within the marketing research function.

The first is the score keeping responsibility. In many organisations this is seen only in terms of the presentation of internal data and accordingly the responsibility of the accounting function. Unfortunately, this approach can easily result in annual sales being determined from the beginning of the financial year rather than the calendar year, making comparison with external market data very difficult. It can be further complicated by being determined in four-week periods rather than calendar months, again making any comparison with external market data difficult. It should be possible to overcome such problems using sensible computer technology. However, this presents another difficulty: the need to justify having differences between the organisation's accounting and marketing data. Closely related to the accounting activity is a reporting responsibility. As a routine activity this is, in many organisation both complex and time-constrained.

The third responsibility is that of maintaining the marketing records of the company. This can include detailed sales and marketing statistical information, competitor information, customer information and any other information which may in some way affect the organisation's products or customers.

The fourth responsibility is that of evaluation. This can be restricted to the routine analysis of internal data and comparison with available external data or can involve specific research using data from many sources.

The fifth responsibility is that of anticipation, which involves using available data to show trends from which rational conclusions can be developed. Anticipating trends is fundamental to any forecasting which attempts to anticipate changes in trends, rather than simply follow them.

The scope of marketing research

Like marketing research itself there have been many attempts to define the *scope* of marketing research. The easiest approach is simply to list research subjects by area. This provides a useful overview and, as is clear from the list which follows, confirms that market research can involve providing information relevant to any aspect of an organisation's activities.

1 Research on markets:
(a) Estimating market size
(b) Estimating segment size
(c) Estimating market share
(d) Studying market trends
(e) Defining customer/user characteristics
(f) Defining characteristics of product markets
(g) Analysing sales potentials
(h) Analysing market potentials for existing products
(i) Estimating demand for new products
(j) Sales forecasting (sometimes considered a separate activity).

2 Research on products
(a) Studying customer satisfaction/dissatisfaction with products
(b) Comparative studies of competitive products
(c) Determining new uses for present products
(d) Product line research
(e) Customer acceptance of proposed new products
(f) Market-testing new products
(g) Packaging and design studies.

3 Research on promotion:
(a) Analysing advertising and selling practices
(b) Selecting advertising media
(c) Motivational studies
(d) evaluating advertising effectiveness
(e) Establishing sales territories
(f) Evaluating present and proposed sales methods
(g) Analysing sales personnel's effectiveness
(h) Establishing sales quotas.

4 Research on distribution:
(a) Location and design of distribution centres
(b) Handling and packing merchandise
(c) Cost effectiveness of transportation
(d) Dealer supply and storage requirements

5 Research on pricing:
(a) Studying competitive pricing
(b) Demand elasticities
(c) Perceived prices
(d) Cost analysis
(e) Margin analysis.

Although comprehensive the list omits many subject areas as important as those listed such as: economic and business analysis, lifestyle research, international and export studies, and corporate responsibility research. Over time, as might be expected, some areas, such as motivation research, have declined in importance while others, such as lifestyle research, have increased.

Such lists also have a serious shortcoming within the organisational context since the value of any research done in many of these areas is likely to depend, at least to some extent, upon the quality of the information resulting from just a few of the others. In particular determination of market size and market share often tend to be interdependent especially when considering product variants rather than product segments. This means in practice that in many organisations the production of useful marketing information involves having full access to an organisation's product sales and other accounting data. This can be a problem, since many private companies and branches of major international organisations treat such information as confidential even within the organisation. It is also a problem which often has to be faced by independent market research companies and can be a major limitation for marketing research carried out by students.

Generally, the importance of market size and share information varies from product to product within an organisation and from organisation to organisation. It is of little importance in markets where there are a large number of competitors, none of which has a significant share. The blank cassette tape could be an example of such a market. It becomes more important when there are only a few competitors in a market segment or when there are many competitors, but one has a significant share of the market segment. It is usually of critical importance when there are many competitors and a few of these have significant market shares. The personal computer is currently an example of this type of market. Since time is likely to affect both the characteristics of a market segment and the relative strength of the competitors in that segment, it is essential to monitor market size and share trends even when these are not of critical importance.

Types of marketing research

Although marketing research can be classified in many different ways most use either one of three basic approaches or a combination of these. The first approach classifies market research in terms of two different methods of obtaining the required information – (a) continuous or (b) *ad hoc* research. The second classifies marketing research in terms of the two essentially different types of information which might be obtained – (c) quantitative or (d) qualitative. The third approach classifies marketing research in terms of three different purposes for obtaining the information – (e) descriptive, (f) exploratory, or (g) causal. As will be seen in the following paragraphs individually the three approaches to classification are interrelated rather than mutually exclusive making classification somewhat complicated.

(a) Continuous marketing research

Marketing information, such as total sales by product variant and geographic region, is gathered on a routine basis so that it can be compared over time. This allows the performance of the marketing activities of an organisation to be monitored and market trends to be determined.

By definition, continuous marketing research supplements existing marketing information and is usually presented on a regular basis as a memo or newsletter. Because of the cost and resources involved, continuous research should be limited to collecting information which is required for routine decisions. In spite of this it is an activity which needs to be controlled since with the advent of computer databases it is comparatively easy to produce more data than can be used by the managers for whom it is produced.

(b) *Ad hoc* marketing research

When research is required for a specific purpose such as investigating the viability of a new product, it is generally referred to as *ad hoc* research as it is carried out only when actually required. Usually this also involves presenting the research findings as a formal report. It is customary for such reports to be sufficiently comprehensive for the information presented to be of value to users who have no relevant intangible marketing information on the subject. This is important since otherwise the value of the information provided is likely to depend more on the user's existing knowledge of the subject than on the quality of the marketing research.

Partly as a result of the comprehensive nature of most *ad hoc* research reports, this type of research is in many organisations seen as the main purpose of the marketing research department. This is generally misleading since, although the presentation of continuous research as a memo or newsletter may not be impressive, it is usually used not only for decision-making but also as the basis for much of the *ad hoc* research undertaken. For this reason it is important that continuous research information is produced in a form that allows detailed analysis, should this be required.

It is also inevitable that most marketing research textbooks and more basic reviews, such as this one, focus mainly on *ad hoc* research. The reason for this is that *ad hoc* research involves a number of well established stages and procedures. In contrast, since continuous research is a routine activity, most of these stages are only necessary when setting up the routine. In practice, most continuous research is, at least in part, subjected to the full research process from time to time as a result of being used in *ad hoc* research. In many organisations such research is also done when preparing the annual marketing planning reference document.

(c) Quantitative marketing research

Quantitative marketing research is one of the two marketing research classifications based on the type of information obtained. Any information which can be expressed using a numerical measure is considered quantitative. It includes not only numerical data such as that obtained from sales and accounting records, but also the numerical aspects of other data, for example, opinion polls regarding voting intentions. Since marketing research is to provide information for decision-making, more than three-quarters is classified as quantitative. Nearly all continuous marketing research comes within this category since usually it is undertaken to provide data for time series analysis.

(d) Qualitative marketing research

Although in practice less that a quarter of the marketing research undertaken can be classified as qualitative, this category is much discussed both with regard to the methods used and resultant findings. It has resulted in the development of many concepts seen as useful in defining and categorising market segments, such as life style. Qualitative research is concerned with information which is based on descriptions and shades of meaning rather than numerical analysis. It is used almost exclusively in the early stages of *ad hoc* research studies. In general, it involves inductive problem-solving techniques which, as explained below are beyond the scope of an introductory text such as this.

(e) Descriptive marketing research

Descriptive marketing research is the first of the classifications concerned with the purpose for which the research is being undertaken. Descriptive research focuses on product performance, market size, trends, competitive strategies and market share. Depending on the objective and context, this could be the result of either continuing or *ad hoc* research.

(f) Exploratory marketing research

The purpose of exploratory research is to identify the nature of a marketing problem. For instance, whether loss of market share is due to the success of a direct competitor or the result of an indirect competitor's success in an associated market segment. Since exploratory research is problem-orientated, it has always to be carried out as *ad hoc* research. Qualitative research techniques are often used in order to minimise the effect that the terms of reference might have on the research outcome.

(g) Causal marketing research

Like exploratory research, causal research is also implemented on an *ad hoc* basis. Causal research is more analytical than descriptive or exploratory research and is intended to reveal the factors critical to the behaviour of consumers or more generally markets. It can thus involve using both quantitative and qualitative research techniques and so is beyond the scope of most introductions to marketing research such as this.

The research process

Since most *ad hoc* marketing research is concerned with the solution of specific marketing problems, it is generally undertaken using what is known as the scientific method. This is an established, standard approach to solving problems using, as far as possible, reproducible numerical data. The scientific method comprises a number of distinct stages. These vary according to the objective of the study, but generally involve each of the following:

1 Define problem.
2 Analyse the situation.
3 Collate problem specific data.
4 Analyse the data to (a) Establish possible solutions to the problem and (b) select most appropriate solution.
5 Prepare report/implement solution selected.
6 Follow up to evaluate effectiveness of action taken.

The deductive approach to problem-solving can only be applied to problems where it is possible and practical to obtain data which is appropriate and reliable. For other problems, the alternative inductive approach to problem-solving is generally more appropriate.

The inductive approach involves establishing concepts by identifying repeated patterns in the behaviour being observed. The validity of the applicability of these patterns is then verified by repeated empirical studies. The results obtained are generally stated as paradigms rather than laws since their application is subject to exception. This is the normal approach used for psychological work involved in, for instance, buyer behaviour studies. It would have been the approach used by Maslow to develop his hierarchical theory of motivation. It is also the basis used for qualitative marketing research. The implementation of this approach to problem-solving requires specialist training and experience and is thus beyond the scope of introductory texts such as this.

The application of the scientific method to marketing research problems

When applied specifically to marketing research problems the framework provided by the general scientific method needs to be adapted to solve this type of problem. It is important to note that all of the original stages are retained.

1 Define the problem.
2 Establish objectives for the study and estimate cost involved in terms of time and resources.
3 Gather information:
   (i) Desk research –
        (a) internal data
        (b) external (secondary) data.
   (ii) Determine and collect required primary data.
4 Analyse data.
5 Prepare report.
6 Follow up implementation.

In the following sections each of these stages will be considered individually in detail.

Define the problem

Problem definition is often very difficult to complete objectively and as a stage in the process is all too easy to omit all together. Generally, an effective approach is to proceed on the basis of an initial definition of the problem and then reconsider the definition after each of the subsequent stages has been completed. While this is good research practice, it has the significant disadvantage of being considered inefficient by pragmatic company managers. It therefore generally needs to be used with care to ensure that the credibility of the study is maintained.

An important characteristic of marketing research is that it is very common for the person who is initiating the research to have considerably more information about the subject at the start of the research process than the person who is to carry out the research. This information is likely to be a combination of day-to-day experience resulting from being involved with a particular market over many years and from receiving information produced by continuous research procedures on a regular basis.

Establish objectives and estimate cost involved

It is generally necessary to establish objectives for the study to ensure the research is properly focused, even when the problem has been adequately defined. Once the objectives for the study have been agreed, the situation should be superficially analysed to establish the availability of existing relevant information. It should then be possible to estimate the likely cost of the research in terms of time and resources. This is essential since it is very easy to agree market research study objectives which cannot be completed within the time available. As a result, it is often necessary at this stage to decide whether it would be preferable for the study to be carried out by a specialist, outside organisation such as a market research agency or by company staff. The decision made is likely to depend upon at least some of the following seven criteria:

1 cost;
2 project urgency;
3 research expertise required;
4 product or service knowledge necessary;
5 objectivity;
6 specialist resources required;
7 confidentiality.

Sometimes the best solution is to use both internal and external personnel for different stages of the work. However, if external personnel are involved at all, it is essential that a formal brief is prepared so that their work can be properly costed and controlled. Time is often of the essence when considering marketing problems. For instance, delaying the launch of a new product in order carry out further research into the most suitable packaging could well cost more in terms of lost sales and product advantage than, at worst, might have been lost by the packaging not initially being ideally suited to the target market.

Gathering information

Information gathering is best considered as three separate activities. These focus on the different sources of information used and are discussed in the usual order in which they are carried out.

Desk research – internal data

Internal data is the information which is internal to an organisation and usually the starting point for all subsequent work. Of particular interest in the context of marketing, is the time series data relating to orders received, products delivered, advertising expenditure, promotional campaigns and so on. Sometimes the information required is available directly from routine continuous research data. However, this is often in some way insufficiently detailed.

Much of the 'time series' data will have been summarised, for instance as sales by day or week or month or even as quarterly or annual figures. Inevitably, detail is lost as the figures are summarised. Usually this is because the summaries are prepared primarily to provide managers with measures of financial efficiency. While such measures are essential in any business organisation, they are likely to use conventions set by the accounting authorities rather than the need to optimise the use of the resources allocated to marketing. Furthermore, public companies are required to publish summary figures and it is important that the published figures show that the company is financially sound and prudently managed. It is also important that as far as possible the information is summarised in such a way as to make it difficult for competitors to gain useful information regarding (e.g. market share) from the information published.

For manufacturing companies financial efficiency has been seen traditionally as being largely dependent upon production efficiency. This orientation led to the development of the production-orientated costing systems which form the basis of modern management accounting practice. Cost accounting as a procedure involves considerable clerical routine and its automation was one of the earliest business applications of computer technology. Because of this, many costing systems retained their production orientation even when this was no longer justified. As a result, it is not uncommon to find that even sophisticated management accounting systems are unable to provide information in the form required for detailed marketing analysis. Fortunately, providing the basic information can be accessed, it is now usually possible to use a personal computer to extract and collate the information in the form required, although it can be surprisingly difficult and time consuming.

An example will illustrate some of the inherent difficulties. Consider a company which manufactures plumbing fittings, e.g. taps, shower mixers, and so on. It is likely that for costing purposes weekly totals of shipments by product type (type A basin taps, type C bath taps, and so on) would be adequate. For marketing purposes this information is likely to be needed not only by product type but also by type of customer (market segment) and geographic region. This is many times more information.

The problem becomes further complicated if the manufacturer decides to offer a range of products in sets – for instance, to house builders. In each set there could be two pairs of basin taps and one pair of bath taps and one kitchen mixer tap. To be attractive to the builder the set would be priced at less than the sum total of the individual items. For invoicing purposes the set would be treated as an individual product. To establish whether offering these sets increased sales sufficiently to cover the associated price reduction would require analysis of total sales by type of tap. This is likely to involve a significant amount of work and care to ensure that the items sold in the sets were not counted twice.

As was mentioned in the section on continuous research, in most businesses only basic marketing data is monitored on a regular basis. Usually this includes sales by product type and delivery area. It may be collated on a daily, weekly or monthly basis according to the product and could also include orders received on the same basis. Sales usually equate to shipments since products are normally invoiced when shipped.

Desk research – external (secondary) data

Although one of the principal objectives of collating internal marketing data is to monitor the performance of the marketing function, in practice this information is of little value for decision making unless it can be compared with the market as a whole. For long term success, organisations need to grow faster than the market during periods of growth and decline less rapidly than the market during periods of decline.

In order to make these comparisons it is necessary to refer to data obtained from outside sources. Many industries have established trade associations and some of these, such as the Society of Motor Manufacturers and Traders, have become the principal source of marketing information relating to their industry. This, of course, is only possible when the members of the organisation agree that it is in their individual best interest to provide information to the organisation and contribute to the cost of its collation. Very often the information produced is only circulated to those companies which have fulfilled their obligation to supply information to the collating organisation. There are also some commercial organisations, such as Systematics International Ltd, which collate information supplied by contributors and provide data on an industry-wide basis under a private voluntary exchange agreement. Of course, the validity of the information produced depends upon the proportions of industry which are willing to contribute to and buy such services.

In the absence of specially collated industry data, more general data has to be used. Much of this is collated by government departments to measure economic and, more especially, industrial activity and the effectiveness of current economic policy. Some of these measures, such as the retail price index, have become newspaper headline news. Others are published quarterly in the *Business Monitor* series.

Although companies are required to provide such information many fail to do so within the time allowed. As a result, the published data inevitably includes estimates and amendments. Furthermore, its reliability is also affected by other important factors. These vary according to the industry concerned although the following two examples may be considered typical.

First, to reduce the cost involved, data is not usually collected from companies which are small in terms of the number of people employed relative to the size of the industry as a whole. Instead, the totals for the industry are calculated by grossing up the data collected by a factor calculated to represent the output of the small companies. Because of this it is possible for market leaders of important market segments to be omitted from the figures. Second, in order to maintain the confidentially of the companies contributing information, product sectors with less than three contributors are combined with other product sectors. This, like the first example, has no effect on the overall industry totals but can make segment totals meaningless.

Thus, although there are numerous sources of external data, most are of only limited value having been originally collected for purposes other than marketing research. It is for this reason that data taken from these sources are generally referred to as *secondary data*. When using secondary data, wherever possible its accuracy should be checked. It is not sufficient simply to show that several sources agree with regard to a particular item of information. All this very often shows is that they all used the same original source or worse still, each other. If it is not possible actually to check the accuracy of the information then an attempt should at least be made to put it into context.

Generally speaking, any secondary data being used within an organisation can be compared with the market held by that organisation. Where the market is being served by a number of small companies total capacity estimates can be compared with market size estimates and any discrepancies investigated. Research done by organisations not involved in a market or by students, for instance, cannot usually use this approach. Instead, reference needs to be made to other information available. If, for instance, information was required about the market for cash registers used in shops, garages, restaurants and so on, an estimate of the market could be made on the basis of the number of retail outlets within a town or the country, the average number of cash registers in each and how often these are replaced. The resulting figure would, of course, be an estimate but would still be useful as a check.

Another approach is to relate consumption to the population as a whole. Reliable population estimates are available for most developed countries since they are required as the basis for many government policies. Generally the population estimates are obtained by means of a census carried out every ten years. In the UK this was last done in 1991. The principal objective of a census is to measure variations in the population relating to the need for public services: schools, healthcare, law enforcement, and so on. Since in the UK the data shows the demographics of the population by area, it can also be used as appropriate to estimate the potential demand for certain products or services. It can also be used as the basis for checking the potential validity of data. For example, you are looking for information regarding the market for jeans in the UK and you find an article in which it is stated that in the UK 47 million pairs of jeans are sold each year and the value of the market is £650 million. If the population of the UK is approximately 55 million and 10 per cent are children there would be about 50 million adults. On this basis the data would suggest that adults buy on average about one pair of jeans per year. Is this reasonable? It is quite likely that many students buy three or more pairs of jeans per year, but then the average student's parents possibly only buy on average one pair per year and the average student's grandparents probably buy none. Taking all this into account, what at least can be said is that while 47 million may or may not be correct, it is clearly not obviously incorrect. How about the value? This suggests that the average price of a pair of jeans is less than £14. Is this likely to be right? A walk round any town centre looking in shop windows might show that there are jeans for sale at £14 but they are not branded and most jeans people are wearing seem to be branded. What does this mean? Either the article was using information which was wrong, or which was out of date, or there was a printing error. There are other possible explanations, the figure could be based on ex works prices rather than the retail selling price, or on some other cost basis such as the value at which the goods were imported. Whatever the reason it is clear that the figure needs to be treated with caution and if used, because it is the only information available, its apparent shortcomings should at least be discussed.

The collation of relevant external data can involve continuously monitoring measures of national economic activity, such as the gross national product, or measures of business confidence such as the Confederation of British Industry poll of business activity trends and investment intentions. Generally, as with internal data, only measures which over time have been shown to be relevant are monitored on a continuous basis. Information required to respond to specific marketing problems is collated on an *ad hoc* basis.

Many marketing problems will only require analysis of either external secondary data or a combination of both external secondary and internal data. Unfortunately, as has been mentioned, it is generally necessary to at least check the validity of any external data used. As with the jeans example this would involve at least a cursory visit to the shops to get some idea of the current price range for jeans. This simple example of primary research will be discussed in more detail in Chapter 10. The analysis of secondary data will also be discussed in greater detail below.

Gathering information – primary data

Primary research has been referred to already and is often referred to as field research in contrast to desk research. It involves using one or more of the following four market research techniques: observation, surveys, projective methods, and experimentation. Each of these is described and discussed in detail in Chapter 10.

Data analysis

To be of value marketing information must be:

- accurate;
- current;
- sufficient;
- available; and
- relevant.

Thus, the objective of data analysis is to ensure as far as possible the information presented meets these requirements. Furthermore, as discussed in the introduction to this chapter, it needs to be understandable to whoever will be using the information. This is often a major challenge for the researcher even though personal computers offer an extensive range of alternative methods of analysis and presentation. Ideally the method chosen should be simple and easily explained to the person who is to use the information.

The purpose of data analysis

It needs to be stressed that the purpose of marketing research is to provide information, not simply to present data. A primary characteristic of information is that it can be understood without prior knowledge or interpretation. This usually involves putting data into context. For instance, the fact that in 1960 a graduate engineer might expect to start work as a trainee at £650 per year, and in 1990 the same graduate would expect to start at £10 000 per year is data. It could be presented as information by showing for instance that in 1960 a new Mini cost 75 per cent of a trainee graduate engineer's starting salary whereas in 1990 a new Mini represented 50 per cent of a graduate trainee engineer's starting salary. Another way would be to state that in 1960 £650 represented 3200 gallons of petrol whereas in 1990 £10 000 represented more than 5000 gallons of petrol. Both of these comparisons would seem to show that the graduate engineer, as a trainee, was more highly valued in 1990 than in 1960. The fact is in 1960, the graduate engineer was unlikely to find a better combination of salary and career prospects than that offered by becoming a graduate trainee engineer, whereas in 1990 graduates with the same degree could have increased their starting salary by 30 per cent or more by using the engineering degree as the basis for entering careers in finance or general management. It is hardly surprising that the following adage is so well known: There are lies, damned lies and statistics.

The same data can, however, be viewed from the perspective of the cost of the new Mini. In 1960 this represented about 2500 gallons of petrol whereas in 1990 it represents about 3000 gallons of petrol. Thus, while in terms of the graduate trainee engineer's salary the car has become significantly less expensive, in terms of the petrol it has become somewhat more expensive. These changes are, however, in the range of 30 to +20 per cent which is minor in comparison with the changes in monetary value of these items which are 1000 – 2000 per cent.

The 30 year time span used in this example was specifically chosen to emphasise the effect of the relative changes in monetary values over time. It also usefully emphasises how products change. The Mini of 1960 was not only crude in comparison with the 1990 version, but required more frequent servicing, was not expected to last as long and was far less reliable. This, to an extent, compensates for the increase in terms of the value of petrol and makes the reduction in terms of salary even more significant.

Because of product and specification changes such as these, market research analysis over extended time periods is generally very difficult without specialist knowledge. This does not reduce the need to analyse any data presented since the effect of changing values is likely to be sufficiently significant to hide trends, especially in established markets.

The analysis of value data

Value data, whether collated from internal or external sources, can potentially be an extremely valuable source of marketing research information. It allows expenditure on different types of product to be combined and trends over long periods to be compared with leading indicators to establish relationships which can be used for forecasting. This type of analysis, however, needs to be done on a constant value basis. The importance is recognised in many tables showing national economic statistics which include constant historical (e.g. 1985) values or a constant value index based on a specific year. This approach is convenient for those preparing the data as new data can be appended to that already published.

It is not, however, the best approach for presenting marketing information. It is inherently difficult to relate the values of even a few years ago to the present and even more difficult to do this with the accuracy needed to draw sensible conclusions. Thus, for business applications, it is very much better to present historic data in present value terms for discussion and analysis.

Example

From the data presented in the following table (which was taken from industry sources and amended for illustration purposes) can anything be said about the market for biscuits in the UK?

The total UK biscuit market, 1988–90

	1986	*1987*	*1988*	*1989*
Sales £000 000 (RSP)				
Chocolate biscuits	276	315	377	437p
Other biscuits	675	698	722	769p
Total	951	1013	1099	1206p
Sales volume (000 tonnes)				
Chocolate biscuits	138	138	170	179p
Other biscuits	455	452	451	456p
Total	593	593	621	635p

p = provisional

It would appear that the market both for chocolate and other biscuits was growing both in terms of UK sterling value and volume of chocolate biscuits as stated in tonnes but static in terms of volume of other biscuits. Would this also apply if proper allowance was made for inflation?

There are many sources for the Retail Price Index, the statistical data presented on one of the back pages of *The Economist* being as convenient as any. There are also many versions of the Retail Price Index since, depending on the source, it may be the figure at the end of each year, the figure at mid-year or the average for the year as a whole. In practice so long as the same measure is used for each year in the series it makes very little difference. This is because the differences are small compared with the overall effect. Another problem is the choice of price index since, in addition to the retail index which is reported month by month as a news item, there are special indices which relate specifically to fuel, food, durable goods, and so on. Where one of these appears to be more suitable, the results obtained should always be compared with those obtained using the standard retail price index and an explanation found if there is any significant difference.

What would be the effect of adjusting the sales figures for biscuits to compensate for inflation ?

When considering monetary values it is always easier to think in terms of present-day values. For this reason, when calculation constant values it is better to state these in the current value terms rather than in an arbitrary historic value as is the usual practice. The reason for this is that most individuals who need to use this type of information for business purposes find it very difficult to relate the values of even a few years ago to the present and are unlikely to judge this relationship with any accuracy.

As an example, the calculations necessary to present the Biscuit Market Data in constant 1989 values will be shown:

	1986	1987	1988	1989
RPI % Increase		4.3	6.4	7.7
Year-on-year factor	1.043	1.064	1.077	1.00
Accumulative factor	1.195	1.146	1.077	1.00
Sales constant 1989 £000 000 (RSP)				
Chocolate biscuits	330	361	406	437p
Other biscuits	807	800	777	769p
Total	1137	1161	1183	1206p

p = provisional

It will be seen from these constant value figures that while the chocolate biscuit sector has shown real growth, the other sector is in real terms a shrinking market. It is noteworthy that this constant value decline was not matched by the decline in volume, which means that the average price of other biscuits must have declined over the period studied. This would suggest that competition had increased in this sector or demand had shifted to either the lower priced brands or product varieties. Over the same period the average price of chocolate biscuits increased as might be expected in a growing market.

The example shows how simply by presenting time series data on a constant value basis provides information about the market which otherwise is completely hidden. It also shows that trends within the data are as might be expected. Had this not been the case it would have been sensible to question the validity of the data. As with any secondary data, it would be sensible before formally presenting this data to attempt to validate it by comparing it with the present situation. At the simplest level this would involve visiting some supermarkets and comparing the price range for chocolate and other biscuits with the average prices obtained from the data adjusted to present-day values, using the same approach as was used to obtain the 1989 values. Another simple but worthwhile check would be to compare the relative amount of shelf space devoted to the two types of biscuits since it would not be unreasonable to expect these to reflect the relative market sizes of the two products.

Prepare report

Unless the information is properly presented it is unlikely to meet the requirement of the person who requires the information. The report should show the objectives of the study, explain how the study was carried out, detail any assumptions made and present the findings of the study clearly. Data, whether directly applicable or as background information is normally best presented in a series of separate appendices. Particular care needs to be taken with respect to the presentation of graphical information. The purpose of using graphics is to make the information easier to understand. It is useful to show trends and differences. Accordingly, it is usually inappropriate where the data is essentially static.

With the availability of modern computer presentation packages it is important to match the choice of diagram to the data being presented. Most packages include facilities for producing graphical data for use in presentations and these are generally unsuitable for written reports. In particular, any diagram which presents two-dimensional data in a three-dimensional format should be avoided. These often look smart, but usually make the data more difficult to interpret properly without explanation. This is not the purpose of a diagram. When in doubt the best guide is to follow the approach used in most basic text books, except where these use three-dimensional diagrams. Common sense is usually a sound guide.

Follow up implementation

This stage need not be formal but should be conscientiously carried out since it provides opportunities to understand how the methods used in the investigation of presentation could be improved on future occasions.

Data sources

There is a list of sources of external secondary data sources in Appendix III on pp 374–6. In addition, the internal data can be drawn from:

- Sales records
- Delivery and stock records
- Prices and quotations
- Sales promotion – price offers, etc.
- Advertising – media and messages – size of budget
- Sales personnel's call reports and assessments of their effectiveness
- Past studies on marketing effectiveness.

Conclusion

Marketing research means providing the information for decisions on marketing activities such as advertising, pricing and distribution. The approach used may vary in terms of time frame (continuous *v* ad hoc), information type (qualitative *v* quantitative), or the research purposes served (descriptive, exploratory, causal).

Whatever the type of research, the demands of budget constraints, research rigour and timeliness will require a methodical, well-managed sequence to be followed, from the initial problem definition and objectives stage, through data collection and analysis, to presentation and reporting of findings.

Marketing information must be accurate, current, sufficient, available and relevant. Further, it needs to be presented and communicated to the user in an understandable format. Statistical information, in particular, needs to be carefully handled, and presented consistently in terms of time series, measures and values.

Examples

Here are some examples for practice. In all cases although the data is based on industry sources it is presented only for illustrative purposes. For these assume that the price of the product being considered has generally changed in line with the RPI and this has changed year-to-year as follows:

	1982	1983	1984	1985	1986	1987	1988	1989	1990
RPI % change on previous year	8.5	4.6	5.0	5.5	3.9	4.9	7.8	7.6	10.4

Example 1

Jeans seem to continue to resist or adapt to fashion changes in the UK as can be seen from the following table:

	1982	1983	1984	1985	1986	1987
UK sales of jeans £m	460	490	540	610	740	820
UK sales of jeans (million pairs)	42.1	44.6	45.1	41.0	42.5	40.6

What are the real trends in this market?

Example 2

Mineral water has for an number of reasons been one of the most unlikely growth products in the UK during the 1980s. This is shown by the following table:

	1985	1986	1987	1988	1989	1990
UK sales of mineral water (£m RSP)	65	78	115	124	225	300
UK sales mineral water (litres m.)	92	106	148	194	315	400

What are the real trends in this market? What is likely to be of concern to the suppliers?

Example 3

US-based companies which dominate the breakfast cereal market worldwide are confident that the UK market still has growth potential though this might be limited. Is this view justified by the following table?

	1984	1985	1986	1987	1988	1989
UK sales cold (RTE) cereals £m RSP	466	490	552	594	641	686e
UK sales cold (RTE) cereals (000 tonnes)	340	322	349	353	357	361e

e = estimated

Example 4

Trainers were for many years almost the only growth product within the whole of the footwear market sector. On the basis of the data presented in the following table is this growth likely to continue?

	1983	1984	1985	1986	1987	1988
UK sales trainers (£m RSP)	197	230	295	340	450	568
UK sales trainers (million pairs)	8.5	10.5	14.5	17.5	26.5	33.4

Example 5

It is believed that the market for lawn mowers is more dependent on the activity in the market for houses than any other single factor. Since this remained buoyant until 1989 can any other trends be seen in the following table?

	1984	1985	1986	1987	1988	1989
UK sales lawn mowers (£m RSP)	86	101	101	119	133	143e
UK sales lawn mowers (million units)	1.16	1.30	1.22	1.32	1.43	1.46e

e = estimated

Example 6

Tea is no longer holds the dominant position it once had in the UK beverage market. Furthermore, there have been some important changes within the UK tea market. Can you identify the extent of these changes from the following table?

	1984	1985	1986	1987	1988	1989
UK sales tea bags (£m RSP)	401	441	402	474	474	475e
UK sales tea bags (m. tonnes)	99.3	99.0	103.7	126.4	127.9	129e
UK sales blended tea (£m RSP)	229	234	194	120	106	105e
UK sales blended tea (m. tonnes)	69.1	65.0	60.7	40.4	36.7	35e

e = estimated

Questions

1 'A problem well-defined is a problem half resolved'. Discuss.

2 Consider the distinctive advantages of continuous research, giving examples of the marketing questions that it might answer.

3 'Qualitative research has obvious value in the insights it can provide, but when over-used it can be distinctly misleading'. Discuss.

4 Taking as an example the manufacturer of any leading consumer product, illustrate the variety of marketing decisions that might be better supported through the effective use of marketing research.

References

Crimp, M, *The Marketing Research Process*, 2nd Edn, Prentice-Hall, 1985.
Moutinho, L, and Evans, M, *Applied Marketing Research*, Addison-Wesley, 1992.
Chisnall, P M, *Essentials of Marketing Research*, Prentice-Hall, 1992.

10

MARKET RESEARCH

Introduction

As already discussed in Chapter 9 the term *market research* as used in this book defines the specialist function of marketing research concerned with collecting primary information through the application of one of the following four primary research techniques:

1 Observation
2 Surveys
3 Projective Methods
4 Experimentation

The European Society for Opinion and Marketing Research (ESOMAR) defines market research as, 'The systematic collection and objective recording, classification, analysis and presentation of data concerning the behaviour, needs, attitudes, opinions, motivations, etc. of individuals, organisations (commercial enterprises, public bodies etc) within the context of their economic social political and everyday activities'. Thus the polls used to monitor the voting intentions of an electorate and the relative standing and popularity of the government and opposition are good examples of an application of a market research technique. Usually such estimates are made on the basis of a sample of about 1000 potential voters and have an expected accuracy of +/- 3 per cent. This is remarkably good when one considers that in the UK this is a measure of the intentions of more that 40 million individuals voting in more than 600 separate constituencies.

Primary data like internal and external secondary data may be collated on a continuing or *ad hoc* basis. Often the results of the voting intention polls are presented to show how intentions have changed over time even though often the research was conducted intermittently. Continuing research involves conducting such research on a regular basis. This is done to monitor the standing of major brands against their main competitors. Like all the major car manufacturers, Peugeot UK, for instance interviews about 100 people regularly to find out how the name Peugeot and it's products are perceived with regard to characteristics such as value for money, economy, quality, performance, sportiness and so on. The results of such surveys are tracked as a moving average and the advertising message changed if for example, the result of a concentration on an executive model has resulted in the perception moving away from the value for money image relative to the competition.

As the two examples show, the term *market research* includes all types of opinion research and accordingly is not restricted to the consideration of markets as is suggested by some authors. In the UK, market research is a specialist activity developed separately from marketing and hence marketing research. The Market Research Society has been central to this development. Founded in 1947 it has, with the Industrial Marketing Research Association, helped to develop the interests and professionalism of market researchers and to maintain an identity which is separate from other aspects of marketing. The two organisations have encouraged the development of rigorous opinion and market research techniques, for which they have earned a justified reputation, as well as the theoretical basis for many of these techniques. Also, by remaining separate from other specialist marketing activities, such as advertising, and from marketing as the profession represented by the Chartered Institute of Marketing, the two marketing research organisations have been able to develop a rigorous code of practice. This would have been more difficult if market research had developed as it did in the USA. There the market research profession is represented both by a specialist section of the American Marketing Association and the Marketing Science Institute of America.

Having separate organisations responsible for marketing and marketing research as in the UK is important since ethical questions are involved not only with respect to the design, implementation and reporting of market research studies, but also with regard to the use made of the results. One aspect of this problem as it relates to surveys is discussed as an example on page 123.

Observational research

The most basic of the four principal market research techniques used to obtain primary data is observational research. At its simplest level it involves conscientiously looking at something. In spite of this apparent simplicity it should be a routine part of all research involving the use of secondary data. This is because any sensible interpretation of data has to be based on a proper understanding of the products concerned. Reference has already been made to this in the sections on secondary external data and analysis. The first example was the validity of the average price of jeans and the second was with regard to the relative size of the different sectors of the biscuit market.

An important feature of many markets which is often only apparent from conscientious inspection is the full extent of the range of products involved. Consider, for example, the market for watches. In jewellery shops, prices are likely to range from somewhat under £20 to possibly in excess of £4,000. In addition there is a discount watch market where prices start at below £2. The characteristic of this market is that in comparison with the price range the size, function and even the accuracy of the product essentially remains the same.

The market for batteries is very different. As a visit to any shop selling batteries will show, there are not only a wide range of sizes but several different price categories in each size range. These represent different qualities and the rechargeable type. In addition there are many special types of battery used in watches, calculators, cameras, hearing aids, and similar small equipment which, although very small, often cost more than a large standard battery. The only common feature of these products is that they use a chemical reaction to produce electric power. The implication, therefore, of this is that for any marketing purpose the market for batteries cannot be realistically considered as a single market. Rather the battery market is made up of a number of individual sectors. What is less clear is how to define these sectors. This is even more difficult when it is realised that in addition to the products available in the shops there is a vast range of technical batteries used in a wide range of equipment ranging from computers to emergency exit signs. Clearly any comments made about the market for batteries which did not recognise these differences would be of little value in a marketing context.

In many markets, observation is essential to ensure the products being offered are competitive in comparison with the quality and price being offered by competitors. A simple example is a supermarket department manager's routine morning walk around a competitor's store to check on the price and quality of the fresh produce on sale. The essential characteristic of such observation is that, unless the routine is reported, the information gathered each day is likely to remain intangible information. This is typical of observational market research. It generally increases the intangible information available within an organisation. It is because of this that managers have always been urged by the gurus of management science to 'spend time in their markets'.

There are, however, formal observational market research techniques which produce tangible information. One example is the traffic survey which involves recording, for instance, the number of vehicles approaching and leaving each of the roads at a junction minute by minute or hour by hour to measure traffic flow rates. Such surveys are often carried out by the Ministry of Transport prior to implementing road improvement schemes. Similar observation techniques have been used in supermarkets to evaluate customer reaction to check-out queues. Another supermarket application has been to plot the routes taken by different types of shopper so that store layouts ensure that in going from one essential or listed item to another involves passing as many of the most likely other purchases as possible. A more sophisticated example of an observational survey has been developed through the use of bar code readers at supermarket checkouts. These, not only can be used to control stock, price the produce and print a detailed list, but also to analyse the goods selected by each individual customer. This information can be used to improve the layout of the store with the same objective as before. Furthermore, in stores where a significant proportion of purchases are made using credit cards, it is then possible to link purchase selections to the home location of the shopper. Using such data advertising can be precisely targeted at specific local areas thereby improving its cost effectiveness.

Another sophisticated observational technique is that used to measure television audiences. This involves having the televisions in about 4500 homes, selected to provide a cross section of the general viewing public, equipped with meters which record when the television is on and the channel selected. This information is then retrieved automatically each night by a computer system using the normal telephone network. To improve the accuracy of the findings the meters are equipped with a means of recording which members of the household are watching the television when it is on.

Surveys

The second, and by far the most important, of the four market research techniques used for obtaining the primary marketing information is the *survey*. These are used extensively to find out all types of information from individuals. As mentioned in the introduction, one well-established use of surveys is to measure voting intentions prior to elections. The surveys are commissioned by the major political parties and by newspapers and often seek to establish the opinions of the potential voters with regard to the relative importance of the issues considered critical at the time of the poll, in addition to voting intentions.

In all types of survey, questionnaires are used to obtain the information required. Accordingly the reliability of the information will depend upon the effectiveness of the questionnaire and the people selected to ask and answer the questions. Before considering each of these factors it would perhaps be useful to consider what types of information can be obtained using a questionnaire.

1   Facts
2   Knowledge
3   Intentions
4   Demographic characteristics
5   Behaviour
6   Opinions
7   Attitudes
8   Motivations
9   Other psychological characteristics
10   Lifestyle.

In the marketing context it is useful to separate facts and knowledge. It should be possible to determine facts precisely for example 'Do you have with you now a phonecard which still has value?'. Knowledge is less straightforward since it is difficult to separate a person's actual knowledge from their perception of this knowledge. Because of this, answers to a question such as, 'Do you know about the Phonecard system?', are likely to depend on how complete the person answering believes his or her information to be on the subject.

It has also been recognised by the market research profession that its standing in the eyes of the public is important. In this respect the codes of conduct which, as mentioned in the introduction, have been adopted by both the Market Research Society and the Industrial Market Research Society are significant. In particular these prohibit the use of market research as a method of screening potential customers. Sadly many doorstep sales personnel have found such an approach can be effective. This bad practice has given market research a bad name.

Questionnaire design

Experience has shown that the effectiveness of questionnaires can be generally improved by following some well-established guidelines. These relate to layout, length and question order. Since the questionnaire is the only tangible link between the person asking the questions and the person answering them, it is important that it is an effective means of communication. It therefore needs to appear at first glance straightforward, well-designed and not too long. As a general guide the length of questionnaires for trade surveys or for use 'in the street' should not exceed one typewritten side of A4; those for use on the doorstep, two typewritten sides of A4. Questionnaires for use in prearranged interviews can be longer since a good interviewer should be able to hold the attention of a respondent for an hour or more.

The layout first and foremost needs to be easy to use. A questionnaire should comprise six clearly defined blocks. The first should be the heading. This should contain a survey title in large enough print to be easily read by the respondent, even upside down; instructions to the interviewers, and the introductory statements the interviewers should use when introducing themselves to potential respondents. Below this there should be four column blocks. The first should be narrow for the question numbers, the second wide enough for the questions, the third wide enough for the answers, and the fourth should be a narrow column for the answer codes. Across the bottom of the sheet or the last sheet there should be a sixth block containing any questions needed to classify the questionnaire in terms of the location, time and date of the interview, the interviewer and any other relevant information such as weather conditions. It should also include a statement which reminds the interviewer to thank the respondent.

The order in which questions are asked is important for several reasons. First, the initial questions should positively confirm the purpose of the questionnaire. Second, they should be sufficiently factual and uncontroversial to allow respondents to gather their thoughts about the subject. Third, they should develop trust between the interviewer and the respondent; this is important since it is through trust that respondents become involved and hence more likely to answer the questions candidly.

Before starting to design a questionnaire and draft the questions it is first necessary to establish:

- What is the main purpose of the survey?
- What information is required?
- Who will be providing this information?
- How will the questionnaire be used: personal interview, telephone interview, or mail?
- What types of information are required?
- Will a respondent consider any of the required information to be either sensitive or confidential?

The next stage is to draft questions which focus on the main purpose of the survey and the other information required. The order in which the questions will be asked should then be considered. The first two or three questions should be simple, interesting, help establish what the questionnaire is about and reassure the respondent by showing that the questionnaire will neither be difficult not take longer than would be reasonable in the circumstances. There should be a logical development from one topic to the next which may involve adding questions which provide links from one topic to the next. This approach allows the respondent to become involved with the objective of the question-naire thereby encouraging accurate answers and a willingness to answer any sensitive questions which the respondent is more likely to accept as being necessary after having completed the majority of the questionnaire.

The wording of questions

Since the purpose of a questionnaire is to obtain accurate information questions need to be worded to ensure, as far as possible, a truthful response. This is only possible if respondents:

1 are able understand the question;
2 are able to provide the information requested;
3 are willing to provide this information.

Does the question 'Do you have with you now a phonecard which still has value?' meet these criteria? Can it be understood? This depends upon the person being asked the question understanding the term phonecard and if so, the interpretation which is applied to it. There are at least three possible interpretations. It could be the British Telecom Phonecard, or it could mean any phonecard, thereby including the BT card, the Mercurycard and any others such the French Telecarte, or it could even mean any card which can be used in a phone, which would include Access and Visa cards. There is enough choice here to produce a confusing result.

There is no reason to suspect that the second of the criteria would cause any problem. From a practical viewpoint anyone who believed that they had a card would probably get another if they found it had been lost or had no value when they next tried to use it. Likewise anyone who had one, but had forgotten would probably not remember to use it even when there was an opportunity to do so. The willingness of the respondent to provide the information is, however, likely to depend upon the need for the information being understood and the respondent being confident that there is no other motive involved. Both of these factors are likely to depend to a significant extent upon the context of the question within the questionnaire and the context in which the questions are being asked.

Just as the effectiveness of questionnaires can be improved by complying with some well-established guidelines, so the wording of questions can be improved by adhering to some simple rules:

1 Ask short, easy-to-understand questions. Often these two requirements seem to be mutually conflicting. The need to be easily understood, however, should always be considered as more important than brevity. Often the easiest way to meet these apparently conflicting requirements is to ask two questions, the first being intended to assist the respondent rather than provide the required information.

2 Avoid leading questions. This requires extreme care both with regard to the wording of questions and the order in which they are asked. It is quite easy for respondents unconsciously to establish a pattern of answering. They are in effect, led on by the previous question. Sometimes this is simply because they are inquisitive about the questionnaire itself and simply want to avoid having it terminated as a result of giving a negative response.

   Some subjects, especially those which have been advertised on the basis of their logic, are often assumed to have become accepted practice. Hence there are many people who, if asked the question: 'Do you use the *Yellow Pages* regularly?', are likely to respond 'Yes' even though they have not used it for months or even years. Further questions seeking to find out how often, are then likely to be answered vaguely or defensively thereby reducing any goodwill there may have been between the interviewer and respondent. One simple device which can be used to overcome this type of problem is to add 'or not' to the question. This reassures the respondent that a negative answer is just as acceptable as a positive one and avoids a situation which otherwise could have significantly reduced the reliability of all subsequent answers.

3 Ensure that respondents are not given motives to lie. This follows from the need to avoid leading questions. A typical example would be a question relating to something apparently peripheral to the stated purpose of the questionnaire for which it is easier to guess the answer than appear ignorant. It has to be emphasised that the purpose of a questionnaire is to obtain information not test the respondents' knowledge, memory or powers of deduction.

Such basic guidelines as these are surprisingly difficult to apply in practice, as can be seen by critically reviewing some of the questionnaires we receive either seeking market research information or for other purposes such as employment applications. The case study at the end of this chapter provides an opportunity to review a sadly not atypical example.

Rationalising the answers

The potential effectiveness of a questionnaire is affected by other factors in addition to the structure of the questionnaire and the wording of individual questions even though these are of prime importance. One of the most important of these other factors is the selection of a rational way by which the answer can be recorded. The choice can both affect the wording of an individual question and the number of questions required. There are two considerations which need to be taken into account: first, 'What information is required?'; second, 'What information can I obtain most easily?' Consider a questionnaire concerning facilities used by students. One factor which could affect the choice of facilities might, for a number of reasons, be age. One approach would be simply to ask 'How old are you?' If asked at the end of a well-designed questionnaire which had developed trust between the interviewer and the respondent and which showed the question was relevant, it would generally get a truthful reply. Fine, but what could you do with this information? Divide it into categories such as <17, 17<18, 18<19, 19<20, 20<21, 21<22, 22<25, 25<35, 35<55, 55+. This would suggest that what is required is not the age of the respondent, but the age category of the respondent. The answer can be obtained by showing the respondent a card with each category identified by a code letter. This could safely be shown early in the questionnaire, thus allowing subsequent questions to be selected according to the age group of the respondent.

It is quite likely that nine data categories are more than necessary. In which case the question such as 'Are you under 25 or not?' may provide all the information required. If greater detail is required regarding those under 25 this could be a secondary question for those answering 'Yes' only.

These examples show the three different types of answer that can be used to collate factual or demographic information and hence the three types of direct question:

1 The open question – How old are you?
2 The closed dichotomous question: Are you under 25? (requiring a 'yes' or 'no' answer).
3 The closed multiple choice question: Which age category are you in? A = <17, B = 17<18, C = 18<19, D = 19<20, E = 20<21, F = 21<22, G = 22<25, H = 25<35, I = 35<55, or J = 55+. The coded list is offered to the respondent on a card.

Of the ten different types of information only two, facts and demographic information, are likely to have unequivocal answers. For all of the others the answer needs to be qualified in terms of degree. Even knowledge should be considered in this category, since as previously discussed, it can be influenced by people's beliefs and attitudes.

Returning to the question relating to phonecards. Assuming that for the purpose of the survey the type of card is unimportant, the original question is likely to identify those who have cards. How could the frequency of use be established? There could be two aspects of this question. First is the perception of how frequently it is used. The second aspect is the user's perception of frequency. It is actually conceivable that some users would consider that once a week was frequent, whereas for others several times a day would be frequent and once a week infrequent. A respondent's perception is often important, especially in marketing, since buying decisions can be strongly influenced by perceptions. Many different methods have been developed to measure the strength of feeling with regard to attitudes, beliefs and opinions. The following three are the most straightforward and are used frequently to measure strength of feeling using a direct question.

First, is the *non-comparative rating scale*. For example:

'How frequently do you use your Phonecard?'

5	4	3	2	1
Very frequently	Frequently	Sometimes	Occasionally	Seldom

This is useful for measuring perceptions and, first impressions and is used in situations where the overall confidence level needs to be investigated.

Where a more specific response is required, the *comparative rating scale* can be used. For example:

'When using a public phone how often do you use a Phonecard rather than coins?'

5	4	3	2	1
Always	Very often	About the same	Occasionally	Seldom

Often it is necessary to investigate a large number of potentially significant criteria or features in order to find the few that are critical. This can be done by wording each question so that the answers can be on a agreement scale. For example:

5	4	3	2	1
Agree strongly	Agree slightly	Neither agree nor disagree	Disagree slightly	Disagree strongly

This is known as the *Likert scale* since it was first proposed by Renis Likert in 1932. It will be noted that the non comparative and comparative rating scales are variations of this basic approach.

With all these first three ways a table can be constructed with the questions in a left-hand column and the answer codes in an adjacent matrix. By this method it is possible to cover a large number of topics quickly and conveniently. The technique is particularly suitable where the questionnaire is being completed by an interviewer and the respondent has been handed a card showing the numbered answers. However, it is important, especially when used in questionnaires that will be completed by the respondent, that there is a random mix of favourable and unfavourable statements, otherwise the result is likely to be affected by respondents who continue to agree or disagree as much from the rhythm of ticking the boxes as from conviction.

The fourth style of questions is *Semantic Differential Scale*. This uses two opposite statements instead of a single statement and the respondent is required to show a tendency towards one or other of the statements rather than to agree or disagree. The effectiveness of the measure depends upon choosing suitable opposing meanings which in practice can be difficult. An example of this approach would be:

'What are your opinions regarding the BT Phonecard? Please place a cross on the line at the point that best indicates your opinion.

	Extremely	Somewhat	Neither	Somewhat	Extremely	
Expensive	——————————————————————————					Cheap
Simple	——————————————————————————					Complicated
Available	——————————————————————————					Unavailable

Reviewing the draft questionnaire

Having drafted a questionnaire it should be reviewed not only with regard to the points already made but also with regard to whether it would:

- maintain the co-operation and involvement of the respondent;
- develop the confidence of the respondent;
- allow the respondent to develop answers;
- minimise bias;
- simplify the task of the interviewer; and
- minimise the difficulty of data collation and processing.

At this stage each question should be reviewed and the critical questions reviewed in detail. This involves considering the likelihood of the question providing the information required. It will depend in part upon the type of information sought. There is no point in asking questions which the respondent is unable to answer. This can be avoided by using filter questions. Hence, before asking whether a person finds parking in the city centre difficult, it would generally be necessary to establish how the respondent came into the city centre on that particular day and whether or not this was a daily routine. Establishing that a respondent is able to answer a particular question is part way to ensuring that the question is answered accurately.

As already mentioned, the type of information can affect the potential accuracy of an answer. In addition to knowledge, questions can be asked with regard to intentions, demographic characteristics, behaviour, attitudes, opinions, psychological characteristics, motivations and lifestyle. Any question which cannot be classified in terms of one of these types of information should be reviewed carefully since it is likely to be misunderstood.

Other causes of misunderstanding are the words used. Generally, technical words should be avoided and where possible, so should words which are not among the 1000 most common words in the English language. Furthermore, as has already been mentioned, every effort should be made to avoid introducing bias through leading questions.

In addition to being used in formal surveys, questionnaires are also used for informal interviews. Often they need to be just as carefully designed but their implementation will be much more flexible and dependent upon the interviewer. Their main purpose is to provide a framework for the interview to ensure all aspects of the subject are covered. They are also used in casual surveys such as those which use guarantee cards, magazine readership surveys and user surveys.

Sampling

Questionnaires are occasionally used in surveys involving only a small total population such as might be the case in industrial market research when all the potential customers for a particular product are included in the survey. This is referred to as a *census*.

Usually, however, this is not practical and surveys involve only a small proportion of the total population. This is referred to as a *sample*. Using a sample has two specific advantages. First it is less costly than a census. Second it is faster which in the marketing context is often of paramount importance.

Defining a satisfactory sample is a three stages process. The first of these is to define the target population. This is the total group about which information is required. It could be the female adult population of the country, it could be the Coventry University student population as a whole or it could be those members of it who have cars in Coventry. The latter is an example where the definition of the population could have a significant effect on the results of a survey since by limiting the population to students with cars in Coventry would eliminate any student who has a car, but does not have it in Coventry because of the difficulty and cost of parking.

The second stage is to specify how the sample will be selected and the third stage is to specify the sample size. Because of the inherent costs of undertaking market research, the most convenient satisfactory sample should be used. Returning to our phonecard question, if for some reason the extent of ownership and use of phonecards among Coventry University students was required then this would be the population. One of the most convenient samples of this population that could be taken during term time would be a class taken at random. Statistics theory tells us that samples of less than 30 should be treated as small samples. Therefore, a method of randomly selecting a class of more than 30 students would need to be used. Let us assume the resulting sample has 40 students. This sample is then asked the question: 'Do you have with you now a BT Phonecard which still has value?' By a simple show of hands it is found that 21 respond 'Yes' and 19 respond 'No'. What does this mean? In theory, not very much. This is because while the class might have been taken at random, it is not the same as randomly selecting the 40 individuals. There is a possibility that for the purpose of the question the members of a particular class share a characteristic which is not shared by the population as a whole. It is not possible therefore to extend any characteristic, such as phonecard ownership of this class, to the population as a whole (all Coventry University students).

Rather than analyse the problem of unrepresentative samples using statistics theory, let us consider the problem logically. It is clear that if we wanted to know exactly how many Coventry University students had valid phonecards one way to do this would be to gather them all together in one place and count those who had cards and those without cards as they left. The accuracy of the result would depend upon the care with which the counting was carried out and the number of students who, due to illness or some other reason, could not attend. Thus, if it was known that at the time of the count there were 10764 enrolled students, and that 8124 had cards, 2257 did not have cards and that 383 did not attend, the best that could be said having carried out this survey is that at the time and date of the survey of the 10764 students enrolled between 8124 and 8507 (8124 + 383) had cards and between 2257 and 2730 (2257 + 383) did not have cards. This means that, even assuming the method of counting was totally accurate, with 100 per cent certainty, card ownership could not be specified more precisely than as being *not more that 79.03 per cent and not less than 75.47 per cent.*

Since any method used to count those with and without cards would have some potential of error the precision with which card ownership could be stated with 100 per cent certainty would be accordingly reduced. That is, if the counting error was estimated as being not greater than ±1 per cent card ownership could not then be stated at 100 per cent certainty more precisely than being *not greater than 80.03 per cent and not less than 74.47 per cent*.

The 5.56 per cent difference between these is a measure of the precision of the measuring instrument used. This precision can only be improved by changing the measuring instrument, which could, for instance, involve tracking down some of the missing 383 students or using a more accurate method of counting.

In most business situations measures based on 100 per cent certainty are neither necessary nor possible. Furthermore, the difficulties involved are clearly evident from the above example. Let us consider a completely hypothetical reason as to why it might be necessary to know the proportion of Coventry University students with valid BT Phonecards. Imagine that BT has developed a card-operated fax system for use in universities and colleges and wished to select the colleges where this would be potentially most successful. Having initially installed the system in a number of colleges on a trial basis, it could have been established by comparing the successful and unsuccessful trial installations that those which had been successful had been in universities or colleges where BT Phonecard ownership was in excess of say 35 per cent.

As with any business venture it is realised that there are factors which affect success or failure which are outside the control of the organisation. Because of this it is accepted that some installations will be more successful than others and indeed that some will fail. The level of acceptable risk is dependent upon the type of business and in particular the investment required and the profit potential of the venture. Considering that it is said that two thirds of new products fail it could justifiably be argued that a 40 per cent expectation of success might be reasonable. Clearly anything which can be done to maximise this would be sensible especially during the initial introduction of a new product.

Accordingly, BT decide that initially they will aim for a 50 per cent installation success rate. That is, of every two systems installed one will be successful and the other, being unsuccessful, will have to be moved to another site. Because of the other factors which were identified during the trials as contributing to success or failure it is decided that the risk due to insufficient card ownership should be limited to 5 per cent. That is, for every 20 card fax systems installed they would expect 10 to be successful and not more than 1 of those to be unsuccessful as a result of insufficient card ownership among the student population concerned. This means that before installing a system in Coventry University they need to be 95 per cent confident that not less than 40 per cent of the total Coventry University student population have BT Phonecards.

Clearly, it is unnecessary to conduct some sort of census which would result in a 100 per cent confidence level measurement of card ownership. Furthermore statistics theory provides a method for specifying the reliability of the information obtained from any random sample used to determine the characteristics of the total population of which it is part. This is specified in terms of the probability that the population as a whole can be defined as being within a specified range with regard to information measured. For instance, from a random sample of male students between 1.75 and 1.85 metres in height, it is possible to be 95 per cent confident that any male student in this height range will weigh between 50 and 90 kilograms.

When the same approach is applied to questions with a yes/no answer such as, 'Do you own a Walkman?', the result would be stated in the form that from the random sample used it is possible to be 95 per cent confident that from 74 per cent to 100 per cent of that population possess a Walkman. For both of these examples it is also possible to calculate the range applicable to different confidence levels. The only information needed to do this is the original sample data. Hence, if in a random sample of 40 students, 21 had phonecards and 19 did not, this information would be used in the following formula to calculate the high-low limits for the population of which the sample is a random part.

At a 68 per cent confidence level

$$\text{High 'Yes' limit (\%)} = \frac{Ny \times 100}{Ny + Nn} + \frac{50}{\sqrt{(Ny + Nn)}} =$$

$$\text{Low 'Yes' limit (\%)} = \quad - \quad =$$

Substituting Ny = 21 and Nn = 19 we get

$$\text{High 'Yes' limit (\%)} = \frac{21 \times 100}{21 + 19} + \frac{50}{\sqrt{(21 + 19)}}$$

$$\text{Low 'Yes' limit (\%)} = \quad -$$

Calculating

$$\text{High 'Yes' limit (\%)} = \frac{2100}{40} + \frac{50}{\sqrt{(40)}}$$

$$\text{Low 'Yes' limit (\%)} = \quad -$$

$$\text{High 'Yes' limit (\%)} = 52.5 + \frac{50}{6.32}$$

$$\text{Low 'Yes' limit (\%)} = \quad -$$

$$\text{High 'Yes' limit (\%)} = 52.5 + 7.9 = 60.4$$

$$\text{Low 'Yes' limit (\%)} = \quad - \quad = 44.6$$

Where the application requires a higher level of confidence than 68 per cent as in this example, it is a simple matter to recalculate the limits for either 95 or 99 per cent confidence levels as follows:

For 95 per cent confidence the:

$$\text{High 'Yes' limit (\%)} = 52.5 + 2 \times 7.9 = 68.3$$

$$\text{Low 'Yes' limit (\%)} = \quad - \quad = 36.7$$

For 99 per cent confidence the:

$$\text{High 'Yes' limit (\%)} = 52.5 + 3 \times 7.9 = 76.2$$

$$\text{Low 'Yes' limit (\%)} = \quad - \quad = 28.8$$

Thus on the basis of this sample the requirement that at least 40 per cent own BT Phonecards at any one time has been met at the 68 per cent confidence level but not at either the 95 per cent or 99 per cent confidence levels.

Since the assessment being undertaken is simple it would be little trouble to repeat the survey with another random sample of 120 students. The total random sample would then be 160. If we assume the proportions with and without cards remain exactly the same then of the 160 students, 84 would have BT Phonecards.

Thus, at a 68 per cent confidence level substituting $Ny = 84$ and $Nn = 76$ in the above formula, we get

High 'Yes' limit (%) = $\dfrac{84 \times 100}{84 + 76}$ + $\dfrac{50}{\sqrt{(84 + 76)}}$

Low 'Yes' limit (%) =   -

Calculating

High 'Yes' limit (%) = $\dfrac{8400}{160}$ + $\dfrac{50}{\sqrt{(160)}}$

Low 'Yes' limit (%) =   -

High 'Yes' limit (%) = 52.5 + $\dfrac{50}{12.65}$

Low 'Yes' limit (%) =   -

High 'Yes' limit (%) = 52.5 + 3.95 = 56.5

Low 'Yes' limit (%) =   - = 48.5

For 95 per cent confidence the:

High 'Yes' limit (%) = 52.5 + 2×3.95 = 60.4

Low 'Yes' limit (%) =   - = 44.6

And at the 99 per cent confidence the:

High 'Yes' limit (%) = 62.5 + 3×7.6 = 64.3

Low 'Yes' limit (%) =   - = 40.7

Thus, on the basis of this four-times larger sample, while the proportion within the sample has remained the same the requirement that at least 40 per cent own BT Phonecards at any one time has been met both at the 95 per cent and 99 per cent confidence levels. It should be noted that it was necessary to increase the sample size by a factor of four to reduce the difference between the high and low limits by a factor of two.

Those readers who recognise that the formula used above is a specific application of the Central Limit Theorem as applied to proportions will have no difficulty in developing a formula for calculating the minimum sample size needed to confirm or reject the proposition that a Phonecard fax system should be installed at Coventry University. For the others, it will no doubt be sufficient to accept that this can be done using the following formula:

$$N = \frac{Z^2 \; p(1-p)}{E^2}$$

Where N = sample size, Z = confidence factor constant (=1 for 68 %, = 2 for 95 % and 3 for 99 %), p = proportion of 'Yes' answers and E = high/low limits /2

Thus, for 95 % confidence Z = 2, 50 % proportion   p = 0.5 and 10 per cent error E = 0.1

$$N = \frac{2^2 \; 0.5 \times 0.5}{0.1^2}$$

$$N = \frac{4 \times 0.25}{0.01}$$

$$N = \quad 100$$

This demonstrates how important it is to understand not only what information is required but also how accurate it needs to be. The calculation of minimum sample size as might be expected is based on the assumption that only half of the class possessed BT Phonecards, the worst case from the viewpoint of calculating sample size, and the error was the difference between half the class having cards and the minimum at which installation was considered viable. That is, –10 per cent at the 95 per cent confidence level. Had the proportion with cards in the original sample exceeded 60 per cent then this result would have shown that the requirements to proceed were essentially met even at a 99 per cent certainty level.

The random sample

The validity of a result obtained from a sample can only be estimated using statistics theory as a measure of a population when a random sample is used. That means that every member of the population had an equal non-zero chance of being included in the sample. This is clearly not the case if the sample chosen is a class. It is equally not the case if every fifth student leaving the union bar is questioned since this would disqualify students who never visit the bar. If additional sites were chosen to overcome this problem say outside the library and outside the refectories, the chance of being interviewed would depend on how many of these facilities a student used.

The only theoretically sound solution would be to randomly select the required number, in the above example 100, using, for example, student registration numbers. It would then be necessary to track down every one of these randomly selected individuals to find out how many were in possession of a valid BT Phonecard. Even in a reasonably compact area such as Coventry this would be very time consuming and potentially expensive. It also assumes that the list of student numbers can be accessed and is up to date.

Another approach would be to carry out the survey by, for instance, selecting a number of classes which include representatives from different types of course, different years of study, and in different subject areas. Then by including in the questionnaire questions relating to factors such as age, year of study, subject being studied, car ownership, and type of accommodation, the sample could be compared with the total population with regard to these characteristics. If it was found from this comparison that the sample was similar to the population as a whole then it would not be unreasonable to assume that it was representative of the population even though it was not a random sample.

Such an approach can be used where the target population can be easily defined e.g. Coventry car park users, but where there is no list from which a random selection can be made. Instead it would be necessary to attempt to obtain a representative sample by ensuring that interviews were carried out at a number of different sites and at different times of day. The representativeness of the sample could then be checked by asking each respondent the registration year letter of his or her vehicle, for instance, and then comparing the profile of the respondents with the profile of vehicles using the car parks. This could be obtained by observation. Another check might be the time of arrival and likely departure or length of stay which could be checked against the information which might be available from the equipment dispensing payment tickets. By comparing this information the representativeness of the sample could at least to some extent be verified or some allowance made with regard to any apparent bias.

This approach has been further refined by all of the established market research companies for specific applications such as forecasting national election results from comparatively small samples. While the procedures used by different organisations will vary they will also have many similarities. For instance, they will recognise that the result will not be affected by any seats held by large majorities. Likewise it is possible that some make assumptions about older voters being more likely both to vote and to vote as they did previously. By this approach it is possible to develop a critical sample rather than a typical or representative sample of the population. This is particularly useful where it is necessary to complete the survey quickly.

Readers requiring information regarding the different types of sample used in market research surveys should refer to any of the standard textbooks on market research. This should, however, be done with caution as it is easy to unjustifiably attribute random sample properties to non-random samples without considering the implications of doing so. Readers wishing to use statistical techniques for market research are also referred to the standard texts. Again, caution is advised since statistical analysis cannot improve the quality of the information being analysed. One of the main values of statistical analysis is to show the potential adequacy of information which is available. This has been illustrated in the BT Phonecard example. Statistical techniques cannot compensate for the limitations resulting from the use of a non-random sample or a poor questionnaire. It is important therefore to beware of false accuracy. There is no point calculating the high and low limits of a proportion which differ by 20 per cent to 0.1 per cent. It is meaningless and was only used in the example to allow figures to be traced by recalculation. In circumstances where the range is large it generally helps to think of the figures rounded to the nearest 5 per cent even though they might be specified for identification purposes to the nearest 1 per cent.

Survey implementation

Having designed the questionnaire, a limited number of copies are produced so that a pilot survey can be conducted. A pilot survey usually involves at the very least having 50 questionnaires completed by experienced interviewers. This will bring to light any problems with regard to the order or wording of questions and the reply cards if these are used. Amendments are then made, and if extensive, another pilot conducted before producing the number of copies required for the full survey. The next stage of the process involves distributing the questionnaires, arranging for them to be completed. Where interviewers are to be used arrangements will need to be made for them to be briefed and possibly also trained. The completed questionnaires will then need to be collected, checked, coded and analysed. With the availability of market research analysis programmes which can be run on personal computers this is comparatively straightforward.

The results of the analysis will then need to be effectively presented in a report. The factors relevant, being the same as for a marketing research report as discussed in the previous chapter.

Projective methods

The interview as a data-collection method has limitations with regard to establishing the way individuals view their place in the world and, as a result, their expectations. Since the advertising and sales promotion functions of marketing are often required to raise the expectations of potential customers, certainly when promoting prestige products, market research procedures have been developed to undertake investigations in this and associated topics.

Many of this third category of market research techniques involve group discussions initiated by a researcher. Some of these groups have existed for several decades in spite of the membership steadily changing over time. For this reason this category of market research has often been referred to as group research. The title projective methods is now generally used for two reasons. First, it is more descriptive since one of the main approaches involves the group participants explaining how they believe other people might react to a particular product, package or appeal. Second, it covers the other techniques essentially used for the same purpose such as word association tests, and the use of cartoons in story completion exercises. This range of techniques is thus generally used to establish the opinions and attitudes held by particular groups of people towards certain types of product. An example of the value of using these techniques was the discovery by Rowntree that none of the available block chocolate products really appealed to the male market. As a result they developed the Yorkie bar and the rest is history.

Experimentation

The fourth category of market research techniques used to obtain primary information is *experimentation* or, as it is sometimes called, *laboratory testing*. The essential characteristic is that one element of the product or marketing design is varied while, as far as possible, the other potential variables remain constant. *Hall tests* (so called because public halls are often used for this type of test) are an important example of experimentation. When Bulmers wanted to introduce a new brand of premium cider they ran a series of hall tests to confirm that customers would associate the shape of bottle chosen with a premium product.

The difference between experimentation and test marketing is in many cases academic since it is the data collection which is critically important in both of these. The value of using such data for marketing decisions was shown in the hypothetical card-operated Fax example on pages 132–4.

Conclusion

While some of the market research techniques discussed and explained in this chapter can be applied fairly simply, generally market research is a specialist activity which requires considerable expertise and experience to carry it out effectively. It is accordingly expensive so it needs to be used to achieve clearly defined objectives.

Questions

1 Consider the advantages and possible disadvantages of observation as a means of collecting marketing information. Give examples of the research settings in which such an approach might be used.
2 The manager of a local leisure centre wishes to collect information to guide future decisions on activity planning, investment in new facilities, promotion and pricing. Assuming a limited budget, what market research methods would you propose he uses?
3 What research approaches might be used by an advertising agency in order to pre-test advertising campaigns?
4 What sources of error might present themselves within the research techniques outlined in this chapter?

References

Crimp, M, *'The Marketing Research Process'*, 2nd Edn, Prentice Hall, 1985
Mautino, L & Evans, M, *'Applied Marketing Research'*, Addison-Wesley, 1992
Chisnall, PM, *'Essentials of Marketing Research'*, Prentice-Hall, 1992

Case study: market research

You have been approached for advice. A good friend has inherited some money and is considering opening a nursery school (for children under five years old). She found premises which could be easily converted for use as a nursery school and are in an ideal location but which would require her to take out a substantial mortgage in addition to her available capital. She went to her bank which agreed to provide the mortgage in principle, but asked her to prepare a detailed business plan. They insisted that this included an independent market research study which showed the project was viable.

The bank suggested a number of consultants who could undertake this study and on the basis of this advice one of these was selected.

Unfortunately the resulting survey indicated the proposal was not viable. This was serious since it meant that the bank would not only withdraw their offer of the mortgage but your friend would have to pay for the survey.

Since there are no nursery schools in the vicinity of the premises selected the result did not seem logical. Your friend thought there might be something wrong with the survey and asked you to have a look at the questionnaire, a copy of which you will find at the end of the case study. As this clearly has many deficiencies you agree to prepare for her a report which:

1 Briefly outlines the functions of a questionnaire.
2 Discusses how the order in which the questions were asked could affect the validity of the answers.
3 Demonstrates the process by which the wording of ONE of the badly worded questions could have been improved.
4 Comments on any other aspects of the questionnaire which ought to have been revised before it was used.

Since it is clear, from even the briefest review, that the questionnaire has many deficiencies you need only use as examples a representative selection of the faults which are likely to have affected the survey result. (Assume that at the time the questionnaire was used the average income of the working population in Coventry was £11,000 per annum.)

SURVEY OF NURSERY SCHOOL PROVISION
IN THE CV3 AREA OF COVENTRY

1 Do you have a child or children?   Yes/No (if No terminate)

2 Are you a working parent?   Yes/No
  a)   Is this full-time/part-time?
  b)   What is your occupation?_____

3 What facilities are offered by your place of work? (Please tick)
  Creche Facilities   (   )   Extended leave with pay   (   )
  Paid Nursery Fees   (   )   Return to previous job   (   )

4 Are you a single parent?   Yes/No

5 What is your household income level?
  Below £15,000   (   )
  £15,000 - £20,000 (   )
  £20,000 - £25,000 (   )
  £25,000 - £30,000 (   )
  £30,000 - £40,000 (   )
  Over £40,000   (   )

6 Do you have a bank account?   Yes/No

7 Which Bank? _____

8 Are you male/female?

9 What is your age? _____

10 Is/are your child/children male/female?

11 What age(s) is/are your child/children? _____

12 Does your child/children attend kindergarten?   Yes/No
    12b   What type of pre-school facility do you use?
    Day nursery (   )   Play group   (   )   Private Nursery   (   )
    Childminder (   )   Nursery School   (   )   Nanny   (   )

13 How much does this child-care facility cost per hour?   £ _____

14 Do you pay by the week, month or year? _____

15 How long did your child/children have to wait for a place at this facility?_____ days.

16 How often does/do he/she/they attend? _____

17 For how long does/do he/she/they attend? _____

18 Why do you use this particular method of pre-schooling?

    _____

    _____

19 Which of the following would be your preferred choice?
    Day nursery (   )   Play group   (   )   Private Nursery   (   )
    Childminder (   )   Nursery School   (   )   Nanny   (   )
    Please give your reasons for your choice.

20 How would you rate the pre-schooling facilities in this area?

	Good	Adequate	Poor
Day nursery	( )	( )	( )
Nursery School	( )	( )	( )
Childminder	( )	( )	( )
Private Nursery	( )	( )	( )
Play group	( )	( )	( )
Nanny	( )	( )	( )

21 How far do you agree with the following statements?

Pre-schooling:	Agree	Disagree	Strongly Disagree
a) Gives children opportunities to mix with other children?	( )	( )	( )
b) Prepares children for primary school?	( )	( )	( )
c) Allows women to return to work?	( )	( )	( )

11

POSITIONING AND THE MARKETING MIX

Introduction

In previous chapters this book has looked at the concept behind marketing, the environment in which organisations operate, customers and sub-segments and how customers behave, as well as the ways of gathering information to help make decisions. The analysis and understanding of the market is important, but only to help make better decisions in the marketing of a particular product or service.

The next section of the book looks at those elements over which the organisation has control, generally called the marketing mix of controllable variables. These variables are loosely grouped together under the headings of

> *Product*
> *Price* } The offer mix
> *Place*
>
> *Promotion* } The promotional mix

A vigorous debate has taken place over the last decade about the dangers of seeing marketing solely as the control of the '4 Ps'. Some authors on service marketing have suggested the addition of three other Ps:

> *People*
> *Process*
> *Physical evidence*

Others have returned to a mix of internal and external factors which usually includes the elements considered important before McCarthy popularised the '4 Ps'. Perhaps it is sensible to list the factors from Borden's paper of 1964, which first used the term marketing mix. These are

Internal

Product policy	Promotions
Pricing	Packaging
Branding	Display
Channels of distribution	Servicing
Personal selling	Physical handling
Advertising	Fact finding and analysis

External

Customer buying behaviour
Trade behaviour
Competitors' position and behaviour
Government regulations

These external items have already been considered and no reader should fail to realise their importance. It is also easy to see how McCarthy was able to condense the twelve items in Borden's original marketing mix into the four major categories.

Mention has been made of Philip Kotler's view of mega-marketing. He suggests that

Marketing is the task of arranging need-satisfying and profitable offers to target buyers. Sometimes, however, it is necessary to create additional incentives and pressures at the right times and in the right amounts for non-customers.

The non-customers are those who can create favourable market conditions for a firm to operate in, or, more negatively, could block the path to target buyers, for instance by government action. While the task of manipulating the environment is outside the scope of this book, all readers can see how lobbying, or political public relations could assist marketing success.

George Bernard Shaw wrote in *Man and Superman*,

The reasonable man adapts himself to the world; the unreasonable one persists in trying to adapt the world to himself. Therefore, all progress depends on unreasonable men.

The basis of the marketing concept is that organisations should match their offerings to the environment in which they are operating, but this could be too close to the reasonable organisation! However, this does not mean that the emphasis should be on mega-marketing and major environmental changes because such successes are rare; but it is possible to change the most important 'world' – the customers and their attitudes, towards your offering, by use of the controllable variables of marketing – that is by arranging 'need-satisfying' offers and promoting them to the chosen target market. This brings us to what is sometimes termed *positioning* of a product or service. Positioning can be seen as the choosing of a segment in which to compete. It goes further in that an organisation could adopt a premium position, or a low-cost position within a segment. Competitive position demands that an organisation considers what it is offering compared to competitors for the same target customers. It must choose a position which enables the organisation to answer the question, *Why should customers buy from us?* This could mean differentiating the offering from competitors by additional features or better availability perhaps. In his article 'Differentiation - of Anything', Theodore Levitt wrote,

There is no such thing as a commodity. All goods and services can be differentiated and usually are... Everybody – whether producer, fabricator, seller, broker, agent, merchant – engages in a constant effort to distinguish his offering in his favour from all others.

Levitt goes on to consider the total product concept which is discussed in the next chapter. It might be appropriate here to consider another view of the levels of an offering (*see* Fig 11.1).

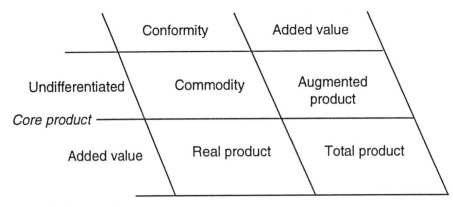

Fig 11.1 Added value and total product concept

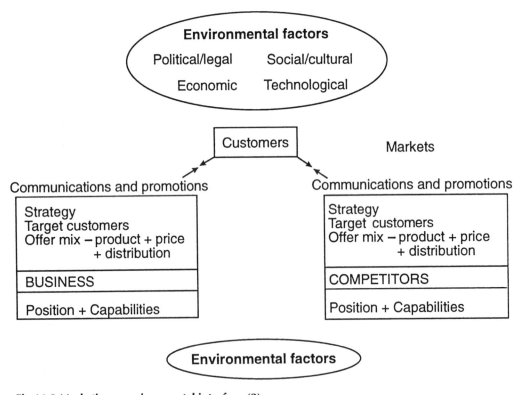

Fig 11.2 Marketing – environmental interface (2)

Two US advertising men, Al Ries and Jack Trout, suggested that

Positioning starts with a product, a piece of merchandise, a service, a company, an institution, or even a person. But positioning is not what you do to that product. Positioning is what you do to the mind of the prospect.

This statement relates to the perception a customer (prospect) might have about an offering, and it is this perception which is critical, not the organisation's view of what it is offering. The role of marketing is to create the right match of satisfying offers, on the one hand, and the appropriate customer perception on the other. The latter task is not the role of Shaw's 'unreasonable men', rather it is the task of reasonable, logical and skilled marketers who understand how the customer's decision is formed and perhaps how it can be influenced (*see* Fig 11.2).

Target marketing

The first task in the marketing process is to identify the market segments which are to be considered. These should be defined using bases relevant to the product category being offered. Within each segment, the key attitudes of the customers towards the product category must be identified. Since decisions will have to be made on which segments offer the best opportunity, it is essential that the descriptors are well chosen.

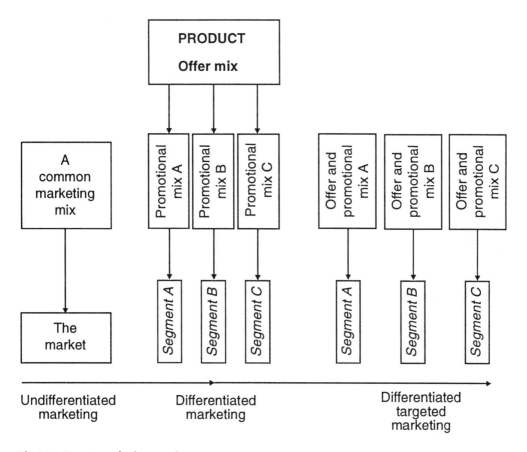

Fig 11.3 Target marketing continuum

Writing in *Admap*, Adam Lury, a controversial Chairman of a UK advertising agency, stated, 'Demographics tell me nothing I want to know'. He argues that the world has changed fundamentally and it is no longer true that you can lump together all the C2s and consider their common wants. He gets very close to a 'product orientation' when he says, 'Brands and Business must be themselves, and let consumers come to them by self-selection'.

As an example he cites the Body Shop as a company who set out what they believed in and let customers come to them. This is, of course, a good example, but there are many unheard of examples of companies whose offerings did not appeal to customers, and are now out of business. Therefore, while agreeing with Lury that demographics and lifestyle are only useful if they can help predict future behaviour of customers, the authors of this book do not follow his advice to reject it completely. The descriptors must be well-chosen, and beyond that care must be taken in applying the criteria used to define a segment. There must be a link between the customers in that segment and the attitudes and product wants of those customers. This is the basis of target marketing.

Figure 11.3 shows the progression from undifferentiated marketing through to target marketing. Undifferentiated marketing is where a single marketing mix is offered to the entire market, but this rarely succeeds because markets are not homogeneous. This is especially true in global markets, where major differences of culture and history can divide potential customers. As an example, Mars, the chocolate company, feature only men in their promotional material in Saudi Arabia because of the Arab views on showing women. Mars is an example of differentiated marketing where the basic product is the same but the mix is varied. Target marketing develops this further, including the total marketing mix with variations to the *total product* offered. Ford Motors now make so many different models of the Escort car that one observer suggested that should all the different models be placed in a line then they could almost go round the globe! Japanese car makers now claim they can personalise a car in all features and so offer a customer the ultimate in personalisation. This is an extreme example of target marketing, and a long way from Henry Ford's bold claim of 'Any colour so long as it is black'. It is certain that new flexible manufacturing systems (FMS) will add to the opportunities open to marketers who, as a result, will be able to define smaller target segments and to interact with these segments more precisely.

Fig 11.4

Service companies have always been able to achieve personalisation as the delivery of the service is inseparable from the production. The delivered service is of course liable to variations, depending on who actually delivers the service. This is why service organisations such as McDonalds, the fast food restaurant chain, pay so much attention to the achievement of consistency in the quality of service given. It is comparably easy to destroy a reputation by a single incidence of poor service which gets broadcast, and such an occurrence would make it very difficult to support a desired position.

Product positioning

Positioning in this context refers to the placing of a product in that part of the market where it will be able to compete favourably with competitors' products. While it is the perception of customers regarding the product that is most important, there must be some consistency between the product's actual attributes and the perception of that product. It is therefore necessary to consider the *total* product attributes which make a product acceptable and affordable to target customers.

In studying the target segments it should be possible to identify those factors which potential customers see as desirable. There may be many such factors and it is only by harnessing the power of computers that multi-dimensional models can be constructed. It is possible, however, to illustrate a positioning map (*see* Fig 11.5) in two dimensions as long as it is realised there may be other key dimensions that customers value. Of course the importance of different factors varies but this can also be accommodated.

A study of CD records found factors such as gives out a very good sound, enjoyable to play, and will not scratch were rated much higher than, easy to store and can program the selections. This study was not aimed at specifically identifying attributes, but rather at seeking consistency in the information from respondents. Reliable and consistent methodology is a technical matter but vital when developing attributes for use in positioning studies and gap analysis.

A positioning map for the US car market was published in *Wall Street Journal*. The axes are reproduced in Fig 11.5. You will see they amalgamate several factors to enable a two-

Fig 11.5 Positioning map for cars

dimensional perceptual map to be produced. It will come as no surprise that Chrysler Motor Corporation research found customers placed BMW and Porsche in the top right quadrant; Toyota, Nissan and Volkswagen were in the bottom right; with Cadillac and Mercedes in top left. Ford was considered as a single entity in bottom left, but if you considered the different models in Europe, it is likely the XR3i would be in a different place from the Orion.

Exercise

You could suggest where to place some other models with which you are familiar, *but remember* it is not your opinion that counts - it is the opinion of the customers in a particular target segment that is important.

For each segment a number of ideal positions and desired levels of attributes will emerge. There will also be specific positions identified for competing brands. If you were designing a new product then the closer it is to the ideal mix of attributes, the better the chance of success. For an existing product it may be a strategy is necessary to try to change its position as perceived by potential customers.

Positioning is in the mind of the customer

An example of re-positioning is the way the holiday resort of Torbay (Torquay, Brixham, and Paignton) halted the decline in visitors by re-branding the resort as the 'English Riviera'. South Devon has Britain's best climate in terms of sunshine hours and temperature, but ten years ago it was attracting a decreasing number of visitors. Visitors came primarily from northern England and were disproportionately from the lower socio-economic groups. The re-branding has created a new image of the area. It has had to be backed up by product improvements as indicated in this quote from Maggie Corke, assistant Director of Torbay Tourist Board. 'If you call yourself a Riviera, you have to live up to it'.

This has meant redevelopment and new amenities. It is, however, the new position of the 'English Riviera' that is credited with the change in perception of the area and the halting of the decline in tourists.

Another attempt at re-positioning an old product was the new image for the British Labour Party. The new position did not attract a sufficient number of voters to win the 1992 General Election. But there is no doubt that a change in the perception of the party has been achieved.

Both these examples involve changing the consumer's perception of an existing product. In both cases changes were made to the product and its promotion although for these examples price was less relevant. Place in the context of geographic location of Torbay is static but place as one of the four marketing P's actually refers to channels between supplier and customer. It can be seen from these examples that place is not a very good category, especially outside the area of consumer and industrial products. In fact physical evidence, as mentioned earlier, is more important for Torbay as this certainly shapes perception, and with a political party the people element is vital.

Mention has already been made in Chapter 1 of 'Mickey Mouse Marketing' and the importance of people, whatever their job, who directly interface with potential customers.

In order to avoid a gap between management perception of what is being offered and customer perception of what is being received, the organisation must ensure proper attention is given to what is called internal marketing.

Internal marketing

The direct link between an organisation and its customers is now being termed *external marketing*. The actual delivery of this involves people, employees of the organisation, and their contact with customers is termed *interactive marketing*. To complete the links there is the way an organisation treats, as well as how it motivates, its employees. This is *internal marketing* (*see* Fig 11.6). Internal marketing has been defined by Christian Gronroos of the School of Economics and Business, Helsingfors, Finland, as:

> To create an internal environment which supports customer-consciousness and sales-mindedness amongst all personnel within an organisation.

Internal marketing also involves other functional disciplines, in particular what is called human resource management. Marketers, however, should have both the research skills to identify employee needs and wants as internal customers of the organisation, and the communication skills to assist the effort. More of the role of internal marketing will be discussed in Chapter 22 on organising for marketing (*see* p 336).

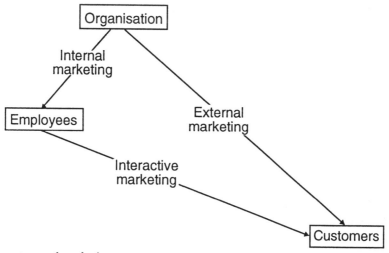

Fig 11.6 Three types of marketing

If all aspects of Fig 11.6 are positive the organisation will offer excellent customer service. The opposite effect could come from the following vicious circle:

Company: The staff treat customers like rabble. 'They need a good talking to'.

Employees: If the company does not care about me – why should I bother.

Customer: I'm not coming back.

Retaining customers

The five principles of good marketing practice described in Chapter 1 are: targeting; positioning; interacting; controlling; continuing to build relationships with customers. There are various estimates about the cost of attracting new customers, but it is probably true that it costs on average up to five times more than the cost of retaining an existing customer. New business is the most expensive because it usually has to be won from a competitor. New customers, for whatever type of product, need to receive a disproportionate level of marketing input which could include product design, promotion, personal selling or any other element from within the marketing mix.

Although a continuum can be constructed based on cost per customer, as in Fig 11.7, it would be inappropriate to offer the same marketing message to all groups. The new business prospects are at a pre-transactional stage. They have to be persuaded about an intended purchase from a new supplier and require re-assurance that the offering is right for them. At the other end there are repeat sales either to loyal or occasional users, where the post-transitional stage exists. These customers may require confirmation that the purchase was right and encouragement to buy again. Repeat customers also act as a source of new business because satisfied customers tell others and such endorsements are worth more than any advertisement.

Fig 11.7 Customer pyramid (2)

Regular, loyal users are therefore extremely valuable to an organisation. At a time when many companies are valuing their brands as assets and incorporating these values into their balance sheets, it is a pity that no way can be found to put a value on loyal customers and include this also among the organisation's intangible assets. Of course the accountants do not treat customers as assets because most buyer – seller relationships are not contractual in a formal manner but rely on the informal relationship between the two parties. However, it would be positive thinking for organisations to value their customer relationships even more than they value their other assets and devise measures to ensure they do not lose them. It is always possible to lose customers if a competitor makes a superior offering or even if they re-position *your* product to make their offering superior.

Winning customers

Ries and Trout offer the intriguing fact that the average supermarket carries 12 000 different products or brands on its shelves, yet an average college graduate has a speaking vocabulary of only 8000 words. As a comparison it does not follow logically, but these facts do indicate how difficult it is to achieve awareness of a product or company with so many different offerings being made on a regular basis. McGraw Hill once published a cartoon with the following copy line

I don't know you
I don't know your company
I don't know your product
I don't know what your company stands for
I don't know your company's customers
I don't know your company's record
I don't know your company's reputation

Now, what do you want to sell to me ?

One creative solution suggested by Ries and Trout is to re-position your competitors. This actually means looking for a weakness in the competition's offering when compared to customer demands, and then to see if your strengths can be used to find an opening. If it is done in an effective way it could not only create awareness for your offering, but also develop a strong position for your product in its market. One of the examples Ries and Trout give is from the market for Vodka in the USA. Pepsico ran an advertisement for their brand of imported vodka headed

Most American Vodkas seem Russian
Samovar: made in Schenley, Pennsylvania
Smirnoff: made in Harford, Connecticut
Wolfschmidt: made in Lawrenceburg, Indiana

Stolichnaya is different. It is Russian.
Made in Leningrad, Russia.

This advertisement assumed the real thing was Russian-made vodka and it exposed the other brands with their pseudo Russian names as frauds – a classic example of the re-positioning of a brand and *de*-positioning of the competition. (Note: The English vodka, Vladivar made a virtue of its origins advertising itself as the 'Vodka from Varrington'.)

An alternative and successful move to win customers was the promotion by Diners Club promotion which offered free membership to anyone sending them a cut up American Express card. Not only did this take out the competition, it also eased Diners Club's task and expense of doing a credit check on applicants. They decided that anyone with an Amex card would also be likely to qualify for Diners Club.

The difficulty with winning customers from competitors is that your competitors do not like it and will probably fight back. Diners Club did not gain any long-term sustainable advantage from their promotion. Stolichnaya did. Writing on sustainable advantage, Pankaj Ghemawat said, 'All of your competitors may be stupid some of the time BUT you cannot count on them being stupid all of the time'. Winning customers is not as simple as a promotional game which you sometimes win and sometimes lose. Sustainable advantage comes from all elements of the marketing mix. Of course sometimes customers get tired of their regular brands and move to an alternative for a brief change. While valuable, these so called change-of-pace sales rarely offer enough business for a viable product. The ideal position is to offer a more acceptable product at a more affordable price as in the lower right quadrant of the matrix in Fig 11.8. It is more likely that any new offering will be in the more acceptable but also more expensive quadrant, or in the less acceptable but cheaper one. It is in these cases that customers have to make a value judgement, with a trade off between features and price.

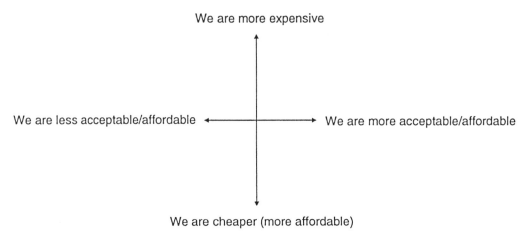

Fig 11.8 Positioning matrix

The offer mix and the promotional mix

The actual offer that an organisation makes to its customers is called the offer mix. It comprises the factors of the total product and/or service offered, the price including all discounts and deals, and the level of availability of the offering. Customers will evaluate the offering using the tests of the '3 As' introduced earlier: acceptability; affordability; and availability. These factors are discussed individually in more detail in Chapters 12 to 15. However, it must be remembered that a customer will evaluate the offer mix as a total package, trading off one element against another in making a buy/no-buy decision. It is always a good discipline for marketers to try to put themselves in the position of a customer and try to see how an offer can be assessed.

Exercise

Think of a purchase you have made recently and note down the reasons why you bought the item under the 3 As mentioned above. When you have finished that think of an item or service that you did not buy and repeat the exercise.

It would be naive to assume that marketing communication in the form of advertising and promotion does not play a significant role in making products seem acceptable. It obviously does. There are three major roles of communications and different elements of the so called promotional mix, and each can play a different part in achieving the best results regarding

- creating awareness of the offering;
- a stimulus to make the purchase; and
- post-transactional reassurance.

Chapter 16 explores the process of communication and Chapters 17 and 18 explore the four elements of the promotional mix which are traditionally: paid advertising; public relations; sales promotion; and personal selling. More recently, direct marketing, which includes direct mail and telemarketing, has developed to rival these elements. This development has enabled the promotional message to be targeted much more accurately and to reach the sub-segments that are developing in many markets. This micro-marketing is possible both in a tailored offering, such as a personalised new car, and in precise delivery of messages to the micro-market. Figure 11.9 now develops Fig 11.4.

Fig 11.9 Target marketing process

Conclusion

In order for a company's marketing programmes to be successful, all of the factors in this chapter should be taken into account – from identification of the target market through to the positioning of the product. These are among the most important decisions that management will take with regards to the actual marketing strategy to be followed.

All of the elements of the marketing mix will have an important role to play. Further details of each of them will be unfolded in the following chapters. However, before putting marketing-mix theories into practice, the objectives of the organisation must be taken into consideration. It is essential that these are identified and understood in order that management can target, position and generally market its products or services to the best of its ability.

Questions

1 Using the matrix in Fig 11.5, position six cars according to your perception. Compare this with another student and explain the differences.

2 Marks and Spencers is a very successful retail store group. How has it achieved a quality position in the market place?

3 If a company launches a new product, e.g. Mars ice cream, will customers naturally place it in a similar position to the original product, e.g. Mars Bar?

4 In a product range, e.g. Ford cars, can a Ford Fiesta confuse the positioning of a Ford 4 x 4 Scorpio?

References

Booms, B and Bitner, M J, *Marketing Strategies and Organisation Structures for Service Firms*, in J Donelly & W George (Ed), *The Marketing of Services*, American Marketing Association, 1981 pp 47–51.

Borden, N, 'The concept of the marketing mix', *Journal of Advertising Research*, 1964.

Cowell, D, *The Marketing of Services*, Heinemann, 1984.

Ghemawat, P, 'Sustainable advantage', *Harvard Business Review*, September/October 1986.

Gronroos, C, 'Marketing orientated strategies in service businesses', *Finnish Journal of Business*, 4, 1979.

Kotler, P, 'Mega marketing', *Harvard Business Review*, March/April 1986.

Levitt, T, 'Differentiation – of anything', *Harvard Business Review*, January/February 1980.

Lury, A, 'Demographics tell me nothing', *Admap*, December 1990.

McCarthy, E J & Perrault, W D, *Basic Marketing*, Irwin, 1990.

Piercy, N, *Marketing-led Strategic Change*, Thorsons, 1991.

Prince, M, 'How consistent is the information in positioning studies?' *Journal of Advertising Research*, June 1990.

Ries A, and Trout J, *Positioning the Battle for Your Mind*, Warner Books, 1982

Shaw, G B, *Man and Superman; a comedy and a philosophy*, Longman, Green & Co. 1956.

12

PRODUCT POLICY

Introduction

Product policy is of fundamental strategic importance in marketing. At its most basic, it involves the organisation in a commitment to a deliberate policy on which markets to serve, with which products or offerings. Though such a policy will doubtless change over time to reflect market dynamics, it should prove robust enough to guide key commercial decisions across the organisation, and should therefore itself be the product of much corporate soul-searching, analysis and preparation. In simple terms, product policy amounts to a 'game-plan' to achieve a product-market match, thereby serving both market requirements and corporate objectives, for the present and into the future.

As products and offerings are the common factor linking the company and its customers, and as the product is the very framework around which other elements of the marketing mix are draped, product decisions reach to the very centre of marketing strategy and management. The product will be an obvious focus of attention for all customers, and for all staff and service functions within the company. It will also, of course, be an object of interest to leading competitors, suppliers, potential customers, intermediaries and many others.

The essentials of product policy

A company's product policy may not explicitly appear in any one policy document or statement, but will likely show itself in those major decisions of corporate and marketing strategy that involve product planning, future development and innovation. Product policy will therefore integrate closely with the organisation's mission statement and any ongoing re-evaluation of 'what business are we in?'. Essentially, product policy will be concerned with:

1 Developing strategic guidelines that direct at once the marketing of existing products and the development of new products. While these guidelines will be associated with company wide objectives such as profitability and growth-market share potential, they will also reflect corporate policy in respect of what is a desirable mix of product offerings. These guidelines will determine the overall strategic direction of the company in terms of product-market development, and will be the concern of senior management and marketing decision-makers.

2 Translating these general guidelines into operational performance at the level of both individual products and the wider product mix. Specifically:

(a) For existing products, this will involve managing and monitoring the marketing of these products in respect of markets served, quality-performance indicators such as profitability and image, sales targets and competitive standing. These tasks will be the core of day-to-day marketing at the product level. While companies will vary in the way in which they staff and organise for these ongoing activities, it is not uncommon to find in larger companies a division of marketing responsibilities according to product lines or brands, by the employment of specialist product managers or brand managers, within the marketing department. (Though a more detailed examination of marketing organisation approaches will be made later, for present purposes it is enough to understand that each product or brand manager looks after the marketing and competitive 'health' of an allocated number of company products or brand ranges.) Product marketing represents the most obvious marketing tasks of the company on a day-by-day basis. While for many company products there will be a comfortable and familiar maintenance job to be done in managing a 'steady tiller' within the marketplace, there will occasionally be the need to engage in more radical changes in marketing plans, and in the very product itself. The dynamics of customer tastes, or the cut-and-thrust nature of competitive marketing or new product activity, may sometimes make it necessary to fundamentally change the marketing of certain products, to re-design and re-present them, perhaps for a different market, or even to delete them from the range.

(b) For reasons of extraneous factors such as competition or market change, or to serve corporate growth or diversification strategies, in due course new products will be added to the product range, and occasionally new offerings substituted for withdrawn products. While the arguments for a market-centred approach to new product development are nowadays accepted by most companies, the successful development and launch of new products involves the commitment of marketing resources to an integrated company-wide innovation effort. As with comparable activities such as product modification and re-launch, new product introduction and marketing involve effectively re-balancing the total product range, and reflect decisions on product policy made at the corporate level. Within such a market-centred approach to new product development, the role of the marketer will be to advise, inform and initiate product change, and to participate in a cross-disciplinary teamwork approach to development and commercialisation.

In summary, product policy represents a key area of corporate and operational decision-making on product offering, that involves marketing in supporting present products, effecting ongoing marketing changes to the product range, and commercialising new products, as part of a total corporate plan. In simple terms, it involves (i) managing and modifying existing products, and (ii) developing and establishing new products. For convenience, the present chapter will focus on the marketer's involvement with existing products, and the following chapter will be devoted to new product development and marketing.

It is necessary at this point to introduce a few basic concepts and definitions, to lay the groundwork for a more detailed examination of key issues in product policy.

What is a product?

While the question is almost rhetorical, it is necessary to see the product from a market perspective, rather than in solely physical or company-centred terms – a mistake often made by production-dominated companies. For marketing purposes, the product is what the customer perceives it to be, so that a working definition might be:

Product: everything that the customer receives that is of value in terms of a perceived want, need or problem.

Though rather broad and vague, such a definition allows that:

1 customers vary in their needs, wants and problems, and how they perceive them - there may be scope for varying product offerings in the market;
2 some products may appear to customers better value or more attractive, for various reasons, almost irrespective of producer intentions, or objective measures of quality or product input;
3 some product offerings will not make the grade with customers, and will fail commercially. Others may survive as weaker or marginal products, while a few, the classical 'brand leaders', will gain commanding market shares.

The term *product* applies not only to physical products, but also to services and other intangibles such as causes and ideas. For example, the major charity organisations such as Oxfam and Save The Children are as actively involved in making product offerings as the ubiquitous widget manufacturer in the West Midlands! Even in the case of an everyday physical product such as washing-up liquid, there will be intangible extras and associations that are offered in addition to the outward product, e.g. the quality assurance of a known brand name and manufacturer source.

Simply stated, the marketer needs to view the product as a multi-dimensional offering, a mix of tangible features and intangible services and attributes, bundled around a basic or core benefit. This multi-faceted view of the product is illustrated in Fig 12.1.

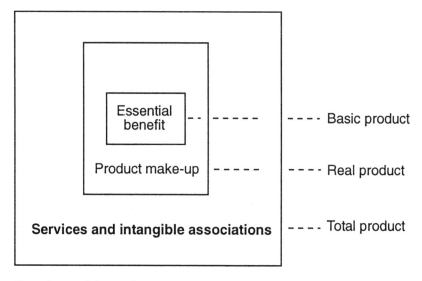

Fig 12.1 Three facets of the product

The *basic product* represents the essential service or benefit on offer, e.g. an easily applied scuff-resistant shoe polish for children's shoes. Usually the basic product will get to the most essential benefit of value to the customer, expressed in a product form. The *real product* will comprise the basic product and an additional 'layer' of tangible features that make up the listed product or service, e.g. design and colour, quality specification, brand name. The *total product* will add to the listed product a number of intangible extras that augment the offering by adding utility through services (eg delivery, customer service), and perhaps subtle qualities and assurances of distinctive value to the customer.

It is probably worth noting that, in an era of increasing buyer sophistication and market competitiveness, marketing success is more likely to be achieved by those companies that manage to develop competitive advantage through original service offerings and combinations associated with the 'penumbra' of the total product and the potential it offers for development and differentiation. Alternatively stated, the critical part of the value chain has shifted from the base product and the production process, to the wider product and the extended organisation that supports it.

A classification of products

For purposes of marketing and strategy analysis, it is useful to classify products into broad types, according to shared characteristics. Figure 12.2 presents a standard classification of products.

Durables ←——→ Consumables ←————————→ Services	
Consumer products	Industrial products
Convenience goods Shopping goods Speciality goods Services	Capital items and equipment Materials and components Supplies Services

Fig 12.2 A classification of products

- **Durability:** a useful distinction is that durable products last some time, while consumables or non-durables are used up in a short time. While services may vary in their durability, in that for instance a repair service may render a repaired item of some further use for a time, services are usually categorised separately.
- **Durable** goods are products that have an extended period of use, e.g. washing machines, cars, lawn-mowers, machine tools. They are usually relatively complex fabrications, higher-priced, and normally bought as part of an investment or acquisition decision. While manufacturers of such products compete over time by continual product improvement and innovation, the marketing task is made difficult by the fact that replacement purchases can often be postponed.

- **Consumables** are products that are literally consumed in the immediate or short-term, after a limited number of uses or doses. While many consumer products such as foodstuffs, drinks, and household products are typical examples, industrial products such as raw materials and nuts and bolts also fall within this classification. From a marketing viewpoint, consumable product markets have high purchase frequency and often require mass distribution to many purchasers; while the competitive nature of the market is often reflected in keener prices and margins, high promotion spending, and product-switching behaviour among buyers.
- **Services** may be seen as specific types of product that offer benefits through performance rather than use, acquisition or possession. The intangibility of services poses particular problems for marketers in promoting and demonstrating value to customers. Other characteristics that typify services are their perishability – an unused tableplace at a restaurant represents an irretrievable commercial loss – and the fact that quality varies according to the efficiency of the provider staff and their organisation. In both consumer and industrial markets, services have grown in importance in recent years, so that in most western economies the service sector nowadays accounts for the major part of the employment market. A detailed examination of the marketing of services will be made later in the text.

Consumer products

Consumer products are products bought by individual consumers or households, for personal use or consumption. The sub-categories introduced in Fig 12.2 are based on differences in consumer buying behaviour, rather than the products themselves.

- **Convenience goods**: These represent the majority of frequently purchased consumer goods, bought with little effort or deliberation, e.g. breakfast cereals, coffee, soap. These products form the classic mass markets, where the total market volume and spread requires convenient supplies, accessible through everyday channels such as supermarkets and corner stores. Within this category, some commentators distinguish between staples, the standard products bought as part of an everyday shopping-list, and impulse goods, bought without any planning at all, often on impulse, e.g. chocolates and sweets sold at supermarket checkouts.
- **Shopping goods**: These are goods where consumers literally 'shop around' before purchasing , in order to compare price, quality, design features and the like. Furniture, clothing, and household utensils would fall within this category. Though comparisons will be made in shopping for these products, they are still common-place purchases with volume markets, so that consumers will expect to find a ready selection in the high street, or even under one roof - search behaviour is therefore not necessarily exhaustive or extensive.
- **Speciality goods**: These are usually higher-quality, higher-value items with a degree of uniqueness that is so valued by consumers that a greater effort will be made to search out the product. Commonly cited examples of such products would include fine chinaware, exclusive designer clothing, sophisticated photographic equipment, hi-fi innovations, high-performance luxury cars. The more limited market for such products, and a supplier concern for an exclusive image, usually means distribution through a smaller number of retail franchises, and a more subtle handling of the marketing task overall.

- **Consumer services**: These represent a wide and growing variety of offerings, from local services of long standing, such as hairdressing and car repairs, to more specialist services offered through a developing professional infrastructure, such as private health care. A more recent distinction, between private sector and public sector services, has resulted in a new-found interest in marketing and customer service, among supplier organisations and consumers alike.

Industrial products

Industrial products, sometimes termed business products, are products bought for use in making other products and services, within a business setting. Unlike consumer goods, they are bought not for their own sake or for personal consumption, but in order to contribute to a commercial manufacturing or service operation. In an economic sense, they are intermediate products or inputs, the demand for which will ultimately be tied to the requirements of final markets, for ordinary household goods and services – a relationship that is termed 'derived demand'. For this reason, industrial markets often experience periodic fluctuations in demand, or industry cycles, that represent exaggerated whip-like reactions to more marginal variations in related consumer goods markets. Figure 12.2 distinguishes a number of industrial product sub-categories, according to their use as inputs to the production process.

- **Capital items and equipment**: These represent heavier but indirect inputs to the supply-delivery process. Capital items will comprise large investments in fixed facilities such as plant, buildings and stationary installations. Such big-ticket investments will be the subject of carefully prepared production plans, design investigations and trials, protracted supplier discussions and negotiations. Marketing such products will involve direct links with prospective purchasers, specialist-to-specialist technical contacts, pre-sale service, and often contractual relationships extending far beyond the installation and commissioning stage.

  Though no hard-and-fast distinctions exist, equipment will typically comprise portable production machinery, tools and accessories, and other items such as office equipment, used in support functions within the organisation. These items individually represent less heavy investments, though in total they will comprise key systems, often built in modular linkages of compatible elements. Technology changes and periodic systems re-design will likely make for a limited in-use life of such equipment, so that purchases will be depreciated over a shorter period than that for major capital items. In marketing terms, equipment markets will be characterised by a number of competing suppliers, offering varying degrees of compatibility at competitive terms. Specialist stock-holding channels and other intermediaries may exist to serve the market at large, while manufacturers may deal directly with major corporate customers.
- **Materials and components**: These will represent the physical inputs to the fabrication or delivery of the final product. Materials may range from raw materials, often bought direct from domestic or overseas suppliers on longer-term contracts, to processed materials such as chemical formulations, sourced either directly or through intermediaries. Contractual arrangements may be preferred by customers where volumes allow, in order to assure continuity of supply and quality standards.

Promotional elements are unlikely to feature heavily in the marketing of materials, as standard grading systems may limit competition to differences in price, contractual back-up and distribution arrangements.

Components may vary from standard items such as valves, pumps and switches, to more specialist or customised items, fabrications and sub-assemblies. While standard items may be bought in by volume-contract arrangements, or multiple-sourced through outside suppliers and distributors, key components and customised parts may be the subject of vertical contracting arrangements. Such sub-contractor relationships may involve close collaboration between customer and supplier, increasingly following Japanese-style linkages through JIT (just-in-time) principles, quality assurance vetting, and computer-aided design (CAD) systems. While company and industry practices obviously vary, it is difficult to generalise on marketing practices within such markets, though recent trends in globalised manufacturing, and parallel moves towards EC integration, spell out a generally tightening competitive scene.

- **Supplies** comprise a variety of items that are indirect inputs into the production process. These may vary from factory floor requirements such as lubricants, abrasives and cleaning materials, to office sundries such as paperclips and notepads, and a whole miscellany of other items needed for various functions within the organisation. As many of these items are standard, purchasing decisions will be made routinely, and perhaps devolved to lower levels throughout the organisation. Marketing of such products is likely to hinge on ready availability through intermediaries, supported by price promotion and regular sales and service cover.

- **Services** in industrial or business markets will be an important though indirect support to the production process. Routine and standard services such as office-cleaning, catering, haulage or vehicle hire are likely for heavy-use customers to be the subject of revolving contract arrangements. Specialist business services such as market research, accountancy, advertising or management consultancy are likely to be sourced and managed through the offices of relevant functional managers, who will select and liaise with the specialist outside supplier(s) chosen. Very large organisations may have sufficient workload in specialist areas such as market research, to justify an in-house subsidiary agency. Similar open-market dealings may be engaged in within other functional areas, where opportunities are seen to market spare corporate capacity, for instance through contracted R & D facilities.

Servicing of key equipment and installations such as computers, will nowadays be integral to supply contracts for the hardware itself, though technology moves have created a ready market for hi-tech advisory services in fields such as expert-systems software development for non-standard applications.

The product life cycle

The concept of a life cycle has over the years become an accepted part of marketing theory, providing a potentially valuable analytical and strategic tool. The basic life cycle pattern borrows heavily on the biological model of successive life stages, from gestation and birth, through adolescence to maturity and eventual demise. The marketing translation of this progression is illustrated in simple form in Fig 12.3.

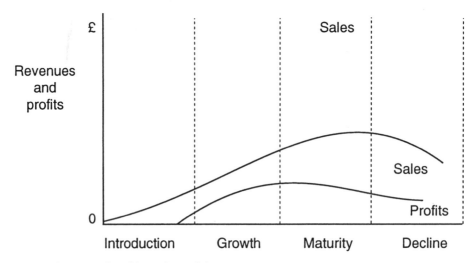

Fig 12.3 The basic product life cycle model

Introduction: In the immediate post-launch period sales build rather slowly, while financially the product has not recouped the resources put into its development, during what is strictly speaking a prior stage, gestation.

Growth: The product 'takes off', gaining market share and an early majority of buyers. Profits grow.

Maturity: For many products the longest period, beginning with continued sales growth that eventually slows as saturation approaches. Profits dip later in this period, as marketing outlays are stepped up to counter competitor entrants.

Decline: Sales may fall drastically, or the product may linger unhealthily for some time. Profits fall appreciably, giving way to, sometimes heavy, losses.

The generic product life cycle (PLC) model is commonly depicted as a bell-shaped curve, though variations are sometimes introduced to illustrate special cases, e.g. the inverted V-shape of a short-lived fad or novelty product, or the scalloped shape that might be associated with a fashion product adopted by 'waves' of followers. Individual products are accepted as each having a unique pattern, in terms of sales-profits volume, gradient, shape and duration. Longstanding brand-leader products are likely to show an extended 'read-out' of ups and downs that reflect market trends, competitor activity and company marketing successes. In practice, of course, most veteran brands will have undergone major product and marketing changes over the years, if only to survive!

Over the course of the product life cycle, changes are likely to be registered in terms of market size and growth, customer types, and the dynamic interactions between company marketing strategies and those of competitors. These differences may both reflect and partly determine the successive stages within the cycle.

Marketing strategies over the cycle are difficult to summarise, though it might be possible to suggest that in the earlier period market development is the watchword, in the growth stage strategy becomes more offensive, while in later stages defensive and consolidation strategies predominate. A more detailed outline of strategy changes over the PLC has been presented by Doyle in his article 'The realities of the product life cycle', and appears in summary form in Fig 12.4. For a fuller treatment, the reader would benefit by referring to the complete article, which has become a landmark in the literature.

	Introduction	Growth	Maturity	Decline
Characteristics				
Sales	Low	Fast growth	Slow growth	Decline
Profits	Negligible	Peak levels	Declining	Low or zero
Cash flow	Negative	Moderate	High	Low
Customers	Innovative	Mass market	Mass market	Laggards
Competitors	Few	Growing	Numerous	Fewer
Responses				
Strategic focus	Expand market	Market penetration	Defend share	Productivity
Marketing expenditure	High	High (declining %)	Falling	Low
Marketing emphasis	Product awareness	Brand preference	Brand loyalty	Selective
Distribution	Patchy	Intensive	Intensive	Selective
Price	High	Lower	Lowest	Rising
Product	Basic	Improved	Differentiated	Rationalised

(Source: P Doyle, 'The realities of the product life cycle', *Quarterly Review of Marketing*, Summer 1976; reprinted in M J Thomas and N E Waite, *The Marketing Digest*, London, Heinemann, 1988)

Fig 12.4 Marketing implications of the product life cycle

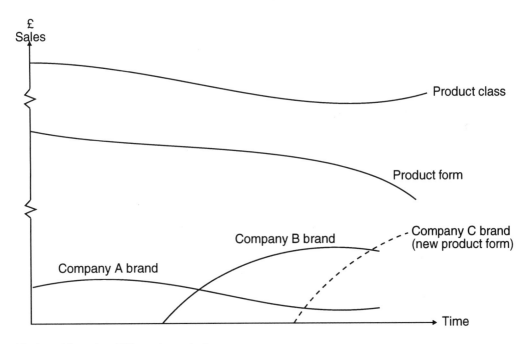

Fig 12.5 Three-level life cycle analysis

Extensions on life cycle analysis

From the earliest interest in the generalised 'product' life cycle, research has moved on to distinguish at least three distinct levels of aggregation: that for the product class (e.g. breakfast cereals), the product form (e.g. health-conscious cereals), and the specific product or brand (e.g. Alpen). Working at an analysis of three levels of market sales, it is possible to more realistically locate the position and prospects of one particular product or brand, and make strategic decisions in the light of market and sector trends, competition and general performance indicators.

Figure 12.5 illustrates such a three-level analysis, showing a scenario with three competitor brands. The picture is one of a product class until recently in slow decline, and a falling product form cycle within which Company B Brand has long overtaken Company A Brand, a product form competitor. More significantly, the arrival of Company C Brand has introduced a new product form, which appears now to threaten the market sector for A and B, and add a new growth source to the total (product class) market. Clearly, Company B in particular will need to re-assess its prospects, and perhaps modify its product or consider entering the 'new form' product market.

Uses of product life cycle analysis

Used carefully and with the support of appropriate research, the PLC provides valuable insights into product strategy and market change. Mapping the path of both company and competitor brands, product form and general market sales, assists the company in reaching decisions about new product development or product modification, as shown in Fig 12.5. Across the life of a product, PLC analysis might enable a company to better exploit product potential, and to avoid projected problems by well-timed strategy changes. Such a situation is illustrated in Fig 12.6, where the company has managed to 'buck' the trend by timely changes in product strategy, so boosting the product's performance beyond the original projection.

Again, studying PLC analyses for the whole range of a company's products, may allow the company a better understanding of where growth opportunities are to come from, in order to better realise company growth objectives. Within the product range, such analysis should assist the company in making priorities and decisions about where resources are to be 'ploughed back' into product development, range extension (or 'filling') and the like, and which breadwinner products have to be supported to fund such initiatives. In resourcing terms at least, products within the company's portfolio are interdependent.

Difficulties with PLC analysis

Companies sometimes create problems of their own making through an over-simplistic interpretation of the generalised PLC model. At any level of aggregation, PLC analysis can only provide a model or theoretical structure. It cannot offer a template against which to naively measure deviations from 'the norm', nor can it make prescriptions about the duration of phases or the requisite strategies to follow or defy the 'normal' pattern.

A common problem is the failure to apply and interpret the appropriate level of aggregation (brand, form, or product class), or to seek understanding through comparison between levels. Research and information sources are sometimes inadequate for the expectations made of an analysis, while sometimes definitions employed, for example

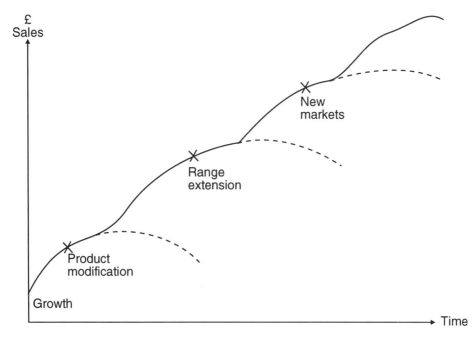

Fig 12.6 Extending the product life cycle

of competitors or substitutes, are inaccurate or subjective. Particularly at the brand cycle level, difficulties are encountered in interpreting phase-to-phase movement or turning-points. While a large measure of subjective judgement is inevitable, it may be possible to approach such demarcation by studying evidence of saturation levels, general profits decline, industry over-capacity, or changes in market responsiveness to price or promotion. Notwithstanding, it would be more prudent to accept the inherent limitations of PLC analysis, and to use it as but one input within a wider auditing exercise.

The product mix

The product mix, sometimes called the product portfolio or product range, is the assortment of different products offered for sale by a company. Most established companies have a mix of products on offer - they are multi-product organisations. New products will have been added over time, and variations on successful products introduced, in order to cater for new or different customer groups, to expand sales and profits, to become a more competitive and credible supplier in the market, or simply to spread commercial risk over a wider product mix. Growth in the product mix may well be the chosen instrument of corporate growth, though the size (or length) of the mix will not guarantee success, and two similarly-sized companies in the same market may have major differences in the number of products that they field. Figure 12.7 illustrates graphically the way in which 3M has grown over the years through product development.

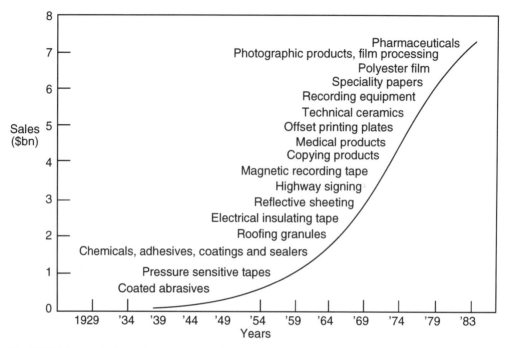

Fig 12.7 3M growth through product development

Product Line: A number of products that are related by being targeted to similar markets or for similar uses, or sold through similar outlets or on comparable terms, e.g. Procter & Gamble has a number of product offerings within its line of detergents, including famous names such as Tide, Bold, Oxydol and Dreft.

A company's product mix can be measured in terms of size or length - the total number of products in the mix.

Width: The number of different product lines within the product mix. Thus, in addition to a sizeable detergent product line, Procter & Gamble also has toothpaste, shampoo, toilet soap and many other product lines.

Depth: The number of different versions offered within each product in a product line, e.g. a Procter & Gamble toilet soap may be offered in two sizes (regular, family) and three colours (pink, blue, white), giving the product line a depth measure of six. Obviously, depth will vary by product line, so for example a newly introduced soap may only be offered in one regular size, and one fragrance.

Consistency: Refers to the closeness of various product lines across the mix, in terms of production methods and materials, target markets, common distribution outlets and the like. It may not always be obvious how or why a company has an apparently disparate mix of products, e.g. 3M introduced Scotch masking tape after its abrasives customers in the motor trade voiced the need for such a product.

Product mix decisions

Decisions on the consistency and dimensions of the product mix will comprise key issues within a company's product policy, and will almost certainly involve senior management (i.e. corporate) decision-makers, as well as functional specialists in the marketing department. Corporate sales growth and profit objectives may be served by, for example, increasing the width of the product mix (i.e. adding new product lines) and capitalising on the company's reputation, or a leading brand name, in a horizontal move to adjacent product markets. For example, the recent introduction of Persil washing-up liquid exploited the strength of the Persil brand name in the detergent sector.

Contributions to corporate growth objectives might equally be achieved through increasing the depth of the product mix, thereby gaining competitive advantage and market coverage, through reaching buyers with differing preferences, in other segments. For example, some time after the successful launch of Jif surface cleaner fluid, for bathrooms and kitchens, Lever introduced Lemon Jif, exploiting the favourable association of lemon-based ingredients with cleaning and grease-removing properties.

By the same token, some companies will, through careful product policy guidelines resolve that the product range must retain a consistency and logic that should *not* be diluted by straying into unrelated product areas. Other companies, after mixed experiences with diversification into other product fields, will tighten up their product policy by rationalisation, withdrawing or selling off products outside their reconsolidated product base. Such product policy moves will be difficult, and possibly costly, and will involve higher-level corporate deliberations and decisions. They will hopefully return to product policy a thrust and focus, and free resources to concentrate on product markets where the company has known strengths. For example, among the many companies to have withdrawn from the computer market in recent years, Honeywell Inc. appears to have little cause for regret, having successfully grown since through a well-managed concentration in fields such as electronic components, controls and instrumentation.

While most large companies have some variety in their product range, they will usually seek a consistency in their total offering, reflecting their key strengths and competences.

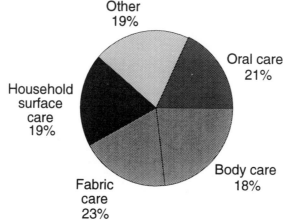

1990 total sales $5.69 bn worldwide, of which, by product field:

Other 19%

Oral care 21%

Household surface care 19%

Body care 18%

Fabric care 23%

Fig 12.8 Sales breakdown by product field: Colgate-Palmolive

As an example, Fig 12.8 shows the product-market sales of Colgate-Palmolive, the US-controlled consumer products manufacturer. This 186-year old company is probably best known for Colgate toothpaste and Palmolive soap, which are represented in the chart under the oral care and body care divisions respectively. While the company has 40 per cent of the world toothpaste market, it has a variety of product interests that range from household cleaners (e.g. Ajax) to mouthwash and other health-care products.

Product range analysis

For both day-to-day marketing purposes, and as a basis for longer-term decisions such as product modification, range extension and innovation, companies need to monitor and analyse key performance indicators for their product mix, and its constituent lines. Of critical concern will be indicators of product-market match, performance *vis-a-vis* leading competitors, identification of market opportunities and challenges, and some ongoing diagnosis/projection of each product's performance in terms of profitability, growth, and resource usage. Such analysis will therefore range from the holistic (i.e. total range) level to a detailed focus on individual product items, pack-sizes and individual product variants. The information bases for these analyses will draw heavily on accounting and costing records and other internal control data, and company market research findings/information which is nowadays increasingly stored and accessed through marketing information system (MKIS).

Figure 12.9 presents a simplified product range analysis for a hypothetical healthcare products manufacturer. Though simplistic and generalised, the analysis gives

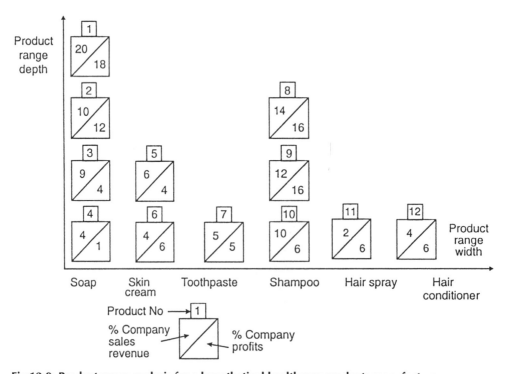

Fig 12.9 Product range analysis for a hypothetical healthcare products manufacturer

some insight into the strategic and managerial issues involved in product policy. In marketing terms, the company is fielding a spread of product lines (i.e. width), offering differing line choices (i.e. depth) to consumers. The sales and profits percentage figures indicate that the product lines make different contributions to company performance, while individual products within the lines themselves differ in their sales/profit profile. It is interesting to note that, even with a limited portfolio of twelve products, sales revenue contribution of individual products ranges from 20 to 1 per cent, while that for profits varies from 18 to 1 per cent of the total.

Clearly, even with only two yardsticks, profits and sales, simple comparison shows that some products are performing better than others. While statistically this will always be the case, especially within extensive product ranges, companies need to understand why and how performance varies, as part of the overall product management and marketing process. For example, in Fig 12.9, Product No. 4 may be facing severe market competition and production difficulties, while Product No. 11 may be a recent addition that has great profit potential, once it is established.

Resourcing and accounting measures such as sales and profits express product performance in terms of internal common yardsticks that enable within- and across-range comparisons, which are vital to product planning and strategy. Figure 12.10 illustrates a

Measure	Measurements
Sales	Volume (units) Revenue (£000) Percentage of total (%) Ranking (1---n) Sales growth (% ± 12 months)
Profits	Total (£000) Gross margin % ROCE % Percentage of company profits (%) Ranking (1---n) Profits growth (% ± 12 months)
Costs	Total (£000) Unit cost £ Overhead allocation (£000) Fixed v variable cost (x:y)
Others	Investment (£000) Capital spending and recovery CASH flow (£000) Plant use Budget X Functions e.g. marketing, transport, service

Fig 12.10 Accounting and resource measures of product performance

more comprehensive list of measures by which a company might conduct an internal product audit, product by product.

The value of such an audit is that it presents an analysis of products across a common set of measures, so that anomalies and problems can be identified, examined and addressed. With accounting data alone, it is possible, for each major product, to present a 'mini' profit and loss account and balance sheet, to indicate financial performance. Certainly larger companies will treat leading products as separate profit centres, and sometimes organise them as product divisions or strategic business units.

For a thorough marketing analysis of products, of course, financial information would need to be supplemented by external measures of how products fare within the marketplace. Figure 12.11 illustrates the various measures of marketing performance that might be applied to products and product lines.

- ❏ Sales and market share v. company target and v. leading competitors...current and historical.

- ❏ Projected product sales potential.

- ❏ Geographical sales - by region v. export.

- ❏ Sales pattern through year - seasonality, cyclicality.

- ❏ Sales x market segment e.g. age groups, income groups etc.

- ❏ Product sales v. overall market/segment growth.

- ❏ Age-maturity of product... life cycle features, trends.

- ❏ Number of current buyers users... and buyer profile (v. competition).

- ❏ Measures of product growth and success e.g. purchase loyalty (v. competitors), repeat purchases, first time buyers v. lapsed buyers.

- ❏ Distribution measures - overall % market cover
                            - stocking by outlet types
                            - % full range stocking.

- ❏ Quality measures e.g. complaints, refunds and returns, late deliveries, damages and breakdowns, sales problems, lost orders and cancellations.

- ❏ Awareness and recall measures of product/brand advertising and promotion.

- ❏ Attitude/image/preference measures v. competition.

Fig 12.11 Marketing measures of product performance

Performers and under-performers

The critical application of sales/profits and marketing measures to the product range will enable a company to identify those products that perform well, and those that patently under-perform. It can then make informed product policy decisions in respect of matters such as product improvement and modification, new product additions and replacements, and product withdrawals. It is probably no exaggeration to state that, even in the smallest of product ranges, products will differ in performance terms. Within larger product ranges, some products may have some common features that make for success or weakness in such a way that broad categories or types may be identifiable.

Peter Drucker, a well-known American management writer, has proposed a broad typology of products that encompasses the following categories:

1 Today's breadwinners.
2 Yesterday's breadwinners.
3 Tomorrow's breadwinners.
4 Others, referred to by such colourful terms as Cinderellas, also-rans, and investments in management ego.

While these descriptions are self-explanatory, if generalised, they do indicate that company performance is closely linked to product offerings, and how these fare in a competitive market. There is also to be found in the writings of Drucker, and other management commentators, clear advice on how companies should plan and manage product policy through informed decision-making and strategic analysis. Too often, managements launch products for the wrong motives (Drucker's 'investments in managerial ego'), or for the wrong market (product-market mismatch), or proceed to mis-allocate resources on 'lost cause' products rather than those with real potential (the Cinderella syndrome).

Portfolio analysis

A powerful facet of product policy is the recognition and exploitation of the dynamics within the product range - the extent to which products support each other, in marketing, resourcing or other terms. If it is a truism that company performance hinges on the product range, it is also to be expected that returns will vary according to the fine-tuning and management of resource-use against and within the range itself. In simple terms, there is a strategic dimension in the way that the product range is managed as a portfolio of (product) investments.

To illustrate this strategic aspect of product policy, and to aid corporate strategy development generally, various techniques of portfolio analysis have been developed, usually based on a matrix (or grid) representation of the products/product divisions within the firm. Figure 12.12 illustrates one of the most popular of these approaches, the growth-share Product Portfolio Matrix, originally developed by the US-based Boston Consulting Group (BCG).

The matrix is based on two principal dimensions: relative market share (i.e. related to the nearest major competitors); and market growth (a proxy for life-cycle development, and subject to interpretation). To apply the matrix, a company would plot its major products in the appropriate cells, positioning them, as in Fig 12.11, by circles proportional to current (or projected) sales income. (Note: the technique makes reference to cash generation, which is a basic and definitive resource, rather than the possibly more nominal and conditional values that might measure profitability). The analysis therefore

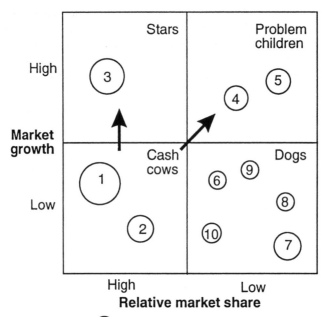

Fig 12.12 BCG's product portfolio matrix

attempts to describe the basic resource interdependencies of products within the portfolio, as reflected in the nature of the four classifications, explained below.

Cash cows: These products are market leaders within mature markets that are no longer as demanding in marketing terms. They therefore generate healthy cash reserves, in excess of the particular product's resource requirements. Significantly, the net surpluses generated can be invested elsewhere in the matrix (the bold arrows in the figure), to fund the developments of other company product initiatives.

Stars: As this colourful term implies, 'Stars' require constant grooming on their way to success. These products may generate major cash inflows through their market share, but this may be more than balanced by the competitive expenditures necessary within a growth market. Barring untoward developments, companies would be obliged to defend and advance star products as an investment, in readiness for the time when they can be treated as cash cows, when the market matures somewhat.

Problem children: Sometimes called 'wildcats' or 'question marks', these products have low market shares in a dynamic market setting. They therefore consume cash and other resources at some rate, and represent a necessary but measured risk in strategic investment terms.

Dogs: These products may constitute a mix of modest cash-earners and costly liabilities, among which will be former cash cows (Drucker's 'yesterday's breadwinners'), fallen stars and problem children. Companies will need to monitor these products carefully, control expenditures, and occasionally thin their ranks (product pruning).

The value of the BCG matrix is that it gives some insight into the resource plough-backs and dependencies that exist within the total product range, or within any mix of company initiatives (the technique could be applied to some effect in analysing a company's mix of export markets worldwide). It highlights in general terms the policy decisions necessary to maintain or change a company's position in respect of both individual product lines and the total product portfolio. As an example, the hypothetical company in Fig 12.12 would need to consider how Products 4 and 5 (problem children) can be promoted leftward by gaining market share, which are the loss-makers and which the cash-earners among Products 6 to 10 ('dogs'), and how long Product 1 (the major cash cow) can be relied on to fund a possibly top-heavy array of less productive investments. Indeed, the company might well be advised to re-examine the criteria it uses to develop and manage product lines generally. As a qualification to the above, it should be stressed that no simple 2 x 2 matrix analysis will cope with the complexities and dynamics of product management and strategy to be expected in a large company setting. Certainly, there are major difficulties and risks in applying and over-interpreting formal analytical tools such as the BCG matrix. While competing and more complex matrix approaches have been developed in recent years, notably by large multi-market companies such as General Electric and Shell International, the same advice applies: the basic merit of these techniques lies in the analytical skills and insight in producing the categories, rather than the development of standard prescriptions or panaceas.

Product strategy

A major impetus of product policy will be the corporate objectives to be attained via the product mix, reflecting that the overall performance of the company is in simple terms the sum total of that of its various product/service offerings. Product strategy will address the issue of how such corporate objectives are to be achieved, both at the level of the individual product, and the total product range.

Strategy implies purposeful, well-researched, well-planned and well-resourced activity. In product strategy terms, the research and planning foundation will depend heavily on the careful analysis and monitoring of existing products' performance, on market research and forecasting, competitive analysis, and a firm understanding of company marketing and resource strengths and limitations. Product strategy can take many forms and variants, at a number of levels, depending on market circumstances, company practices and the like. For simplicity, the present treatment will deal with only the major, more generic, strategy alternatives. It should be stressed that product strategy does not operate by product dimension alone as certainly market factors have to be considered in parallel.

A useful perspective on product strategy that reflects this product-market focus is the product-market scope matrix developed by Ansoff, illustrated in Fig 12.13. Four broad strategy alternatives are identified within the product-market scope matrix:

Markets	Products	
	Present	New
Present	(*) 1. Market penetration	(**) 3. Product development
New	(**) 2. Market development	(****) 4. Diversification

(Key : * = indicative degree of risk in each strategy)

Fig 12.13 Strategy alternatives within the product-market scope matrix

1 *Market penetration* – basically the company follows the advice of Peters and Waterman in 'sticking to its knitting', competing with the same product types in existing markets. This might involve increasing sales to existing customers, finding new users within present markets, or taking market share from competitors through more effective marketing.

2 *Market development* - here the company offers the same products to new markets or segments. A classic example of this strategy was the case of Johnson and Johnson's Baby Powder, which the company successfully targeted to women purchasers, when facing a projected fall-off in demand in the primary babycare market. Companies building export markets would also exemplify this strategy.

3 *Product development* - entails the introduction of new products, aimed at the same target market. Here the company is exploiting its basic marketing strengths and familiarity with customers, in order to widen its product offerings.

4 *Diversification* - here the company moves into both new markets and new product sectors, perhaps involving major changes in technology and marketing methods. As indicated in the risk star-rating (*) in Fig 12.13, this strategy involves the greatest risk of the four strategies outlined. For this reason, companies will often seek to contain or reduce their risks in some way, for example by licensing in technology or products, buying products and market share through acquisitions, or building on some familiar experience, e.g. in distribution channels or supplier links. By way of qualification, it should be pointed out that the rewards of risk-taking through diversification may be proportionately higher, while it is a truism that without risk-takers pursuing such strategies, most really innovative products would never see the light of day.

Product positioning

Positioning is a term sometimes used loosely among marketers. It can refer either to the company wide strategic stance or 'mission' taken on where to do business, and with what competitive advantages, or it can be confined to a more tactical concern with how individual products are targeted and positioned within a particular market or segment. The former, policy-level positioning issue might better be termed strategic positioning, though it is certainly in general terms relevant to product policy at the corporate level.

Product-level matters of positioning, product positioning proper, revolve around the way in which customers perceive a company product in relation to competitive products and/or their preferences and ideal product attributes. In a real sense, both levels of positioning are related, and it may well be that company experience of positioning, or re-positioning one product may lead to major lessons and strategy changes that involve new product development, fundamental re-design exercises or product deletions, and decisive changes in marketing strategy.

Informed product positioning will depend on reliable research into the position of the product(s) in relation to competing products, and to 'ideal' attributes elicited from respondents. A first stage would be to identify, through experience or preliminary research, a listing of products or brands competing with those of the company, and then to isolate the major attributes or characteristics that customers hold to be significant in making purchase choices within the product field. A set of detailed ratings and rankings might then be obtained in relation to these attributes, across the named products, and against 'ideal' products that respondents are asked to envisage. Through such procedures a comprehensive set of research information should be generated, so that multi-dimensional comparisons may be made of competing products and ideal positions, usually with the aid of dedicated software packages. To illustrate the value of such an exercise, Fig 12.14 shows a positioning 'map' of a hypothetical study of hotel groups, displayed for simplicity along two dimensions only.

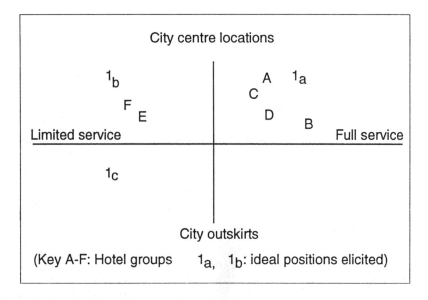

Fig 12.14 Product positioning map

From the positioning map it can be seen that existing hotel groups have clustered themselves about the two upper ideal positions. Proximity to the ideals might imply that groups A and F are leaders in their respective segments - something to check against known business volume. It is significant that one ideal position (Ic) is not catered for at all, perhaps revealing a market opportunity for 'basic board' overnight accommodation for short-stay travellers. Obviously, two-dimensional information on position and preferences should be supplemented by data on other attributes such as price, non-urban locations, accommodation style and the like. The mapped positions of course reflect only respondent perceptions, and it might be of value to check these. For example, Group D may have a number of out-of-town hotels, somehow not familiar to respondents, implying shortcomings in the company's communications programme.

Product modification

Product financial returns, portfolio analyses or research studies like the perceptual mapping exercise in Fig 12.14, may highlight the need for a company to revise a product to a greater or lesser extent. At one end of the spectrum such revision may entail no physical change to the product itself, but a re-positioning job, perhaps through changing the marketing programme, the advertising strategy, or the platform or proposition on which the product is presented. Re-positioning might require a redirection of the product to new target groups, perhaps for new uses or occasions. A now classic example of re-positioning was the case of Lucozade, which was successfully re-marketed from a remedial tonic drink to a leading 'soft' drink, targeted at younger health-conscious consumers.

Modification might take the form of other changes in marketing variables, such as price reductions or higher volume channels, in order to increase sales and market share. More fundamental changes to the product itself might be indicated, however. These could take the form of design face-lifts, to improve the product aesthetically and achieve a more contemporary image, as commonly happens with 'white goods' such as cookers and refrigerators, where such cosmetic changes are necessary to stay abreast of fashion trends. More radical still might be a complete re-design of the product, encompassing both bodywork restructuring, changes in functions and materials, and perhaps major changes in technology. While such a major product revision would entail the development of a new, second-generation or replacement product, it is a moot point at which level of revision a product modification has to be classified as a new product development strategy.

A practical issue in both product modification and replacement activities, is the timing of the new product and the phase-out of the old, since decisions about production plant, old-model stock depletion and spares, and the promotion and selling-in of new models will need to be handled carefully to ensure a co-ordinated operation.

Strategy for marginal products

One of the major lessons of both portfolio analysis and PLC monitoring is that there are dynamic resource interdependencies among a company's product range. Simply stated, a company cannot afford to have too many loss-making or marginal products. Sooner or later, radical action will be called for, in the interests of the company as a whole. This is not to deny that some marginal products may be knowingly maintained for a time, in given circumstances, e.g. newly-launched products in promising sectors, or older products performing a market-holding operation until a planned replacement issues off the assembly line.

Again, some products with specialist features or a strategic significance, perhaps among key customer groups, may be given a period of grace in which to be managed back to solvency. 'Special' products, sometimes heatedly defended by sales managers, might be re-priced at 'special rates' in order to return profits. In other cases, a concentration strategy might enable the company to re-group product marketing activity about the strongest segments, or through the most viable channels.

Products identified through portfolio analysis as cash-earning dogs ('cash dogs') will be left alone while producing returns. More particularly, loss-making 'dog' products would require serious consideration. While loss-makers are known drains on company resources, it is often the case that their loss-making is under-recorded, since they may give rise to continued quality and other problems that take disproportionate managerial time, thereby indirectly affecting the prospects of more healthy products. For some of these products it may be possible to engineer a temporary break-even or small profit, through drastic cut-backs in support, increased prices, or both - a harvesting strategy. Exceptionally, if the product sector generally is depressed, this might buy extra time within which some competitors might pull out, effecting a further, if temporary, improvement.

Sooner or later, though, decisions will have to be made to cut out the 'deadwood' products and eliminate the clutter in the range. Though statistically unproven, there is a consensus that the 80:20 rule operates as forcefully within product policy as elsewhere. Eighty per cent of the company's profits (or losses?) are attributable to 20 per cent of the products. The product deletion decision itself might take the form of an immediate discontinuation, or more commonly, a planned phase-out over a short period to complete order commitments. Occasionally the product, its brand name or associated production facilities may be successfully sold to other interests, perhaps smaller concerns more able to cope with diminished volumes and margins.

Branding

Branding is the practice of giving a distinctive identification - usually a name, symbol or design - to a product or range of products, and through usage and promotion establishing this identification in the marketplace. Products or product lines so identified are termed brands, and are the object of marketing activity that is often referred to as brand strategy. Though distinctive symbols, corporate logos and packaging may accompany the brand, it will usually be most readily identified through a brand name. For legal purposes, brands and brand and product names have to be protected from unauthorised use by a trademark. An equivalent legal safeguard for less tangible properties such as literary and artistic works is the establishment of a copyright.

Branding has a long history, probably most commonly associated with the maker's stamps and hallmarks used by artisans through the ages. From a marketing perspective, branding has become more commonplace since the turn of the century, developing alongside the emergence of marketing itself. Brand names give products an identity among customers and intermediaries alike, distinguishing them from standard commodities, and particularly from competitor products. Brand names are adopted by customers as a shorthand identification of the product, and taken as an assurance of the general quality and characteristics of the product. Research studies employing 'blind' product tests, of branded versus unbranded and control products, repeatedly show respondents to have preferences for branded products, and a willingness to pay more for them. It is not surprising, therefore, that companies nowadays assign asset values to brand names, or that the owners of famous brand-names such as Rolls Royce or Coca-Cola go to great lengths to legally protect their properties.

In many markets, brand names are used by buyers as convenient signposts during search and shopping behaviour, where favoured brands are mentally ranked at the top of a 'choice set' of contenders. Marketers will be concerned to maintain and develop such brand loyalty. Though branding has recently become more popular within industrial markets, the most well-known brands are still almost exclusively among consumer goods and service markets. In choosing brand names and developing a branding strategy, manufacturers may opt for:

1 *Multiproduct brands*, or 'family' brands, where the company uses one standard brand name, often the company name, for all its products, e.g. Heinz, Walkers, Colmans. Multiproduct branding can offer marketing economies where a favourable brand name carries across a whole product assortment, to the benefit of otherwise weaker products, and assisting in the acceptance of new products by consumers and intermediaries alike. Equally, a problem or failure in one product could work to the detriment of the whole brand 'family'.

2 *Multibrand products* involve a manufacturer assigning different brand names to different products, or even to various products within a product line. This practice is commonly seen in consumer good sectors such as biscuits, detergents, and cigarettes, where companies field a variety of products that are often individually developed and targeted at specific segments, or for particular uses or occasions. In other instances, less through design than circumstance, large manufacturer groups will find themselves with an extensive mix of competing brands, taken on board through a series of corporate acquisitions.

3 *Retailer own brands* predominately associated with consumer retail chains where 'own-label' brands have proved a useful source of supplementary business for some manufacturers (though some more brand-conscious companies have a deliberate policy of dismissing such ties as a threat to their brand franchise). Those entering own-brand contracts may value the extra sales involved, with little promotional outlay and at planned volumes and delivery dates, offering production economies through segments otherwise closed to them, or supplied by competitors. However, the cost of such business may be strict adherence to contract terms that include quality inspections, production-vetting and no-question returns policies, at prices that demand strict cost controls for often thin margins.

Indeed, aside from their commanding position in own-label contracting, leading supermarket groups have, through concentration, become so powerful in recent years that even large branded products manufacturers may have to make cost concessions to avoid the threat of their brands being 'delisted'.

Conclusion

Product policy is an area of key strategic significance within marketing management, as it represents the crucial area of decision-making where a company's resources are shaped to market requirements. At one level product policy pivots on the individual product, in all its facets, while at a more aggregate level it concerns itself with corporate performance issues related to the product mix, its dimensions and consistency. While approaches such as product life cycle analysis may be of some value in managing the individual product, techniques such as portfolio analysis have been developed to assist in strategic product decisions concerned with product withdrawal, range extension and innovation.

Questions

1 Consider the vale of product life cycle analysis for a specialist producer of business software packages.

2 'There is little a company can do with a product that is in the decline stage of the product life cycle'. Discuss.

3 'The brand is more important than the product'. Discuss.

4 Under what circumstances might it be desirable for a company to eliminate a product from its range? Using relevant examples, illustrate the marketing issues presented by such a product withdrawal, and how they might be handled.

References

Ansoff, I, *Corporate Strategy*, Revised, Edn., Penguin, 1989.
Boston Consulting Group, 'The product portfolio', *Perspectives on Experience*, 1971.
Doyle, P, 'The realities of the product life cycle', *Quarterly Review of Marketing*, Summer 1976.
Drucker, P F, 'Managing for business effectiveness', *Harvard Business Review*, 41, May 1963.
Peters, T and Waterman, R, *In Search of Excellence: Lessons from America's Best Run Companies*, Harper & Row, 1982.

Case study: Priestman Arts Centre

As a successful Marketing Executive with a national grocery chain, you have just embarked on a voluntary six-month secondment to a community arts project. Your salary increments and career progression have been guaranteed by your employers, who have a longstanding reputation for social work within a range of activities as diverse as wildfowl protection and arts sponsorship.

Your secondment assignment is to act as Marketing Consultant to the Priestman Arts Centre in Weardale, a large industrial town in the North-East of England. Now in its seventh year, the Centre operates within a somewhat broad brief of providing 'support and promotion of the Arts in general within and around the Borough of Weardale'. The Centre's well-appointed premises comprise two exhibition galleries, a 250-seat theatre with cafeteria, a flexible work studio accommodating a weaver-in-residence, and an Arts bookshop.

The Centre offers a programme that ranges from exhibitions of paintings, pottery and glassware, to live performance events such as dance sketches and poetry readings, chamber music evenings, and comedy playhouses. Though not strictly monitored, attendance figures tend to vary significantly. While a conventional painting exhibition might generate an encouraging through-traffic, other scheduled events, such as music recitals may prove disappointing in spite of the performers' names.

The menu of activities on offer has recently been endangered by financial circumstances. For the coming year the Centre will suffer heavy cuts in its Arts Council Award and its Borough Council grant, both of which have been important supports in an otherwise loss-making picture. In the words of Miles Berenson, the Arts Centre Manager: 'This is a heavy blow. We've always made a policy of attracting the best events within the budget. This will be more difficult than ever now'.

Within the terms of your 'appointment' as Marketing Consultant, you are expected to analyse the operations of the Centre and produce and activate a plan for its future marketing activities. As one preliminary step towards the plan, you are invited to comment and advise on product policy issues of relevance to the Centre, its activities and offerings.

13

NEW PRODUCT DEVELOPMENT

Introduction

New product development is a vital part of product policy for all companies and organisations, as it represents one of the key means by which corporate renewal is achieved, and a future secured. As it is a future-directed activity that affects the whole company and its commercial prospects, it follows that new product development should serve corporate objectives, and their expression through strategy. It will therefore be at the centre of much corporate deliberation and decision-making, and in most well-managed companies it will be the focus of a planned development programme.

Marketers have a major role to play in new product development, for a number of reasons. First, product development is itself a material part of marketing strategy, and a route to both increased competitiveness and customer satisfaction. Second, marketers are, perhaps uniquely, in the position to direct and assist the development effort, through their market knowledge and research capability. Furthermore, it will be the role of the marketing function to launch and successfully commercialise the new products, once readied for market.

The case for new product development

The most obvious case for product development is the strategic need to innovate and change in response to, or preferably somewhat ahead of, market change. While companies will innovate at different speeds, and with varying success, some will appear more competitive and forward-thinking in their product development activities, and others more reactive and conservative. As in business generally, product development is an undertaking concerned with opportunity-seeking, but beset by risks – statistics vary, though conservative estimates would indicate that at least 50 per cent, and maybe 60 to 70 per cent, of new products fail within their launch year, while a high proportion of the remainder never become major successes. However, *risk*, and *risk-taking*, are necessary ingredients of the innovation process, as summarised in the adage: 'The biggest risk of all is to take no risks'.

In simple terms, one of the most telling implications of the product life cycle model is that a company must ensure that a succession of new products is coming on-stream, to cover the commercial ground lost through the demise of older products, at the other end of the life cycle. Certainly, the prospects would be rather weak for a company with a product range hemmed within the later stages of the life cycle. Appropriate to the biological analogy of the life cycle model itself, new product development can therefore be viewed as a form of plough-back, an investment for the future.

The growing body of research on new product development has shown that the rationale for product development will vary among companies, depending on factors such as market conditions and company performance. Among the strategic objectives that companies follow in their innovation programmes, the following are perhaps the most common:

1 To increase or defend market share. Given the evidence that market share has a strong association with profitability, through competitive mass and production economies, this rationale for innovation is closely tied to profit-seeking.
2 To develop or enter a future new market or segment, perhaps as a pre-emptive strategy to outpace competition.
3 To maintain a lead position as an innovator. While this objective is competition-related, those companies that operate in fast-changing technology fields, such as electronics, will find themselves almost carried along by a constant stream of product and process innovations.
4 To diversify into new product markets, as a strategic hedge against over-dependence on a limited product range: the classical 'third leg' strategy.
5 To exploit distribution strengths, to stimulate distribution channels, or to cement a firmer trading relationship with intermediaries.
6 To make productive use of slack resources, e.g. in sales or production capacity, or perhaps to remedy seasonal or cyclical dips in activity.
7 To exploit company experience in working with a new technology or new materials, or otherwise to commercialise spin-offs and by-products of the company's primary endeavours.

Whatever local policy guidelines companies set for themselves in product development terms, it has become a commonplace observation that dependence on new products for sales and profits growth is increasing steadily over time. Innovation-watchers might argue that the rate of change is multiplicative, making for a continual growth in product innovation. Such a view could certainly be supported by reference to factors such as the dismantling of trade barriers and the globalisation process, the convergence of technologies (e.g. telecommunications and computing), and the growing sophistication and innovativeness of customers generally.

Types of new products

Product development represents a wide spectrum of activity, spanned at one end by the painstaking development of products and technologies through basic research programmes, and at the other extreme by the countless variations and improvements to existing products that are everyday features of 'busy' markets such as grocery products.

'Newness' is a relative term, and most products introduced to the marketplace are developments or variations on existing product formats. The norm for most markets will likely be a constant drip-feed of incremental product improvements, with the occasional 'splash' effect of a major product innovation that re-groups the market and redirects technological development. In line with such a process, most major companies will subscribe to both ongoing product improvement and longer-term programmes of fundamental research. The variety of 'new' products to be met with will therefore encompass the following broad types:

1 **Major innovations**: Products involving radical new combinations of technology, formulation or user benefits, with the potential to form entirely new markets and even whole industries – television, X-ray, the microprocessor and VCR technology would typify such innovations. By definition, such innovations are rare gems and not without major development and commercialisation risks, e.g. the build-up of a customer base can itself be a key issue, as instanced by the commercial difficulties of the Concorde supersonic aircraft joint venture.

2 **Product improvements**: At one end of the scale, these products may represent major innovations in existing markets, with the potential to marginalise other competitors. A good example would be the succession of 'system' products that have effectively created new segments in markets as diverse as writing instruments, wet-shaving products, cameras and lawnmowers. In these and other markets (e.g. cars, washing machines) it is possible to trace a thread of development through to second- and third-generation products that consolidate updates in design and technology.

   At the other end of this category would be the more everyday, marginal improvements and modifications that are regularly incorporated through features such as product redesign, re-packaging, and formula and ingredient changes. A particular marketing variant on the improved product is the *re-positioned product*, an existing product that is re-targeted, often unchanged, to a new market or segment.

3 **Product additions**: Products without major claims to innovation or novelty, usually imitations of current market leaders, or simply line extensions of product ranges that a company already markets successfully. Certainly below the brand leadership 'skyline' in the marketplace, most product entrants are likely to fall within this category. Not surprisingly, most product failures occur within the ranks of these 'me too' products. However, exceptionally it may happen that a largely imitative or indistinctive product, perhaps entered as a diversification move by an established company from another market, assumes market leadership through better marketing.

Note: A key point to make about new products is that 'newness', like beauty, is in the eyes of the beholder – in marketing terms, *customer perception* is the ultimate judge of whether a product is new or not.

The product development process

The corporate setting

The development of any new product, or service, is usually a lengthy, costly and risky process. While 'lucky strike' discoveries of new products and formulations do happen, they are very much the exception to the general rule: 'success comes from 1 per cent inspiration and 99 per cent perspiration!'

Most companies will seek to create their own 'luck' by adopting a disciplined, commercially-directed programme of new product development that follows key corporate objectives (market share, growth, profitability), and is consistent with whatever product policy guidelines these imply (as discussed in the previous chapter). Such a programme will depend for its success on a number of firm prerequisites:

1 An up-to-date summary, or shared understanding, of key corporate priorities for development.
2 Shared knowledge of company resources, capabilities and limitations.
3 Market, competitor and other external knowledge and information sources, e.g. for checking the commercial potential of projects.
4 Commitment to a base level of specialist resourcing, projected forward against target activities and projects.
5 A known and agreed set of procedures and decision criteria against which to assess and progress development projects.

In some companies these elements may be mirrored in corporate mission statements, annual plans and product policy guidelines, or even formally laid down in dedicated development or R & D plans. While over-formalisation may hinder rather than help, what is important is that at the appropriate levels in the company informed decisions are made and strategic criteria followed in respect of assessing and advancing development initiatives.

Stages in the product development process

While the gestation period for different products will doubtless vary according to technological complexity, resourcing issues, corporate priorities and the like, an attempt will be made to present a generalised sequence of the development process. Figure 13.1 illustrates a simple 'funnel' model of the process, in which new product ideas are initiated, screened, commercially assessed and progressed further, rejected or set aside for later re-working. The product development stages outlined in the model are examined in some detail below.

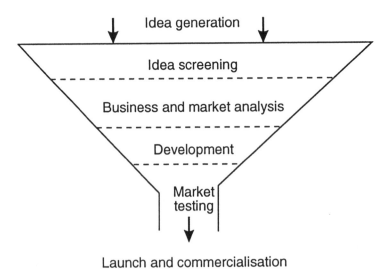

Fig 13.1 The product development process

Idea generation

This stage, the logical beginning of product development, represents for most companies an *ongoing* effort of accumulating and generating development ideas, rather than a discrete once-and-for-all step or process As worthwhile ideas are at a premium, a *continuous* effort is necessary to tap creativity from a number of sources.

The number of ideas necessary to support successful product development has been illustrated by research studies conducted by the US consulting firm Booz, Allen and Hamilton. In a landmark 1968 survey among American manufacturers it was estimated that 58 ideas were necessary to sustain a successful new product launch. This figure had been reduced to seven when the consultants conducted a duplicate survey in 1981, indicating that manufacturers had improved their development performance through stricter management and investment procedures. Even so, the research indicates that most product ideas fail to 'run the gauntlet' of successive stages and filters within the development process. Moreover, as no company can claim any monopoly on creativity, it would make sense to consider potential product ideas from a variety of sources.

Internal		External	
R & D **Design**	} Basic research	**Competitors**	– Imitation or improvement
Engineering **Manufacturing** **Purchasing**	} Development & Operations	**Customers**	– Trade customers, intermediaries, consumers Feedback, complaints, suggestions.
Marketing **Market Research** **Sales Personnel** **Customer Service**	} Market studies, analysis of previous research, product testing	**Specialists**	– Design houses, consultants, advertising and research agencies
Senior Management			
Other sources - employee suggestions, inter-departmental efforts eg brainstorming		**Others**	– Suppliers Joint-venture partners, overseas contacts, licensing partners

Fig 13.2 New product idea sources available to a company

Figure 13.2 presents a summary of idea sources available to a typical company. In most companies product ideas will come from both internal and external sources, though certainly in technology or science-led fields such as pharmaceuticals or electronics there will at any time be a feedstock of ideas and formula alternatives that stem directly from ongoing research programmes. Even in these cases, though, there is a strong case for drawing on problem 'cues' from users and customers, trade channels, competitor intelligence and sales force feedback. Without such market direction there is a danger that development efforts lose their focus and become directed solely by the forces of 'technology push'.

Whatever the product field, ideas for new products, and product improvements, can come from anywhere within the value chain, inside or outside the company. Within the company, multi-disciplinary efforts, drawing on specialists from a number of departments, may prove especially effective. The logic of these approaches is that a more balanced spread of ideas may be generated, and that political or inter-departmental rivalry is reduced by eliminating the NIH ('not invented here') syndrome. Such team-work efforts may take many forms, from the regular employment of creative techniques such as brainstorming, group problem-solving and discussion sessions, to more permanent organisational mechanisms such as venture teams, 'think tanks' and new product committees.

Idea screening

Given a number of development ideas, it is necessary to put them through a standard screening method to select only those with apparent business and development prospects. This first-level screening will usually rate and compare ideas across a number of key factors held to be important in terms of company/product fit, such as compatibility with company technology and manufacturing capability, marketing resources, distribution channels, research/design capability and the like.

Figure 13.3 presents a simplified example of a rating sheet that might be used for comparing development ideas across such a screen of weighted factors. The score profile illustrated in the table is quite encouraging, though in practice most development ideas would score quite modestly, while still others would be rejected as too middle-of-the-road to justify retention – too high a 'pass-rate' might dilute development resources and prejudice the real potential winners. While the shortlist criteria and their weightings will vary from company to company, and over time, the important consideration is that a consistent and agreed set of benchmarks is used from the outset.

Product selection criteria	(A) Weighting	(B) Criterion rating 1 2 3 4 5 6 7 8 9 10	(A X B) Weighted idea score
Corporate objectives	4	* (9)	36
Financial capability	4	* (9)	36
Marketing compatibility (including export)	4	* (8)	32
Relation to present products	3	* (8)	24
R&D/Engineering	2	* (7)	14
Manufacturing	2	* (8)	18
Suppliers/Sourcing	1	* (9)	9
	20		169

Weighted score key: 0–89 poor; 90-139 fair; 140+ good.

Fig 13.3 Development idea rating screen

Business and market analysis

The development ideas that survive the initial screening illustrated in Fig 13.3 will effectively enter a more rigorous series of checks and analysis within the next filter, as it is after this stage that 'green light' decisions will be made to authorise and commit costly resources to development projects.

The business and market analysis stage is concerned with establishing a viable commercial rationale for development products, as both a guide for development work and a first-level business planning statement. The assessments made will involve market and marketing investigations, financial projections and costing/scheduling estimates. These investigations are likely to be carried out by separate departmental specialists, though the final business assessment will depend on some information interchange between parties, e.g. sales estimates will be required to assess revenue/profit calculations.

The marketing information required within the business analysis will likely come from a combination of existing market data and previous research findings, frequently supplemented by specific qualitative research exercises designed to validate the market attractiveness of shortlisted product ideas. Usually the ideas will need to be translated into alternative product *concepts,* i.e. succinct statements of the essential dimensions, attributes and rationale of the proposed product, expressed in customer language. The most common means of concept testing is via group discussions, where a small number of potential customers are exposed to alternative concepts, sometimes supported by pack mock-ups or models, asked questions and led in discussion on issues such as concept acceptability, apparent uses and benefits, advantages over existing products and the like. The findings of such research, though highly tentative, give some early insight into customer reactions and perceptions, and usually a means of selecting the more viable concepts, together with the benefits to incorporate into their further development. Alongside existing market data, and information on matters such as buying and switching behaviour, it should be possible to estimate preliminary market and sales forecasts, as an input to financial assessment work.

The marketing assessment of a successful product concept is commonly summarised in an outline marketing rationale, which will include overall comment on market volume, target segments and product positioning, together with specific guidelines on product attributes and qualities, indicative price-bands, and performance targets versus likely competition. These latter details will serve as an early product specification and a development brief to be followed by R&D.

Business analysis of product ideas is likely to be expressed through financial reports, which will combine aggregates such as sales forecasts, investment requirements, functional outlays and costings, and profit projections. These broad indicators in turn may break down into detailed components such as investment appraisal/payback summaries over an assumed product life or depreciation period, direct-indirect cost structures and departmental estimates, pricing and break-even calculations, and other financial arithmetic necessary to compare the viability of alternative product proposals.

Development

The development stage proper is really a succession of overlapping activities, orchestrated as a teamwork effort. While in most companies the responsibility for development work will be located within the R&D department, or an equivalent function such as Design or Product Engineering, in practice a variety of inputs are needed from other functions in order to ensure that the final product or service is both marketable and commercially viable. Figure 13.4 illustrates the complexity of inter-functional working within the development stage.

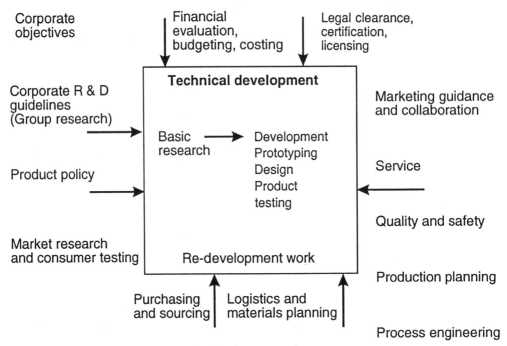

Fig 13.4 Multi-disciplinary inputs to the development task

In scientific sectors such as medicines, the development stage will be lengthy, and usually divided into sub-phases, starting with pure research in pursuit of chemical/physiological reactions, leading to a development stage proper, itself divided into laboratory and clinical phases. In other science-led or high technology fields such as aerospace and electronics, development may be equally complex, speculative and costly. The scale of resourcing and effort at risk within the development stage therefore makes clear the case for co-ordinated teamwork, planning and controls.

In the interests of co-ordination many companies have adopted particular forms of organisation for product development. These will be discussed later in the chapter. As previously stated, marketers have a particular guidance role to play in product development, if only to ensure that customer realities remain a focus of the development task. The experience of many marketers is that R&D personnel, unsupported by market guidance, fall prey to a 'technology myopia', an interest in the (research) chase itself rather than the (marketplace) end product. During the development stage, therefore, marketers need to stay close to development staff, by ensuring for instance that prototypes are developed to market guidelines and assessed through customer research, and by generally advising on the maintenance of deadlines, cost, quality and design guidelines.

During the development period a succession of product tests will be made, on a number of product formulations or prototypes in order to develop and 'fine-tune' a finished product ready for ultimate production and launch. For manufacturing planning purposes alone, varying tests will be made among alternatives in terms of materials specifications, design-performance configurations, production-assembly approaches and cost estimates, quality and safety assessments, supplier sourcing and the like. Logically, marketing specialists will need to stay abreast of these activities, and where necessary offer comment and advice on commercial and marketplace aspects of the decisions to be made.

Parallel to these 'internal' tests, there will usually be the need to subject successive product designs to customer tests, in order to check on market acceptability, decide on yet unresolved issues of product attributes (e.g. colour, materials, user controls, design aesthetics, minor design changes), or to make performance comparisons through in-use tests or trial placements.

A marketing-centred approach to development is therefore an *iterative* process, involving a dialogue with outside parties, primarily potential customers, *and* internally with various functional specialists within the organisation. It is worth stressing that both external *and* internal sides of the dialogue are critical. Furthermore, in today's competitive climate they are also interdependent. The increased zeal with which companies now embrace initiatives centred on Total Quality Improvement, just-in-time (JIT), design for assembly (DFA), and Simultaneous Engineering – to name but a few 'new wave' approaches that have gained a deserved respect within manufacturing and engineering – demonstrates that real market advantages can be won through internal improvements in production efficiency, quality and accelerated development.

Market testing

After the various product performance, functional and customer preference tests of the development phase, most companies will subject the, by now market-ready, product to a final assessment under *market conditions*, prior to full-scale launch. The objectives of doing this will be to reduce commercial risk by uncovering unforeseen product problems, fine-tuning the marketing and distribution programme, and making more accurate projections of sales, market performance and profitability.

The ultimate form of market test will be to conduct a formal *test marketing* operation, usually in some test market area(s) or town(s) chosen as representative of the total market-area. Tests in TV regions, urban areas (e.g. London) and provincial cities are quite common for consumer goods. Test marketing would be undertaken as a scaled-down version of the intended national launch, involving similar advertising media and campaigns, distribution and sales cover, promotion and pricing elements of the marketing mix. Sometimes variations (e.g. in price, advertising intensity) may be tested in different test locations, in order to optimise the launch marketing mix, and to more accurately project sales volumes, purchaser profiles, buying volumes, first-time and repeat purchases. While marketing activity 'on the ground' will be most obvious in

Table 13.1
First-time and repeat sales combinations during test market

% Trial purchase	% Repeat purchase	Possible diagnosis
High	High	Marketing and product successful.
Low	High	Poor marketing threatens good product.
High	Low	Product unsatisfactory.
Low	Low	Both marketing and product unsatisfactory?

sales and advertising terms, the value of the test market will rest as firmly on the research conducted at trade and household level, through retail consumer audits, sales force feedback and other sources. It may, for instance, prove necessary to buy in research in a *control* area outside the test market, in order to compare sales effects on competitor products, and to eliminate market wide variations. Of particular interest to the marketer will be the recorded incidence of initial sales (penetration) and repeat sales (re-purchase), which, together with purchase size, will indicate the likely success of the eventual full launch. Though generalised, the trial-repeat patterns set out in Table 13.1 would indicate varying degrees of success.

Limited market testing may be conducted instead of a full test-marketing operation, perhaps where:

- product and production variables have to be finalised well in advance, e.g. with cars and other durable manufactures;
- the product does not represent a major launch or commercial risk, e.g. as with a range addition or minor variation on a trusted formula; or where extensive previous in-development research assures confidence;
- competitive urgency may drive for an accelerated launch, or there may be the real risk of competitors spoiling test-market results (e.g. by under-pricing, intensified sales and promotion), or the loss of competitive surprise, or even copycat products appearing;
- other reasons might involve budget constraints, or a need for marketing information limited to restricted areas, e.g. brand-switching patterns, promotional effectiveness.

Limited marketing testing might take various forms, for example, 'mini'-test markets involving selected stores or a regional chain, where test products are 'placed' by the company for a period of time. In other cases, commercial market and research test services will be used, perhaps involving panels of households that are recruits to a shopping circle involving catalogue choice or home delivery. Comparable, though less strictly commercial, are the simulated 'shopping laboratories' operated by a number of research companies.

Market testing *industrial products* is usually conducted on a more controlled basis, for example through trial installation with selected customers, or through invitation to demonstration events, company showroom and test facilities and the like. Arguably, heavy investment industrial products are more likely to be developed through continuing contact with prospective customers, so that many of the 'grey areas' covered by test marketing may be already resolved.

Finally, it is worth noting that, with growing internationalisation, large global companies are increasingly conducting test-market operations in selected countries, prior to regional and international market launch operations.

Launch and commercialisation

This represents the end of the development process, and the full-scale introduction of the finished product to the marketplace. The resource costs and risks attending this stage are significant, as shown in the simple development-expenditure relationship outlined in Fig 13.5. The commercial risks riding on any major launch justify the careful analyses, tests and preparations involved in the development process, and also the marketing professionalism required to support market entry. Competitive realities should ensure that the company makes *objective* decisions based on test-market results – even if the decision is to abort or delay product launch. Given a 'green light' decision to proceed, however, the company will still need to maximise the lessons of the test market, and ensure that launch activity proceeds methodically to the marketing plan developed. Given that production volumes will require scaling-up from the pilot plant levels of the test market, many companies will decide on a gradual 'rolling' launch region by region, or compromise by stock build-up to shorten the release period and increase launch impact. Critical to the success of the launch will be the monitoring of market research indicators, and generally the quality of managerial decisions taken on the basis of the controls built into the launch marketing plan.

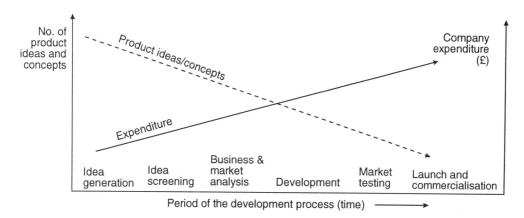

Fig 13.5 Company expenditure over the product development process

Product adoption and diffusion

Of direct relevance to the process of new product development, segmentation and target marketing is the issue of *how* products are received and adopted on release to the marketplace. There is a consensus that new products penetrate or *diffuse* into the marketplace at differing rates, among different groups of buyers. The most notable theoretical contribution to this issue has been the work of the American researcher Everett Rogers who proposed that, at least in relative terms, first-time purchasers of new products could be classified according to the innovativeness of their adoption behaviour. Rogers presented the adoption behaviour of purchasers of a new product as a time-dependent phenomenon that could be plotted within a normal distribution curve, as illustrated in Fig 13.6.

The five adopter groupings statistically identified by this analysis might suggest that buyers vary somewhat in terms of innovativeness, openness to new propositions, conservatism, loyalty and related behavioural dimensions. While there are a few research findings that indicate innovators to be younger, better educated, more cosmopolitan and open-minded, there has yet to emerge any set of *general* findings, or any reliable and practical indicator of innovativeness that might help marketers in the obvious interest that they have in identifying and targeting these innovation-prone buyers.

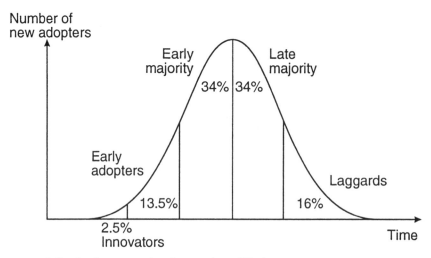

Fig 13.6 Normal distribution curve showing product diffusion process

Organisation for new product development

Of no small significance to the success of a company's innovation efforts will be the way in which it organises and manages the development effort. Research studies indicate that top management involvement and leadership are critical determinants of the 'entrepreneurship' shown by the whole organisation. Rigidity, bureaucratic rule-making, demarcation and interdepartmental conflict are major obstacles to success in new product development. In order to avoid these problems and to encourage teamwork and co-ordination, progressive companies have evolved separate organisational arrangements for their innovation programmes. Figure 13.7 outlines a number of the more common organisational 'solutions' to be met with, though it should be stressed that structural preferences vary from company to company.

- The **Product Manager** system, commonly found in large consumer goods companies in particular, meets with mixed reports in terms of product development. The major reason for this is that product managers have enough pressing problems dealing with established products, so that, excepting more simple line extensions, new product development may suffer by comparison.
- The **New Product Manager** position has evolved from the product manager system, specifically to allow the full-time efforts in innovation that product managers rarely manage.
- **New Product Committees** are commonly used in large companies, usually for policy-making, review and product selection purposes, rather than full-time innovation management. Though composed of representatives of different functions, it may suffer the common committee malaise of bureaucracy, lethargy and political infighting.
- The **New Product Department** represents a more visible and dedicated solution for development than a new product committee, and will usually be headed by a senior manager experienced in product development, supported by a multi-disciplinary

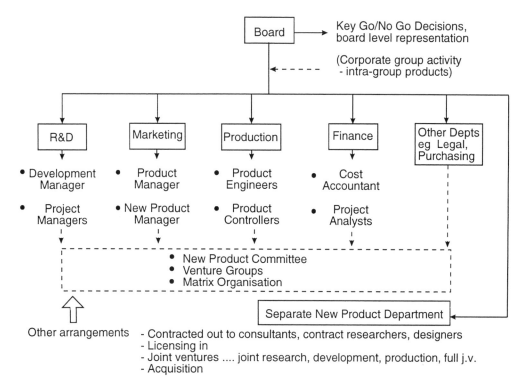

Fig 13.7 Organisation for new product development

team of specialists. Properly managed and resourced, such departments can be the driving force of innovation throughout the company.

- **Venture Groups** or teams represent a multi-functional task force grouping assigned to particular projects, or *ventures*. The efficacy of such a teamwork approach has been confirmed by its major proponents, which include such large companies as Dow, Monsanto and 3M.
- **The Matrix Organisation** represent a radical, company – or division-wide restructuring of staff and management in order to 'kick-start' innovation through improved communications, integration and working relationships. In simple terms, staff and functions are reorganised so that dual reporting relations impose closer collaboration across departmental boundaries.

While all these structures represent *internal* organisational mechanisms for new product developments, there remains a number of *external* sourcing avenues that companies use, for reasons of cost, or time-saving, or in order to 'import' creativity and innovation. In high-cost research environments such as proprietary medicines, licensing-in is a supplementary means of staying abreast of developments, or accelerated entry to new product sectors. Joint ventures and strategic alliances have the merit of risk-sharing and resource-pooling, and appear to be growing in popularity at the international level, especially in technology-led fields such as automobiles and aerospace.

Conclusion

New product development is of key strategic importance, as it represents the opportunity for a company to introduce 'fresh blood' into its products and services, and thereby strengthen and widen its opportunities in the marketplace.

Logically, from a marketing viewpoint, new product development should *start* with the idenitification of the needs and problems of customers, and the means to offer them enhanced performance and improvements over competitive offerings. Commercially, the innovation process generally is both costly and risky. Companies therefore need to adopt a managed approach to product development, ensuring informed decision-making co-ordinated efforts and effective returns on the investments involved. The marketing function has an important part to play in the general development process, and in the successful commercialisation of new products.

Questions

1 The 'right' organisation is often argued to be a critical factor in a successful programme of innovation. Comment on this view and evaluate the alternative means by which the product development function could be organised in a company manufacturing domestic and industrial refrigeration equipment.

2 'Test marketing is wasteful, inconclusive and unnecessary - if a new product is going to succeed, it is in the real market that success will be achieved'. Discuss.

3 Taking as a focus any recently launched new product, present in summary form a marketing rationale for its introduction, a broad view of its position relative to other products marketed by the company, and a brief listing of leading competitor products.

4 Consider the strategic role of new product development for a company operating within the service sector.

References

Booz, Allen & Hamilton, *New Products Management for the 1980s,* Booz, Allen & Hamilton, 1982.
Everett M Rogers, *Diffusion of Innovations*, 3rd Edn., The Free Press, 1983.

Case study: Linley Engineering

Linley Engineering Services is a small Coventry company providing a range of sub-contract metalwork and engineering services including welding, profile cutting, flamecutting, grinding and fabricating. It also undertakes intermittent contract fabrication of a range of trolleys, an outwork arrangement made five years ago with the trolley manufacturer, a Birmingham-based company specialising in palletisation and materials-handling systems. This work, never particularly profitable or reliable, has for the last two years amounted to no more than an occasional batch order from the Birmingham company, which is itself now troubled by recessionary difficulties.

In 1988 Linley had a monthly turnover of approximately £60 000 and had 22 employees. However, since that date it has suffered severely from the effects of local recession, and has not markedly recovered in spite of a short-lived industrial upturn. It now has only ten employees and turnover has fallen to £28 000 per month. It has recorded a small loss in each of the last three years.

There are some 1100 accounts in the sales ledger but only 120 have been active during the last twelve months. Of these, ten accounts produce 70 per cent of the company's sales. Order sizes vary from 'one-off' jobs costing £100 to a longstanding contract worth £10 000 per month. Profits per job are known to vary somewhat, though the company has not succeeded in its periodic attempts to plan profits or purposefully provide for future growth.

Sales contacts are currently handled by the Managing Director, John Linley. Apart from a listing in a local trades directory the company spends no money on advertising or publicity. The company has a secretary/works accountant who costs all jobs and prepares estimates and quotations. Design, production and purchasing is handled by a production foreman, under the direction of John Linley.

In recent months John Linley has been giving serious thought to the strategic avenues open to the company, and especially to the possibilities that might exist in new product fields and markets. He believes that, if only for survival purposes, the company needs to move away from dependence on the depressed sub-contract sector, and the 'metal-bashing' image that sticks to it. In particular, he feels that opportunities lie in the development and commercialisation of a credible range of company-manufactured products, supplied to the open market. In this way, he reasons, the company would be in more direct control of its own destiny.

To this end, he has resolved to make a careful assessment of the company's situation, its strengths and limitations. From this he means to develop a shortlist of possible new product ideas for the intended line of manufactured products. Advise John Linley on the issues and guiding principles he might consider in developing a plan for the design and commercialisation of any new product line.

14

PRICE, QUALITY AND VALUE

**There is hardly anything in the World that some men cannot make a little worse
and sell a little cheaper**

John Ruskin (1819-1900)

Introduction

In 1992 the inflation rate in Peru reached 1400 per cent per annum. Similar events are occurring in Eastern Europe, as restrictions on the Russian rouble are removed. In the UK, we cannot contemplate prices doubling every month, but we can appreciate the problems it causes for both suppliers and customers. In some areas of Peru people have so little faith in money that they rely on exchange of goods, such as chickens for clothes, and eggs for firewood. Their exchanges are dictated by the desirability of what is offered by the two parties. They have little to do with the cost of production.

Barter deals, also called counter trade, were commonly used in some controlled economies. An example is one international soft drinks firm selling drinks in Bulgaria, but receiving payment in soft fruit such as raspberries (used for jam making in another UK company), and Black Sea holidays. There were times in the past where barter was more common than it is now. By considering how it can be used, we are able to appreciate the value of products or services. This is the concept of 'affordability' described in Chapter 7.

Of course the pricing of products must be put into context. Tickets for the 1992 opening ceremony for the Barcelona Olympics had a face value of £150, but they were changing hands at £800 on the day before the ceremony. At the same time, tickets for a long running West End comedy show were on offer at half price at the Leicester Square ticket booth.

In this chapter we will look at the whole aspect of price, value and cost. There are different strategies where price can be used effectively within the marketing mix. These can vary as new products require different strategies from those appropriate to existing products. Also, different strategies are necessary for different market conditions, and at different stages of the product life cycle. There is no doubt that pricing decisions are vital for any organisation, after all it is the only element within the marketing mix which creates revenue for your organisation. A survey by the Chartered Institute of Management Accountants in 1988 suggested many organisations still use cost as a basis of fixing price levels. This chapter is designed to show how such policies can restrict the flexibility of decisions relating to this powerful marketing tool.

When it comes to low price as a strategy it is as well to remember that anyone can give money away. Anyone can cut the price of their product, but price rarely offers a *sustainable* competitive advantage. If your competitor loses sales due to your price cut, then a similar price reduction redresses the balance. Of course the customer gains in a price war at the expense of company profit. However, this can only continue while profit is still possible.

Exercise

If you live outside London examine the ways of travelling to London (if you live in London consider a journey to Birmingham).
Write down five ways of travelling and find out the *cost** of a return journey. Then explain the advantages and disadvantages of each type of journey and explain why they are all used by different groups of travellers.

e.g.: Coach
     Train (peak time)
     Train (off peak saver travel)
     Hire car
     Own car

* Note cost to you is the price charged by the supplier.

Components of a price

It will be clear, from the exercise above, that price has more components than the money actually charged. For instance, if you pay for your ticket by credit card rather than by cash, you have an extra few weeks before paying the account. This could benefit you in a number of ways, although British Rail pays the credit card company a small fee which adds to British Rail's costs. If you decide to drive to London you will have to include petrol and perhaps car parking charges, not to mention the problem of apportioning depreciation and tax/insurance. Alternatively, if you use a student travel card you get discount on your coach or train travel. There are other pricing situations where other components are involved. For instance, in many industrial situations the parties negotiate stage payments, and also additional benefits such as service levels, as part of the contract.

In deciding between alternatives, we should also cost the time required during the search for suitable products. In assessing benefits time is also important. Compare the different times experienced in delivery. In our travel example, for instance, trains are faster than coaches; air freight is quicker than sea for overseas orders. A fleet car purchase manager will probably look at a lowest total cost model when deciding what to purchase. This could include: manufacturer's recommended price; discount offered; payment terms (when payments due); additional features offered (service deals or radio cassettes fitted free, for example); delivery terms; cost of use (routine maintenance and running costs); convenience; reliability; lifespan; and resale value of cars at end of use by fleet. In addition, such aspects as acceptability to users, image and other psychological issues, and affordability will be considered.

It will be apparent, from these various examples, that it is almost impossible to list all the elements which will be considered by a purchaser. You might like to think of a recent purchase, and write down all the costs incurred by you in the *total* purchase.

From a marketer's point of view, it is vital to understand the way a potential buyer is likely to behave. You can then offer the right deal to attract purchasers for your product. In the 1970s Japanese cars were offered with fitted car radios, while most UK companies made their customers pay (then £20) for a radio. The actual cost of fitting in the factory was only £2, so for a small extra cost customers received a real benefit. This was one reason for the attractiveness of the first Toyotas because the company realised that most purchasers fitted radios when buying a new car.

The economist's price

In an economist's view of the marketplace, price is seen as the major factor determining the level of sales of a product. The theory suggests that demand for a product will rise dramatically if its price is reduced. The actual amount of change in demand is a factor of the 'elasticity' of the product (*see* Fig 14.1).

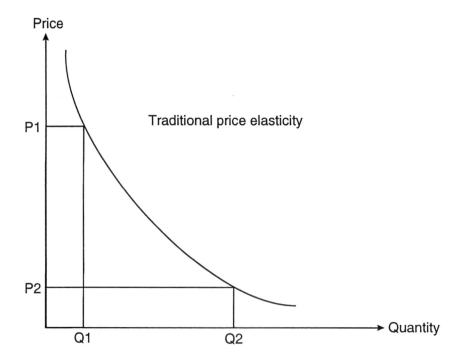

Fig 14.1 Traditional price elasticity

The demand for a product is said to be inelastic if the quantity sold hardly varies in spite of a substantial price change. This can be the case where there are few substitutes available. Such a product is heating oil for an oil-fired central heating system. It is too expensive to replace the system with gas, and, in cold weather, heat is required for the home. Hence the heating oil is purchased when required in the cold weather. Price is less important than the temperature in assessing the volume to be sold in the UK. However, even this example it is not completely straightforward. A study by a major oil company showed that householders in Germany, where they have larger domestic storage tanks installed, were very good at studying the oil market and buying when prices were low. In the UK, consumers generally purchase when the tank is nearly empty whatever the price, even though the difference of 1p/litre could mean £10 on a typical bill. So the UK market is more inelastic than the German market.

An elastic demand certainly occurs where a price rise is likely to frighten off a large number of customers who either do not buy at all, or purchase a substitute product.

$$\text{Price elasticity of demand} = \frac{\% \text{ change in quantity demanded}}{\% \text{ change in price}}$$

Of course, there are products which do not follow the basic economist's model. Perfume is an example. When 'Tweed' by Lentheric was re-launched in the 1970s the price was increased dramatically and a new presentation, including advertising, supported it. Volume *rose* by 40 per cent to make it then the UK's largest selling fragrance. There are also products such as 'Stella Artois' beer which are advertised as 'Reassuringly expensive'. Would volume increase if price was reduced or would consumers believe quality had also declined? More importantly, as profit is a multiplication of volume and margin, would total profit increase or reduce?

The traditional economist claims that prices should be set to maximise 'short-term' profits. This is said to be when 'marginal revenue', the increase in revenue for one extra unit of sale, is equivalent to 'marginal cost' of one extra unit of production. However, while this has a mathematic integrity, it fails to understand the marketing role of price in a competitive marketplace.

Example

The World's Most Expensive Perfume

In 1981, Thomas Fairfull left his work as owner of a small print shop in Ontario (Canada) to begin a cosmetics company, L'air D'or International Limited, which manufactures the world's costliest perfume. L'air D'or retails for $275 an ounce and contains flakes of 23-karat gold that leave traces on the wearer's skin. However, the company's eau de parfum, which retails for $59, makes up 80 per cent of the company's sales. L'air D'or has clients in London, the USA, and the Middle East, but the company is failing miserably in Canada, primarily because Canadians are wary of buying an unfamiliar product. Fairfull cannot afford the kind of advertising that Calvin Klein or Christian Dior buys. The Company is also subject to a law suit charging its name is too similar to Nina Ricci's L'Air du Temps brand. The presence of the top-priced product has, however, gained the company a great deal of free publicity so the role of price can be seen here in a different light.

Source: Canadian Business, January 1987

Price and competition

One reason for changes in both volume and price is action by competitors. The basic demand curve assumes all other facts remain constant. In reality they rarely do. At its simplest there can be a vicious circle as shown in Fig 14.2.

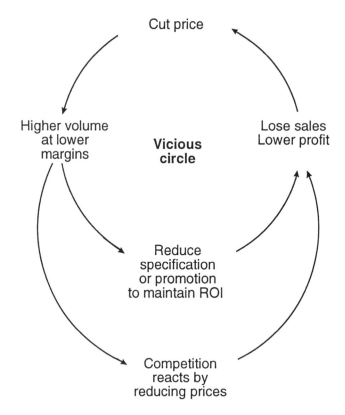

Fig 14.2 Vivious circle of prices: price-value cycle 1

It can easily be seen that such a competitive reaction, leading to a price war, would have a disastrous effect on an organisation. However, if you consider the situation from the point of view of one of your competitors, they do not want to lose sales because of *your* price cut. From your customers' position it all depends upon how they perceive value. This can be considered in the framework of buyer behaviour which is discussed in Chapter 5.

It is important that pricing decisions are made within the overall context of the marketing mix. Products rarely offer directly equivalent features, and, in fact, it is one of the roles of marketers to find ways of differentiating their product. This could be achieved through offering additional levels of service, so the customer can decide to place a value on the total offering, rather than directly comparing identical products. The subject of real, and total products is covered in Chapter 12. In the customer's decision process, the perceived value is a function of required features, and the price paid. The object is to achieve a virtuous circle (*see* Fig 14.3).

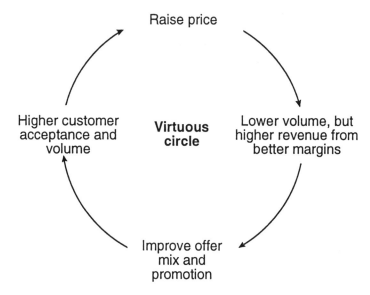

Fig 14.3 Virtuous circle of prices: price-value cycle 2

The level of competition varies from one product market to another. Some will have a large number of competing firms, other relatively few. Where there are many competitors, price (and other marketing) competition will be very severe. The other extreme is a monopoly, and perhaps that single supplier could fix his own price. The price set by a monopoly is, of course, modified by legislation and the Monopolies Commission.

In some competitive markets one or two companies emerge as leaders. The level of prices they charge can become the norm for the market. Smaller firms take their lead from these larger organisations without direct collusion, but most only move price when the leaders change. A study of the price of petrol will show how such a market operates.

To show that a competitive price does not always ensure a sale we could perhaps look at the fmcg (fast moving consumer goods) market for a product such as instant coffee. Some shoppers search for low-priced brands, or own label products, while others remain loyal to premium brands, such as Maxwell House or Nescafé. This could be because consumers think Nescafé is a better product; after all Nescafé advertise that their instant coffee is 'better' than shop's own label. It is not necessarily better, as companies such as Marks & Spencer or Sainsbury have very high quality standards which they impose on suppliers of products, including instant coffee. However, there is no doubt about the good quality of Nescafé instant coffee, but even Nescafé offer different blends at different prices. Of course, another reason for the success of Nescafé is the marketing strength of the actual brand name. This will be discussed elsewhere, but the value of a brand name is being recognised by some companies who are valuing brand names and including the valuation on their balance sheets.

The major accounting bodies also now realise the marketing value of brand names as an asset to a company. It is surprising, therefore, that in relation to the offering to the customers, there is still a blinkered view in many companies that prices must be based on costs.

Price and costs

Decisions on price are of crucial importance to all organisations since, as stated already, it is the only element in the marketing mix which brings an input to the company. It is too important to decide price on some automatic formula based solely on cost. It is also too important to be left to accountants, or salespeople, or even marketing managers in isolation. Charles Dickens gave good Victorian advice when Mr Micawber, having been through a debtors prison, says to David Copperfield:

> Annual income twenty pounds, annual expenditure nineteen nineteen six, result happiness. Annual income twenty pounds, expenditure twenty pounds ought and six, result misery ... and in short you are for ever floored.

Of course costs must be used to set a bottom line below which prices cannot go. Organisations can just as easily be floored if they spend more than they receive. But there can, of course, be a case for including a loss leader in a range, and using such products to develop customers while making profit on other items. The use of portfolio planning to ensure an overall profit for the company will be considered later.

Another area where low prices are justified can be the hope of high, extra sales reducing costs, so allowing profits. This could be possible in a new product situation. But price is still a marketing issue. The benefit of volume on costs is part of the total budget for a company. It is difficult to always make profits immediately upon launching a new product. In particular, development costs can be high and will probably take time to recover. The proper planning of profit-making and loss-making products is covered in Chapter 21 on marketing planning and control.

A variety of cost-based formula have been developed by organisations. The survey by CIMA, mentioned earlier, shows these are still widely used. The simplest version is to calculate the total cost, including all overheads, and add a set percentage for profit. This is known as 'cost-plus' pricing. This is justified on the basis that a satisfactory profit can always be achieved. But although this method seems straightforward, it does rely on the ways costs are calculated in an organisation, as well as reflecting any inefficiencies in operating that organisation. The biggest problem lies with allocating overheads since the basis for this allocation is, at best, arbitrary. Another area of uncertainty comes with the volume estimates, since the cost of producing 1000 units will be considerably different from producing 1 million units.

The biggest drawback with cost-plus pricing is that it takes no account of how customers might value a product, nor how competitors might price their version of the product. The National Health Service in the UK is currently suffering from this type of problem as different hospitals try to work out the price to charge for basic operations. The cost of a simple operation can vary by over ±£600 on a £1000 average across a number of hospitals. It is, of course, necessary to work out costs accurately to help efficient running of organisations. The message, however, must be:

Costs are about PRODUCTION
Prices are about VALUE

One important calculation relating cost, prices, and volume is the calculation of the so called break-even point for a product. This can be explored in standard accounting texts and we will look at a sample break-even calculation here. Figure 14.4 illustrates the break-even point.

The break-even point is the level at which the cost of producing a product or service equals the revenue from selling it.

Assume a manufacturer has fixed costs of £1m. He sells his products at £3 each and the variable costs of manufacture and sale are £2. He will make £1 (£3 less £2) on every product sold. To 'break-even' and to cover the fixed cost he will have to sell 1 million units.

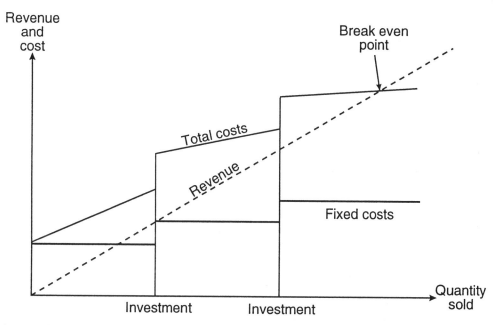

Fig 14.4 The break-even point

To use break-even analysis effectively, it is necessary to calculate a break-even point for several alternative prices. However, great care must be taken in using break-even analysis as it does assume inelastic demand. This might be a fair assumption over a small change in price, but not over a large variation.

The calculation of break-even allows us to look at another cost-based pricing method called 'marginal cost pricing'. The marginal cost, or variable cost, of a product is the extra cost an organisation suffers in producing one more unit of that product - in our example above, £2 per unit. We could decide to add an agreed mark-up to this to determine our price. So if we suggest a 50 per cent mark-up then, given a £2 marginal cost, the mark-up will be £1, and the final price £3.

(£2 + (50% x £2) = £2 + £1 = £3)

Some retailers use a version of this when calculating prices. However, experience, when dealing with companies like major high street retailers, suggests they sometimes start with the price they want to sell at and then work back. They calculate the necessary margins on selling prices of 99 pence for instance. They are then able to tell suppliers what they will pay for supplies. This is only possible because of the strength of the large supermarkets, compared to some smaller companies who supply them. Marginal price deals are sometimes done, with selected customers, to stimulate demand, or to develop business with those chosen customers. The problem with marginal costing is that it only guarantees a gross profit per unit, but it does not guarantee a *net profit* from *total sales*.

John Winkler, a noted authority on pricing, states that if 'cost-plus pricing will generally keep you in business, marginal costing can easily put you out of it'. He goes on to suggest: 'Never do it if it will set a precedent for the long run with your biggest customers', 'Never do it if news of low price deals will spread in the market', 'Never do it if it commits you to extra capital cost in the short run, or long run', 'Never do it if it uses up scarce resources you need elsewhere', 'Never do it if you have to sacrifice some full profit business to fit it in', and 'Never delegate discretion on marginal pricing decisions down the line. Anyone can give products away, the aim of marketing is profitable business'.

To re-emphasise the point that costs are related to supply, and prices to demand in the competitive marketplace, we can look at the recent recession in the UK car market. Sales in 1991 were some 20 to 30 per cent below 1990 levels. Many more cars were built than could be sold. If costs were based on manufactured volumes, then there is no guarantee that margins from sales will be sufficient to cover overheads, and in fact most companies made a loss during the year. To stimulate demand the manufacturers tried a number of short term offers. Many of these involved prices. For instance, Ford reduced the price on small models by up to £1000, and on Granadas by £2000. Vauxhall offered a US style 'cash back' of up to £1500 with every car sold. A Vauxhall spokesperson said, 'this method means we don't have to change the list price so that residual values (car's value at resale) are not affected'. Other manufacturers took alternative action, for instance Renault offered a 'Diamond Deal' promotion offering a reduced rate of VAT, zero per cent financing and optional extras.

Although reducing prices stimulates demand, it must be handled very carefully. Remembering the advice from Mr Micawber, say a car is priced at £10 000 and the manufacturer makes a gross profit of 18 per cent and net profit before tax of 7 per cent. If price is reduced by £1000 (just 10 per cent of reduction in price) we get the following effect.

Revenue	£10 000	£9000
Cost of goods	£8200	£8200
Gross profit	£1800 (18%)	£800 (8.9%)
Other costs	£1100	£1100
Net profit before tax	£700 (7%)	(£300) (loss of 3%)

You see a reduction of 10 per cent in price turns a healthy profit into a loss.

To conclude this section on costs, it should be clear that costs have a role in the determining of price. However, costs alone should not determine selling prices. The costs provide a bottom line to guide the pricing decision.

Price and organisational objectives

Marketing decisions must be consistent with the total organisational objectives. Pricing decisions are just one of the marketing decisions. Obviously, if the organisation has a target return on investment, you can see the link to pricing. However, organisational objectives could be: 'Pile it high and sell it cheap' as coined by the founder of Tesco, Sir John Cohen. If your organisation has this latter objective all its operations must be designed to supply volume at low prices. More recently Tesco has changed its philosophy to compete more effectively with Sainsbury's. Sainsbury's position is encapsulated in the line, 'Good food costs less at Sainsbury's. This slogan includes both price and quality in a statement of value directly related to customers.

Example

Pricing a service

Two former secretaries have set up a secretarial and bookkeeping service on a local trading estate. It offers basic services to the small companies on the estate. The major expense is the salaries of the two partners, and one employee, a word processing operator. Overheads include office rent and rates, and the maintenance of office equipment such as computers, fax machine, answerphone, etc. There is also the interest on the bank loan used to buy equipment. The organisation is really offering 'time' carrying out routine tasks. They calculate the overheads are £15 200 per annum, the employee is paid £6000 (including employee-related costs) and the two partners draw £1000 per month each. Total running costs for stationery, telephone bills, postage are a further £10 000 giving a total £55 200 per annum.

There are 230 working days per year if we eliminate weekends and holidays. But no-one works at 100%; 80% is still good, so if we assume 184 days each (80% x 230) for the *three* productive workers there are 552 working days each year. To just break even they need to charge £100 per working day. What do you think they should charge clients?

Price and quality

The eight dimensions of quality proposed by David Garvin in a 1987 article in the *Harvard Business Review* are:

- **Performance** – which refers to a product's primary operating characteristic.
- **Features** – the 'bells and whistles', those characteristics that supplement basic functioning.
- **Reliability** – the probability of a product malfunctioning during a specified time period.
- **Conformance** – the degree to which design of operating characteristics meet established standards.
- **Durability** – a measure of product life with both economic and technical dimensions.
- **Serviceability** – relating to the ease of maintenance.
- **Aesthetics** – how a product looks, feels, sounds, tastes or smells - personal judgement comes in here.
- **Perceived quality** – as consumers do not always have complete information to judge a product or service (amateur buyer), perception of quality, reputation or other intangibles are important in judging how customers rate your offering in their value equation.

You might offer your own measures of quality and how they help to add value to an offering. These dimensions, however, are a good basis for such discussions. Figure 14.5 shows a balance between quality of offerings and the benefits for an organisation.

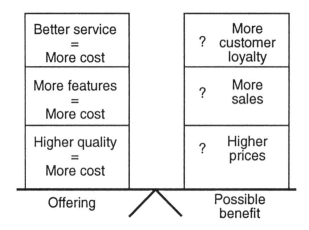

Fig 14.5 The trade-off between the quality of offerings and the benefits for organisations

There is a trade-off between price and quality at the basic level. To add features can cost money and this is not always recovered in profit in sales. However, the relationship is not that simple, and programmes such as zero defects are often very positive when assessing costs. But price should not be dependent on costs, but on customers' evaluation of value. Of course some aspects of quality can increase this evaluation; others will not do so. The balance between quality and price should be considered in the context of profit, level of sales, and organisational positioning. It is not an easy equation but it is vital in an integrated marketing offering.

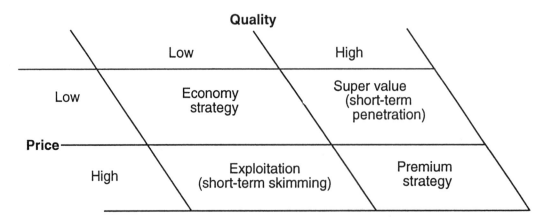

Fig 14.6 Price/quality strategies

Pricing strategies

Figure 14.6 links the *price* to the *quality* of an offered product or service. Quality is a very difficult factor to measure. However, you should now realise that other elements of the marketing mix add to the 'quality' of value of the offering. It is useful to remind ourselves that: **'quality' is remembered long after the 'price' is forgotten**.

Premium pricing

A 'premium strategy' uses a high price, but gives good product/service in exchange. It is fair to customers, and, more importantly, customers see it as fair. This could include food bought from Marks & Spencer, or designer clothes, or a Mercedes car. We should remember that customers for consumer goods are often *amateurs*. They do not really know how to judge value. They build up a perception of such value, and sometimes use price to help establish levels of 'quality'. If you saw a new Mercedes car on offer at your local garage with a sign saying 'half price offer' you might be suspicious about what you are being offered. If the offer were a Zil, which is a Russian luxury limousine, you might perhaps have less scepticism if it were offered at half price. But then you would worry about servicing and reliability.

An industrial buyer could have more knowledge of the technical characteristics of his purchases. In many cases tight specifications on the performance of machinery are used for buying in this area. But not all industrial purchases are professionally assessed, although no-one should underestimate the ability of customers to assess value. Nevertheless, sometimes the benefits of a product need to be presented in a way that will help a buyer to make a buying decision. Remember, marketing is about making it easier for the customer to say 'yes'.

In considering which car a company should use for its sales force, the car fleet manager mentioned at the beginning of this chapter might consider the lowest total cost over the life of 70 000 miles. It might be the resale value of a Ford Sierra which gained it a superior rating to an equivalent car from another supplier. The car fleet buyer might be a professional, but might still require help to appreciate the total value of what is offered to him.

Penetration pricing

'Penetration' pricing is the name given to a strategy that deliberately starts offering 'super value'. This is done to gain a foothold in a market, using price as a major weapon. It could be because other products are already well established in the market, maybe at high prices. Alternatively, penetration pricing could be used as an attempt to gain a major share of a new market. It can also deter competitors who see no profit in the market.

As time goes on and the product is established prices can be raised nearer market levels. Alternatively, the supplier's cost could come down as volume increases. In this case the consumer benefits by a continuation of the low prices.

Example
British Motorcycles dominated the world market in the 1950s. In 1970 only 1 per cent of the UK market was 'made in Britain'. Honda, Yamaha, Kawasaki and Suzuki now supply over 90 per cent of the market. Honda first achieved recognition by taking

the manufacturer's prize in the Isle of Man TT races in 1959. But their market entry was achieved with small motorcycles, sold at low prices that competitors could not match. In 1975 the Boston Consulting Group studied the industry worldwide on behalf of the British Government. Table 14.1 shows the production levels they found.

Table 14.1
Motorcycle production levels worldwide

Country	Company	Output	Motorcycles per man/year
UK	Small Heath/Meriden	38 500	12
Italy	Motoguzzi	40 000	13
USA	Harley Davidson	50 000	15
Germany	BMW	25 000	20
Japan	Honda	2 000 000	280
Japan	Yamaha	1 000 000	200

While figures are not directly comparable, the high volume has dramatically reduced Honda's costs. They can make a good profit, and still retain their low prices. This lower price has now become the new normal level for pricing motorcycles, not only in the UK, but also worldwide.

Penetration pricing must be used carefully as it is very difficult to raise prices to catch up with the market levels. There are many examples of products launched at a low price, but which lost significant sales volume when prices rose. It is sometimes possible to offer customers an initial discount to gain business provided you make it clear prices will rise later. Building societies have been offering discounted mortgages to first time buyers at 1 per cent reduction for the first twelve months. But after that they rise to commercial rates.

Economy price

'Economy pricing' is a deliberate strategy of low pricing. It could be that you are offering a 'no frills' product/service, with a price reflecting this. However, before such a product is launched, it is important to decide the position it will have in the marketplace. That position is how you want your customers to perceive it. A product that competes purely on price is vulnerable to attack from more established products.

This happened when Sir Freddie Laker launched his 'Sky Train' trans-Atlantic flights in the 1970s. Competitors such as British Airways, Pan Am, and others, reduced some of their prices. Laker found he could not sustain his flights profitably as passengers chose the most convenient of the cheap flights available. Laker went bankrupt, although later the receivers for his company claimed damages from other airlines. More recently 'Peoples Express', an American carrier – has also suffered from an unsustainable economy policy.

The Victorian philosopher John Ruskin (1819–1900) once said

It is unwise to pay too much, but it is unwise to pay too little. When you pay too much, you lose a little money, that is all. When you pay too little, you sometimes lose everything, because the thing you bought was incapable of doing the thing you bought it to do.

The common law of Business Balance prohibits paying a little and getting a lot. It can't be done. If you deal with the lowest bidder, it is as well to add something for the risk you run. And if you do that, you will have enough to pay for something better.

Of course, there is legislation, such as the Sale of Goods Act, which demands a product must be fit for the purpose for which it is sold. Nevertheless, Ruskin's point is taken sensibly from a customer's position, and all suppliers would do well to take heed of it.

Price skimming

We do not need to discuss 'exploitation' in detail. Customers won't pay if they don't think they are getting value. However there are times when high prices and large margins are appropriate. It is certainly easier to reduce prices than to raise them. A policy of 'price skimming' is often used for products at the introductory stage. Here the price is initially pitched high, which gives a good early cash flow to offset high development costs. If the product is new, and competition has not appeared, then customers might well pay a premium to acquire a product which is offering excellent features. The launch of many home computers showed this pattern. As competitors came into the market, and new features were added by the new entrants, prices dropped for all products.

Another market with high margins is the drug market. The prescription drug market uses fairly cheap basic ingredients. The cost of developing medicines is high, and made even higher by the cost of testing, and gaining approval, from the regulatory bodies. The prices are high when new drugs are launched and they are protected by patents. When the patent runs out, 'generic' drugs come in to compete and prices fall. This official monopoly, based on the legal protection of a patent, is a reflection of the unique effort in developing a new drug. It is certainly justified by the costs involved.

Psychological pricing

'Psychological' pricing is designed to get customers to respond on an emotional, rather than rational basis. It is most frequently seen in consumer markets, having less applicability in industrial markets. The most common is the use of prices such as 99 pence or £9.95 which can be seen in many retail outlets. We all know that 99 pence is £1.00 less 1pence, and £9.95 is £10 less 5pence.

Why do you think such prices are used?

In some markets companies are over sensitive about price levels. Cadbury's were conscious of this with their bar chocolate. To maintain prices, as raw material costs rose, they reduced the thickness of the chocolate blocks. The result was thin chocolate bars. Rowntrees spotted this and decided Cadbury's had gone too far. Rowntrees saw an opportunity for a chunky product. Yorkie was launched with great success.

Petrol companies were very worried about the effect of prices rising above £2 per gallon. They could not give reduced volume but had the advantage of metrication. New prices are often given in pence per litre (£2.00 per gallon = 44p per litre). Now as prices approach 50p per litre we are seeing prices such as 49.9p rather than break the 50p barrier. It is likely that once past 50p prices could rise without such a worry.

Product line pricing

'Product-line' pricing is a strategy which involves all products offered. There may be a range of normal price points in a market. A supplier might decide to design a product suitable for all price levels, offering opportunities for a range of purchases. For instance, a basic Mars bar retails for about 24p (local CTN), a multi-pack of five bars 94p (Sainsbury), and a multi-pack of mini-Mars bars at £1.99 (Sainsbury). The price points are 24p, 94p and £1.99. (These prices were correct in early 1992. You should check the prices now, and see how each price level fits into the range of Mars products available.)

Pricing variations

'Off-peak' pricing and other variants, such as early booking discounts, stand by prices and group discounts are used in particular circumstances. They are all well-known in the travel trade but it is also appropriate to use different prices such as these in other industries. You could argue that an off-peak journey, say a rail journey to London one Tuesday afternoon, is not the same 'product' as one during the morning rush period. In the customer's eyes it is a different product. If you have to be in London by 9.00am you cannot travel in the afternoon. Certainly, 'stand-by' prices represent a different product as there is no guarantee of travel. The opposite is an early booking price which not only ensures travel is reserved, but can offer the supplier a guarantee of a known demand.

Pricing in industrial markets

Industrial products can be ones purchased for resale, or they can be raw materials which can be incorporated into manufactured products. Alternatively, they can be installations or consumables used in industrial operations. When dealing in this market, there are other considerations affecting all aspects of the marketing mix, including pricing strategies.

Consumables are the convenience goods of the industrial market. However, there is no need for fancy packaging to attract shoppers like in a supermarket. They therefore tend to have basic packing for protection, and can often be supplied in multiple packs. The price will reflect this. In addition, there may be a quantity discount, although this is more usual with raw materials. Certainly the business is usually done on credit, but it is common to offer discounts to customers who pay their invoice within (say) ten days.

Installations are more likely to be negotiated, with all the requirements costed to give a price specific to the customer's requirement. There is no role for psychological pricing, but it is common for the sales negotiators to be given some freedom in the price to be charged. In these types of negotiated situations the sales force can be rewarded according to profit achieved, and they certainly need to know the limits within which they can negotiate.

Raw materials will be regular purchases, and it is probably more important that suppliers are reliable. Customers will be prepared to pay a little extra to a known, and trusted, supplier rather than risk supply problems. Of course, a customer may operate a policy of dual sourcing so as to compare competition prices. If the supplier builds up a strong relationship with the customer, then a good exchange of information takes place, and prices are continually discussed along with other issues. There may be an annual contract between supplier and customer which confirms price for the whole year. The contract might have a rebate clause which allows for a discount if volume exceeds an agreed figure. As industrial markets are distinguished by smaller numbers of partners and larger orders, many of their contracts are individually negotiated and over-riding discounts are built into the agreement.

Many of the above pricing methods are possible because industrial markets have much more direct contact between supplier and customer through the wide use of direct personal selling in these markets.

There is one very difficult area of industrial marketing where direct selling is not a factor. This is when suppliers are invited to submit a tender for a contract offered by a large customer, who may be a local authority or a government department. In this situation the customer specifies what they want, and asks a number of suppliers to submit a bid. In this situation it is necessary not only to carry out detailed costing on what is required, but also to understand who else is bidding. Then a policy can be worked out based on the knowledge of competition, as well as how badly your organisation wants the contract. The final price is therefore a marketing decision, and not based solely on costs.

Recently the TV area franchises were put out to tender for 1993. Central TV correctly surmised they would be unopposed so put in a very low tender. However, TVS failed to hold onto their franchise in spite of submitting a bid well above the competitors. This was because the awarding committee felt it was too high for the company to continue to provide the level of quality required in the future.

Distributor pricing

Many producers are not in direct contact with their customers. They will use indirect channels of distribution, perhaps via wholesalers or other intermediaries. No product is finally sold until it reaches the eventual consumer. So it is the final price to the final purchaser which is the measure of value. You might have recently bought a birthday card for one of your friends, maybe paying, say, 89p in a card shop. This might seem expensive for a small piece of printed cardboard, and an envelope. Even if we know 13p is the VAT charged by the government, it still seems a lot. But remember the printing company will probably have sold the card at 38p (excluding VAT) allowing the card shop to double the price. In this business 100 per cent mark-ups are usual, and can be justified by the relatively low turnover of individual designs. Also, as customers consider the purchase in relation to a more expensive present, the price is considered acceptable in spite of the retailer mark-up.

The problem many producers face is how to control the eventual selling price of their product. At one time it was possible to insist on the final selling price, but now this is not possible in most industries. Therefore producers must understand the way distributors add margins so that they can judge the effect on the final selling price of any action taken further up the distributive chain.

Pricing and its relation to the marketing mix

In this chapter price has not been considered in isolation but as one key part of the marketing mix. The word 'affordability' was used at an earlier point, but although this introduced the customer view it does not encompass the full area of value. The price is what is paid as part of the exchange process (see Fig 14.7), being passed from customer to supplier either as money or in kind. What is received by the customer is the composite of the other elements of the marketing mix. This is an acceptable product, conveniently available so that the customer feels it is well worth the price asked. It is therefore essential that price is put into the wider context of the total marketing mix. If a product is made more attractive (added value by additional features), it makes that product more valuable to customers. Similarly, a service could be made more readily available and thus more valuable to customers. In this case it might be possible to raise prices to reflect the increase in value. Alternatively the enhanced value could lead to additional sales. The decision about additional features must be taken by managers who realise the way consumers measure value, and not simply by saying the additional features have increased costs hence prices must rise.

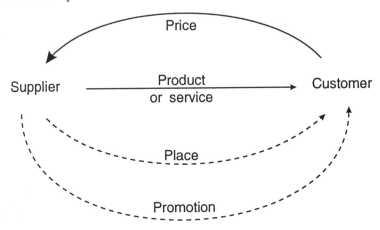

Fig 14.7 Price in the exchange process - the only element of the marketing mix received by suppliers

Accountants are used to cost/benefit analysis in other parts of their work, but where price is concerned it is essential to do a cost/benefit analysis *for the customer*: cost to the customer being price from the supplier; benefit to the customer a measure of quality offering.

Price and the product life cycle

You have already studied how a product develops through its product life cycle. At different stages there are different competitive pressures, and differences in the way customers evaluate a product/service. For a new product (the first in the market) a 'skimming' policy could be appropriate. However, in a competitive, declining market with a mature product a different strategy is relevant.

Exercise

Select a product you have bought in the last month. Decide where it is in its product life cycle. What is the range of prices for competitive products and where does the product you bought fit in?
Why do you think this is so?
What pricing strategy do you think the supplier is pursuing?

Conclusion - the art of pricing

Pricing is a management decision with a large marketing input. It also involves accountants, salespeople and probably the Managing Director. The objectives for the organisation will influence management policy. All organisations need to establish a framework within which to operate. This will provide the limits for their decisions. Figure 14.8 is quite useful in this respect.

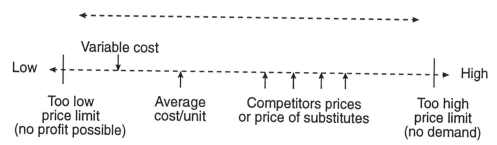

Fig 14.8 A pricing framework

The actual limits for the high and low points are still a matter of judgement, but the key points of competitors' prices can often be established to give reference points. But it is not always possible to establish the real price competitors charge as the 'price-list price' only tells part of the story. Winkler lists ten ways to 'increase' prices without increasing prices. These are

1   Revise the discount structure.
2   Change the minimum order size.
3   Charge for delivery and special services.
4   Invoice for repairs on purchased equipment.
5   Charge for engineering, installation, supervision.
6   Make customers pay for overtime required to get out rush orders.
7   Collect interest on overdue accounts.
8   Produce less of the lower margin models in the product line.
9   Write escalator clauses into contracts.
10 Change the physical characteristics of the product.

Obviously not all these are available in every market. However, the fact that such a list is possible shows how involved pricing decisions really are.

Questions

1   Some companies price a product at £9.99 or £19.99. What are the advantages and disadvantages of such prices?

2   Why do customers sometimes believe high prices indicate high quality products?

3 Explain the reasons behind 'off peak pricing'.

4 What are the drawbacks to using penetration pricing as the main strategy in entering a new market?

References

Boston Consulting Group *Strategy Alternatives for the British Motorcycle Industry*, HMSO 1975.
Chartered Institute of Management Accountants *Survey on Price*, 1988.
Garvin, D A, 'Competing in the eight dimensions of quality', *Harvard Business Review*, Nov/Dec 1987, pp 101-99.
Winkler, J, *Pricing in The Marketing Book*, pp 251–70 (Ed M J Baker), Heinemann, 1987.

Case study: price, quality and value

St Thomas' Island Hotel

James Clarke had just completed his first year as Manager of the St Thomas' Island Hotel on the south coast of Cornwall. Although not on an island it was situated on a headland next to an excellent sandy beach with magnificent views of the coast and out to sea. It was also close to a local sailing centre where many boats were moored. For James this had been his first management job after a degree in Hotel Management and four years' experience with the Moat House Hotels group. The hotel itself had recently been run by receivers after the previous owner had gone bankrupt. It had now been purchased by a Cornishman who was also a top London banker with romantic dreams of his birthplace but a hard headed attitude to business. At the interview when James had been appointed the objectives had been made clear.

'The hotel must break even in the first twelve months and go into profit thereafter. I am sure you will understand that if you fail to achieve this your position as Manager will not be tenable.'

The hotel itself had 70 rooms all with ensuite facilities. It had been owned by a number of different proprietors in the last ten years and each had added to the facilities without spoiling the front appearance of the hotel nor the ten acres of woodland which it owned on the northern approach to the building. It had two tennis courts, and a croquet lawn outside, and a fitness room, sauna, and a billiards room in the west-wing extension, which also contained 50 of the bedrooms. The main building housed two excellent bars – the Pirates and the Swag – along with a restaurant capable of seating all guests at the same time.

John was now considering his first year-results where he had just met his target, but not because the occupancy rate was anywhere near break even level. At the beginning of October when no guests were actually booked, a conference organiser had phoned having to relocate following a fire at one of the bigger hotels. All rooms full for seven days in October, was a real bonus, but James had still felt it proper to charge *in excess* of the full room rate, especially since he had to hire in a marquee as a temporary conference hall. Luckily the weather had been kind and the event had gone very well.

The results for year one are shown below. Much of the bar profits were as a result of the conference delegates who did a lot of business in the bar.

Receipts	£	
11 500 room nights @ £35 per night (average)	402 500	(half board)
Conference one week @ £60 per night	29 400	(full board)
Bar profits	15 000	
Total	£446 900	
Expenses		
Staff and related costs	210 000	
Food and drink	135 000	
Utilities		
Building maintenance	60 000	
Other supplies		
Advertising and brochures	10 000	
Miscellaneous items	30 000	
	£445 000	

For next year James realises he cannot rely on a repeat conference. Anyway the hotel is not really equipped for such events. However, he has received a request from a national coach company for three months' block booking (May to July) at £2000 per night for up to 65 rooms, including dinner, breakfast and a packed lunch for all guests. While James is aware this will put his food bill up he hopes he will recoup some of the cost with increased bar profits. Although the £184 000 would be useful guaranteed revenue against only £140 000 taken during the same period in year one, James has some doubts.

Many guests on leaving after their holidays had told him how much they had enjoyed the hotel and the excellent service they had received. He even had a number of pre-bookings from guests who wished to return during the spring and summer, and he wondered how they would react to a coach party. He would also need to achieve again the full bookings for August and Christmas, which contributed a quarter of the year one's revenue. However, the figures also showed that from the end of October through to March the hotel was rarely more than 20 per cent full except for the Christmas period. This obviously offered opportunities for growth.

James has until the end of the week to decide on the coach company contract. What would you advise him to do?

15

MAKING PRODUCTS AVAILABLE

If you build a better mousetrap the world will beat a path to your door
Ralph Waldo Emerson

Introduction

The quote above, by an American philosopher, is far from the truth in markets where supply exceeds demand. Obviously it is important to communicate with potential customers about your products, and the key benefits they offer. There are only a few products which customers will make the effort to seek out. For this to happen it has to be a product that the purchaser really values. Such a product, one which potential customers value, could be based on exclusivity, for example, a designer dress, or an individually crafted piece of jewellery, or perhaps another type of 'aspirational' product. There are really very few products where customers will beat a path to your door. It is therefore very important that products are made readily available to customers. Marketing has already been described as 'Making it easier for your customers to say "yes". Certainly the decision to purchase can be helped by making products available where potential customers can find them.

If the product required is specialised, or maybe one that needs to be made to an individual design as is common in industrial markets, then experienced purchasing officers will use all their skills to locate a potential supplier with the necessary abilities. Here they might 'beat a path to your door'. But this is unusual and this search is not necessarily going to find all organisations which can fulfil the requirements. It will be more likely to find those organisations which take positive action to develop channels linking them to potential customers.

The purchasing department must procure the right goods, at the right time, in the correct quantities, at the right price. The key decisions of the purchaser or the purchasing organisation regarding which goods to purchase will be taken to meet the objectives of the purchaser or the purchasing organisation. You might consider the role of a buyer for Sainsbury responsible for jams and marmalade and how his or her actions would affect both a major supplier and a customer for this product.

Example

Let's say that you were trying to purchase a jar of jam. You would probably go to your local grocer's shop. In the price list published by *The Grocer Magazine* there are 13 suppliers listed, but in an outlet of Sainsbury visited in early 1992, there were only the following five brands in stock.

Sainsbury own label
Robertsons
Duerrs
Nelsons
Wilkins Tiptree.

Hartleys is one of the brands not stocked by Sainsbury. The problem Hartleys have is how do they reach potential customers, especially those who do most of their shopping at Sainsbury. Certainly few, if any, of these potential customers will try to visit the Hartleys factory in Cambridge. So Hartleys have either to change Sainsbury's decision regarding the brands the supermarket group are prepared to stock, or find an alternative way of getting close to potential customers.

This example considers how to make products easily available to customers, and it might suggest a sales-based solution. In fact it also highlights the fact that while Sainsbury's are a potential customer for Hartleys, the final consumer is in fact a customer of the retailer. The term *trade marketing* is used regarding that part of the exchange process between supplier and intermediary. It is as important a marketing job as dealing with final consumers. The specific role of the intermediary will be discussed later in this chapter. But this example also highlights what are called distribution channels (*see* Fig 15.1), which are the links connecting (marketing) organisations and through which goods or services are transferred from the original producer to the final consumer.

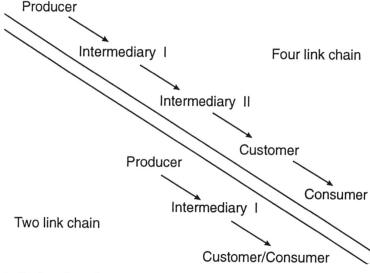

Fig 15.1 Distribution channels

Distribution, when considered by a marketer, is not merely concerned with physical distribution. It covers:

- the choice of channels – direct or indirect;
- decisions on whether to use a single channel or several different (complementary) ones;
- decisions on how to make those channels available;
- decisions on building relationships with intermediaries;
- ownership and investment within the channels.

The problem of channel choice is not restricted to physical products alone, but can just as easily apply to a service. Consider a student insurance policy made available through an insurance broker, such as Endsleigh Insurance. It is covered in the 4 Ps of marketing by the word *place*. But place really does not describe all the elements involved in the task of making products easily available to customers. These include:

1 Bringing customers into contact with offered products/services.
2 Offering a sufficient choice to meet customers' needs.
3 Persuading customers to develop a favourable attitude to a particular product.
4 Maintaining adequate levels of sales both for your organisation, and if appropriate, for the intermediaries.
5 Providing appropriate services and information to help purchase decisions.
6 Maintaining an acceptable price, including the payments to members of the distribution channel.

Selection of channels

The prime aim of any marketing decision relating to distribution channels is how to reach the relevant customers. This must be in the most appropriate way given the following four major considerations:

1 Potential customers' requirements
2 Your organisational resources
3 Competitors' and distributors' actions
4 Legal constraints.

Peter Chisnall wrote in his book, *Strategic Industrial Marketing,*

Products of all types must be readily available to customers. Established firms are likely to have well defined channels of distribution, with which they may have particularly strong links because of efficient servicing. In other cases, a widespread network of exclusive distributors may be very difficult for a newcomer to challenge, or build up from scratch. Perhaps a *non-traditional channel* of distribution may offer new entrants an opportunity to develop business.

Established firms do indeed have well-defined channels. These channels often establish the norm for that particular market. While such channels will clearly differ from market to market, the channels themselves develop from the exchange between suppliers and customers. They then come to fit the needs of many customers and again become the expected norm. Such arrangements are usually of a long-term nature, and can prove a challenge to new entrants as described by Chisnall.

Customer requirements

The choice of efficient distribution channels relies on a knowledge of a particular market. But more specifically, on the needs and wants of customers. It may not be possible to satisfy everything a particular customer wants, but that customer's decision is likely to be based on issues such as cost, convenience, and availability. We could look at the different ways in which varying types of food retailer might offer a particular food item for sale.

Example

An out-of-town hypermarket might offer two different brands at a good price (especially if one is its own brand). The hypermarket will support it by long opening hours including an increasing number of outlets open on Sunday (in spite of the complicated law on Sunday opening in the UK). In fact the term *place* does not just refer to the location as might be imagined, but also such issues as opening hours which are equally critical to *availability* and, therefore, to customer decisions.

The problems facing most customers are (a) travel to the hypermarket which could be difficult without a car, and (b) the long queues at the checkout if your visit is at a busy time.

A town-centre store such as Marks & Spencer will offer only its own brand, but it is likely to be slightly more expensive. Marks & Spencer trade on their quality position and not their price. The store might be more convenient to a customer being in a town centre, but that is not always so. Also, Marks & Spencer is not open especially late, and not open at all on Sundays. A neighbourhood store, owner managed but perhaps a member of a buying group like Spar, will have limited choice. They probably stock just one branded product, offered for sale at its recommended retail price. But such a store could be near urban housing, and is likely to be open for even longer hours than the hypermarket.

The decision facing potential customers is how they rate the different elements of cost and convenience. The supplier of the food product will perhaps see no conflict in supplying all three types of retailers. The attempt by the supplier to obtain maximum coverage is termed intensive distribution. This is the strategy of giving the product the maximum exposure possible, so that it has the best chance of being found by a customer. However, the supplier is likely to put greatest effort into trying to develop the channel which offers the greatest return. In supplying the hypermarket it is likely that a direct approach will be used. But to supply the neighbourhood store they will probably supply in an indirect way via a wholesaler or Cash and Carry.

Opening times are relevant to the availability decision of customers for such diverse organisations as public libraries and supermarkets. The restrictions on local authority budgets has been blamed for shorter library opening hours, as well as a more limited 'product' due to less spending on new books. However, the visible result is fewer books are being borrowed. It is possible to argue that the reason also has something to do with the ever increasing presence of substitute products such as TV or video. While marketing is not a term used by many in the library service, the need to satisfy customers is still a key requirement. The use of mobile libraries over many years was one way libraries found of increasing availability. The reduction of opening hours in some towns is the opposite.

Opening hours are also a key competitive issue and Sir Dennis Landau of the Cooperative Wholesale Society commented on it when discussing illegal Sunday trading: 'There is no virtue in remaining legal and going broke in the process'. It might be interesting to discuss this in relation to competitive business in general.

The maximum availability of food products, via all chosen channels, is desirable for the food supplier. If the product is not on sale when required then potential customers could buy an alternative (competitor's) food item. Here there could be an alternative for the customer but the supplier loses a sale. In the library example, a customer might be annoyed if the product was unavailable when required. That could influence future behaviour and decisions.

The situation is very different in an industrial setting for a specialist component required by a manufacturer. The production line could be brought to a halt if the component is not available when required. In the past, firms invested working capital in buffer stocks, but such costs are increasingly being reduced as companies change to sophisticated supply chain systems such as JIT (just in time). This type of supply chain can only work if there is a close partnership between supplier and customer. Decisions by the customer on whether to source locally, or perhaps import cheaper components, would be determined by issues of convenience and availability. Hence such a situation provides an interesting challenge for the marketing department of a potential supplying company. For this reason knowledge of customers' behaviour is critical to decisions on suitable channels of distribution.

Organisational resources

The choice of channels has to be consistent with the needs and capabilities of the organisation as well as meeting the needs of customers. It might be considered necessary for a qualified person to install a more technical product such as a gas fire or a heavy duty machine. In this case suitable channels might be restricted to those where such a service is available. The producer could, of course, set up a network of wholly owned outlets. That is, however, very expensive. It may be beyond the resources of a producer and it could also be an inefficient way of achieving the objectives.

An organisation will normally first make decisions on the market segments to which they want to offer their product. However, as has already been discussed, there is likely to be an ongoing need for market information to be fed back to the original supplier. In view of this, it could be decided to work with a particular type of channel which will facilitate the process. The channels used by major car companies to distribute their products have recently been in the news. Nissan are attempting to replace an agent who has sole rights to market Nissan cars in the UK with a new network controlled by the Japanese parent company.

Many companies admit they are better off working through intermediaries because they can provide the resources to cover all the potential customers in a cost-effective way. In fact this is another reason why food manufacturers market via retailers rather than direct. In other cases intermediaries are in an excellent position with regards to customers. This is why certain life insurance and pension companies operate via solicitors, accountants or banks rather than recruiting large direct sales forces. The intermediary gives credibility to the product.

Imported products can also benefit from indirect channels which is why French mineral water, Perrier, is distributed in the UK by Bulmers, the cider company. Both organisations benefit: Perrier from an efficient transport system, and Bulmers' large professional sales force; Bulmers by being able to include a very desirable product in their portfolio.

One problem arising from the use of intermediaries is that it almost invariably leads to some form of loss of control over the way markets are served. Obviously, it also involves lower margins, but this needs to be set against the costs of direct distribution, and the breadth of potential customers that any channel can achieve. Of course, if our manufacturer of the food product wants to reach regular customers of Marks & Spencer he cannot do it without losing identity and control supplying an own brand product. This now gives Marks & Spencer a very powerful position in part of the supply chain. But companies who successfully work with them, such as Northern Foods, can gain very large sales by co operating in this way.

Market considerations

The example above is also relevant when considering which channels are (a) suitable for customers, (b) acceptable to the organisation and (c) feasible within light of existing market conditions. (The test of suitability, acceptability and feasibility is used in another context by Johnson and Scholes as one of the tests of corporate strategy.) Control of the distributive channels is a very effective barrier to entry in many markets. Even if it is possible to gain access to a general distributor alongside competitive products, it will not be enough if the distributor constantly recommends a competitor's product rather than your product.

An interesting phenomenon is that brands with small market shares suffer, in what Professor Ehrenburg calls, the 'Double Jeopardy Effect'. This is reflected by their customers being less loyal to that brand in regular purchases, hence emphasising the poor sales. This effect makes it very difficult for minor brands to compete effectively.

Example

However, opportunities do exist to develop sales in any market as the example of Canon Photocopiers shows. This was an effective market entry strategy. Rank Xerox used to dominate the UK photocopier market. They offered a range to meet almost every need. They supported this with a very large direct sales force and a national service network.

Canon broke this dominance by a strategy of producing reliable standardised machines which, although not as sophisticated, initially were cheaper. Canon offered their range through independent distributors who could undertake their own service requirements. A much cheaper operation than the Xerox sales and service teams.

Of course Rank Xerox have fought back and Canon have developed from their initial strategy. However, the role of alternative channels in Canon's market entry strategy was vital.

Another case, where the use of alternative distribution channels was introduced to avoid direct competition with established products, is the way Avon cosmetics use thousands of direct sales agents rather than sell via retail outlets. Avon have a turnover of £250m. in the UK and make an excellent profit on their business.

Legal issues

The legal environment was discussed in Chapter 3. There are obvious issues such as product liability laws, which affect all offerings. These restrictions vary from country to country. It is equally important to appreciate legal issues when developing channels for distribution. Key legislation such as the Sale of Goods Act puts responsibilities on retailers. In structuring the channels support must be given to the retailers (your customers) even if they are not the final consumers. Policies on returned stock, and replacing faulty goods is a key element of distribution policy and customer service.

There are many laws restricting business. The legal environment relating to your customers and your customer's customers is part of the environment that must be considered when making products/services available.

Types of distribution channel

Channels can be long or short, single or multiple (hybrid), and can achieve intensive, selective or exclusive distribution. The length of channel could have any number of intermediaries or be direct to customers (*see* Fig 15.2).

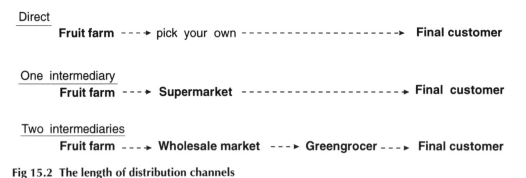

Fig 15.2 The length of distribution channels

Exercise

For each of the situations in Fig 15.2 write down the advantages and disadvantages to the fruit farmer. The issues you are likely to consider are ones of control, cost, feedback, customer service and how likely it is that the supplier will achieve particular objectives.

Direct channels

A direct channel is said to exist when there are no intermediaries between the supply organisation and its customers. Such an arrangement could be

Direct:

Insurance Company   ⟶   (own sales team)   ⟶   CUSTOMERS

Indirect:

General trader	➤ mail order catalogue	➤ CUSTOMERS
Garden bulb supplier	➤ direct mail leaflet	➤ CUSTOMERS
Clothing manufacturer	➤ party plan	➤ CUSTOMERS
Library service	➤ mobile library	➤ CUSTOMERS
Small bakery and cake shop	➤ own retail outlet	➤ CUSTOMERS

The last is also an example of vertical integration. In these examples the supplier will decide all aspects of the contact with the customer. This could include how often the sales person should contact the customer or how frequently to send out a catalogue. In this type of *direct* channel there is no doubt who has control of the many decisions regarding the exchange. The situation is more complicated in *indirect* channels. There are many reasons for using *direct* channels, but equally there are a number of reasons why such channels are not always used. Some of these are listed in Fig 15.3.

FOR	AGAINST
Small market easily reached	Wide geographic market spread
Need to demonstrate a technical product	Financial resources may be better used elsewhere
Inability to persuade intermediary to accept product	Lack of retailing skills or know-how
High intermediary profit margins	Limited product range which is not economical for direct sales

Fig 15.3 'Going direct to market'

Indirect channels

The conventional channel structure is shown in Fig 15.4. The roles of wholesaler and retailer could be filled by any of the intermediaries relevant to a particular market.

The links are important with a *marketing exchange* taking place at each stage. The link provided by negotiation is not necessarily formal, but it certainly takes place in the legal sense of an offer and acceptance.

It is important to realise the effect of the indirect nature of the channel, and the supply pipe line, on these indirect channels. One well known British company launched its product into the USA with apparently great success. It more than met the year 1 estimates of sales. In year 2 sales did not increase, in fact they fell. On investigation it was found that many wholesalers had bought large quantities in the first year, being encouraged by attractive promotional deals. However, the retailers and consumers were not buying, and so the pipeline was blocked by large stocks of the old product. It was an expensive lesson as the British company attempted to sort out the problems. This example shows the importance of information and feedback from all parts of the distribution channel. It also illustrates the problem of loss of control that a supplier can have in an indirect channel.

Another common problem is the extent to which products are 'out-of-stock' at one level in a distribution chain. The longer the channel, the more difficult it is to cope with

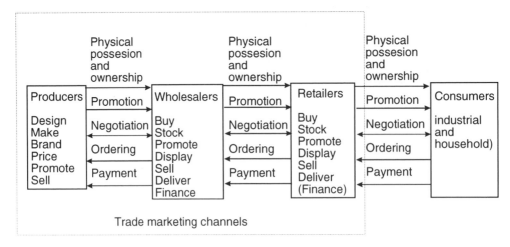

Fig 15.4 **Full channel structure**

the variations of consumer demand. If a product is not available when required it could lead to a lost sale. This again emphasises the need for monitoring all levels of any indirect channel.

Hybrid channels

There is no reason why a supplier should stay with a single channel. Educational toy supplier Early Learning started with most sales via its mail order catalogue. It carefully monitored sales in large areas of population and, when it considered the time was appropriate, a retail outlet was opened in a secondary shopping area. Note these areas were not in the prime High Street sites. It was considered customers would be prepared to seek out an Early Learning outlet because the company felt they offered an unique type of product. So it was decided there was no point in paying the highest retail rents for prime High Street sites. The catalogue still continued and sales justified both channels running alongside each other.

Figure 15.5 represents the channels used by a well-known UK confectionery company where maximum distribution (intensive) is vital for sales of impulse purchase items.

There can be problems with mixed channels as the following example illustrates.

Wang Computers tried to base its distribution activities on a combination of its direct sales force, in conjunction with dealers.

In 1985 the company lowered the sales commission rates of its sales force for sales made jointly with dealers. Consequently, the rates for these sales were below those for sales made directly by the sales force without involving dealers. Inevitably Wang's own sales representatives began to compete with, rather than cooperate with, their resellers – some Wang dealers even filed lawsuits because of this policy. Apparently it is now difficult for the company to re-establish its channel relationships as a residue of ill-will remains with the dealers towards the Wang direct sales operation. Obviously Wang failed to manage a workable hybrid channel strategy.

(*Note*: in August 1992, Wang filed for protection from bankruptcy in the USA.)

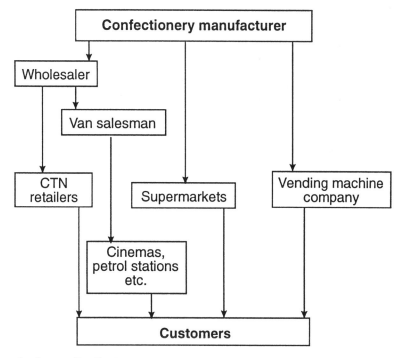

Fig 15.5 Confectionery distribution

Intensive, selective and exclusive distribution

Intensive distribution involves maximising the number of outlets where a product is available. This wide exposure means more opportunities to buy. It is typified by confectionery, soft drinks and other fmcgs (fast-moving consumer goods).

Selective distribution is used where the choice of outlet or service offered is specifically relevant to the buying situation. Examples are electrical or photographic specialists who can offer professional advice or plumbers who can install purchases. However, this type of restricted distribution is becoming less common, with supermarkets, chemists, as well as department stores, offering ever wider ranges of household and electrical goods.

Exclusive distribution is much more restrictive. In this case there is often only one exclusive company in any one geographic area. The major car main dealers offering sales, service, repair and warranty facilities come into this group. They receive the benefit of exclusivity which reduces competition. It is likely that the relationship will be formalised with a legal contract including targets, and obligations on the distributor. In return for acting as the local distributor for Ford or BMW or Rover, the distributor could receive promotional help.

The role of intermediaries

Many markets are subject to dynamic change and in some the functions of channel members are being modified. Nevertheless the common roles of the *intermediary* remain important. The most basic role is to reach customers at a lower cost per unit than the supplier can achieve directly. Perhaps the role could include reaching the target in a more effective way, given the buying habits of customers. This could be achieved by simply buying in bulk from the supplier and selling individual items on to the customers. The supplier concentrates on production, and delivers in quantity to the intermediary who becomes the supplier's customer. The intermediary will obviously take a share of the profit from a product/service, but it might still benefit the supplier because the intermediary could well be responsible for

- stock holding costs;
- transport and delivery to final customers;
- breaking bulk and consolidation of orders; and
- providing local services such as display or service.

It is also possible that the supplier would be paid more quickly by the intermediary rather than the final customers. Certainly, use of intermediaries can reduce the number of transactions involved in reaching customers (*see* Fig 15.6).

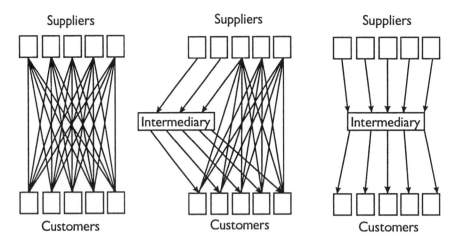

Fig 15.6 Reducing transactions using intermediaries

There are many different types of intermediary such as those listed below. One key difference that should be noticed is whether the intermediary takes ownership for the products in transit as a merchant, rather than acting as an agent who just puts buyer and seller in contact.

1 **Agent:** primarily concerned in the identification, conduct and negotiation of sale of goods either direct or through intermediaries. Agents do not take title or ownership of goods, nor do they often become involved in the physical handling of goods.
2 **Merchant:** takes title (buys) and resells merchandise. Wholesalers and retailers are the two main types of merchant.
3 **Wholesaler:** buys and resells products to retailers and to major industrial institutions and commercial companies. Normally sells little directly to the consumer.
4 **Retailer:** a merchant dealing primarily with the final consumer.

5 **Dealer:** buys and resells merchandise at wholesale, retail or both. Thus dealers take ownership, are involved with stock, and usually have close market contacts within a particular area.

6 **Distributor:** often confused with dealer. More precisely distributors are closer to the wholesaler role, often controlling independent dealers for retail distribution.

7 **Jobber:** is a term widely used to designate a distributor or wholesaler. In the UK it usually carries the connotation of specialist knowledge or franchise with a particular market sector.

8 **Franchisee:** is basically a licensing system under which the owner of a product or service grants an independent local operator the right to trade under the umbrella of the brand owner's name, offering the brand owner's product.

Recently much has been written about the power of food supermarket buyers in the selection of products (*eight* chains now represent 57 per cent of the UK grocery trade). They are offered hundreds of new products every year and have room for only a small proportion on their shelves. Therefore the power of the buyer for the retail outlets is vital in deciding which products should be added and which delisted, or which will never be bought. In these decisions a strong brand name can be an extremely powerful lever to persuade a major supermarket to stock a product. Once a relationship is formed it can be a long term partnership. A recent article by Knox and White on the subject of fresh produce concluded

> We have observed that these relationships are both highly interdependent and concentrated. Because of the increasing volume of high quality produce required by the retailer, they are obliged to work with a limited number of large suppliers who are capable of producing sufficient volume to meet these needs. As a consequence, there appears to be a reluctance to make rash changes in either supplier or retailer affiliation. Consequently, the average duration of a buyer-supplier relationship in the horticultural market was found to be about eight years. (*European Journal of Marketing*, vol 25, January 1991, p 51)

Certainly channel choices are long term and the interdependence of the parties is obvious. But in some markets the intermediary may lead the marketing and promotional effort; in others it is the supplier.

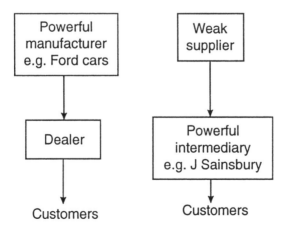

Fig 15.7 Channel leadership

Vertical marketing systems

The model of powerful suppliers or intermediaries competing for control of a distribution channel is now being challenged by what is termed *vertical marketing systems* (VMS). Certainly conflict can arise in a channel where channel members have their own distinct objectives which may not complement those of other channel members. Figure 15.8 suggests these differences.

Producer	Retailer (Intermediary)
Marketing objectives	**Objectives**
Sales levels	Return from shelf space
Market share (product)	Comprehensive product range
Consumer loyalty	Market share (all consumers)
Financial contribution	Financial return
Distribution requirements	**Supplier requirement**
Coverage of market	Producer support
Location of display space	Best deal available
Investment in inventory'	Limited local competition
Service levels	Product demand created by brand owner
Active promotion of product by retailer	

Fig 15.8 Different objectives, different requirements

The companies in Fig 15.8 represent separate businesses, and each is seeking to maximise its own profits. The problem is that conflicting actions could reduce the effectiveness of the total system. But the companies are also interdependent, as the Knox and White study discussed. Hence it is really not sufficient to count intermediaries and measure/monitor members performance. Not all channel systems have members who see themselves as part of a system. This does little to enhance the quality and effectiveness of service. The idea of a vertical marketing system is that producers and intermediaries make a serious attempt to co-ordinate the channel of which they form a part, and to eliminate conflict between individual members.

A survey of such relationships by Dawson and Shaw (*EJM* 1989) used a structured survey of 42 large British multiples and 60 suppliers in four very different product areas. Findings indicated that there are many examples of retailers and suppliers entering into long-term arrangements to do business together. Both parties invest heavily in the development of the relationship. It is interesting that 43 per cent of the retailers and 92 per cent of the manufacturers agreed that they preferred to remain with the same supplier/ customer from year to year whenever possible. Factors acting to increase the stability of relationships included

- a need for consistent quality;
- a need for a flexible response;
- joint product development work; and
- specific delivery requirements.

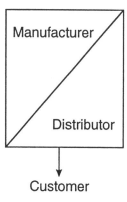

Fig 15.9 Vertical marketing system

Even if no formal VMS is developed it is still important to build strong relationships between channel members.

- Any manufacturer that can appeal to the channel partners' self-interest will find its influence over distributors or retailers probably higher than if its programmes are totally self-interested. This is providing benefits – the basis of marketing. For example, Levi Strauss jointly developed a computerised order processing-inventory management system with its retailers, the advantage of this being that retailers found themselves in a more favourable position in terms of profit. However, these information systems require closer partnerships.
- Knowledge about the actual balance of power may be helpful to prevent wrong decisions with serious consequences. Attempts to drop the dealer network in order to sell directly from company-owned sales branches may end in a situation where former dealers join with competitors and successfully work against a manufacturer.
- Furthermore, channel arrangements should be based on adequate compensation. A distributor's response to a margin squeeze may be to cut back stocking levels to shift inventory-holding costs back to the manufacturer's side. In the long term this can only have negative effects on both parties.
- Manufacturers should be sensitive to the possibility of horizontal channel conflicts. These may be caused through increasing the number of outlets/intermediaries to intensify distribution. Increased margins, for example, may be helpful to prevent such a conflict.
- The manufacturer's own sales force is a vital link to distributors. Training the sales force to support the distributors' sales forces may improve the overall channel performance.
- As a general guideline manufacturers should treat their channels of distribution as strategic assets.

Vertical integration and franchising

It will be apparent that there are two themes running through the subject of channel choice. First is the different operational roles of channel members at different levels in the system. The other is the co-operation and control of these different members within a total system.

To overcome the problems of control, the most obvious solution is for an organisation to combine the different levels in the distribution channel under a single ownership. Such an arrangement is usually called *vertical integration* although now sometimes termed a *corporate vertical marketing system*. It is more costly for the supplier, but this can be offset by the higher revenue from not having to fund distributors' margins. Costs and control of distribution channels is illustrated in Fig 15.10. Examples of this are the development of manufacturing units by the Co-operative Wholesale Society, or the way Laura Ashley, which started as a design and production operation, developed its own retail outlets.

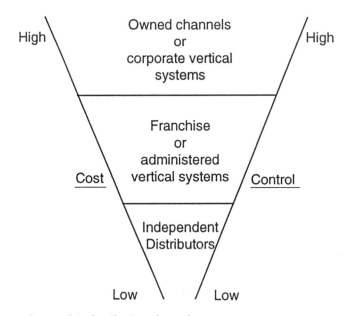

Fig 15.10 Cost and control in distribution channels

An even longer integration was the Union International group run by the Vestey family. They combined companies to supply the Dewhurst Butchers chain which they owned. These included Weddel Meat Wholesalers, The British Beef Company (which also imported meat via the wholly-owned Blue Star Shipping line), Thornhills Poultry (sold in 1987), Union Cold Storage and many other related companies. For several decades the advantages were of great value. Now the increasing trend by consumers to buy less in traditional butchers and more in supermarkets has led to problems of integrated companies which are difficult to solve. In fact none of the three companies have been particularly successful recently. Although when they first developed vertically there were real advantages such as

- economies of scale;
- savings in transaction costs;
- close supplier relationships;
- barriers to entry; and
- efficiency.

And for a time all companies performed very well. The problems have come in the dynamic, changing competitive world. The lack of flexibility, the stifling of competitive forces and the lack of focus by the organisations have been reflected in performance. Laura Ashley plc has completely altered its business to concentrate on design and retailing, dramatically reducing its manufacturing operations in Mid-Wales. CWS has been losing share to other food operations for many years; and Union International have been on the financial pages, although property was partly to blame for their problems.

Management guru, Tom Peters, advises companies to stick to the basic business which they are good at (stick to your knitting). This would suggest that companies who try to both manufacture and retail products could be spreading their activities too broadly. One way of obtaining the advantages without all the problems is to use a franchise arrangement.

It is often believed that franchising started in the USA. However, the concept is a development of the tied-house arrangement used by many British brewers, which has lasted for over 200 years. Strangely, this tied-house arrangement has been challenged as restrictive by the 1989 Monopolies Commission report on Beer and Brewing. At the same time as this report restricts the franchises available in beer retailing (public houses), other franchise arrangements covering such companies as Body Shop, Pronto Print, Dyno Rod and Benetton are increasing rapidly. In 1990 the National Westminster Bank reported that total annual sales by franchise business in the UK amounted to £5.24 billion, employing almost 200 000 people. They expect this figure to more than double in the next five years.

A franchise has a proven greater survival rate than other small businesses. It is therefore usually a better option for a small businessperson than starting a new business in an untried area. This is because the franchisor should have been through all the learning processes and expensive mistakes that can affect a new business. Franchisees find it easier to raise the necessary capital and they take on a tested formula. The advantage to the franchisor is that they can expand business with lower capital commitment, and yet gain highly motivated franchisees keen to benefit, and sharing both risks and rewards.

Distributor quality and service

Most intermediaries offer a level of service to add to the original supplier's product. Service organisations are dependent on people and processes as considered earlier. The major problem is the level of commitment from employees in such service industries. A recent survey in the USA suggested over 80 per cent of employees in service industries are really in dead-end jobs. The problem of ensuring the quality, and service levels, offered by your intermediaries is therefore a key element in channel decisions. We have already seen such solutions as franchising, but this is not always a possible route. In such cases it is very important to find ways of achieving the right level of support for your product. When a distributor is offering your product as well as your competitor's product you may have to offer incentives to the distributor's staff to get them to promote your offering. This can get like an ever-increasing costly spiral. It is an area that will be of vital interest to the sales force responsible for ensuring that products are sold *through* the distributor rather than just *to* the distributor.

Getting products into distribution - the push/pull methods

There are two ways products get into a distribution channel. The first is the efforts of a sales team to convince distributors to stock a product. Here a product is being pushed into the distribution channel. The sales techniques are covered in Chapter 19. A good sales-person will not overload distributors with products, but will try to ensure the right level of product is available to meet requirements of the distributors' customers. To do this successfully a partnership needs to be created between salesperson and buyer. In some organisations the use of increasingly sophisticated electronic data and control systems could mean a product will not be purchased until it has been entered into a computer. The use of bar codes (article numbers seen on many products) means that purchases and sales can be tracked efficiently and in some cases re-ordering of products is automatically controlled.

There is no point 'pushing' products into distribution if it does not move on to the final consumer. The customers can create demand, 'pulling' products along a distribution chain. Perhaps you have wanted to buy a particular book, but found it not available in your local bookshop. By ordering it you create 'demand pull'. However, before you can initiate such a chain of events you will need to be aware of the existence of the required book. Perhaps your awareness came from advertising or a recommendation from one of your lecturers.

In practice most markets have a mixture of both 'push' and 'pull' techniques acting on the distribution chain. They are both necessary to keep the flow of products and services moving. At different stages in a product's life cycle there will be different emphasis on the balance between 'push' and 'pull'. You might like to consider the following examples in this context.

> Example 1. A well-known national confectionery manufacturer such as Cadbury's when they launch a new product, e.g. Wispa.

> Example 2. The launch of 'Proton' cars (from Malaysia) into the UK using exclusive distributors.

> Example 3. Insurance policies, specially designed for protection of student posses-sions while in college/university halls of residence.

The role of overseas agents and distributors

The basic role of agents and distributors does not change in overseas markets. However, they usually are given more detailed consideration. Market entry is vital and the distances involved, together with cultural differences, mean a local intermediary is often beneficial. It is possible to set up a wholly-owned channel, but agents and distributors are the most common in terms of numbers of exporters, although not of course with volume of goods. When volume gets high enough a supplier will be tempted to replace the agent with a corporate representation. However, to be fair to agents, and to get the best from their efforts, the partnership must be developed in an honest and open way.

An alternative arrangement, which is always worth consideration, is the joint venture or, even further, a strategic alliance. Such arrangements can be immensely beneficial, not only in one overseas market but, if well-constructed, for the mutual development of both organisations.

Physical distribution management

This chapter should have convinced you of the vital role played by choice of effective distribution channels. However, this could all be wasted if the physical distribution of a product is not organised as efficiently as possible. The recent example of the former Soviet Union, where food shortages existed in major cities, should be contrasted to perishable food rotting in state warehouses. It is a sharp example of the need for good logistics. Although not normally the role of marketing, it is vital that the right level of customer service is achieved, hence the need to consider what an organisation is really capable of achieving. It is not subsidiary to the task of selling, nor is it purely a cost to be borne by an organisation. It is a key element in creating satisfied customers.

Peter Drucker suggested the difference between efficiency and effectiveness was that the former was 'doing things right' and the latter 'doing the right things'. If for the sake of efficiency you do not dispatch a delivery vehicle unless it has a 100 per cent full load, it could save costs. The delays involved with customers receiving the product late could lose sales and materially affect future business. The choice of levels and quality of service will be influenced by both what customers expect, and by what competitors are prepared to offer. If costs of delivery increase then it must be viewed as a way of 'augmenting' the total product offering as discussed earlier in Chapter 12.

Physical distribution management is concerned with transportation, materials handling, packaging, warehousing (and locations of depots), inventory policy, stock control and order processing. It is not the role of this book to discuss such issues in depth. However, it is essential that you see how added value can be achieved through distribution policies and appreciate the necessity of a marketer understanding the role of logistics and physical distribution in the total product.

Conclusion

There are many ways of making a product available to potential customers. The marketing role is to identify the target market and to understand how the target customers make purchase decisions. This can then be translated into an 'availability' strategy that matches these requirements.

The decisions on channels are long term. If intermediaries are used then the relationships developed between suppliers and distributors can be critical to the effectiveness of the channel.

It is the effectiveness of the availability strategy that should be the prime concern of marketers. Within this, channel decisions can give a competitive edge with one organisation reaching customers and gaining sales because its products reach customers in a more appropriate way than those from competitors. An example of this is Coca-Cola, the case study at the end of Chapter 1. The product is an impulse purchase product and, by being available in more outlets, Coke is able to outsell Pepsi.

Other types of products require different distribution strategies. Think of the most suitable strategy for an industrial product or a consumer durable or one of the other categories discussed in Chapter 12.

The one certainty is that it is unlikely that customers will 'beat a path to your door'. In a market with excess demand, availability strategies play a vital part.

Questions

1 Why might an organisation choose not to use an intermediary in its efforts to reach its customers?

2 In retailing, the 4Ps of Marketing are often said to be Place, Place, Place and Place. Explain why this might be said.

3 Suggest three products that might benefit from intensive distribution, and explain how this might be achieved.

4 What are the advantages of franchise distributors as opposed to other distributors?

References

Chisnall, P, *Strategic Industrial Marketing*, Prentice-Hall 1987

Ehrenberg, A S C, Goodhardt, G J & Barwise, T P *'Double jeopardy revisited'*, *Journal of Marketing*, July 1990

Knox, S D & White, H F, 'Retail buyers and their fresh produce suppliers', *European Journal of Marketing*, vol 25, Jan 1991

Dawson, J A & Shaw, S A, *'The move to administered vertical marketing systems by British retailers, European Journal of Marketing'*, vol 23,1989

Case study: making products available

Free range eggs (Notts and Derby) Ltd

Frend Ltd is a medium-size deep-litter egg producer based in a village close to Bakewell, North Derbyshire. Prior to August 1988 it supplied over 20 000 dozen eggs each week to outlets as far away as Manchester, Leeds, and Leicester. However, 70 per cent of the business comes from the counties of Nottingham and Derby. Most of their customers are small independent outlets offering food products which appeal to the 'green consumers'- healthfood shops, greengrocers, independent butchers, and farm shops. Customers pay for the eggs on a cash-on-delivery basis. The average order is now for 5 trays (5 x 2½ dozen) although no minimum is enforced so orders range from 1 tray to 20 or 30 trays per visit. Frend use eight small vans to distribute the product. In spite of the company's excellent image sales levels slumped by over one third following the salmonella scare after a comment by a government minister. Sales have gradually recovered and have now reached 80 per cent of previous levels, but even four years later they seem to have stuck at this level.

Frend Ltd have carried out exhaustive tests and are certain their flocks are free from disease. However, if sales remain at the current depressed levels they will be bankrupt due to depressed prices and the high distribution overheads. In fact the only way they have survived up to now has been by reducing the flock by 20 per cent and accepting a grant from the government scheme to cover part of the cost of this cut back, as well as cancelling orders for replacement vans. But higher servicing costs are affecting cash flow and two vans are thought unlikely to pass their next MOT test.

The owner of Frend Ltd has asked you as a marketing expert to advise him on the following:

Should he change his distribution policy and impose a *10-tray minimum* order on his customers. He is sure this will save money and encourage customers to place larger orders.

Current costs are:

Sales 16 000 dozen @ 50p doz	£8,000 per week
Feed supplement for hens	£1,000 per week
New hens (replacing old birds)	£440 per week
Egg trays	£400 per week

Basic farm costs - maintenance
                      - agricultural mortgage
                      - overnight houses (inc heat)
	£50,000 per year

Labour to collect eggs and maintain flock	£50,000 per year
Egg packing (5 part-time employees)	£15,000 per year
Delivery drivers and other staff	£100,000 per year
Van licences; diesel; insurance and servicing	£80,000 per year
Banking and accounting, records etc	£5,000 per year

16

MARKETING COMMUNICATIONS

Introduction

The quote at the beginning of Chapter 15 is equally applicable to the communication process. Successful marketing relies on customers being aware of the offers being made to them. Marketing communications involves effectively providing information about an organisation and its products to chosen customer groups.

Example

Imagine you have a hobby that you find very enjoyable; let's say cabinet making or dressmaking. Family and friends are impressed by your skill and regularly ask you to make things for them and pay you for the work done. As a result of word of mouth recommendations from your friends and customers, the number of orders you receive each month has increased steadily.

Realising this could be a profitable venture, you decide to concentrate on your hobby, invest some of your savings in a commercial machine which will enable you to increase your output dramatically, and start in business for yourself. At this point you need to increase the rate at which the number of orders has been growing. This means you can no longer rely only on word-of-mouth recommendations. How do you increase this rate of growth?

You realise from comments made by your existing customers that many of them knew that you were a cabinet maker or dressmaker, but had not considered asking you to make something for them until they had seen an example of your work. It thus seems that to increase the number of customers involves both increasing the number of people who know what you do and also the number of these people who have seen examples of your work.

This chapter considers the need to set marketing communication objectives such as these and reviews the many approaches which can be used to achieve these objectives. It involves applying the basic principles of good communication. It is therefore useful to consider the basic elements of the communication process before applying these to marketing and looking at the media that can be used for marketing communications.

The communication process

A typical definition of communication would be: 'The act of making known; intercourse by speech, correspondence, and messages'. The communication process is the foundation of any relationship whether in the commercial or personal field, and it is on this that the success or failure of any relationship depends.

Communication is more than a message being sent. For communication to have taken place it is necessary for the message that is received to have been understood in the way it was intended. This means that the sender of a message has to have a response to know whether communication has taken place. The response or feedback enables the sender to develop the message thereby ensuring that it is understood by the receiver. Communication is therefore a 'two-way' rather than a 'one-way' process.

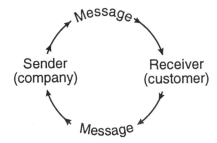

Fig 16.1. A two-way communications model

It will be seen from the two-way communications model in Fig 16.1 that the transfer of a message from a sender to a receiver involves a number of distinct stages. Each of these provides an opportunity for the message to be altered from that originally intended. Furthermore, at each stage of the communication process the message can be affected by 'noise'; for example a physical background sound, such as is normal in a disco, may make it impossible to hear what is said. Similarly, 'noise' can be electronic interference on a telephone line or radio transmission which has the same effect. In the context of communications the term 'noise' has a wider meaning and is used to identify any extraneous factor which can affect the transfer of a message.

It is perhaps easier to understand the communications process by considering how we as individuals respond when meeting someone for the first time. Generally, we are able to respond to the person appropriately without being aware of our response. We automatically note aspects of the person and assimilate unconsciously the information these provide. For example, we note posture, gestures, facial expressions, eye movements, eye contact, the style and quality of clothing, and perhaps status symbols, such as jewellery. Such non-verbal messages are as important a factor in the communications process as the spoken message itself.

Usually when the person speaks what they say is in keeping with the impression we have formed about the person speaking. Occasionally when this does not happen, such as when someone dressed casually speaks with unexpected authority, we are taken by surprise and as a result completely miss what was said. This is an example where the non-verbal messages can be considered to be 'noise' since they have had the same effect as the physical sounds examples of noise given earlier, i.e. they have affected the transfer of the message.

Noise can thus take many forms, all of which have the effect of drowning or distorting the message. In addition, the message can be distorted directly as a result of the processes involved in getting it from the sender to the receiver. In the first instance, the sender may not have the information that should be included in the message: as a result the message may be incomplete. Secondly, the sender may not know the precise words that should be used in some aspect of the message: it may be vague. Thirdly the sender may choose the wrong medium for sending the message: the telephone is used when a letter is needed; an item is described verbally when a drawing is needed. These are examples where the message is distorted by the sender. It can also be distorted by the receiver. If a drawing is used to send the message the receiver will need to be able to interpret it. If words are used, the receiver will need to know what they mean. If the message is written, the writing needs to be intelligible.

In normal person-to-person communications the problems which arise as a result of the message not being heard or being distorted are corrected as the communication progresses. This can be done because the sender is able to revise the message according to the receiver's responses. By the nature of two-way communication this can be done even though these responses are, of course, subject to the same distortion and noise problems as the original message.

How can the two-way communications model be applied to marketing communications? Let us imagine that a message is to be sent to a potential group of customers and television is selected as the communication channel. For the message to be sent via television it must be first *encoded* in the form of words, pictures and images; it must then be broadcast as television signals. Those signals will be received by every television tuned to that channel. The message will not, however, be the same on every television. Not only will the quality of the image and sound vary according to the quality of the television and reception, but the message will also be affected by the size of the picture and whether the picture is in black and white or colour. As a result some of the people watching the television will receive essentially the original message, while others will receive something quite different. It is one of these that is either ignored or *decoded* by the the viewers. Those who decode the message may then either react to the message or just store it for future reference.

It is important to remember that each one of us is different. People differ psychologically and physiologically. They vary in intelligence, education, religious beliefs, social background, and experience. These differences mean that different people *decode* messages in different ways. This is a key factor which makes *two-way* communication preferable to *one-way* communication.

Imagine the following scenario. A student one evening is sitting studying from a textbook. The television, which is in the same room, is on, albeit at a low volume. When a lively commercial starts, the student 's attention is caught. The advertisement shows a friendly group in a pub enjoying an alcoholic beverage. This could stimulate the desire for a drink. It could even more specifically create a desire for the brand featured in the advertisement. There is no guarantee of this link as we all have our preferred brands. Creating what marketers call 'brand switching' requires more than one commercial.

Do you think such an advert would have any effect on the student, or could it be ignored?

In this example we can see a message was *coded*, transmitted via a particular communication channel, the television, then *decoded* by the viewer. The subsequent feedback could be the purchase of a product. Messages sent via a medium such as television can create immediate action. Some examples are the well known television and radio charity appeals such as 'Children in Need', or 'The Week's Good Cause'. These, however, are exceptions. It is unusual for advertisers to get direct feedback from their message through action taken by their audience. Normally, to measure the effect of television advertising messages, advertisers have to use marketing research techniques to track customer attitudes and behaviour. This information can then be used as a measure of effectiveness in terms of sales by establishing a link between the general public attitude to the company or to a specific product and the level of sales. Most major advertisers are able to do this.

Since it is imperative that proper attention is paid to feedback in communications, if no obvious feedback exists then ways must be found of measuring the results of any primary communication. It is only by doing this that the organisation can know whether their communication is on the right track, and if changes are required, know whether these should be to the benefits being offered, the message that is being sent, or the media being used.

The whole picture of the communications process is illustrated in Fig 16.2.

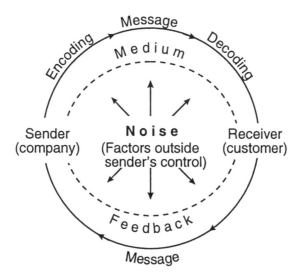

Fig 16.2 A full communications model

Marketing communication

Having outlined the basic communication process the specific factors relevant to marketing communications can be identified. Instead of considering what happens when you meet someone for the first time, consider what happens when you encounter a new product for the first time. This could be in an advertisement, a window display or being used either by someone you know or a stranger. Just as clues were used to establish how you should react to the person you meet for the first time so you use clues to classify the new product. These would include:

- the situation – the type of advertisement/shop/user;
- the type of product;
- brand;
- apparent quality;
- price; and
- packaging.

It is on the basis of clues such as these that a judgement as to the relevance of a product is made. Consider an advertisement for a computer. If the advertisement shows the computer in an office being used by people who are formally dressed, you as a student might well assume that it was designed for business use and accordingly it would be expensive. Alternatively, if it is shown in what is obviously a student environment you may assume that it has limited capability. Accordingly, you are unlikely to consider either of these advertisements relevant to you. If both are featuring the same computer they may well be relevant to you when you realise this.

The preceding example illustrates both the truth and the fallacy in the famous remark about advertising, which in the UK is attributed to Lord Leverhulme, the first Chairman of Unilever, and in the USA to the retailer John Wannamaker:

> I know that half of what I spend on advertising is wasted; but the trouble is I don't know which half!

This raises the wider issue of whether advertising works at all. The subject of advertising effectiveness has been a contentious issue for a very long time. One study, undertaken by advertising man Alex Biel using the substantial PIMS database of over 3000 companies in USA and Europe, looked at comparative advertising to sales ratios related to market share. The results are shown below.

Relative Ad/Sales compared to direct competitors	Average share of market (%)
Much less	14
Less	20
Equal	25
More	26
Much more	32

While these results could be simply reflecting the fact that major brands can afford to spend more on advertising than minor brands, the numbers and diversity of the firms investigated would suggest a correlation between advertising expenditure and market share. These results must be seen against research by Abraham and Lodish who concluded that only 46 per cent of the established brands they studied received a positive sales impact from advertising. The researchers found a higher figure of 59 per cent for new products, but of course we must remember that over a third of new products 'fail' so this figure perhaps refers to those new products that have 'succeeded'.

Exercise

Think of television advertisements which you have seen recently that have encouraged you or anyone in your household to take action by doing something or purchasing a particular product. What was it in the advertisement that really stimulated action? Was there already some prior knowledge or propensity to that action? What part did the advertisement play in the process?

A related problem which could affect the result of an advertisement is the credibility of the message, which can be linked specifically to the media in which it is presented. A beautifully photographed advertisement for a Christian Dior exclusive dress might be appropriate in Vogue magazine but would be out of place in a cheap tabloid newspaper. It would certainly grab attention in the newspaper but credibility would be low. So context can aid or detract from the credibility of a message. Credibility can, of course, be enhanced by the endorsement of a well-known personality. An endorsement can create a halo effect where the presenter 's attributes enhance the product or message. Daley Thompson was used successfully to re-launch Lucozade. Pepsi Cola have used major recording stars such as Michael Jackson and Tina Turner.

Sometimes advertising is not very credible. You can, perhaps, think of an example.

It can be seen that communication is very important to marketing, both in the initial stages after a product has been launched, and sometimes more importantly as a follow up to the initial contact. It therefore follows that marketers and their companies should have an understanding of the communication process. This study will show that while the message sent to the prospective customer is vitally important, the way in which the message is sent is equally important. In both the sending and the receiving of messages, misunderstandings between customer and client must be avoided. And to get the best chance of acceptance the message should not be too complicated.

An acronym much used by marketers is KISS, which means 'keep it simple'. The initial impact of the communication is vital so concentrate on a few elements which will have the greatest effect.

In marketing communications the structure is often basically *one way* – from supplier to target. Organisations then have to develop their own ways of obtaining feedback to check how their messages are being received, and how their marketing objectives are being met.

Communication objectives

In general the objectives of communication will be from one of the three categories below:

- **Informing**: giving information, building awareness that a product/service exists, what the product does, where it can be obtained.

- **Persuading:** creating a favourable attitude, providing a stimulus to favour one brand over another, or one point of view against another.
- **Reinforcing:** dispelling doubts about an action already taken, building support/loyalty to a point of view or purchase, ensuring a good climate for future sales.

An equation can be developed, as shown in Fig 16.3.

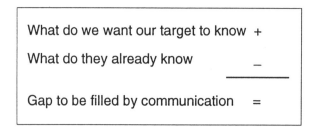

Fig 16.3 Communication gap

The equation must be followed through before the implementation of communication plans is decided. The overall objectives can cover any of the main categories of informing, persuading, or reassuring. The gap is the perceived difference with the actual situation. It is only by setting clear goals in this area, as in all parts of business, that successful execution can be assessed.

One of the key studies in covering both objectives and assessment is the DAGMAR work by Russell Colley. This study was undertaken for the Advertising Research Foundation and an obvious but key conclusion was that in order to know how successful your advertising is you must first understand clearly the objectives you want to achieve. This may seem very basic, but it is surprising how often it is forgotten. There is a feeling that all advertising must be good, maybe akin to the show business dictum that it does not matter what critics write about you as long as they write something. **DAGMAR** stands for Defining Advertising Goals for Measured Advertising Results. In his study Colley lists over 50 possible advertising objectives. A fuller discussion on the subject of feedback in marketing communications is included in Chapter 17 on promotional planning.

Marketing communication media

One of the basics of communications is the selection of media to be used to transmit the communication to the target group. In general media can be split into two categories: personal and non-personal. Very often it happens that several different media need to be used in conjunction with each other in order to convey the message effectively.

If we imagine ourselves working in a large organisation, there are many methods of communication we can use internally: we may send a memorandum to another department and if after several days find that there has been no reply, back up the written word with a telephone call thereby reinforcing our original message. In fact the re-inforcement of messages is often appropriate in communicating information. However, it is important to know when the receivers of your message have heard enough. Some advertisements really irritate when seen for the twentieth or thirtieth time.

Personal channels

Personal channels occur when there is an element of personal contact, that is, where one person, or even several people, take part in an exercise that communicates something to someone. Here the content of the message can be fine-tuned to the particular receiver of the message. A major advantage with personal channels of communication is that the communicator involved can gauge the reaction of the recipient, and depending on the feedback that is received, quickly amend the approach. There is obviously an increased chance that the content will be both heard and understood.

Perhaps you are a student who has to attend lectures and seminars. During these periods something is being conveyed to you. How much you learn is affected by 'noise' elements and interference discussed earlier. It could include how receptive you feel, how good the lecturer is, or even the quality of teaching materials such as slides and handouts.

Personal channels for marketing communications can include everything from telephone selling to office memos. The major areas of interest are:

- internal company communications;
- personal selling;
- personalised marketing – telesales/telemarketing, direct mail;
- trade fairs and exhibitions.

Internal communication

Some people see communications as something done for outsiders. However, every part of an organisation is regularly in communication with other parts of the organisation. Most internal communication is of a personal nature, i.e. letters, memos, telephone calls, face-to-face meetings, presentations, etc. Remember, the most potent method of communication is by word of mouth where colleagues, friends or family make personal recommendations to you. The desired result is to produce an offering acceptable to external customers. This is a situation where internal marketing is necessary. Remember, every employee is a potential part-time marketer. The quality of internal communication will have a direct input on the effectiveness as well as the efficiency of an organisation.

Personal selling

The personal sales approach is the most direct and potent way of selling many products. It ranges from door-to-door insurance salespeople to assistants in your local department store. To be successful salespeople must understand the use of body language, eye contact, asking questions and how to build a relationship with their clients. It is not about smart-talking salespeople who can talk their customers into submission. Rather, a good salesperson will use questions to discover needs and then show how their offerings fulfil those needs. Of course atmosphere is important in creating the right conditions for a sale. Party-plan organisers, Tupperware, know this and are very successful exploiting a social gathering for selling. However, personal selling is a slow and expensive way of doing business. The cost of a sales call will be considered in Chapter 19. A less costly way is to adapt to what is called 'personalised selling'. This is not really personal (no body language!) but it is adaptable and individual.

Personalised marketing

Telemarketing

One advantage of telesales or telemarketing is that it is a much cheaper way of reaching the target audience than sending a salesperson to call. It is common in industrial and other business-to-business situations, in particular those concerning regular repeat orders. For example, in the bakery trade it is common for the flour supplier to telephone the bakery, the order can then be noted and dispatched very quickly. A representative from the flour company would then only be required to call at infrequent intervals in order to maintain good customer relations.

For teleselling to succeed, the companies involved must try to make the approach as personal as possible. Normally the target market is well researched, even if it is only to make note of their prospective customers' names from the telephone directory. Using someone's name, even as a potential customer, makes the telephone call seem more friendly. It is thus more difficult to disregard immediately. If a company relies entirely on telesales there is a problem in that the salesperson rarely establishes a close personal relationship with the customer. However, skilled telemarketers are able to project their personalities over the telephone. The medium has to be used with care as some people view unsolicited telephone calls as intrusive. It is much more common in the USA than in the UK.

Direct mail

Direct mail has become more popular in recent years with over 2 billion items sent in the UK in 1990. When direct mail is sent naming the target customer personally, then it moves into the realm of a personalised communication. The ability to use a more personalised approach has come about due to the advanced technology afforded by computers.

Many people claim they are not influenced by 'junk mail'. However, a response rate of a few percentage points is often enough for a mailing to be considered a success. The economics of direct mail depend on the complexity of the actual item mailed, and the postage which can be up to a third of the cost. The address list must be relevant to the offer, and the mailing itself must create attention. One company sent a mailing from Moscow. This not only dramatically reduced postage to 24 roubles per letter (8 pence at that time), but the letters from Russia created interest among recipients to the benefit of the sender.

Exercise

Over the period of about one month note any correspondence that is sent direct to a named person within the household. The correspondence being of a type which informs about or tries to sell a product.

Trade fairs and exhibitions

It has been said that if a salesperson visits a customer they have *gone to sell*. If the customer visits the supplier they have *come to buy*. The latter is a much stronger position for the supplier. A half-way situation is a trade fair or an exhibition. The advantage is that suppliers meet customers on neutral ground away from the formal office environment.

The shows are generally industry- or trade-specific. Examples are the Smithfield Show and the Royal Show which are mainly for the farming and agricultural industries, whereas the Motor Show is for those interested in the car industry. There are now many large exhibition centres throughout Britain, Europe and the rest of the world, which attract a large number of exhibitors, both home-based and from overseas, to regular events. On a smaller and more localised scale this category could also include local craft fairs and perhaps could be extended to the popular 'car boot sale'.

Exhibitions and trade shows give organisations the chance to show how they compare with their competitors who are often present at the same event. The budget required to participate in such events can be substantial, so any involvement must be well planned, and probably communicated to potential customers in advance. Salespeople will always be in attendance to give advice, explain any complicated features, as well as trying to sell the product. New products cannot only be seen, but also tried and tested and compared to other similar products; but competitors are doing the same. Companies often use major exhibitions as an opportunity to launch new products. It can be important for a company to attend the major exhibitions in their product area so as to show all potential customers that it is still thriving in this particular market.

Exercise

List personal channels of communication which have been directed towards you recently. How did they differ in the effect they had upon you?

Non-personal channels

Non-personal channels of communication 'exist' where there is no personal contact involved. The communication is completely external to the audience. Non-personal channels include the use of one or more of the following channels of communication: commercial television; the press and other print media; radio; cinema; outdoor media; point-of-sale displays; and packaging

Within these channels, techniques of advertising, publicity (PR), sponsorship, and sales promotion can be used. These are considered in Chapters 18 and 19.

Commercial television

This is the most important non-personal communication channel with very wide coverage to its audience. How many people come home from a day's work, have something to eat and then sit watching a television for the remainder of the evening? If they watch a commercial television station they will be subjected, during the course of an evening, to many commercial breaks, on which a large variety of products will be advertised. There is some exposure of products on the non-commercial channels especially with sponsored sports events. However, recently BBC television has been restricted from advertising its own magazines during its programmes. This followed a complaint from a major magazine publisher who considered it unfair competition.

The television stations research in great detail the type of audience expected to watch each of their programmes. Similar detailed research is also carried out with regard to the other non-personal media and their audiences. For television it is to be expected that toys will be advertised during the period when children 's programmes are screened, whereas products like cars might be featured in the evening say around the 'News at Ten'slot.

Television does not offer lasting images, but it does combine sound and moving pictures in a very powerful way. Advertising, using television as the medium of communication, is considered one of the quickest ways of ensuring that your product is known to a wide audience. In Britain almost 97 per cent of homes have a television set, of which 94 per cent are colour sets. Major 'soap' serials get regular audiences of 10-20 million viewers, although specialist programmes such as 'gardening' are more relevant for particular products. The UK commercial television stations are regional. It is therefore possible to use geographic segmentation, as well as including other demographic and psychographic segmentation features related to programmes when timing commercials. There are countries which do not have commercial television stations; Norway was one. Her people used only to see television advertisements if they subscribed to cable or satellite television.

In recent years satellite television has gained in popularity in Britain as the price of receiving equipment has fallen. The cable networks have increasingly drawn on the products of the satellite companies and the actual ownership of satellite dishes is increasing steadily. The householders who subscribe to satellite spend some 30 per cent of their viewing time watching these programmes. This is likely to increase the pressure on the major channels which have seen overall audiences fall over this period. Within the last ten years teletext has also been available. Oracle (on independent television) carries advertisements of a static nature, whereas BBC/Ceefax has none at all.

An extension of television advertising is product placement. This is where the company pays the broadcaster a fee to ensure regular exposure of its product within the context of a specified programme. Any such exposure is felt to be beneficial. Television is such a powerful medium for images and associations that a saying has emerged in the industry: 'Television to sell, Newspapers to tell'. This, of course, links to the objectives of a communication campaign.

The press

The press includes all forms of the following: newspapers both local and national; magazines; directories; and year books. If it is 'press to tell' the fact that twice as much is spent on newspaper advertising compared to commercial television will show the importance of the printed media.

Newspapers

The advertisements carried will obviously depend on whether the newspaper has national or local distribution. With local papers there is always a large section of classified advertisements. There are usually so many advertisements placed by the general public and small local firms, that they are split up into different categories and displayed in groups.

Exercise

Find out how much it costs to advertise in your local newspapers. Is it much less than in a national newspaper?

There are a wide variety of daily newspapers on sale in Britain. To some extent it is possible to divide their readers into broad political and socio-economic groups. At the time of writing the most popular daily paper in Britain is the *Sun* which would appear to veer slightly to the right on the political front. Most readers have a brand loyalty to the paper of their choice and will buy it each day. It is therefore easier to segment the readership and target specific groups with certain advertisements. Many newspapers have developed a strategy where specific days of the week are used regularly to advertise certain things on a larger scale, sometimes jobs, sometimes cars or perhaps property.

Almost 90 per cent of the population has access to a newspaper, but in order for the same advertisement to reach this population, a tremendous number of advertisements would have to be placed; that is why knowledge of the readership is so important. As a medium for target marketing it is very powerful.

There is a great deal of flexibility in newspaper advertising – size, appearance, and more recently colour, are a few of the variables. Colour magazine supplements have been a bonus in advertising and many newspapers now produce a good quality supplement. Initially supplements were usually sold with the Sunday newspapers, but gradually they have become a regular feature on other days. Sunday continues to be the most popular day for newspapers and advertising rates for Sunday papers reflect this larger readership.

In general, the public have a greater propensity to believe the written word. Certainly a lot of information can be given in a newspaper advertisement. A disadvantage with placing an advertisement in a newspaper is that it is likely to have a very short life span – newspapers tend to be read on the day they are published, and are then soon discarded.

Magazines

There are a great many magazines. They range from those covering general topics of interest, to ones on highly specialist subjects. For practically any hobby or interest, it is possible to find some magazine which caters for those enthusiasts. Magazines offer a more selective audience and there is an obvious link between the magazine and the lifestyle of its reader. It is much easier for organisations to segment and target their audience via magazines. For example, someone buying *Prima* magazine is likely to be interested in fashion, craft, knitting and beauty, and have far different interests from someone buying the computer magazine *PC Plus*, unless of course they have an interest in both subjects. It is also relatively easy to segment magazines catering for predominantly male or female readers.

Magazines do not suffer from the disadvantage of being discarded on the day they are published, many are saved for several years by the people who buy them and used as a source of reference. They may be passed from friend to friend until the copy is battered and torn, or they may be stacked in the doctors' or dentists' waiting rooms. They are normally read and digested at a more leisurely pace than newspapers. *Vogue* claims that every copy is read by an average of eight people so a circulation of 200 000 means a readership of almost 2 million. Compare this to the Sun newspaper with a 4 million sale and an 11 million readership.

Exercise

List places where old copies of magazines are placed. Do many people have access to them? Are they read?

Many products can be enhanced by good quality colour advertisements in magazines – most food products would fall into this category. However, high quality does mean high production costs but the results can be worth the expense.

Exercise

Find out the cost of advertising in your favourite magazine.

Directories and year books

Directories and year books range from the *Yellow Pages* directory to the *Daily Mail Year Book*, and would even include diaries promoted by a professional organisation. They include a tremendous amount of information and promote many different fields of interest. Despite being relatively inexpensive as a vehicle of communication, they can be highly effective. A local plumber having a large entry in the local *Yellow Pages* directory can win many customers. If the advertisement is good, and the plumber then proves to be a reliable worker for the customer who chose him from the directory, the plumber will be recommended to others and thus expand his business.

Exercise

Examine your local *Yellow Pages* directory. What size and kind of advertisements gain most attention?

Radio

In Britain commercial radio started to be home-produced in the 1970s, but previously had reached British homes from stations such as Radio Luxembourg and Radio Caroline. There are now many local radio stations, and even a travelling motorist can see road signs which give information on the wavelength of local radio stations.

Radio commercials are much less expensive to produce than television commercials, but do not have the same advantages: there is no visual presentation, so only the aural senses are assailed. However, the medium is used by both local and national companies. Local organisations are able to target their message very precisely and at very reasonable costs.

The appeal of a radio commercial depends to a large extent on how the message is conveyed and it is not uncommon for famous personalities to lend their voice to the advertisement. Another fairly recent development has been the sponsorship of programmes. Sometimes before a particular programme, the announcer will say 'This programme is brought to you by courtesy of ... (a certain organisation)'. By hearing this announcement frequently it is easier to recall that organisation's name.

Radio messages are usually short lived. They do not have the impact of television. Radio is sometimes described as 'noisy wallpaper'. It accounts for only 2 per cent of all advertising spending. Repetition is often necessary to create attention. But if the right message is developed it might have the same dramatic effect as, for example, Orson

Welles' famous broadcast 'War of the Worlds', on US radio before World War II. The audience believed that the USA was being invaded from space and it was so realistic that it nearly caused a riot. But of course that was before the current dominance of television.

Cinema

As a vehicle of communication cinema has had a chequered past in that its popularity has moved with the times. In Britain the cinema was very popular in the 1940s and 1950s, but its popularity waned in the 1960s and 1970s when audiences fell to an all-time low. There has been a recovery in audience figures in the last decade with the advent of the new multiplex screens. Advertising in the cinema has many of the same advantages of sound and moving pictures as television. Perhaps the cinema audience is slightly more captive. The majority of cinema goers tend to be in the age range 14 to 34 and it is therefore possible for precise target marketing to take place. As a medium cinema is popular with local businesses such as restaurants that are in relatively close proximity to the cinema.

Recently there has been a novel development in cinema advertising dubbed 'interactive cinema'. It involves a dialogue between a member of the audience (a paid actress) and the screen image. This, of course, is almost guaranteed to capture the interest of the rest of the audience.

Exercise

Next time you are at a cinema, note the type of advertising that is shown. Would the advertising vary from screen to screen if one was showing a Walt Disney film and another an Arnold Schwartzenegger film?

Outdoor media

Outdoor advertising can be a very effective channel of communication, it is also one of the cheapest, in terms of cost per thousand (CPT) of the adult population reached. Most of the adult population have the opportunity to see (OTS) posters every day. Not only does outdoor media include large posters, but also outdoor features such as parking meters and litter bins can act as host sites to advertisements. Other outdoor hosts occasionally used are tethered balloons, perhaps on the site of a new shop or shopping area. Airships and aircraft with trailing banners have also been used, but they tend to be expensive to commission, and so do not enjoy tremendous popularity.

Exercise

What outdoor media other than posters are you aware of? How effective as channels of communication are they?

Transport advertising on the sides of buses has become very popular, and other commercial vehicles advertise company names and telephone numbers. However, advertising is not limited to the sides of larger vehicles. Taxis always have their telephone number displayed prominently, and now often feature advertisements for local firms pasted on to a convenient viewing position for the passengers to study. Other captive audiences are passengers in trains and aeroplanes. Both are used extensively.

Exercise

Study the advertisements on as many modes of transport as possible. Compare the variety of products which are advertised. Is there a common theme?

Another example of captive audience advertising is on the London Underground. The tube stations have a very captive audience, and unless people want to study each other, the only entertainment available is the posters displayed on the station walls. Another similar example is where bus shelters play host to posters. Adshel bus shelters have been erected in many parts of the country. In return for supplying and providing upkeep of these bus shelters at no charge to the council, Adshel ask to be allowed to display a poster on them. In August 1992 there was a large number of thefts from Adshel sites of posters advertising Sony Walkmans. On investigation it was found that students were removing the posters to use in their college rooms. Sony were said to be delighted because it both emphasised the attractiveness of the poster and provided additional advertising in student rooms. Adshel, faced with repair bills of up to £2000 per shelter, were not so pleased.

Exercise

Make a study of any bus shelters and the posters on them in your area. What posters are on them and are they Adshel shelters?

The positioning and site of the outdoor media is very important. The 1980s in particular saw a massive increase in poster popularity, the relatively low CPT being a contributing factor to this. There has also been a change in emphasis in the type of products advertised, away from alcohol and tobacco, to a more evenly balanced cross section of products.

The size of the posters also varies, but from 1992 there is going to be a concentrated effort by the advertising agencies to try to standardise the size of posters to ninety-six, forty-eight and six sheet size and also increase poster illumination. Mechanised posters which change picture are also on the increase.

The sites chosen to display posters are of paramount importance, the aim being for as many people as possible to see them. Sporting events are popular sites, especially if they are in areas which may be televised such as first or premier division football grounds. Competition for good sites is fierce. Even the use of the football grounds' electric scoreboards for advertising is an example of an unusual medium that is now being used with success. Advertisements are also found on supermarket trolleys although this could be considered a type of point-of-sale promotion.

The use of outdoor media can therefore be seen to be a dynamic and expanding vehicle of communication.

Point-of-sale displays

The material used for point-of-sale displays can prove to be a very effective vehicle of communication and can help to tip the balance in a product's favour at the precise point where and when decisions between alternatives are being made. Often the material for point-of-sale displays is not only supplied by the producer of the products, but is also placed in position and restocked and generally looked after by a regular salesperson. But this is becoming much harder in the major supermarkets as they use their powerful position to control activities of suppliers.

Point-of-sale material can include all or only a selection of the following: shelf edging; dummy packs; display packs; display stands; mobiles; and posters.

Exercise

In your local supermarket note the different kinds of points-of-sale material used.

Packaging

Packaging, which is sometimes called the 'silent salesman', is the ultimate point-of-sale communication tool. It is a non-personal channel of communication, which has become an increasingly important part of the communications mix. Most grocery products are now purchased from a self-service supermarket, and so the need for good packaging has increased with the growth of self-selection. The packaging of a product involves the following functions:

1 Give protection.
2 Contain the product.
3 Be convenient.
4 Give information.
5 Have display advantages.
6 Convey any brand image.
7 Be seasonable when appropriate.

Give protection - contain the product - be convenient

In order for the product to reach the consumer in perfect condition the packaging must offer basic *protection*. Protection is especially important when the product is very fragile, i.e. eggs. The protection must also safeguard against damage from rain, heat, cold, in fact against all the elements of the environment. This function relates more to the total product concept and quality of the offering rather than communications. However, just as a person's appearance is one of the initial communications in a personal situation, so the appearance of a package is an initial communication regarding a product.

As well as providing protection the packaging must contain the product – whether it is a bag of sugar or a bottle of wine or an aerosol deodorant. It would have been possible in the 1950s and 1960s to purchase four small nails loose from an ironmonger; today's consumer is more likely to find nails at the local DIY superstore and they are sold pre-packed in tens. There are many different kinds of containers for products, e.g. toothpaste can either be in a tube or a pump dispenser. You might consider if this is really meeting the needs of the customers? Remember the convenience of the packaging is important but it is the overall value to the customer that is paramount. Some products such as multipacks of drinks have been improved by having a ready-made handle attached, making it easier for the consumer to carry the product home.

Product tampering has become a threat, as happened with baby foods where it was discovered that glass had been put into the food. The manufacturers' reaction was quickly to change the design of the baby food containers, so that it would be obvious if a jar of baby food had been opened. Manufacturers have spent much money and time in designing tamper-proof containers.

Other product factors could be the size of the package – it may be a carton of pot noodle or even individual tea bags or a small one-person portion of custard. Is the size of the package right for the consumer? Giant family packs of cereal or washing powder can be useful when large amounts of the product are used, but they are not so convenient if they don't fit on any of the shelves in the customer 's kitchen. The product packaging should also be suitable for shelf display at the relevant retail outlet.

Packaging that is reusable has increased in importance with the growth of the 'green revolution'. Many products are now being designed so that when the original container is empty it can be filled again. This is common with many of the Body Shop products. With fabric conditioner it is also possible to buy refill packs. The original container for the fabric conditioner may be plastic and would cause a pollution problem when disposed of, whereas the carton container with the refill can be disposed of with much less harm to the environment.

Give information - have display advantages - convey any brand images

Packaging now gives much more information about the product than was given a decade ago. It is now expected that the following information will be given as standard on food: ingredients, country of origin, sell by date, calorific values and a bar code, which can be used both as a stock control and pricing mechanism. However, much of the information on packaging is to attract customers, even if some of it is to meet the legal requirements.

A packaging should have display advantages especially if it is to be sold via interme-diaries. In this case it should be sufficiently attractive and eye-catching to interest the consumer as well as serve the needs of the members of the distribution chain.

One of the most important features of packaging is that it can convey the brand image easily. This has become easier with the advent of new processes and materials within the packaging industry, as more and more products are capable of being packaged. The last fifteen years has seen an almost revolutionary change in packaging and distribution across many product ranges.

Exercise

Name five products of which the brands are easily recognised by the colour or shape of the packaging alone.

Packaging can be very important when a company is portraying a corporate image. They can use the same or similar designs and colours for all products and the packaging is constant over the whole product range.

Be seasonal when appropriate
Seasonal packaging is linked solely to a promotional opportunity that might be present. Sometimes these promotions can be very effective. Scandinavian soft toilet rolls are edged with miniature sprigs of holly and mistletoe at Christmas, at other times of the year the edging is little red hearts. In Britain it is mainly Easter and Christmas, and to some extent Valentine's Day where seasonal packaging is most relevant.

Although packaging can carry out functions of protection, the communication and promotional aspect are of tremendous importance. It would be very dull indeed to go shopping and not be assailed by all the different colours, shapes and sizes of products in their various packaging. One of the reasons why Radion washing powder was so successful after its launch was that the packaging colours were so noticeable with orange and lime green. This factor alongside the abysmal, old-fashioned television advertisements, assured it was noticed in the marketplace, and from this, it became a successful product. However, it is not recommended that other companies follow this route to success with their products as it is a very dubious one.

Conclusion

It is important that a company is aware of the channels of communication that it has at its disposal, and utilises them in the correct way. The medium chosen to convey the message must be appropriate. The appropriate medium depends very much on what the product or service is, and to whom it is targeted. If the product is of high value and aimed at the industrial market, a personal channel may be best – an example would be a fork-lift truck salesperson calling on a potential factory customer. However, if the product is of low value and aimed at the consumer market, a non-personal channel may be more effective. Washing-up liquid on a television advertisement is a more realistic scenario here. Other non-personal channels include the price, media and broadcasting.

We can therefore understand that a message must be sent via a channel from the organisation to the ultimate customer. This, however, is only half of the communication process. In order for it to function well it should also give a feedback, which we could perceive in the form of increased sales, if the product were successful, or even decreased sales if the communication was bad and conveyed the wrong message. The feedback should be a definite reaction of some type to our message.

As we have seen, the message is sent via a channel, an appropriate medium. Perhaps you will remember a message sent by Benetton a while ago to its customers via a billboard, the billboard posters showed a newborn baby still attached at the umbilical cord. The feedback received by Benetton from its audience, the general public, was swift and sure, they found the posters to be in bad taste and wanted them removed immediately. It was an example where both the message and feedback were loud and clear, and although perhaps not to Benetton 's liking, they had to appease the audience by launching a new poster showing babies that were washed and fully clothed. One thing is certain, Benetton's posters were a talking point and people who formerly had not known of the company then developed an awareness of them. Not only an awareness of the company, but especially an awareness of Benetton's advertising campaigns, which subsequently showed a nun and a priest kissing, and another with a patient in bed dying of AIDS. In 1992 the Advertising Standards Authority upheld that Benetton had shown 'disregard for the sensitivity of the public' by displaying posters showing a car in flames after being bombed by terrorists.

Exercise

Think of recent communications from organisations that have attracted your attention and made you more aware of that organisation. How did they do it?

Questions

1 Think of a recent communication from an organisation that has attracted your attention. Explain how this has affected your views about that organisation.

2 What is meant by encoding? How might an advertising agency help an organisation to encode its messages?

3 What are the advantages of personal communications over non-personal communications?

4 Why is packaging sometimes called the silent salesman?

References

Abraham, M and Lodish, L, 'Getting the most out of advertising and promotion', *Harvard Business Review*, May/June 1990.

Biel, A L, 'Strong brand-high spend', *Admap*, November 1990.

Colley, R H, *Defining Advertising Goals for Measured Advertising Results*, New York Association of Advertisers, 1961.

Coulson-Thomas, C J, *Marketing Communications*, Heinemann 1983.

17

PROMOTIONAL PLANNING

Introduction

Promotional planning can be viewed as a sequential process aimed at deciding the strategies and necessary action plans to achieve communication objectives. The four members of the promotional (or communication) mix which are described in Chapters 18 to 20 are:

- Non-personal – **1** Advertising;
  - – **2** Publicity;
  - – **3** Sales promotion; and
- Personal – **4** Personal selling.

It does not matter whether the company is production-, product-, selling- or marketing-oriented, it will at some time use one, or perhaps a combination, of these elements of the promotion mix. The type of product or service offered by a company will have a bearing upon which elements are used. Of course the budget which an organisation can afford to spend on promotions can influence decisions. The process is shown in Fig 17.1

The objectives of a promotion campaign were introduced in Chapter 16. They are very important; they are the targets that a company will wish to achieve with regard to the three possible groups of objectives:

- informing;
- persuading; and
- reinforcing.

It is only when the objectives have been analysed and decided upon, that the company can set about deciding how best to achieve them. Objectives must be linked to the target audience, and, in particular, the stage they have reached in the purchase cycle – pre-transactional (before a purchase), transactional (at time of purchase) and post-transactional (after a purchase).

Potential customers can go through these stages in deciding on a purchase. However, the objectives of communication could also refer to any of the pre-transactional stages a potential customer goes through before reaching the point where they make a purchase. Effectiveness of communication can then be judged against the customer's stage of development. The AIDA model was developed in the first part of the century when considering the psychology of selling. It reflects the stages prospects move through in the purchase cycle above.

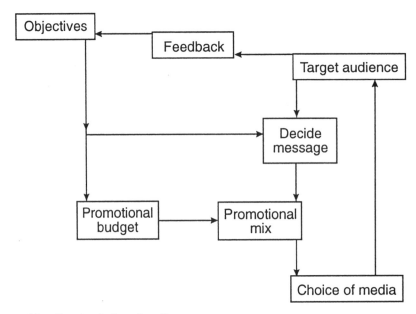

Fig 17.1 Decision flow in choice of media

Attention – Gain attention of the audience.
Interest   – Kindle interest in the product/service on offer.
Desire   – Arouse desire for your product above any desire for your competitor's product.
Action   – The customer buys the product.

The usefulness of this model has been questioned in recent years. Other models such as 'Lavidge and Steiner' (*see* Fig17.2) have been developed and it is now shown that AIDA is not robust when considering the success of advertising with all types of products. It will be possible in many instances for a product to create *interest*, perhaps by the very nature of the advertisement, but this in itself is not enough to create *desire*. Also AIDA does not cover the important post-transactional stage when further purchases are considered.

The more inexpensive and frequently bought products do not always require purchasers to go through all the stages of the model. Items like baked beans are regular consumer products and only the *action* stage is necessary. When you run out, you buy another tin of your regular brand next time you go shopping. For this type of repeat-purchase product, advertising covers only the reinforcement role of keeping the customer permanently aware of the value of the brand. Top-of-mind awareness for brands such as Heinz are reinforced by the slogans: in this case, 'Beanz meanz Heinz'. Shopping goods, which are more expensive and less frequently purchased, e.g. dishwashers or televisions, require more stages in the purchase decision. They may indeed require all the stages of the AIDA model. Nevertheless, a communication can be considered a success if it moves a potential customer from *attention* to *interest*, or from *interest* to *desire*.

It is possible to see an association in most of the alternate models which have been developed to show the progression of involvement. In general they can be classified under the three general headings of knowledge, attitudes and behaviour.

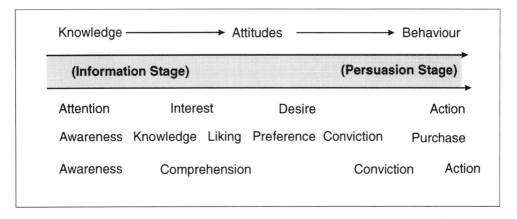

Fig 17.2 Stages of conviction models

The top line represents the AIDA model, the middle line the six stages of the Lavidge and Steiner model. The bottom line shows the four steps described in the DAGMAR (Defining Advertising Goals for Measured Advertising Results) study. Other models can also be fitted into this progression. The starting point for different products will be different and so the measure of effectiveness requires a clear statement of the objectives within a specific context. At the pre-transactional stage the need could be for information such as: announcing a new product; explaining product features; describing available services; suggesting new uses; correcting false ideas; and informing of a price change. Here potential customers would probably be at the *awareness* or *interest* stage on the AIDA scale.

The transaction might not be an actual purchase of a product. It could be just the acceptance of a sales call. However, at the stage leading to the transaction the element of *desire* has to be developed and then extended into *action*. *Persuasion* is most important here and objectives could be arranging a sales appointment; enhancing company image; changing perception of product; building brand loyalty; stimulating a purchase decision or encouraging brand switching.

In the post-transactional period the need is obviously for reinforcement and reminders. Major objectives could be reassuring that the purchase was right; maintaining top-of-mind awareness; or encouraging recommendations to friends. Within these objectives it is essential the goals are set so results can be measured as in the DAGMAR (*see* Chapter 16) process. This forms part of the feedback function shown in Fig 17.2.

Promotion as an investment

Promotional expenditure is not usually considered in the same category as *research and development* or *training,* but in considering the effect of various expenditures on the future of an organisation it is just as important. R&D can be seen as producing the products of the future, without which a company could struggle. Certainly these efforts need to be directed to meet the predicted requirements of target customers. But R&D is the investment in the offering side of the exchange process. Training, and the ever increasing realisation of the benefits of customer-care programmes, concerns the delivery of the offering. A key ingredient in the long-term satisfying of customers.

Promotional expenditure should not be seen as a short-term effort to gain sales. Because there can be an immediate return from some types of promotion there is an assumption in some organisations that promotion should always be treated in this way. This forgets the full benefit of communication. It is an investment in the customers, hopefully creating positive attitudes towards an organisation or a product/service. In Chapter 11 'positioning' was described in the words of Ries and Trout as what happens in the mind of customers. Those authors are professional advertising executives, and they realise how communicating with customers is investing in the development of customers' attitudes and beliefs.

A great deal of promotional investment is future orientated in exactly the same way as R&D and training. It should be treated in this way inside an organisation. If an organisation understands the exchange process, then they will appreciate how both sides of the exchange can be influenced by marketing action.

The target audience

A promotion strategy developed by a company will aim to accomplish an improvement in the way that the company, and its goods and services, are perceived. In order to achieve this, some of the following stakeholder groups will be reached either directly or indirectly:

- specific target customers;
- the general public;
- present and potential distribution channel members;
- present and potential employees;
- suppliers of finance; and
- present and potential shareholders.

It is possible that some communications could be seen by stakeholders who are not the prime target. This fall-out must be appreciated when placing advertisements. In addition, competitors often learn from advertisements. However, all communications must be aimed primarily at those publics identified in the marketing and promotional objectives. Precise targeting of the communication can both save money and ensure an effective response.

An audience of 10 million for a TV commercial could cost £120 000 for a 30 second spot. This is £12 per thousand viewers. For £20 000 you could buy a full page in the *Financial Times* with a 200 000 circulation. This is £100 per thousand. On first appearance the TV is more expensive but better value. But if all *FT* readers were in the target group, but only 10 per cent of the TV audience were acceptable targets, the equation changes. Of course it is not as easy as this. The TV programme reaches one million relevant people, which is five times that reached by the *FT*. If the object is to get coverage of the greatest number of target customers then maybe the TV is still excellent value. But value, costs per thousand (CPT) and coverage all must be considered in the context of the most appropriate medium for the message. It is possible neither television nor press are really suitable to carry the message, it could be a direct mail shot offers a more appropriate medium even if it is more expensive than either.

Therefore marketing communicators must start with a clear view of the target group. But in particular they must decide both: how comprehensively the group is to be covered (coverage is the percentage of total target who are able to see a particular communication or series of communications); and what type of message and media is consistent with the communication objectives. Within the target group the role as user, decider, or influencer will also have to be understood in order to develop a suitable campaign. This also enables the message to be developed at the right level and the selection of the most appropriate media to convey that message effectively to the chosen audience.

When considering promotion there can be two ways of creating demand. Either products can be demanded by consumers who approach suppliers and pull the product through the distribution chain. The alternative is the traditional selling of products into distributors thus pushing products towards the customers.

Pull strategy

A pull strategy is used by many companies. Basically, it is a strategy which by heavy use of advertising and promotion encourages consumers to demand the product. This strategy can be particularly successful when applied to goods which are sold through supermarkets or newsagents, etc. In 1992 the pull strategy was used for a children's lollipop, called 'push pops'. These were advertised so heavily, that the children's interest was greatly aroused, and subsequent demand so heavy that the retailers' demand on wholesalers soon made supplies run out in many areas. The manufacturers did not sustain the initial heavy advertising campaign which could have kept the demand high for a longer period, and the manufacturers' response time to channel demand was not quick enough to meet the initial interest. With time, however, stocks of push pops became plentiful in shops, but the interest in the product had by then been substantially reduced.

Occasionally there is a similar pull strategy when new magazines are launched, especially magazines of a specialist nature, such as *Do-it-Yourself* or *Sewing and Knitting*, which by means of heavy advertising encourage consumers to demand that their local newsagents stock that particular magazine for them.

Push strategy

A push strategy works in the opposite direction to that of a pull strategy. It is the push from the producer to the distribution channel members and from them to the customer which increases demand for the product. Instead of aiming heavy advertising and promotional campaigns directly at the customer, the producer will specifically aim at the people and organisations selling the product to the final consumer. Examples of push strategy are very common in the industrial sector and also in the field of medicine. Medical sales representatives push products very strongly to doctors and back up this push with strong promotional measures. The doctors then prescribe the drugs to the patients who are ultimately the customer.

Avon, the cosmetics firm, is a well-known user of the push strategy. Salespeople call directly to the homes of customers to sell the products. Often companies will offer some kind of incentive to salespeople, to push their product more than their competitors' products. This can occur with many different kinds of goods and services, from insurance to sports equipment.

It is difficult to measure the effect of either the push or pull strategy or to see how efficient they are. Many producers of goods and services do not want to take any chances and run both strategies simultaneously in order that they can reinforce any effect one or the other may be having. Figure 17.3 shows how the push strategy and the pull strategy differ.

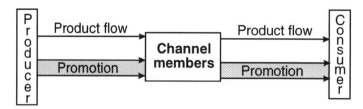

Fig 17.3 (a) The push strategy

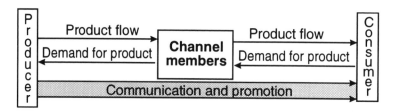

Fig 17.3 (b) The pull strategy

Promotion funding

An economist might suggest promotional expenditure should be raised to the point where the marginal return from additional spend matches the marginal cost of that spend. However, this is not only impossible to measure, but it also forgets the long-term return of promotion. The benefits of a sustained campaign do not always come in the form of immediate results. A more appropriate plan is to set the expenditure based on objectives to be achieved and task to be done (see below). Some companies establish the amount of funds they feel able to allocate to promotion (affordable method). Others decide how much they need to spend separately on the various promotion tools, and then add the totals to arrive at a total promotion requirement. Whether a top-down or bottom-up approach is used, arriving at promotional budgets is a very inexact science. There are four major ways in which companies can calculate their total promotional budgets.

1 The objective and task method (zero-based budgeting).
2 The affordable method.
3 The percentage of sales method.
4 The competitive parity method.

However, for all its faults, the percentage of sales method is generally the one most commonly used. Crosier aggregated the results of a number of studies up to 1985 and found that the objective and task method was being used by 18 per cent of companies, the affordable method (or executive judgement) by 21 per cent, the percentage of sales or A/S ratio by 44 per cent and all other methods were being used by 17 per cent. There is no general model which allows sales increases to be forecast based on promotional spend. Therefore organisations choose methods of allocating budgets with which they feel comfortable.

The objective and task method

The objective and task method with its zero-base approach takes time to calculate and involves the setting of promotional objectives. It is closest to the real need within the promotional programme. The company decides what it would like to achieve with future promotions and works out several alternative ways of attaining these objectives. These will be costed and evaluated before the final decision about which approach to undertake is decided upon. This is a very logical process, but again is not without its disadvantages.

1 It is very difficult to determine the exact response to any particular expenditure on promotion. Although objectives have been set there is no guarantee that they will be met by following any one specific approach.
2 This method does not categorically take into consideration whether the company can afford to follow the objective and task method. The company may know the promotional objectives it wants to attain, and perhaps how to attain them, but is the company financially able to do it?

Unfortunately the method is rarely applied in its entirety.

The affordable method

The affordable method is very easy to understand and basically means that the company will spend on promotion what it thinks is reasonable and can afford. It is often based on either the previous year's spend, or what is available when the forecast revenue and required profit have been fixed. There is very little to commend this method except that the company is most unlikely to spend above its limits. The disadvantages far outweigh the advantages. Some of the disadvantages include the following:

1 Any type of long-range planning is almost impossible. The company cannot guess exactly the funds that will be available in the future to spend on promotion.
2 In times of recession or hardship for the company, very little will be able to be spent on promotion, and yet this is most likely to be the time when spending in this way would prove to be of most benefit.
3 When the economy is especially buoyant or times are very good for the company, it is most likely to be able to afford to spend a lot more on promotion. This is the very time when it may actually be possible to reduce spending on promotion and perhaps increase investment in an alternative, say capital expenditure.
4 In situations where the company is spending only what it can afford, it is likely that other departments in the company are also competing for these limited funds. This will cause the managers to have very little goodwill or harmony between themselves. Instead of all aiming for a common goal, the good of the company, they will be more likely to try to satisfy only their own personal empire-building or departmental goals.

5 There is little opportunity to plan good promotional campaigns, i.e. making sure that the correct target audience is aimed for and using the correct media, message and promotional tool in general. The funds available under the affordable method can change from one day to the next depending on the activities of the company. Usually it is a reduction in the budget.

The percentage of sales method

Perhaps the classical approach, the percentage of sales method, is generally well liked by accountants as it is easy to calculate and therefore a precise amount can be allocated for promotion. A percentage of current yearly sales can be determined and this amount spent on the promotion mix, or a percentage of next year's forecasted sales can similarly be appropriated for this task. However, again, there are more disadvantages than advantages with this system.

1 There is no calculated theory to say what the percentage of sales should be. Whether a high or low percentage is correct, it is merely left to the discretion of management and may perhaps depend on how well the marketing manager can argue a case against, say, that of the finance manager.
2 If the percentage is fixed there is little opportunity to respond to any action by the competition or to any environmental demands that may arise. There is therefore the danger that valuable market share may be lost to a competitor should that competitor launch an aggressive promotional campaign which the firm cannot, because of lack of funds, respond to.
3 It is impossible to calculate what sales are won in relation to promotion spend if the spend always relates solely to the past or present sales figures.
4 Long-range planning for promotion over a period of more than a year is difficult to forecast, the budget is unlikely to remain at a similar level each year, unless the marketplace has remained fairly static.

The competitive parity method

The competitive parity method is where the amount allocated to be spent on the promotional mix is directly affected by how much is spent by competitors. It therefore aims to achieve a 'share of voice' similar to the company's market share. In fact there is some evidence to suggest that market shares are roughly in line with long-term share of advertising spend in some industries. However, this is not always so.

It is thought by those who engage in this method that the amount spent must be about right as it is almost an industry norm. Organisations feel more comfortable not being the odd one out. But there are many abnormalities inherent with this approach.

1 All companies do not share the same objectives. Some companies may have the sole objective to become market leader, others may wish to become more profitable and although these are not mutually exclusive objectives, it is rare to be able to achieve both simultaneously.
2 It is suggested that this method diminishes the chance of promotional wars. But there is no logical reason to suppose that promotional fights will not happen. It is much more likely that all of the companies in direct competition, if they are all following the competitive parity method, will keep their spending patterns match-

ing the others. This is likely to happen even if spending is at a much higher level than that which would exact a reasonable return.

3 The comparative parity method makes it less likely that a *follower* product could become a *market leader*. There are other aspects of the marketing mix to consider. Promotional activities cannot be considered on their own. But a *challenger product* is likely to require above parity promotional expenditure as part of its marketing mix.

The promotional message

Having decided on the communication objectives and the target audience, the next decision is the content of an effective message. This is necessary before deciding upon the balance of the promotional mix. The message has two components: content and mood. The content will reflect the requirement to communicate some particular information or relevant encouragement. This will be what the communicator hopes the receiver will do or consider following receipt of the message. The mood refers to the way the appeal is made to the target audience. Some moods are more appropriate than others for different types of message. Sometimes the mood is modified further when the media is chosen and even when professional creative teams start to work on the actual advertisement. Relevant moods could be: rational, emotional, or moral.

It is here that a good knowledge of the personality traits and attitudes of the target audience can be invaluable. Use could be made of psychographic variables such as the activities, interests, and opinions suggested by Plummer and listed in Chapter 6. Alternatively, the 'inner directed' groups suggested by McNulty, also in Chapter 6, would show the rational to be self-explorers; the emotional to be experimentalists; and the moral to be social resisters. In some ways the credible emotional appeal is the most powerful. You can probably think of wholesome images shown to support Hovis bread, or the delight of the Andrex puppy, or the humour of John Cleese with respect to a well-known chargecard. Humour is not proven to be more powerful than rational appeals. In fact in can become boring very quickly once the joke is known. Nevertheless, it is an excellent attention-grabber and the need to gain attention is obviously the first need for an effective communication.

The AIDA sequence is critical here. The types of headlines which can grab attention must be consistent with the progression of the message. As already mentioned, it may not be necessary to take the target audience through all AIDA stages for a repeat purchase decision, but for the communication itself, all stages are relevant. Your communication must:

Grab	ATTENTION
Excite	INTEREST
Create	DESIRE
Prompt	ACTION

In terms of the total content the rule KISS (keep it simple) is good to remember. Adding too many messages into one brief communication generally dilutes the effectiveness of the primary content. Do not let detail get in the way of a good strong message. And in internal communications a good summary on a couple of pages of A4 is often more effective than a complex report. If people want the details they will ask for them.

Pre-testing of messages using specialised marketing research techniques is highly recommended. The research might study the format/layout of the advertisement. For instance, one technique tracks the movement of an eye across the page when reading an advertisement. This can be used to ensure the key messages are correctly positioned in the copy. However, the simplest techniques are just as important. Show the proposed advertisements, perhaps in rough form, to a sample of your audience and ask them what they make of the message.

Promotional mix decisions

Consider your own personal communications – when do you send a letter or make a telephone call rather than calling on someone in person? How do you decide which is the best way to get your message across? A similar dilemma exists internally within an organisation. The decision to send a memo could be because it is more effective than a notice on the company notice board. But in another situation an article in the company newspaper could be more appropriate.

The same dilemma faces organisations in deciding between each of the promotion mix tools of advertising, publicity, sales promotion, and personal selling. If there are only a small number of customers then perhaps a sales call is best. For mass markets there is a need to use mass media. Advertising is good at creating awareness and interest. Public relations can fulfil the same role as media advertising except there is a loss of control over what is published. This can be countered by the increased authority an editorial item might seem to have as opposed to an obvious advertisement. Sales promotion can be an immediate stimulus influencing a purchase but it can also be used effectively to encourage repeat purchase. Personal selling is expensive but very direct.

Depending on the type of product marketed, an organisation may wish to spend more on one of the promotion tools, say advertising, than another, say selling. Alternatively, an industrial machinery producer could find that personal selling is the most important tool, whereas a toy manufacturer may well be interested in media advertising and sales promotion.

The next two chapters discuss the merits of the major promotional methods. It is obvious that personal selling is a personal medium that offers direct contact with customers. The non-personal methods can be divided between advertising and publicity, which are indirect contact, and sales promotion which supports in a complementary way. Usually a mix of methods is used. This balances the push/pull requirements of reaching customers. Personal selling and sales promotion are very effective as 'push' techniques. The benefits of personal selling are that it is interactive, responsive and flexible. The drawback is that it can be very expensive. But selling should not be seen solely as a 'push' technique; it is also a major tool in developing long-term customer relationships and is part of the customer investment. Sales promotion can reinforce a position for a product or organisation if the promotion is well chosen. Money-off promotions can achieve significant short-term sales growth, but they do nothing for a brand's image. A link to a relevant celebrity could enhance a brand personality.

Advertising and publicity are definite investments. They may be indirect and non-personal, but they can be very intrusive. But for that to be achieved they must reach their target. The media is very overcrowded, and it was once suggested that we all receive over one thousand media advertising messages every day. Nevertheless, every reader of this book should be able to list a number of advertisements they remember well. These are ones that have been received.

The decision on how much to spend on each part of the promotional mix is a standard question, which does not have a standard answer. It really does all depend on the job to be done. It also depends on the budget. And it depends on the necessity of an advertisement or communication message to gain attention. If there is insufficient budget to gain attention using conventional media then any money spent is wasted. The overriding need is to deliver the message effectively. The budget allocated to any method should be judged on the basis of this task.

Problems of budget allocation arise more when organisations do not use the objective and task method of calculation. This 'bottom-up' approach allows a mix of promotional methods to be considered in an ideal context. The alternative 'top-down' approaches inevitably mean a compromise has to be made in the promotional mix allocation. The outcome of this is the mix of promotional methods illustrated in Fig 17.4.

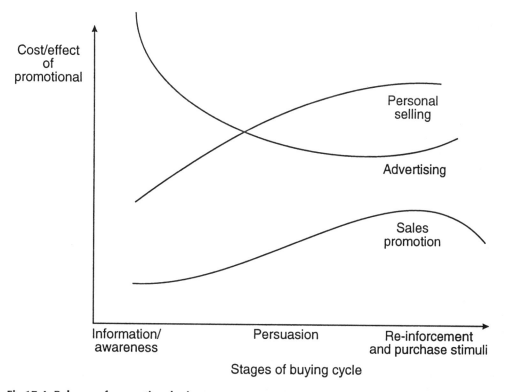

Fig 17.4 Balance of promotional mix

If heavy advertising can increase the size of a market then sometimes an organisation is faced with a version of the marketer's dilemma. If your company 'A' increases advertising, will the increased demand also benefit competitor 'B'? It certainly will if 'B' deploys extra salespeople. But if 'B' also advertises, the market could grow very fast and both companies will benefit if they can get the products to the customers. There are two other scenarios shown in the matrix in Fig 17.5. How would you approach this problem?

	Company 'A'	
	More advertising	More sales people
Company 'B' — More advertising	Market grows fast. Both benefit in line with market share	Market grows 'A' gains more than 'B'
More sales people	Market grows 'B' gains more than 'A'	Market static both lose due to cost of sales staff

Fig 17.5 Advertising/sales dilemma

Measuring effectiveness

The communication is not always tested before it is used, although such an action is recommended. But after it has been used the strategy needs to be assessed and, if required, refined. Two of the most common reasons given regarding why a promotional campaign should be monitored are:

- To show that the money has been well spent, and not wasted on something that is not worthwhile.
- To show that promotion has contributed to sales, that changes in demand were not just environmental factors.

Both these are somewhat negative reasons. They do not measure up to the principles of the DAGMAR study which links feedback to clear communication objectives. Perhaps the problem is that so much of business is carefully controlled by capital payback periods and tangible purchases. Careful study will show that money spent on wages and salaries is not necessarily any more accountable than investment in promotions. But the fact remains that promotion is not directly related to sales in a one-to-one model. Promotion is an investment in customers' perceptions of products, but the return from such an investment is difficult to benchmark. When the judge in a notable pornography trial was asked to define 'pornography', he replied he could not define it but could point it out when he saw it. Good promotion has an element of this qualitative judgement about it, but the aim of feedback is to learn from your experience rather than develop a 'feel good' factor that the money was well spent.

Usually some form of attitudinal research or a continuous tracking study is carried out. Certainly 'benchmarks' can be established for targets such as level of unprompted awareness, level of message recall, stated brand preference and knowledge of facts included in the advertisement. These measures are mainly to do with measuring the effect of the communication. Even brand preference, as measured following a campaign, does not link precisely into actual sales. For many business the bottom line from their promotional investment is increased sales.

Example

For the UK Government Health Education programme different objectives apply. These could be changing peoples behaviour because of the risk of AIDS. The research carried out following the second major AIDS campaign showed that the awareness of AIDS had exceeded the targets set. The worry was that few people said they had or were about to changed their behaviour in spite of the new knowledge. If you look at the anti-smoking campaigns over many years it will be seen that behavioural changes happened very slowly, even though levels of knowledge had changed.

The problem is not how to give information, but how to persuade the target audience to act. Because of this it is usually inappropriate to measure the desired actions. It is more appropriate to measure against objectives related to the message. There are occasions where direct response is obvious. Say a charity advertises for donations to meet a particularly severe problem of malnutrition in Somalia. They can immediately measure donations and they do not worry if these are new gifts of money, or donations which would otherwise have been made to an alternative charity. The short-term effect is easily quantified. There is also a long-term effect, for although the effect of a particular communication reduces with time, there will be some lasting subconscious residue which could mean you donate to 'Save the Children' again next time. This long-term shift is not so easily measured.

Work by Stephen King showed the gap between the desired action and the various ways of measuring advertising effectiveness. He suggested a scale of responses dependent on the task to be undertaken (*see* Fig 17.6).

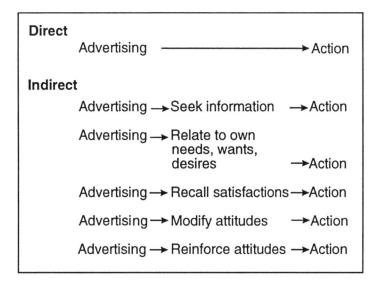

Fig 17.6 A scale of advertising responses

In order to gauge the attitudes and behaviour of donors or customers it may be necessary to go to the customer to find out. This is an action promoted by Tom Peters, who regards it as essential. He states, 'Marketers should be in the field at least 25% and preferably 50% of their time.' You might sympathise with a charity worker who claimed they should not spend time with donors when there is other – *'more important'* – work to do. But this confuses the different roles within a charity. The charity worker will benefit from the revenue achieved by the *'professional fundraisers'*, who could be seen as the marketing managers in the organisation. These fundraisers certainly do spend a great deal of time among potential donors.

Peters gives general advice suggesting all managers should go to the customer, look, listen and provide feedback. The need to listen is a necessary way of providing feedback on what has already been achieved. It is also a necessary preliminary to what still has to be achieved. Listening, like so many simple actions, is anything but simple. Peters advocates going out with a 'naive' mind set to gauge customers' reactions. He is incensed by statements like 'we've got to communicate better with our customers'. On the face of it there is nothing wrong with the statement, but all too often it implies a one-way conversation. Have you ever heard a person in a foreign country trying to get a local to understand them? At each stage of confusion the foreigner speaks more loudly! It doesn't work. That is not communicating better. To communicate you have to do it in the recipient's language. And it is all the better if it is relevant to the recipient's stage of development.

When listening you can ask limited questions, but ask them and then say no more and listen to the answer. You may not be able to listen to all of your potential customers, but the only way to measure need and effectiveness is to listen 'naively' to as many as you can. It is the relationship that an organisation builds through constant interaction with its customers and clients that is the measure required. Communication is the prime way of establishing this relationship but the requirement is for the contact to be *two-way*. If a two-way link is established then there will be no problems in measuring the effectiveness of communication.

Promotion and the demand curve

Demand curve shifting to the right

Chapter 14 looked at how price and quantity define the demand curve. However, price changes only move demand along the demand curve. Promotional activities can help to shift the total demand curve, as well as sometimes changing its shape. Promotions can create a new environment in which buying decisions are made.

It is rare for organisations to have complete knowledge about their competitors' plans. But companies need to make decisions for the future and to aim to gain competitive advantage for their offerings. Companies cannot gain sustainable advantage simply by decreasing the price. If price elasticity of demand existed, then more of the product would be bought if the price was lower, and if the price was increased, less of the product would be bought. This would only cause a movement along a demand curve, and not a complete shift of the demand curve. Also, competitors could soon follow to create the vicious circle described in Chapter 14.

It is possible to create or develop product differentiation by sustained promotional campaigns. This will produce a shift in the demand curve by changing the competitive situation. The movement will be easier to understand if we look at a few examples of products which have actually had a shift in their demand curves in recent years. One of the best British examples is the increase in healthy eating and organically produced food. Healthy eating has been promoted heavily on the back of government reports such as that of the Committee on the Medical Aspects of Health (COMA). The promotion has been supported by communications which range from leaflets in doctors' surgery waiting rooms, to articles in newspapers and advertisements on television. The increased awareness of the issues has caused a shift in the demand curve over a wide range of so called healthy foods. Some examples are yoghurt, brown bread, muesli, and porridge, where the demand for the product has shown a marked increase.

Porridge oats show a definite shift to the right in its demand curve over the last five years. In Scotland and Northern Ireland porridge oats have always been a popular breakfast cereal, especially in winter. Even at other times of the day porridge was used as a snack or as a good food that was filling, and helped keep one warm. Porridge has now become more popular in England, not because it was popular in Scotland, but purely because of the promotion that took place. This promotion let the public know that if taken regularly, porridge oats could help lower the cholesterol level, and bring down the risk of heart disease. The sales of porridge oats have soared. Whatever the answer, the demand curve for porridge has definitely shifted to the right.

A demand curve shifting to the right is illustrated in Fig 17.7.

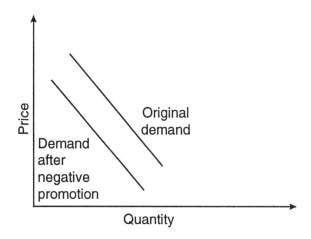

Fig 17.7 Demand curve after a negative promotion

Demand curve shifting to the left

The examples above show how good publicity can shift a demand curve to the right. It can, of course, move in the opposite direction when products are affected by bad publicity. A few years ago Mrs Edwina Currie, then a junior minister for health, announced that egg production in Britain was affected by salmonella. This was potentially life threatening to young children and elderly people, although not from properly cooked eggs. Nevertheless, there was a dramatic effect on the public at large, and the sale of eggs plummeted overnight. The egg industry suffered badly for many months, and some major producers even threatened to take a private prosecution against Mrs Currie. The demand curve for eggs shifted dramatically to the left. Even now, some of the British public feel insecure and have permanently reduced their egg consumption.

A similar example of a demand curve having a dramatic shift to the left was seen recently with the British beef industry. This followed the revelation that some cows had an infection known as BSE or 'mad cow disease'. The situation was so serious that schools, colleges, and hospitals took beef off their meal menus. Prices dropped and so did demand. Some farmers faced financial ruin. So powerful was the worldwide publicity about British 'mad cow disease' that, in 1992, a Russian city, faced with food shortages, refused to accept a consignment of British beef until it could be proven that none of the beef was contaminated.

It is therefore evident that the demand curve can be caused to shift either to the left as an effect of bad publicity, or to the right after good publicity or promotion.

Altering the shape of the demand curve

Not only is it possible to shift the demand curve but it is also possible to change its shape. This can happen when demand elasticity is effected. The company hopes that with a price rise the demand for a product will be inelastic, that is, the same quantity will be demanded even when the price has increased. The opposite is hoped for after a price decrease when more of the product will be bought, thus showing that the elasticity of demand has increased.

Conclusion

This chapter has considered the planning of communications and the different elements in what is termed the promotional mix. The most important lesson from the material presented is that communications are vital as a link between an organisation and its customers. Those customers can be internal or external to the organisation. In all cases two-way communications are preferable. The goals for a communication must be well thought out before proceeding further. This is like the notice seen on a student's door, 'engage brain before speaking'!

However, in measuring the specific effect of a communication the measurement must be restricted to the communication's objectives and not to some more obtuse relationship. If good two-way communications are established with customers, other requirements for a satisfactory marketing exchange will be revealed.

Questions

1 What problems can be caused by trying to include a complex message into an advertisement?

2 How might an advertising budget be calculated for an organisation?

3 Why might an attention grabbing advertisement fail to achieve its objectives?

4 Suggest a suitable situation for a 'pull' strategy as opposed to a 'push' strategy?

References

Colley, R H, *'Defining advertising Goals for measured advertising results'*, New York Association of Advertisers, 1961.

Crozier, K, 'Promotion' in *The Marketing Book*, ed. M Baker, Heinemann, 1987.

King, S, 'Practical progress from a theory of advertising', *Admap*, October 1975.

Lavidge, R and Steiner, A, 'A model for predictive measurement of advertisement effectiveness', *Journal of Marketing*, October 1961.

Peters, T, *Thriving on Chaos*, Macmillan, 1988.

Strong, E K, *The Psychology of Selling*, McGraw-Hill, 1925.

Case study: Mercia Glass

Mercia Glass is a small company just set up by John Wilson, a fifty-year-old glass-blower recently made redundant by a large Nuneaton glass manufacturer. Determined to make the best of the only opening available, John Wilson decided to put to practical use his £10,000 termination settlement by forming a business based on his extensive skills and experience in glass. With funding contributions from two other former glass-workers, now fellow directors, an initial investment of £25,000 has been supplemented by generous grant aid through the local Borough Industrial Office, and a low-rent first-year lease on a newly-commissioned factory workshop at a Bedworth industrial estate. A further 'fitting-out' allowance from the Borough and bank borrowings for working capital have enabled the 'partners' to purchase suitable secondhand equipment and sufficient materials stock to provision them beyond their first six months of full operations.

The product line that the company will initially produce consists of a variety of hand-crafted glass ornaments and giftware, ranging from decorative blown flowers and frosted-glass fruits to stained-glass ashtrays and ships-in-bottles. Though other product ideas are under consideration, the opening range has been restricted to fifteen items, to simplify production start-up and offer a representative product mix for market launch. While no formal market research has been carried out, Wilson and his co-directors have met with largely enthusiastic comments on showing early product samples to friends and neighbours, and a number of local giftware retailers. In the business plans submitted to support their grant and loan applications, the three directors had anticipated they would confidently market all they produced through using local part-time 'party-selling' agents working on a commission basis. These arrangements appeared to produce no cause for comment from their financial sponsors, in spite of the £90,000 first-year sales target the company had subsequently committed itself to.

Now, two weeks before the planned commencement of trading, John Wilson has become concerned about the marketing side of the operation. Assisting part-time in planning the party-sales arrangements, his wife has confided to him the doubts that she now has about finding the right quantity and quality of party agents to move the planned volume of product. In considering the possibility of having to sell over an area wider than the Nuneaton-Coventry district, Wilson draws small comfort from the £700 provision for advertising that he recalls building into the Year 1 budget. Though neither he nor his associates have any sales or customer-contact experience, he feels confident that the product range should almost 'sell-itself', once the immediate marketing arrangements are finalised. Somewhat irritated by this untimely distraction from his production planning schedules, he determines that whatever marketing the company does must, of necessity, be on a shoe-string budget.

Advise Mercia Glass on how to undertake the marketing side of the operation, given the obvious constraint of a limited budget.

18

ADVERTISING AND DIRECT MARKETING

Introduction

Advertising and direct marketing are two types of primary marketing communications but each uses different approaches. Both are controlled by the sender, who pays for the media used. Direct marketing differs from mass-media advertising by virtue of

- the media used;
- the precise targeting of the customers; and
- Interaction with those customers.

In a recent interview, Philip Kotler suggested that 'the death knell for mass advertising is growing louder'. However, he sees a rapid growth in Europe of direct marketing as companies look for more precision in building their customer dialogue.

Such a prognosis is too radical. There will always be a role for mass-media advertising for mass-media products. There are also excellent 'one-way' media such as specialist magazines, and targeted television which uses media schedules chosen to maximise coverage of specific segments. Nevertheless, directly targeted messages are now very possible and so no organisation should ignore the full scope of communication techniques available.

Both media advertising and direct marketing can be considered as 'above the line' expenditure although the phrase pre-dates direct marketing. *'Above the line'* is a term still widely used in marketing which derives from the historical way advertising expenditure was treated in marketing budgets. Main media expenditure was shown *'above the line'* because it represented actual expenditure, as opposed to sales promotion which was shown *'below the line'*, because much of the cost of such items came from a reduction in revenue, e.g. price cuts. Most advertisements run on behalf of a commercial organisation will be placed by an agency, who buy the space and pay the media owners. The agency then receives a commission from the media owners, but charge the full cost to the advertiser. It is not the same as placing a classified advertisement in your local newspaper where you would pay the media owner yourself. *'Above the line'* is no longer specifically related to the accounting conventions, but the term is still widely used to encompass money spent for media coverage. As such it can apply to the total advertising and direct marketing expenditure.

Campaigns for *'above the line'* expenditure are often planned as a whole, to achieve a regular series of messages about a company or a brand throughout a full year. PR is discussed in Chapter 19. However, the definition of PR from the Institute of Public Relations is 'the deliberate, planned, and sustained effort to establish and maintain mutual understanding between an organisation and its publics'. This definition is included here because it is important that not only publicity, but the total communications programme, is seen as a *deliberate, planned and sustained* effort. All the tools of the *promotional mix* should be used in a continuous effort to achieve the *communication objectives* of the organisation.

The scope of advertising

Advertising has a very wide scope. When someone places a card in the local newsagent's window with an item for sale it is an advertisement. This can be contrasted with a major company's commercial shown on television. Each of these examples may be successful if they achieve their objectives, namely moving potential customers closer to the point of purchase for a particular product or service.

Advertising is perhaps the first thing that people think about when considering marketing. You will already know that it comes at the end of the marketing process after a great deal of effort to ensure the *marketing offer* is worth promoting. However, it can be the most visible part of the marketing process. Main media advertising with multi-million budgets is undertaken by major consumer goods' companies. These are only a small number of the total organisations who use advertising to communicate with their publics. For the major companies large amounts of money are involved. The impact of their advertising creates strong recall. Advertising is a major part of their activities. For instance, Guinness have traditionally been high spenders. Guinness state the reason for their spending is the need to promote their product more than other major brewers, as they do not own any pubs, unlike Ansells, Bass or Whitbread. So we can already see a relationship with other parts of the marketing mix, in this case the channels of distribution.

Other high spenders that will immediately come to mind are companies like Procter & Gamble, Coca-Cola, Pepsi Cola, and Cadbury. Their expenditures on advertising are important in maintaining a high profile for the various brands, thus keeping them firmly in the minds of consumers.

Over the last decade the major consumer brands have been displaced at the top of the spending league by financial institutions such as banks and insurance companies, as well as major High Street retailers like Dixons, Woolworths, and J. Sainsbury. This shift reflects both the competition faced by these companies, and the way retailers have taken the lead in many markets. Another major advertiser has been the Government, particularly in promoting the various new share issues as state industries were sold to the general public. Promotional budgets of up to £10 million were allocated to individual privatisation campaigns. The result was not only the successful sales of shares, but also an increased awareness of share-owning in general among a wide spectrum of the British public.

It should be realised by now that advertising covers more than the persuading of a consumer to buy something. It is also a means of trying to influence behaviour and beliefs. This is the case with the following types of organisations:

- political parties;
- local authorities;

- charities;
- churches; and
- pressure groups, such as Greenpeace.

Each of these organisations have a 'product' that they want to 'sell'. The advertising of their 'products', which could be their policies and beliefs, is how these organisations hope to influence and gain the support of the general public. Actually changing behaviour is very difficult, as discussed earlier in Chapter 17 regarding the Government Health Education programme.

You will remember that the objectives of communication fall into the three categories:

- informing;
- persuading; and
- reinforcing.

In general, media advertising is most effective when introducing new brands, or announcing modifications to existing brands. The research of Abraham and Lodish, quoted in Chapter 16, indicated 59 per cent of new products received a positive impact from advertising, compared to 44 per cent of existing brands. The exact figures are not important, but advertising is much more effective at an early stage in the purchase cycle. When a product has lost its novelty factor, having been on the market for some time, consumers will have had time to make a balanced judgement about it. It is always difficult to change firmly held opinions and the advertising task therefore becomes more difficult. The objective of communication may change to one of trying to attract customers from different market segments; or perhaps introducing a new, improved version of the original product. Examples of changes to existing brands include Mr Sheen furniture polish which has been advertised as having a new pot-pourri fragrance, while Brooke Bond have now introduced instant tea granules.

Exercise

Over the period of a few days make a note of any new products or modifications to existing products, the advertising for which has been in magazines or on the television.

The stage of the product's life cycle will have a marked effect on the type of advertising and promotion that is carried out for a product. At the introductory stages of the product's life, advertisements are designed to creating an awareness of the product. After the product has moved into the growth stage of the life cycle, building interest will be of paramount importance. Later, when competition becomes more intense, the benefits of the product, against those of competitors' products, will be stressed, and perhaps the emphasis will switch to other types of promotion, maybe sales promotion.

Advertising considerations

There are many factors which should be considered before advertising is undertaken. Advertisements should first be considered as part of the total communication process discussed in Chapter 17. The objectives, message, and likely budget could well have been determined. Decisions now have to be taken on the role of advertising as part of the promotional mix. Primarily it revolves around the balance between advertising and personal selling, as these are usually the elements where most money is committed. Often decisions will be taken on the basis of the previous year, rather than a proper objective and task evaluation. It is not easy to switch between personal selling and advertising, as salespeople are usually employees with consequent rights. Even if an organisation does not employ a salesforce but uses commission agents, there is still the human problem of reductions. However, you will remember from Chapter 17 that the cost/effectiveness of advertising reduces as customers move through the stages of the purchase cycle. This is also carried into a similar relationship with the stages of the product life cycle mentioned above. Advertising is more important at the early stages. Nevertheless, it is not advisable to stop all advertising in a competitive marketplace, as customers soon move on to new products.

Following a Monopolies Commission report into washing powders, both Lever Brothers and Procter & Gamble each stopped advertising one brand. The Commission claimed that advertising costs contributed to unacceptably high prices. For the chosen brands, advertising was stopped and prices lowered. The sales of both brands began to fall, and one of them has now disappeared altogether. This does not prove advertising works, as other factors were also at work, but it does warn against radical changes in advertising support.

Because sales force costs are less directly variable than expenditure on advertising and other direct promotion, there tends to be more unplanned fluctuations in advertising budgets. Keith Crozier suggested that 65 per cent of promotional budgets are based on either the percentage of sales or the affordable methods (*see* Chapter 17). Both these methods are subject to fluctuations, and so when cuts come they fall on advertising rather than sales costs. This makes the effect even more pronounced.

To plan an advertising campaign the following must be considered.

1 The type of product or service offered.
2 The key benefit offered (why that product should be bought ahead of its competitors).
3 The objectives of the communication.
4 Who the target market consists of.
5 The advertising message and how it relates to other communication messages.
6 The amount to be spent on advertising within the context of the total communication spend.
7 The media chosen to carry the advertisement.
8 The prevailing marketing environment.

The environment, especially including everyone who might see your advertisement, can influence an advertising campaign. Recently, Benetton advertisements raised a storm of protest by the controversial and topical subjects they used. They certainly caught the public attention, and probably did a lot more for the company. However, the use of similar 'shock' advertising tactics by other organisations has sometimes backfired: for example, the 'death scene' advertisements used by the RSPCA (Royal Society for the Prevention of Cruelty to Animals) were withdrawn after much public outcry.

Advertising campaigns

The campaign planners will already know the answer to *who* the target market is? and *what* message is required? They need to decide *when, where,* and *how* they can reach the target in media terms. *When* because timing is a key variable and advertising must be co-ordinated with other communication plans. Also, other marketing plans need integration, as there is no point advertising heavily if there are not sufficient extra stocks available with distributors. *Where* and *how* is the media choice linked to the message. If the organisation is using a major advertising agency, they will have access to a wealth cf statistics linking media to target groups, as defined by segmentation variables.

In organising for advertising very few organisations design their own advertisements. If they do, media facts are available from media owners, but these do not give comparative facts, nor are they able to link together a campaign using several media to calculate the total coverage. However, the range of skills required for advertising are better bought in from a specialist agency. You might be able to put together a good internal team with the necessary skills and, of course, doing it in-house can be seen as reducing costs, but does it really work out cheaper when considering the opportunity costs of staff time and the other risks involved in this specialist area? Another benefit from using a professional agency is that they are able to stand back and review your communications plans in an objective way. If you do not like the agency you are working with you can always change them. But agencies offer a service, and, as in all service marketing, interactions and the building up of personal relationships can be rewarding. Advertising agencies should become an extension of an organisation's own marketing department.

It is still important to have someone responsible for briefing the agency and approving plans. In small companies dealing with local agencies this can be done by the overworked marketing manager, who is trying to carry out all the marketing roles himself. Larger companies might use more than one agency and maybe even a specialist media buying service. These companies tend to have large advertising departments, not to produce advertising, but to compare the different agency performances. Sometimes they get involved in media buying to ensure the buying power of a major company like Cadbury Schweppes can be used to get good discounts across all its brand advertising.

The prima donnas of advertising agencies are rightly the creative talent. This is the key reason for using an agency, because an 'everyday product' has to be presented in a way that takes the target market through all its stages of attention, interest, desire and action. The very best agencies combine creative talent with first-rate business planning.

> Coulson-Thomas, in his book *Marketing Communications,* suggests that on being told how much a client is prepared to pay, an agency will develop a media schedule giving details of which media should be used and why, how many insertions of what length should be made and so forth. In the case of a major campaign, an agency is likely to draw up a proposal which will set out campaign objectives and show how these can be furthered by sending certain messages along selected channels to priority identified target groups. A breakdown of the budget may also be given, showing how much is spent on creative development and on buying space and air time.

This seems to miss the point regarding objectives and integration. Advertising is not a function where a budget is stretched as much as possible and therefore a good brief and clear objectives are the most important issues. There will be a type of interactive process where media choice, message type and budget availability are continually studied against the coverage of the chosen target group. However, it is sometimes better to reduce coverage but present a full message with the preferred number of opportunities to see (OTS) for those reached, than to reduce OTS yet still try to reach everyone in the target.

The agency will try to answer the *when*, *where*, and *how* questions through a mixture of message presentation and media selection. The two are inextricably linked, as reflected in the saying that 'the medium is the message'.

Advertising messages

The message will usually emphasise the key facts that an advertiser wants to communicate. This is part of the content described in the previous chapter. Sometimes there will be an attempt to find a unique selling proposition (USP) – something tangible or intangible that the brand can claim as its own. In some advertisements it is sufficient to just get over the brand name. This is sometimes forgotten in the creative enthusiasm. There have been some notable occasions when the recall of an advertisement was high, and the contribution of the actors involved was well received, but the recall of the brand was minimal. This does a lot for the actors but gives little return on the advertising investment. There have been a number of brands that have succeeded in gaining brand recall without using brand names. Cigarettes such as Silk Cut, and Benson and Hedges Gold have achieved it, while in the past, Cadbury Smash ran successful advertisements without names. Where these succeeded was that the receiver had to work hard to understand the advertisement. Having worked out that the cut piece of purple silk represented the cigarette brand, the recall was stronger than if the brand name had been given and the receiver had not had to work it out. This is a clever approach to receivers but one that few brands dare risk. Another effective no-mention advertisement was just three words: *'Beanz meanz WHO?'* You ought to be able to guess the brand.

It is often said that to be effective an advertisement must be read, understood, believed, remembered, and finally acted upon. Allowing for the fact that TV cannot be read, this is a good list when developing and testing a suitable message. It is another variant of the AIDA progression already mentioned on several occasions. It leads into the question of repetition of messages. Do you remember a message on the first hearing, or does it take several repeats to really understand? For an advertiser there is no firm rule. Some messages for some audiences require a number of opportunities to see (OTS), others are remembered on the first showing. But the requirement needs to be established before the media planning stage, so the media schedule neither undershows nor over-exposes an advertisement.

An issue in campaign planning that is often ignored is the need for consistency in the messages offered. You will remember from Chapter 11 how important it is for a brand to gain a suitable position in its market. The communication is part of the development of this position. Also, it is very difficult to change opinions held about a mature brand. It is, however, very easy to confuse customers through inconsistent messages. Sometimes a new marketing manager is appointed, and to create activity he/she changes the advertising. This might bring a new, fresh image to the product. It is acceptable if it is part of a well-thought-out campaign, but all too often it is confusing. If a new campaign ignores past messages and is inconsistent when placed alongside them, it has to work that much harder to achieve the desired result. Recent examples which you can judge for yourself are:

Volvo cars believe its safety message is well established and does not need repeating again. The new campaign looks at other features such as drivability, appearance and style. (*Campaign*, 19 June 1992)

Pizza Hut wants to reposition itself away from being a fast-food chain into a restaurant experience. They have parted company with ad agency JWT because the current campaign was said to emphasise a price orientation, and say they hope a new campaign will build an 'emotional bond' with the customers.

(*Marketing*, 27 August 1992)

One final point regarding the advertising message is its role in *reinforcing* a buying decision. In Chapter 5 the need for re-assurance in the post-transactional period was mentioned. If a customer has just bought a major product, then interest in that product category continues beyond the actual time of purchase. Advertisements featuring both the model purchased and competitive models will be studied with interest. Even if the real purpose of an advertisement is to *persuade* rather than *reinforce,* the high probability that recent purchasers will see it must be considered. The key benefits need to appeal to this group, as they can also influence future sales by their word-of-mouth endorsement of the product – a very useful addition to any marketing communication programme.

The selection of media

You cannot select word-of-mouth as a communication medium, although it is a very effective medium, and a supplier can hope everything else in the offer is sufficiently attractive to ensure good personal recommendation. The media that can be used are discussed in Chapter 16.

Advertising revenue forms a large proportion of the income for most media owners, so they have to 'market' their 'product' to potential customers, agencies and advertisers. The benefit offered by the media is access to the relevant target customers, that is, the one the advertiser is trying to reach. To help identify the relevant groups the media owners supply very detailed profiles of their readers/viewers. The matching of these groups with the target audience has been greatly increased by the use of computers, and media planning is a very professional business.

Several years ago most advertising agencies offered a full service of account handling, research, planning, creative, and media. Over the last fifteen years more specialists have developed, concentrating on just one of these functions. The most successful are creative hot-houses, and media planning specialists. If a company wished to do its own creative work it could still use a specialist agency to buy the media.

Decisions on media buying cover the right medium for the message, and then the inter-related question of *frequency* versus *coverage,* that is, how many opportunities to see against the percentage of the target market reached (covered) by the advertisement. The figures produced by the media planning packages are usually the averages. If an average OTS is 10 then that inevitably means some people see it on more occasions and some less. The ideal is never obtained. Also a highly concentrated campaign where there is an OTS of 10 over a period of a week or two, will have a different result to one where the 10 OTS are spread out at one per month.

The vehicle for advertising is mass-media. Each insertion of an advertisement is directed at a group of people and not an individual. As it is also *one-way* communication, there is an inevitable lag before any feedback can be obtained. Therefore there is rarely any opportunity to modify a campaign after it has been launched. Pre-testing must involve both the message and the media as the two are inseparable in the actual campaign.

The choice between the different media will be taken based on the different strengths of each: that is, not only the ability to reach the target group efficiently, but the effective way in which that message is delivered. The issue of cost per thousand (CPT, a measure of media cost divided by audience) is only relevant when comparing two media of equal effectiveness. There have been times when TV airtime was so scarce that advertisers who had booked a spot were being bumped out by one offering a higher payment. There is a difference between a fixed-time TV spot during a specific programme, and buying a *'package'* where the TV company guarantees a minimum number of rating points (a measure of audience used in television media). Some advertisements on the latter system will be at favourable times, others will be placed according to availability. The same is true of newspapers and magazines. A key position on the cover or facing a key editorial page will be sought after as being better than other positions. Premium prices are charged for these positions compared with discounts for a *'run of paper'* (i.e. where there happens to be space) position. The choice is therefore both the media used and the relevance of the timing or position in that media.

Lead times are also important. Newspaper advertisements are quick to produce and can be very topical. Such advertisements appeared for Renault the day following Nigel Mansell winning the world drivers' championship. There are other examples that you could find. Lead times for monthly magazines tend to be very long. Also in this category is space in the weekly Sunday newspaper colour magazines. Television also cannot be rushed, although the use of modern video rather than film means there are opportunities here. Although all these aspects are relevant, the key decision still is the one concerning 'the right media for the message'. This is an extension of the one liner, 'TV to sell, Press to tell'.

Advertising agencies

An advertising agency should be an extension of an organisation's marketing department. It can bring specific skills to the partnership, and these should enhance the ability of a company to get the most from its advertising. Agencies can be large, London-based, high-profile operations with international connections, or small, local but equally professional set-ups. The skills they have are related to communication in media. Since no two advertising problems are alike, each needs to be considered separately and in detail. Agencies can be what is termed *'full-service'*, offering all services to their clients. However, there is an increasing number of specialist agencies, concentrating on just one function.

As in any rewarding relationship, honesty and trust are needed to work towards the best solution. The agency skills are in projecting messages either visually or in words. The main functions in a full-service agency usually consist of the following.

1 A selection of *creative teams* comprising an art director and a copywriter, each team specialising in particular media. Agency reputations are often built on their creativity. These groups work closely with the production groups who translate approved creative ideas into finished commercials.
2 The *account supervisor/director* function, really a key account manager who builds and maintains the relationship in the same way as a sales manager might in another

organisation. They also get involved with specialist areas such as advertising research, and other services directly relevant to the client relationship.

3 The *media planning and buying* function which contributes in this vital area.

The clients work directly with the account team, but there is no reason why they should not meet and help brief the other functions. However, clients should not try to do the agency's job. The way to be a good client is to give a clear brief, and when evaluating work, to do so fairly but as a total package.

It must be remembered, however, that agencies are in business, and sometimes are very profitable. They started as agents for the media owners and that is the basis of the commission payments they receive when booking space. The Institute of Practitioners in Advertising recommend that contracts from full-service agencies should allow a 15 per cent net (17.65 per cent gross) margin on media. Even after the Office of Fair Trading ruling that the fixed 15 per cent standard rate commission represents a restrictive practice, many agencies still benefit from increased media spend by their clients. There are other elements of the promotional and marketing mix which compete for marketing investment, and sometimes agencies forget this. Some agencies do offer a range of additional marketing services alongside the advertising role. These could include marketing research, marketing planning, precision marketing/direct mail, publicity/PR, and sales promotion. At times these will be offered from the main agency, and sometimes from a separate agency in the same group. As with the basic agency relationship, a lot will depend on the interaction between the marketing manager for the client, and the account supervisor in the agency. One client might feel comfortable with various services from a single group, others might use separate researchers or promotional groups.

The idea that a full-service agency can save the Marketing Director time has rightly been challenged. Certainly such one-stop-shop agencies should be able to offer a more integrated approach to client needs. But not all clients (advertisers) need to achieve this

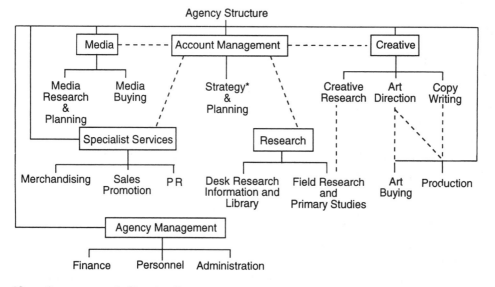

*Sometimes a separate Planning Group

Fig 18.1 The structure of a typical advertising agency

by buying from a single source. However well the agency is briefed, it is still an agency. The advertiser knows the product intimately and can assess the requirements. The different services can all be bought separately, but increasingly it is the media buying function which is being placed with a specialist. Figure 18.1 shows a traditional advertising agency structure. Roger Parry of media specialists, Aegis, gave a hint to the reason when he said:

> The only real economies of scale are available on the media side, and here they are massive. ... To be credible you have to do research into the media marketplace – the more you understand, the more effective you will be. ... If your knowledge is superior to any other planner or buyer, then you will get better prices.
>
> (*Marketing Business*, June 1992.)

For other elements of the promotional mix such as direct marketing, publicity or sales promotion, there are both separate, independent agencies and members of large communications groups. The structure of creative, account handling, and delivery of message are still present in these agencies. They need to be judged as any supplier on the basis of their abilities. If an organisation decides to use an agency then a proper briefing is appropriate.

Briefing an agency

This section refers primarily to briefing a specialist advertising agency. However, the issues can easily be adapted to cover any agency retained to advise on part or all of the communications mix.

Before appointing an agency, it is necessary to go through a selection process. This can involve a competitive pitch, where several agencies are given the same brief and asked to present their plans. These presentations can be very elaborate and expensive for the participating agencies. Sometimes the clients offers a payment to subsidise the agency costs, but for very large accounts agencies are prepared to invest, in the hope of landing a profitable account. There are some agencies who refuse to participate in this competition, preferring to let their past record indicate their abilities.

When briefing a new agency an advertiser has to give rather more background information than would be given to an incumbent agency which would already have the basic data. In his book, *Marketing*, David Mercer gives an excellent study on the process of developing advertising from a good brief. He states

> ...the client's brief to the agency, and how it is translated within the agency, is the key determinant of a successful advertisement. No matter how brilliant the creative treatment, it will not succeed if it fails to meet the marketing objectives.

This obviously points to the need for a structured brief starting with clear objectives. Although the list below was given earlier in this chapter, it gives the key headings necessary for a good brief. Of course, item 7 – media – might be left to be discussed with the agency.

1 The type of product or service offered and issues from the elements of the offer mix such as channels of distribution and price/value.
2 The key benefit offered – the USP. (Why that product should be bought ahead of its competitors.)

3 The objectives of the communication mix and the advertising role within it.
4 The target market profiled using the appropriate segmentation data.
5 The advertising message and how it relates to other communication messages.
6 The amount to be spent on advertising within the context of the total communication spend.
7 The media chosen to carry the advertising.
8 The prevailing marketing environment, including competition.

A brief will give details about all these issues and should also include any historical issue that could affect the responsiveness of the target group. It is also important to share any up-to-date and relevant research data with the agency to ensure they are able to work as full partners.

The issue of budgets, mentioned earlier, is a tricky one. Certainly no company has an open cheque book, but a guide can be given. However, if an organisation wishes to adopt the objective and task method of budgeting, the agency must be asked to draw up their recommendations aimed at meeting the objectives set for the advertising.

Direct marketing and precision marketing

Direct marketing is the use of direct media to reach a target. There have always been opportunities to use direct mail, door-to-door, and telephone communications. The actual media is wider than these but the growth in direct marketing has come about because of the

- development of database marketing;
- proliferation of new products;
- multiplication of distribution channels;
- demassification of markets; and
- decrease in the 'efficiency' of mass media.

These subjects are discussed in the excellent book by Rapp and Collins which used the term maxi-marketing. Maxi-marketing is the requirement of marketing to achieve

- maximum efficient reach to target customers;
- maximum chance of marketing sales; and
- maximum opportunity to develop relationships.

Direct marketing is much more personal than mass advertising, and so it can be a key part of the development of relationships with customers. In 1983 Levitt suggested that 'the future will be a future of more and more intensified relationships, especially in industrial marketing, but also increasingly even in frequently purchased consumer goods'. Now a decade later relationship marketing is a reality.

Technology is developing fast in the area of communications, but so is the skill base to use it effectively. Jane Bird suggests that in the next five years there will be two types of company: those that use the computer as a marketing tool and those that face bankruptcy. This might be an over exaggeration but harnessing the skills of 'database marketing' to the 'direct marketing media' is producing 'precision marketing'. The distinction between 'direct marketing' and 'database marketing' is well-discussed by Keith Fletcher and his colleagues. They suggest Shaw and Stone's definition of database marketing as an interactive approach to marketing communication, which uses individually addressable communications media (such as mail, telephone and the sales force) to: extend help to a company's target audience; stimulate their demand; and stay close to them by recording and keeping an electronic database memory of customers, prospects and all communications and commercial contacts, to help all future contacts.

The high quality, computerised database must then be linked to direct response media, which includes everything from the so called 'junk mail' to statement stuffers and electronic media. The advantages are:

- better targeting;
- powerful *personal* communications;
- flexibility;
- creative opportunities;
- controlled timing; and
- controlled input.

Jane Bird describes a mailing to thousands of customers of the Nationwide Anglia Building Society. Obviously each letter is personalised to a named recipient. The additional element is that each letter offers a personalised offer based on detailed segmentation and geodemographics (see Chapter 6). Therefore the mailing is designed to give a different message to each different segment, so that this should be of much greater relevance than a circular sent to all customers.

The key to success in any communication is access to the audience, reaching the chosen target. However good the message, if it fails to reach its target recipient, it is wasted. It used to be thought that a poor message reaching the right target could do some good – witness the general circulars and junk mail still in use. However, the wrong message can leave the relationship with the receiver if not neutral then actually harmed. The retaining of customers, and building of deep, profitable relationships can only be achieved if customers believe you know them and their needs. David Jones, formerly of Grattan Mail Order, said 'you don't send a gardening catalogue to someone living in a high rise flat'. All mail order companies are developing sophisticated databases, and most importantly, they are continually refining them to keep them up to date. Figure 18.2 shows the types of media and the messages they give.

When assessing media cost the role of 10 x applies. The following rule is a rough guide to costs in 1992. Even television cost varies from below £3.00 in the Border TV region to almost £10.00 in London.

1 Television maybe can cost as little as £5.00 per thousand.
2 Magazines vary greatly but maybe cost £50.00 per thousand (5p each).
3 Direct mail is again ten times more expensive – £500.00 per thousand (50p per contact).
4 Telemarketing costs £5,000.00 per thousand (£5.00 each contact).
5 Personal direct selling can be in excess of £50.00 per call.

However, it is not the cost that counts but the *effectiveness*. A telesales operation replacing regular weekly sales calls could save £45 per customer per call. But the sales call still produces more business so it is a real saving. On the other hand, if a well targeted direct mail shot sent to a well chosen segment brings more enquiries than from a magazine

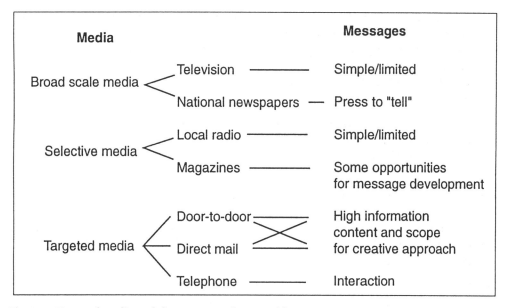

Fig 18.2 Types of media and the messages they provide

with a much larger circulation, there is a real gain. The gains are much greater however. Every reply adds information to the database, and that can be used next time to improve the performance yet further. It is this constant development which really brings long-term gains in effective communications.

Advertising feedback

The need to measure the effectiveness of communications was described in general in Chapter 17. The subject of feedback from advertising and direct marketing is addressed again here because the investment is often substantial, and, unless the return from that investment is reviewed, the whole basis of investing in customers can be challenged.

In 1920, Daniel Starch suggested that to be effective an advertisement must be *seen, read, believed, remembered,* and *acted upon*. This related to print advertising, but it is a useful checklist that can be adopted for all advertising. Tests can be devised to cover each of these stages, and they can also be carried out at different times before, during, after and well after a campaign. Media planners will want to confirm the advertising has received the planned coverage. Figures on circulation of newspapers and viewers for television are gathered by industry bodies (Audit Bureau of Circulation and Broadcasters Audience Research Board) in the UK. These are well covered in Norman Hart's book, *The Practice of Advertising*. The real test required is that related to the effectiveness of advertisements. Advertisers have to monitor effectiveness themselves. Here, it is as well to remember that it is difficult to isolate the effect of a particular advertisement from all other marketing inputs relating to the market as a whole, including competitor actions. The objectives of the advertising will be any of those introduced in the previous chapters. Therefore advertisers use a range of techniques, ranging from *ad hoc* questionnaires to tracking studies among a sample panel. The techniques are designed to meet the specific objective and this type of research is a major study in its own right.

Advertising controls

In the UK controls are exercised by the Independent Television Commission (ITC) for television and independent-related media and the Advertising Standards Authority (ASA) for other media. The slogan associated with the ASA is perhaps the best summary of the aim of the controls: 'An advertisement should be legal, decent, honest and truthful'. While neither the ITC nor the ASA have legal powers, they both have strong positions to enforce their codes. The ITC can refuse to allow commercials to be broadcast, while a recommendation from the ASA will stop a press advertisement. Both react to complaints from the public, these being investigated in detail. Surprisingly, many major companies have been censored by the ASA. These are published in a monthly case-report, which is available through libraries and direct from the ASA.

In addition to a general Code of Advertising Practice (CAP) published by the ASA, there are particular codes of conduct regarding the advertising of alcohol and also advertisements aimed at children. The up-to-date codes on these are available from the authorities. Of course tobacco advertising is banned from UK television as well as the media in many other countries. Such restrictions mean that the millions of pounds that would have been invested in TV commercials are now spent in sponsorship of high-profile sporting events. The brand names, therefore, are not completely missing from the television. This type of control is well known. However, the full scope of the work carried out by industry regulators is much more important. It is the basis of maintaining the overall standards of claims made when advertising products through clear codes of conduct such as the CAP, mentioned above.

When considering database marketing there is a legal requirement to conform to the Data Protection Act 1984. The full implications of this act on direct marketing and direct mailing are published in a guidance note from the Data Protection Registrar. The major thrust is to define the principle that 'Personal data shall be processed fairly'. A good summary of the Data Protection Act, and how it affects marketers, is an article by Phil Boyd published in the May edition of *Marketing Business* magazine.

Conclusion

This chapter encompasses the traditional media used to communicate with customers and the developing media of the future. The marketer has to decide how to achieve communications objectives in the most effective way. In spite of dramatic statements regarding traditional media, these are still able to make a major contribution to communications. The problem of 'one-way' communication is that it cannot be used to build good interactive relationships with customers. As relationships are becoming increasingly important, any ways of assisting the development must be properly considered in an integrated marketing communications plan.

Questions

1 Why was the 'Beanz Meanz who?' campaign so successful?

2 Explain the reason why it is said TV to sell, Press to tell?

3 Why do organisations use direct marketing when it can cost a thousand times more than television for each person reached?

4 Why should an advertiser use an agency to create and place advertising?

References

Aakers, D A and Myers, J G, *Advertising Management*, 3rd Edn., Prentice-Hall, 1987.
Advertising Association Marketing Pocket Book 1992, NTC Publications Ltd.
Bird, J, 'Pinpoint accuracy', *Marketing Business*, April 1992.
Boyd, P, 'Data Protection', *Marketing Business*, May 1992.
Coulson-Thomas, C J, *Marketing Communications*, Heinemann, reprinted 1990.
Fletcher, K, Wheeler, C and Wright, J, 'The role and status of UK database marketing', *Quarterly Review of Marketing*, Autumn 1990.
Hart, N A, *The Practice of Advertising*, Heinemann 1990.
Howerd, W, *The Practice of Public Relations*, 3rd Edn, Heinemann, 1988.
Levitt, T, *The Marketing Imagination*, The Free Press, 1983.
Mazur, L *Silent Satisfaction*, Interview with Philip Kotler, *Marketing Business*, December 1991.
Mercer, D, *Marketing*, Blackwells, 1992.
Miles, L, 'Going solo', *Marketing Business*, June 1992.
Oxley, M, *The Principles of Public Relations*, Kogan Page, 1989.
Rapps, S and Collins, T, *Maxi-marketing*, McGraw-Hill, 1987.
Shaw, R and Stone, M, *Database Marketing for Competitive Advantage*, Long Range Planning, 1987.
Wilmshurst, J, *The Fundamentals of Advertising*, Heinemann 1985.

Case study: advertising and direct marketing

Giftworld Ltd

Giftworld Ltd are manufacturers of silverplated gifts and importers of other items to enlarge the range of products available to a wide range of customers. These customers ranged from a large supplier of thermal underwear who this year offered a small silverplated tray with their direct mailshots, through to many organisations who bought items to use as gifts for clients. In these latter cases Giftworld often used an in-house engraving facility to add the customer's name or logo to the gift so that it could be used as a key part of that customer's promotional plans.

Many regular customers placed large orders at key occasions such as Christmas when over 60 per cent of all Giftworld's sales were made. The company also exhibited at the International Spring Fair in Birmingham's NEC every February and this, together with advertisements in *Promotion and Incentive Magazine*, provided additional new customer enquiries. However, many of the new customers only wanted gifts for Christmas, so there was an increasing problem of maintaining level of work for the rest of the year.

Over the last few years a silverplated 'Mother's Day' tray engraved 'For Mother' has been advertised in a number of consumer magazines and has proved successful both in the level of sales orders and in filling the post-Christmas slack time in production as Mothering Sunday is in March. This product was the idea of one employee who remembered the immensely successful 'Charles and Diana Wedding' tray more than a decade ago but unfortunately such high profile events occur infrequently.

The problem Giftworld have is how to ensure they use their silverplating tank to its full capacity at the other times of the year. It is believed the mailshot by the thermal company will not be renewed in future years and so from March when the 'Mother's Day' trays finish to September when production starts for Christmas orders there is the prospect of very little work, except low value subcontracting orders.

When visiting this year's Frankfurt Gift Fair, the Sales Director established contacts with an Indian company which produces tea sets in brass ready to be finished by silverplating. These can be brought into the UK, plated and then sold as 'Made in the UK' because the final manufacturing process took place in England. The problem Giftworld have is that they do not have any sales contacts with companies who retail silverplated tea sets. The Giftworld name is not known in this market. The Indian supplier will only supply in full container loads, paid for in advance by irrevocable letter of credit. And there are only six months when the Giftworld silverplating operation is not fully used.

You are recruited in the new role as Marketing Assistant reporting to the Sales Director. You have been asked to suggest what Giftworld should do with regards the marketing and promotion of its products and potential new products.

19

PUBLICITY, SALES PROMOTION AND SPONSORSHIP

Introduction

This chapter brings together three separate elements of promotion. Publicity and Sales Promotion are part of the traditional promotional mix introduced in Chapter 18. Sponsorship is a form of promotion which not only rewards study in itself, but must be viewed as an opportunity for publicity as well as a type of sales promotion. The expenditure on sponsorship has risen dramatically over the last decade but now organisations are trying to evaluate the return.

All these three forms of promotion are seen as effective but perhaps not excessively expensive. They all are difficult to evaluate and yet many case studies exist to show substantial benefits. It is therefore appropriate that this chapter considers all three ways of promoting an organisation or its products/services.

PR and publicity

Advertising has been described as a primary method of communication which makes use of mass media. Publicity also uses mass media but the results are not directly controlled by the sender, and so it can be deemed a secondary communication for which no direct payment is made. This does not make publicity any less valuable, it does mean it is sometimes harder to achieve a desired result.

Publicity is something that most people can recognise, but the recognition of publicity is often associated with famous people. Whatever well-known entertainers, politicians, or members of the royal family do in their private lives, it is soon reported in the press. It appears that publicity, in this sense, is strongest when it is regarding the personal lives of the people concerned. The general point is that any story has to appeal to the readers of the newspaper, otherwise it will not get printed. The same rule applies for any story which is not a 'paid-for advertisement', a point often forgotten by organisations. Any publicity item must contain issues of general interest to the readers or viewers, and not just to a particular organisation. Making a story relevant is one of the key skills of successful publicity specialists.

The role of publicity, in a promotional budget, is to obtain positive and relevant mentions. These can be of most benefit if they are achieved to complement other promotional efforts. The definition of PR was given at the beginning of the last chapter, but shall be repeated here:

> PR is the deliberate, planned, and sustained effort to establish and maintain mutual understanding between an organisation and its publics.

Good media relations can also be of benefit to avoid unwelcome publicity. The best publicity specialists know the relevant newspaper editors well, so they are sometimes approached before an unfavourable story is published. In such a case it might be possible to mitigate the negative effects.

Publicity can be aimed at any of the stakeholder groups introduced in Chapter 3. It is not restricted to customers, but can cover any of the other groups such as suppliers, employees, lenders, or the general public. The objectives of publicity can be any of the three roles of communication: informing, persuading or reinforcing.

In some situations there can be a direct link between advertising and publicity. Trade magazines will sometimes offer editorial coverage to a good advertiser, although the magazine will still retain editorial control. The issue of editorial freedom is very important to the major media. Editors and reporters would object strongly to any influence, whether to give positive mentions or suppress negative ones, from any organisation, even if it was a large purchaser of advertising space in a particular publication. Editorial opinion does carry more authority than 'paid for advertising' because of the impartial nature of such comment. Some advertisers try to benefit from this by producing advertorials - adverts laid out in the same form as the editorial matter, with the heading 'advertising feature' written as small as allowed by the publication.

Areas of public relations activities

There are four major areas that can be relevant in achieving good public relations. These are

- media relations;
- editorial and broadcast material;
- controlled communications; and
- face-to-face events.

Media relations

Media relations involve taking news to the editors, taking editors to the news, creating relevant news stories and managing the news. Building good relationships with the media is obviously a benefit. The personal contact with editors is covered in the first two tasks above. The other two relate to the need to produce a regular supply of news items as part of the *deliberate, planned and sustained publicity effort*.

Editorial and broadcast material

Editorial and broadcast material is the 'product' of public relations. It covers press conferences, news releases, personal interviews, feature writing, case histories, press visits and journalist briefings. News releases and press conferences are the most commonly used methods of gaining publicity, but as you can see, there are many other techniques which can be used.

1 Press conferences. A press conference is held in order to brief members of the media about a major news event. You might be familiar with these conferences being used by a political figure, or maybe by the police during an enquiry into a serious crime. The technique is equally applicable to PR for a company or product. Editors and feature writers receive many invitations to such events. They are, therefore, selective about which press conferences they choose to attend. The subject has to be particularly interesting or topical, or maybe the conference/presentation is attractive because it is held in an interesting location. The cider makers, H P Bulmer used to own the steam engine, King George V. They used steam-train runs as a location for press conferences, and always found a willing audience.

2 News releases. A news release is an item circulated to the media in the hope of getting it placed in a publication. It is the mainstay of publicity and, if published, can be of considerable value. Editorial matter is seen and read by more people than advertising in the same magazine or newspaper. The contents of an article also gain credibility by having the implied support of the publication. Whereas advertisements are seen for what they are, editorial comment is often considered objective and unbiased. The drawback of relying on publicity, is that the editors decide what will be published and when it will appear. If a news release is set out in a way that is unsuitable for the publication, then it might be modified before insertion. This modification could change the balance and meaning of the release. The release could, of course, be rejected. Rejection is more likely with a major publication which is inundated with releases. Specialist journals, however, are often pleased to receive items about product successes, new contracts, innovations, export achievements, or people in the industry. In some cases the specialist journals could be the best media to reach your target.

News releases are a *'one-way'* communication, which do not give an opportunity for questions. Press conferences do give an opportunity for *'two-way'* exchanges but only with the media editors, not with the eventual target audience. They are often used to support a news release where it is felt the story could be enhanced by contact.

Controlled communications

Controlled communications is the area of publicity material for company use. It includes annual reports, educational material, leaflets, audio-visual presentations, and any material that could be successfully placed to support organisational objectives. This low-cost material is a luxury for some organisations because of the time required to plan and prepare it. The benefits are even more difficult to measure than advertising or other main media publicity. But such channels should not be ignored. The less usual ways of reaching consumers could prove effective just because they offer a different approach.

Face-to-face events

These include other ways of reaching the chosen audience direct. Conferences, exhibitions, lectures, shopping centre events, demonstrations, open days, public visits and many more are examples of activities used to facilitate contact. The environment for such contact is a key ingredient. Then the event has to be structured to give the right level of interest linked, to the communication message for the event to be considered worthwhile.

Exhibitions are an excellent way to present an organisation to its customers. They have already been mentioned in Chapter 16. They can be expensive, but can also be a simple, low-cost 'shell' construction. Whatever the cost, it is important to ensure that an exhibition is as effective as possible. This means being pro-active in inviting visitors to your exhibition stand, rather than reactive, waiting for visitors to appear. The role of PR, as well as direct mail, in attracting visitors must not be ignored. The cost of such an exercise is only a small proportion of the cost of the exhibition as a whole, and usually is money well spent.

Financial and corporate PR

Financial PR has been given a separate section because it is a major area of importance to public 'quoted' companies. The share price of companies, and their financial credibility, cannot be separated from an organisation's trading success. The key measure with financial backers is confidence - the confidence the 'Money Men' have in the management of an organisation. This includes institutional investors, professional financial advisers and the financial media. It is naive to suggest an organisation is judged by its published performance. The role of financial PR is to directly influence the relevant individuals and institutions, and to develop good relationship with them. The media used is highly specialised, including the use of screen-based electronics news – the CNS (company news service) established by the Stock Exchange. Because this is so specialised it is perhaps outside the scope of this book.

In-house or agency?

The decision on whether to handle PR internally, or to appoint an agency, can depend on the way PR is perceived. In a small organisation it is often the Managing Director who takes control, but there are three other options: to train an existing manager to handle PR; to appoint professional PR staff; and to use an external agency. It is always possible to use a combination of these options to deal with the *planned* programme. However, there are always the *unplanned* events which have to be handled in-house. Just as every member of staff is a part-time marketer, so they are also all part-time PR people - anyone can accept an incoming enquiry from the media. In some 'sensitive' industries, for instance Nuclear Electric, there are nominated executives who are trained in dealing with tough media reporters, and all incoming enquiries are routed to these selected managers.

For the basic decision on in-house or agency PR the trade-off is between intimate knowledge of the company, its products and services, and the wide range of experience and objective advice from a PR consultancy. A compromise is often used whereby a small PR department, or just one nominated individual works with an external agency, the agency being paid a retainer related to the task required.

The advantages and disadvantages of publicity

Advantages

Publicity should be an important but subtle part of the promotional mix, not just an adjunct to advertising. The most important advantages to be gained are:

- **Credibility:** If the public are made aware of the benefits to be gained from a company's products from an independent source, and that source is not being paid by the company in question, then the credibility factor is that much greater.
- **Greater readership:** When glancing through a newspaper it is seldom that a great deal of attention is primarily paid to advertisements, much more attention is given to editorial or news sections. Similarly, people are more likely to divert attention from the television to do other things while the advertisements are being shown.
- **Contain more information:** Publicity is able to impart more information to the

public than advertisements can. A glance is all that is usually given to an advertisement, whereas publicity, when presented as news, is given more attention and is therefore able to contain much more detailed information.

- **Cost benefits:** No direct payments are made to the media for publicity. There are obviously costs involved, but PR budgets are far less than those for advertising.
- **Speed**: Publicity has an advantage of speed. Information on a major development can often be issued and reported in a short space of time. Publicity can also be flexible and reactive.

Disadvantages

Publicity is generally looked upon as being of benefit, but sometimes both companies, and famous personalities, wish that they could avoid publicity. If there is a major accident on the premises of a company, or an oil leak from one of the oil companies installations offshore, that company will be on the receiving end of some very bad publicity. They can try to minimise this by breaking the news to the media themselves, and being as helpful as possible, but damage to their reputation will still be incurred.

- **Message distortion:** A company has no control over what the media report about them. A press release, which a company hopes is reported in full, may in fact not be used at all, or may have only a small portion of it reported. If the publicity given is untrue or libellous, of course, the organisation will have recourse through the judicial system, but such action is expensive, and creates a difficult situation for the future. With good relations, and a good understanding of the type of release required, the risk of distortion can be dramatically reduced.
- **Repetition:** With advertisements a company can ensure that there is frequency of the message. Publicity does not have this advantage and the message may only be given once, if at all.

Introduction to sales promotion

Sales promotions have grown in importance during the last two decades. In part this has been a reaction to the ever increasing cost of media advertising (higher than the rate of inflation); and in part it has been a reflection of the effectiveness of sales promotions in creating additional sales in a very direct manner. The Advertising Standards Authority's (ASA) Code of Sales Promotion defines sales promotion as:

> those Marketing techniques, which are used, usually on a temporary basis, to make goods and services more attractive to the consumer by providing some additional benefit whether in cash or in kind.

The code covers such forms of promotions as: premium offers of all kinds; reduced price and free offers; the distribution of vouchers, coupons, and samples; personality promotions; charity-linked promotions; and prize promotions of all types. In fact, almost any promotion that is not main media advertising or publicity can be grouped under the general heading of sales promotion. Mercer (1992) suggests that sponsorship should be considered as part of sales promotion.

The term *'below the line'* is applied to sales promotion as opposed to *'above the line'* for advertising. However, both sales promotion and advertising are key parts of the promotions mix. There was a time when advertising agencies were critical of the use of promotions. Now *'below the line'* techniques have become increasingly sophisticated and effective; they are seen as an important complement to advertising. In fact, many campaigns use advertising to support promotions. Also promotional offers, while not slavishly following the *'above the line'* theme, are often chosen to support the brand positioning.

There is a difference between promotions that really do benefit the promotional message and those that just bring forward sales to an earlier period. The latter is described by market research company Neilsen, as 'mortgaging' of future sales. This occurs if no overall sales increase is achieved. That is, the increase during the promotion is lost by lower than expected sales in following periods. Another criticism of sales promotion is that they can be easily copied by competitors. In this case a vicious circle, similar to a price war can occur. A recent article on the cost of sales promotion by John Philip Jones said this vicious circle is described at Unilever as:

Promotion ———▶ Commotion ———▶ Demotion

Jones considers the role of promotion in a large number of mature markets which exhibit what he calls, the lack of market vitality, as growth rates decline. He suggests that if

> after giving advertising every chance, there is no perceptible short- or long-term effect. . . [then] manufacturers should cut their losses. A brand can be maintained in effective distribution by a minimal level of promotional support and with only enough theme advertising to keep the brand name in front of the sales force and the retail trade. And sometimes no theme advertising at all.

The implicit objective that long-term profitability is the main aim, is fine. But there can be other marketing objectives. However, when products reach the later stages of their life cycles, the suggestion that some mature products should receive minimal support is a consistent marketing strategy. Doyle's article on the product life cycle and marketing strategy was mentioned in Chapter 12 (*see* Fig 12.4). Doyle suggests marketing expenditure should be reduced. The emphasis should be on brand loyalty and the defence of market share. Within this, good sales promotion, rather than poorly thought-out short-term offers, do give an extra dimension. The problem is how to choose the right mix of promotions to meet the need of a given brand. To make some sense of the chaotic variety of sales promotions they have been grouped to reflect the target market.

- Consumers.
- Trade customers/intermediaries.
- Sales force incentives (discussed in Chapter 20).

Consumer promotions

Most sales promotions make one of the three ageless appeals: Save! Win! Free! There are several satellite appeals, too: Give! Now! Fun! Re-assurance! The Motivations appeared to lie deep in the human psyche, and show themselves in many forms in our society:

- Most people like a bargain
- Most people will jump at something for nothing

- Most people like to indulge some skill, or 'have a flutter'.

This was how Chris Petersen, an early practitioner of sales promotion, started a chapter of his book, *Promotion in Action*. Although published in 1979 it captives the essence of consumer promotions. Of course, Petersen is talking about the various themes used in promotions. For a promotion to be suitable it must be consistent with the overall objectives of an organisation. These are often listed as:

1 **Extra sales volume:** The original aim of sales promotion, it is usually short-term, but extra profitable sales is the ultimate aim of most commercial organisations.
2 **Point-of-sale impact:** Linked to increase volume, this objective is to gain maximum exposure at the time of purchase and at the point of decision on whether and what to buy. The joint tasks of persuasion and reinforcement can be enhanced by effective point-of-sale promotion.
3 **Repeat purchase**: The role of marketing as described in this book is building satisfying exchanges with customers. These will, hopefully, lead to increased levels of repeat purchase as well as gaining product advocates who will recommend a particular brand. Techniques such as collector schemes which build ongoing repeat business, can lead to developments of future habits and loyalty.
4 **Sample purchase or product trial:** One of the most difficult marketing jobs is to get people to try a new product, ranging from the test driving of a car to the sampling of a new chocolate bar. If a potential customer tries a product then at least they can evaluate the product properly. They might like it, or consider it is not as good as their current product. But trial is far superior as a basis of consumer judgement to ill-informed customers who have never tried the product.

Malcolm MacDonald suggested a more structured classification based on direct versus indirect appeal, and whether the offer was based on money, goods or services (*see* Table 19.1).

Table 19.1
A classification of direct and indirect appeal of promotional materials

	Direct	Indirect
Money	Price reduction	Coupons Money equivalent Competitions
Goods	Free goods Premium goods Free gifts Trade-in offers	Stamps Coupons Vouchers Money equivalents Competitions
Services	Guarantees Group participation & events Special exhibitions and displays	Co-operative advertising Stamps Vouchers for services Event admission Competition

Money-based consumer promotions

Money is the most widely acceptable type of offer but it suffers from the criticism of short termism described by Jones. For instance, goods might not appeal, as not every purchaser wants the item offered. But, by offering 'money off' the purchaser is presumed to make a saving. They can, therefore, decide what to do with that saving, while the value of the product is enhanced. Money can be offered: directly as a price-cut; indirectly as a coupon linked to a product purchase; or as a money prize in a competition where proof of product purchase is required.

However, there are problems with both coupons and competitions. Major supermarket groups will accept coupons without the customer purchasing the relevant item. This negates much of the benefit from a coupon promotion. Competitions are controlled by the Lotteries and Amusement Act (1976), one of a number of legislative controls affecting sales promotions. Such laws can cause problems for ill-informed organisations.

The four major problems of 'money off' promotions are:

1 They are expensive, with the reduction in revenue coming directly from profit.
2 A significant proportion of customers are 'price-off' buyers who buy only during the reductions.
3 Regular price reductions can damage the quality image of a product or company.
4 'Money off' promotions are easily copied by competitors.

However, in a competitive marketplace, it can be difficult to resist competitive pressure. For example Marks & Spencer for many years refused to run 'money off' sales. With the problems of retail volume they now compete with other major department stores running sales events. In August 1992 they announced a promotion termed 'Outstanding Autumn Value', with a spokesperson stating, 'we are really looking to sharpen up our value everywhere'.

'Money off' schemes are appropriate in many situations such as to create sampling of products. In launching a new food product the first requirement is to get potential customers to try it. A coupon or reduced price will help to achieve this. These offers can also encourage possible multiple purchases. Another use of 'money off' is to bring purchases forward, for example, an early booking discount for holiday booking. In another context, however, the example below shows a problem with this type of promotion.

Example

The fertilisers division of a major international chemical company used to encourage early purchase by offering an early purchase discount every year. Fertiliser is used primarily in the spring when it has maximum effect. One year sales were lagging so much that, in spite of the earlier price promotion for early orders, the company dropped prices dramatically during the season. Early purchasers were in fact worse off. Next year the early promotion was a disaster as customers had lost complete confidence in the company and its quality image. The fertiliser division never recovered from this effect.

'Money-off' promotions are widely used, but perhaps they are the easiest promotion to criticise due to the obvious problems. Therefore, such promotions should be used very selectively, and certainly not be an automatic first-choice method.

Goods- or merchandise-based consumer offers

Value can be offered by goods and merchandise, without the same risk of damaging brand images. For example, free product (500 grammes extra free) costs relatively little to producers, and certainly does not change pricing structures. Also, merchandise can be bought in bulk at very heavy discounts. Consequently, excellent offers can be made either free or what is called *'self-liquidating'* (i.e. at cost). By linking to purchases of the main brand then promotions can build brand loyalty and repeat purchase in a very direct way.

It was suggested earlier that goods/merchandise might not appeal because the item offered might not be desired by the target customers. It is a risk, although it is possible to offer a range of items. One example of this is a choice from a catalogue offered by a major petrol company. The mechanics of the promotion is that sales are recorded in the form of points recorded on a swipe card. The points are then exchanged for a wide range of products, from a catalogue. This is just one attempt to offer value, and also to reduce the problem of restricted choice.

In considering how promotional offers influence behaviour. Ask your student friends why they choose to open a bank account at a particular bank. It might be the convenient location of the branches, the overdraft limit, the fact their families use that bank, or the promotional offer made. It could be that more than one issue influenced the decision, but it would be interesting to find out the role of the promotional offer.

Exercise

How many students open a bank account because of the offer of a free £10 record token valid at 'Our Price' record shops, as offered by Barclays Bank in 1992?

All major banks make offers to encourage students to open an account. Check the offers from Lloyds Bank, Barclays Bank, Midlands Bank and the National Westminster Bank. Ask a group of students to see what offers they value?

The offers made by banks to attract students are often well chosen and very relevant to the needs of this group. The choice of offers is very important to the success of any promotion. You will be able to find evidence of this in many of your local retail outlets. However, sometimes the promotional offer can give problems which reflect badly on the product being promoted. Some years ago a brand of Table Jelly offered a 'free goldfish' as a promotion. Major problems resulted in dead fish being delivered to customers, and the resultant complaints affected the brand concerned. The Code of Sales Promotion Practice is particular on the subject of suitability of promotional products.

Promoters shall not offer promotional products which are of a nature likely to cause offence or products which, in the context of the promotion, may reasonably be considered to be socially undesirable.

Particular care should be taken in the distribution of free samples to ensure that children or other particularly vulnerable groups are not harmed.

Consumers should not be led to over-estimate the quality or desirability of promotional products. Particular care should be exercised where the recipient has no opportunity to examine goods before taking delivery.

It might be interesting to find some current promotions and see how they adhere to the code.

Services as promotion

Promotions of this type are very varied: a guarantee, or a 'no-quibble' exchange are excellent in building strong positions in markets; new retail store openings, often featuring a major personality, can create high initial awareness; famous authors signing their books can draw large crowds; charity-linked promotions can show a brand as caring (for example, by linking with 'Save the Children Fund'). The scope is enormous. Events and sponsorship might be covered in part under this heading, although they also come under publicity. The subject of sponsorship cuts across all three areas of consumer, trade and sales-force and so have been included in a separate section at the end of this chapter.

The benefit from services promotions is usually the provision of additional and specific benefits (added value), point-of-sale impact and enhanced product personalities. In many cases the benefits are qualitative and difficult to measure. But the effect they can have will usually last for longer than a short-term 'money-off' deal.

Industrial and trade promotions

This sector of Business-to-Business promotion can be subdivided into:

1 Industrial customers who are users of a product.
2 Trade intermediaries who sell the product on.

The first group will be receptive to some of the techniques discussed above under 'Consumer promotions'. However, the person who raises the sales order, in an industrial company, is not always the end user, nor necessarily the influencer of the purchase decision (*see* Chapter 5). It is therefore very important to understand the role and position of the person who could receive the promotional benefit. There is a problem of deciding what is fair promotion and what is bribery!

Examples

- An executive collects 'Air-miles' from his company travel trips. Should he use the benefits for company business or his next family holiday?
- A purchasing manager has placed a series of good orders with your organisation. You give that purchasing manager an expensive desk diary, embossed with your organisation logo. Is this good promotion?
- A purchasing manager has placed a series of good orders with your organisation. You are offering a free case of whisky for large orders. Should the purchasing manager receive the whisky for his personal consumption?

There are many other examples and they all start because the expenditure and purchase order is from the customer *company*, but the promotion is often received by an *employee* of that company. The Code of Sales Promotion practice states:

> No trade incentive which is directed towards employees should be such as to cause any conflict with their duty to their employer, or their obligations to give honest advice to the consumer.

Similar dilemmas are faced with respect to trade intermediaries. But where do you classify a meal purchased by a sales representative, who invites a buyer to that person's favourite (expensive) restaurant as a 'reward' for a particularly large order?

The ethical issues are brought into sharp focus because of the clash of people and their employing organisations. It is worth considering the type of promotional objectives a supplier organisation might have with respect to trade buyers. Writing about the promotion of durable products, Quelch *et al* suggested objectives might be:

1 To persuade existing outlets to:
   - maintain existing floor/shelf space;
   - stock additional models or promotional versions;
   - provide additional floor/shelf space;
   - provide special displays and features;
   - increase inventories of specific brand.
2 To persuade new outlets to stock brand
3 To insulate the trade from consumer-price negotiations at the point-of-purchaser
4 To insulate the trade from a temporary sales reduction that might be caused by an increase in price.
5 To compensate the trade when the traditional retail margins have been eroded by price competition.
6 To identify which items in a product range the dealer should push during particular periods. (Quelch *et al, Sloan Management Review*, Winter 1987)

While Quelch's article discussed durable products, this list could equally well apply to non-durable products. Petersen suggests the objectives of promoting to a retailer are:

- to gain, and/or to consolidate, distribution;
- to achieve required stock levels in outlets;
- to get display and other activity around the brand; and
- to get noticed by the retailer.

All of these objectives can be satisfied by the category of 'push' techniques which typifies many sales promotions. The types of promotion aimed at an industrial or trade buyer can again be: money-based; goods/merchandise-brand; or services-based. MacDonald lists some specific techniques in his book, *Marketing Plans*. The detailed study of such techniques is, however, the subject for a book in its own right. Some of the issues are covered in Chapter 20 on selling.

Tailored promotions

Many organisations sell to a mix of different intermediaries. A 'tailored promotion' is a promotional offer that is made to a particular intermediary. It is a highly focused strategy, chosen to apply to a single customer, or small segment. The promotion is designed to meet the specific objectives the supplier might have towards that particular segment. Such a promotion could be a general offer of the sort already discussed, such as a 'money-off' deal with a particular customer only. But this sort of deal can cause real friction with other customers, if they feel they are loosing out. 'Tailored promotions' are most relevant to major customers, or ones that could be significant. For such outlets a promotion specifically designed for that outlet has a strong appeal. It could link a consumer promotion with trade incentives but still restrict the offer to a particular intermediary. The use of techniques which are wider than 'money-off' promotions with a particular intermediary has a definite appeal. For instance, a drinks company will run special events with individual public houses to promote new products. Alternatively, a cosmetic company could offer the services of a trained beauty consultant to a particular department store in return for extra sales.

Tailored promotions can involve a similar level of effort to national promotions. However, the return in sales could be higher and they can certainly be used to help build relationships with the intermediaries.

Sponsorship

A promotional offer can be something tangible like 'money off' or a free gift. It can also be less tangible, for example in the form of an endorsement. Sporting equipment is often enhanced by the endorsement of a world-class performer, e.g. Nick Faldo Golf Clubs. Such products are able to sell at premium prices due to the association with a personality. The link here is direct and the benefit to the product is obvious. In return the personality will be paid for the endorsement.

From this point, it is a small jump to associating a personality with an unrelated product. The personality does not need to be a famous sportsperson, it could just as easily be Mr Men Yoghurts. The attraction of the character makes the product more acceptable to target consumers. The exchange process is apparent in both these situations with visible benefits to the products from the 'halo' effect of the association. It can also work effectively when a company name is displayed on sporting equipment, e.g. Benetton Formula One racing cars.

In too many companies, sponsorship is seen as some form of charity donating money to a person or organisation. Last century a report in the *Blackburn Times* stated that 'a local iron foundry owner had sponsored a football team by a donation of £100'. More recently, another wealthy steelman has invested millions of pounds in Blackburn's football team in an effort to buy success. This is not sponsorship. It does not have the benefit of a 'two-way' exchange.

But, let us consider another football team, say Manchester United. The team receives money from Sharp and, in return, the players wear the company logo on the team shirts. Maybe this is advertising using a novel medium; it is also a good example of sponsorship.

A definition of sponsorship might be:

> Sponsorship rates placed when a payment, either in financial or natural terms is given in return for some consideration or benefit. Sponsorship should give benefit to both parties.

There are other definitions of sponsorship but many fail to grasp the exchange process and the WIIFM (what's in it for me?) factor. This definition includes endorsements and related product links, but the growth in sponsorship has come from deals linking all sorts of companies and brands to sport or the arts. Sport is generally thought to account for over 75 per cent of all expenditure, including sponsorship of major events, teams, and individual performers. The total spent in such deals in the UK alone is estimated at £500 million.

Sponsorship benefits

When considering sponsorship as part of a promotional campaign an organisation must assess the benefit they receive for the money spent. First must be the 'extra dimension' gained by association with a person or an event. The very act of sponsoring says something about a sponsor in a way no advertisement can. However, there are other positive advantages. Sponsorship can offer real opportunities for advertising or PR. In fact, one rule of thumb suggests a company shall spend as much again on publicity as they commit to the basic sponsorship. But the chance to gain publicity at a pre-arranged time can be very valuable. Media coverage, especially television, can be gained for products such as cigarettes. This is only a small part of sponsorship, although it might be the area with which most people are familiar.

Sponsoring an event could give a company publicity but could also give them an opportunity to link to corporate hospitality. Inviting major customers to 'the company event' is much stronger than other events. Special ticket allowances are common practice. Promotional opportunities featuring the sponsor link can extend to merchandise, e.g. golf umbrellas. It will certainly be featured on event-related material. The link could go further so that key personalities meet customers or visit employees. Employee interest can also be enhanced if they have a team or event to follow. Again tickets can be used very effectively.

The key to successful sponsorship is to make it fun for all concerned. Also to view sponsorship as a partnership which can yield benefits for a significant period of time.

Sponsorship and promotional planning

Sponsorship should not be considered as a cheap alternative to media advertising. In most cases it is not done as a way to circumvent advertising restrictions. Sponsorship is not something to be offered to the first interesting project you are offered.

The first thing in all areas of promotion and communication is to sort out clear objectives. Sponsorship can become a link between all the elements of the promotion mix – advertising, publicity, sales promotion and selling. It provides a theme which can be exploited in many ways. However, sponsorship is expensive in terms of time, money and people. To benefit fully an organisation must clearly know what it is trying to achieve and where it is now. If the aim is to enhance the corporate image, then first explore what is the current perception of your organisation and, also, of the intended sponsee. Then follow up by exploring if the link is credible.

One issue often forgotten is the effect of ending a sponsorship deal. The end can receive as much publicity as the commencement. The announcement that your company has decided not to renew a sponsorship needs to be handled well or the negative publicity could undo all the positive benefits previously achieved. But, perhaps the biggest risk with sponsorship is that it is a very difficult area to predict. It is difficult to forecast the level of media coverage. It is difficult to forecast the way an event or a personality will interact with a company or brand name. It is difficult to know if the target audience will see, and respond, to the sponsors. Nevertheless many organisations are prepared to take this 'risk' because the 'return' from successful sponsorship can be substantial.

Conclusion

Advertising is not the only way to promote a company or its products. All techniques need to be considered together in order to deliver a sustained and regular series of planned messages to target audiences. The objective of the communication element in a general marketing decision is derived from the overall Marketing objectives. The delivery of the messages is a specialised function requiring highly skilled functional people. There are so many messages being broadcast that it is difficult to stand out from other communications. Creativity is needed to deliver a message that grabs attention and leads to action. Therefore no organisation should fail to consider the rich variety available with publicity, promotion and sponsorship.

Questions

1 How does corporate PR differ from publicity for a product?

2 What are the advantages and disadvantages of price based sales promotions?

3 How might an organisation evaluate the success of a sales promotion?

4 Suggest a successful sponsorship, and explain why you consider it to be successful.

References

Bidlake, S, 'M&S in pricing U-turn', M*arketing*, 27 August 1992.
British Code of Sales Promotion Practice, Advertising Standards Authority, Code of Advertising Practice (CAP) Committee, September 1984.
Howerd, W, *The Practice of Public Relations* 3rd Edn. Heinemann 1988.
Jones, J P, 'The double jeopardy of sales promotion', *Harvard Business Review*, September/October 1990.
McDonald, M, *Marketing Plans*, Heinemann, 1984.
Mercer, D, *Marketing*, Blackwell, 1992.
Miles, L, 'Going solo', *Marketing Business*, June 1992.
Oxley, M, *The Principles of Public Relations*, Kogan Page, 1989.
Petersen, C, *Sales Promotion in Action*, Associated Business Press, 1979.
Quelch, J A, Neslin, S A and Olson, L B, 'Opportunities and risks of durable goods promotion', *Sloan Management Review*, Winter 1987.

20

PERSONAL SELLING

Introduction

It is often easy to confuse selling and Marketing. This is because the two disciplines are linked in many companies and Sales Marketing functions are easly found. But selling is not the same as Marketing. It is, however, a key part of the Marketing role and many of the skills of a good salesperson in understanding customers are required by good Marketers.

The publicity material for a national sales training roadshow suggests that 'No matter what business you are in, there ARE people out there waiting to buy. Lots of them. All you have to do is to find them before your competitors do.' There is nothing wrong with this statement *if* it is then developed into the full range of marketing activities as discussed in the previous chapters of this book. That is:

- identify target customers;
- discover needs; and
- develop ways of fulfilling those needs.

Where it could go wrong is if the presenter lives up to one description as 'the Mohammed Ali of the Selling Profession'. Selling is not a way of beating your opponents by having the biggest punch (for those readers who do not know, Mohammed Ali was former heavyweight boxing champion of the world). Selling is:

- identifying target customers;
- discovering needs; and
- matching offerings with needs.

This sequence is almost identical to the one above regarding marketing. Both have an element: *'find needs - fill them'*. The differences are that *marketing* can usually work with all resources of a company, and aim to create satisfying exchanges with all potential customers. The *offer mix* of product, price and distribution can be planned by the marketer to be acceptable, affordable and available. In fact, a good marketing organisation will focus the entire company on its customers, with a medium- or long-term perspective.

Selling is more of a micro-relationship. The product is often given and restrictions on price and distribution can exist. The salesperson has less flexibility with the *offer*, and has to get sales *now*. But immediate sales are often made possible by existing relationships. What a salesperson must do is build on these personal relationships. They can do this by:

- augmenting product delivery in an appropriate way; and
- creating a more receptive attitude from potential customers by using a combination of information and persuasion.

The idea of a sales orientation was introduced in Chapter 2. Direct selling is a widely used way of reaching individual customers and can be defined as

The process of identifying potential customers, informing them of a company's offer mix, and finding a match between the benefits offered and customers needs through personal communication.

Selling is very much part of the communication mix. It is *two way* and *personal*. This means salespeople have the maximum opportunity to find the connection between benefits and needs, and so to persuade the customer to change needs into wants.

Sales representatives are *company advocates* to the customer. But they can also be *customer advocates* whose detailed knowledge can be fed back to their company regarding future opportunities. Therefore, while selling is not marketing, it is wholly consistent with marketing. It is simply that part of marketing which deals with individual contacts with customers, and short-term achievement of sales with an existing offer mix.

The scope of selling

There are a wide number of roles which can be classed as personal sales. These range from shop assistants and door-to-door salespeople, through to major account managers who work with customers that place millions of pounds of business. There are three main roles involved:

- prospecting or cold calling;
- selling; and
- account maintenance and development.

Prospecting or 'cold calling'

The role of these prospectors is to seek out new customers, establish contacts, and determine needs. They also need to identify the decision-makers and influencers who must be convinced if a sale is to be made. These salespeople work in the early *pre-transactional* stage with a new customer.

The skills required in finding potential new customers are very different from building relationships with existing customers. It is much harder to persuade a customer to buy for the first time than to get a repeat order from a satisfied customer. This is because it involves an element of the unknown (*see also* Chapter 11).

Even if the customer knows the company or product, they may have to be convinced to change from a competitive product. Prospectors have to deal with customers who say they are not interested. They have to move these potential customers into making a first appointment. Having achieved this, they must remember that *they never get a second chance to make a first impression*. This is why one group of potential customers -lapsed users and former customers - can be even more difficult to win back. Former customers already know your company and its products but have decided to trade with your competitors. It may be a simple evaluation of product features and price which a new offer mix would change. It may, however, be that your company let the customer down, gave poor service or somehow upset the relationship. Undoing the past can be much more difficult than starting from a situation where nothing is known.

Perhaps the most powerful weapon a prospector can use is personal recommendation. When contacting a new customer it can help if you can say that an existing customer suggested the contact. In some industries, such as life assurance, the salespeople are trained to follow up with existing customers to get recommendations to new prospects. Life assurance is a product that is not purchased regularly, so salespeople are always trying to find suitable new prospects who have reached the right stage in their life cycles to require the product.

Selling

This is the *transactional* stage. A customer could be:

- a 'hot prospect' - someone who is close to making a first purchase decision with your organisation;
- an occasional customer, who conducts limited business with you;
- a regular repeat customer; or
- an advocate who goes out of his or her way to trade with you.

The transactional stage is the most important as far as current performance is concerned because current sales are what keeps the organisation going. The process of making a sale is discussed later, because it is not solely the application of persuasive skills.

In some situations the customer *comes to buy,* for instance in a retail outlet, or a visit to a manufacturer's factory. Here the salesperson has an advantage in that they are working in a familiar location. The disadvantage for retail sales staff is that they often have no knowledge of the potential customer, the customer background, or any previous history of a transaction with that particular customer. The salesperson has to find this out by suitable questioning.

In other situations, the sales representative or sales engineer can be visiting the customer. The seller will have researched the customer, have some knowledge of the customer needs and the previous history of transactions. But the customer will be on home territory. The salesperson has *gone to sell.*

Issues such as the salespersons' attitudes, their beliefs in their products as well as their negotiation or persuasion skills are relevant in achieving success when selling. Chapter 2 included a short case study on the day of a travelling salesman. It will be apparent from this that the time spent actually face to face with a customer is comparatively short - sometimes less than 10 per cent of the salesperson's day. There are many other roles, like administration, that a salesperson needs to do. The need to make the *contact time* most effective is a critical role of a professional seller.

A good salesperson will have objectives for each individual customer. These objectives will lead to an individual strategy for the sales contact period with the customer. Such objectives could be:

- for a new customer/hot prospect – an objection that has to be overcome;
- for an occasional user – to discover why they are not regular customers and find ways of increasing sales frequency; and
- for a regular customer – to introduce an additional product line to complement existing purchases.

The objectives and strategy should be thought out in advance, but the very nature of personal selling means that issues will be raised during a meeting that will require the plan to be modified. In this situation salespeople are on their own. They are the representatives of their organisation to the customer. They cannot continually refer back to Head Office for instructions, and so must fully understand the flexibility they may have to vary the offer mix. They must beware that they do not make promises that *cannot* be kept, such as priority delivery dates. Of course they can make offers and promises that are possible. It is in this situation that a salesperson can be said to be at the *sharp end* of a company's operations.

Account maintenance and development

The building of relationships with customers is the key to future profitable sales. Therefore the process does not normally finish with a successful sale. *Post-transactional* activities start with successful delivery, on time, but move through to many activities which forge strong relationships for the future. These could go as far as using computerised marketing, and even distribution data to track relationships. Such benefits can be part of what is now called *direct marketing*. It could mean establishing electronic links for future re-ordering such as that which links the production planning department of JCB excavators to its suppliers, to really produce 'just-in-time' ordering; or it could mean a simple note in a diary for a follow-up meeting. Figure 20.1 shows the continuum from a sale taken in a competitive market through to a close relationship, contractual link or dealing with an in-house supplier.

Losing customers is much easier than winning customers. The consulting firm Bain and Company, has researched the situation, and concluded an increase of 2 per cent in the retention rate has the same effect on profits as cutting costs by 10 per cent – a worthwhile target. In cruder terms *Business Week* suggested:

> Smart selling means building relationships with customers, not just slam-dunking them on a single sale.

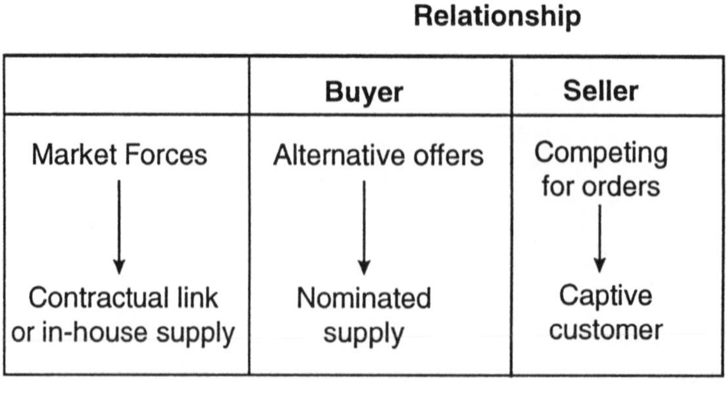

Relationship

	Buyer	**Seller**
Market Forces ↓ Contractual link or in-house supply	Alternative offers ↓ Nominated supply	Competing for orders ↓ Captive customer

Fig 20.1 Different aspects of buyer and seller relationships.

The elements of what is sometimes called relationship marketing were given by Christopher Payne and Ballantyne as:

- focus on customer retention;
- orientation on product benefits;
- long timescale;
- high customer service emphasis;
- high customer commitment;
- high customer contact; and
- quality is the concern of all.

It can be seen that in building of strong relationships there is a key role for personal salespeople.

The principles of selling

The role of a salesperson is often that of a solitary representative of an organisation, who visits other organisations. There are occasions and industries where team selling is appropriate (and, of course, there is the related issue of sales management), but many of the half million UK sales people work alone. The different roles of selling were discussed in the previous section, but, for all groups, the principal role is to be an effective link between a supplier organisation and a potential customer.

The stereotype salesman, depicted by Arthur Miller in his play *Death of a Salesman*, is a back-slapping, joke-telling individual who drops in each season to show his products. This is still a reality in some industries and can be a relevant way of doing business in some instances. But, at a cost in excess of £50 for each sales call, it is a very expensive way of 'entertaining' customers. There are many other ways of bringing products to the notice of customers.

The principle of personal selling is that personal contact is a very powerful way of communicating. Blake and Mouton, who are best known for their work on management and leadership styles, produced a grid for the two elements of the selling role – concern for the customer and concern for achieving the sale (*see* Fig 20.2). Salespeople can fill all these roles. The relevant one for any particular situation is the one that matches the buying style of the customer.

The idea of a 'customer's friend' could be: 'I want to understand the customer and respond to his feelings and interests so that he will like me. It is the personal bond that leads him to purchase from me'. This takes relationship marketing too far. However, it has more long-term opportunities than the 'hard sell': 'I'm in charge of the relationship and will pile on the pressure to get the customer to buy'. The 'hard sell' approach may seem appropriate to a commission salesperson who only gets paid when a sale is made, but it can go against the basic principle of identifying customer's needs and satisfying them.

Neither of these positions really reflect the principles of modern selling. The better positions lie along the shaded diagonal in Fig 20.2, the actual position varying for different selling roles.

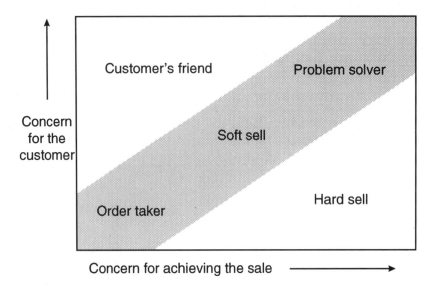

Fig 20.2 Grid for sales excellence

The selling process

Selling is best thought of as a seven-stage process. The same process applies to prospectors, sellers and those responsible for future sales. In fact, there is no reason for all stages of the process to be the responsibility of a single individual, although it is often all carried out by one person. The stages of the selling process are:

- Research   } preparation
- Objectives
- Problem identification
- Objections   } negotiation
- Benefits
- Close   } relationships
- Follow up

The middle stages of *problem identification (asking questions), meeting objections and explaining benefits* do not take place in a formal sequential manner during sales contact. New objections can be raised, or questions asked, at any time during a negotiation. The objections often show that the customer is still interested in matching needs with a suitable offer. This middle stage is the negotiation/presentation period. It is the most critical part of the selling process. However, a well-researched solid foundation is a necessary starting point. There have been too many occasions where salespeople have caused themselves problems by failing to prepare properly.

Research

The research stage involves obtaining information on four key elements.

1 The product/offer mix.
2 Competitors' products/offer mixes.
3 The customers.
4 The relationship between the organisation and the customer.

The first item seems obvious but it relies on proper internal communications in an organisation, so the salesperson fully understands what is being offered. There have been times when a customer has seen details of a new product, maybe in a trade journal, before the salesperson. You can imagine the embarrassment this can cause when a customer tells you your business. It is also important for salespeople to know the constraints on how far they can negotiate. Buyers are well informed and this must not be underestimated. But the object is a win-win deal when both buyer and seller are satisfied. The limits needs to be established well before negotiations start, hence the need for consistent and clear information.

Individual salespeople often learn a lot about their competitors and the directly competitive offerings being made. These individuals can, therefore, be a good source of such information, and they are able to utilise this knowledge in their selling. But organisations should not believe that *all* salespeople will have full information on *all* issues in their marketplace. Collection and dissipation of information on competitors to all salespeople can be linked to suggestions on how to counter the claims that competitors could be making.

The third element is again obvious but necessary. It is the studying of the prospect organisation, and this helps to reveal opportunities and threats which could arise. The customer still should know his own organisation better than the salesperson, but if there are plans for expansion, or contraction, or other developments, then prior knowledge can help in setting objectives, and in the face-to-face meeting. Additional information is obtained during the selling at the problem identification stage.

Prior knowledge is equally necessary for the relationship between suppliers and their customers. Maybe there have been problems in the past, or perhaps there are reasons above normal trading that binds the organisations together. All previous contacts will affect the relationship, so they must be known by the salesperson who can then decide a negotiating strategy with regard to such information.

Issues of power in negotiations can come from any size of organisations, but these can also come from the control of information itself. The sophisticated article number schemes used by retailers often give the retail trade more information than a salesperson on the product sold through these intermediaries. In dealing with intermediaries such as food retailers, the suppliers are at a disadvantage unless they can gather similar information.

Objectives

Setting objectives is necessary for businesses as a whole, and for individual negotiations. A strategy for a meeting with a customer will have objectives - let's say, for example, to get an order for 500 items, or to get machine X in the customers' plant for a test period, or to increase prices by 10 per cent and keep the business. But objectives must not be rigid. Selling is about negotiation. In the UK we rarely negotiate in private life. You are unlikely to succeed if you offer to pay 10 per cent less for your grocery bill when you reach the supermarket check-out. That is because the check-out operator has no power to negotiate. In other circumstances, in a retail store, it could work – try it! In some countries this type of bargaining is well established.

The requirement in setting objectives is to have an acceptable 'fall back' position of alternatives which could be offered; not just price but perhaps payment terms, or special after-sales service, or free merchandising help. Such alternatives can be introduced during the negotiation, if appropriate, with a view to making *an offer* that is acceptable to the customer. There will be other objectives for a meeting, such as to introduce a new product to an existing customer (*see* the Ansoff Matrix, Fig 12.13), or even to discover the names of potential new customers for existing products. These objectives are illustrated in Fig 20.3.

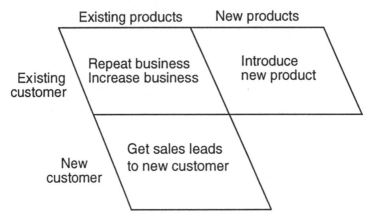

Fig 20.3 Three types of objectives (derived from Ansoff's Matrix)

Problem identification

Objectives are a necessary preparation for a sales contact, but when that contact actually takes place it is still necessary to re-establish the facts from the customer. It is obvious that a cold caller will need to ask questions to establish the needs a prospect may have. The same is also true of regular sales contacts because changes do happen and a sales presentation will fall flat if there has been a fundamental alteration in the needs of the customer's organisation.

Questions need to be open ended to allow customers to respond and to volunteer information that can be used in the subsequent presentation. Open questions are typically ones such as:

- In what way does this machine fail to meet your requirements?
- What are the main reasons for your interest in this service?

Closed questions, such as the ones below, do not give opportunities for enlargement.

- Does your company use a three-tonne press?
- Who currently supplies this service?

A good list of question types can be found in Lancaster and Jobber's book, *Sales Techniques and Management* (page 82). Questions should be used to identify problems. But they can also be used as a way of keeping control of the situation by dictating the agenda. The one question that should never be used, on an exhibition stand or in a retail store, is

'Can I help you?' The obvious response is, 'No, thank you'.

Objections

The experience of all the authors is that objections are a natural part of the sales process. They can come during the initial approach for a meeting right up to the point when the salesperson is trying to close the sale. If no objections are raised, even an experienced salesperson will worry that something unknown is wrong. Objections are not excuses but genuine statements of interests, while revealing some issue to be discussed further. Objections can highlight issues of direct importance to a buyer, but equally they can be 'false objections'. In these cases the salesperson has to dig for the real problem.

When dealing with objections it is essential that the salesperson does not take any objection personally. It is not a personal rejection and, if considered to be so, could be demoralising. Objections can be countered. Rebukes such as 'I'm too busy to see you' can be countered by saying, 'Of course, I appreciate you are a busy person, but what I'd like to show you will only take ten minutes of your time'. This technique *agrees* with the prospect but then *counters* with a reasonable suggestion. Other techniques for dealing with objections are discussed in Lancaster and Jobber's excellent book.

It is vital to respect the customer during negotiations. Do not interrupt and certainly do not argue with a prospect/customer: if there is an argument and the customer wins you have probably lost the sale; if the salesperson wins the argument he has definitely lost the sale.

Benefits - the solution to the problem

It will be noticed that the sales process described here does not specifically include a sales presentation. That does not mean such presentations are not used. They are. The need is for the presentation or negotiation to address the customer's needs, and to describe the *'offer'* in terms of benefits as seen by that customer. An offer must be: *acceptable, affordable* and *available*. Since the customers are the judges of these factors, it is preferable to present the customers with benefits they can understand, not technical features that could confuse. Benefits can be described at two levels.

- the benefits offered by a particular product or service; and
- the benefit of dealing with the salesperson's organisation.

The way to describe the benefits will come direct from customers and will use the customers' own language, something all successful salespeople are able to do. In the earlier questioning stage, the benefits required will be probed. Later in the meeting, the objections and other needs will be revealed. A good salesperson uses the customer's own words to describe why a particular product best fits that customer's requirement.

'Closing'

Closing is a word from sales jargon. It relates to the key requirement of closing the sale - getting the order, or meeting the objectives of the sales contact. To close, finish, bring to an end, conclude or complete is the last stage of a sales negotiation. But this is not a sudden action, at some pre-arranged time. It is a logical development that can take place at any time. Skilled salespeople look for signs, called buying signals, that the customer is ready to close. The body language is important in a personal sales situation, and it is often said that the whole period of contact is an attempt to bring the situation to a satisfactory 'close'.

There are all sorts of devices for forcing a 'close', and successful salespeople have an instinct as to when they should use these. They know when to ask for an order, and then *the golden rule is to shut up*. By doing this, they do not talk themselves out of an order after the event. The use of silence is powerful in forcing customers to either accept the proposal or raise another objection. If a new objection is raised following an attempt to 'close' (get an order), then the process of dealing with that objection, such as offering compensating benefits, is repeated. And then, perhaps, a new 'close' can be attempted. A successful 'close' might be the end of a particular sales contact but it is only the start of the next important stage - the follow-up.

Follow-up or after-sales service

It will come as no surprise to readers of this book that after-sales service is stressed. Of course, some delivery issues might be in the control of another department but, even if they let the customer down, it is the salesperson who has to visit the customer again next period. The salesperson is the real point of contact, and good after-sales service can mean increased business. It can also lead to contacts with new prospects. Poor service is likely to do the opposite.

Six things to avoid

Salespeople must carry out the various elements in the sales process effectively. However, there are six major mistakes that can be made even by successful salespeople.

1 Not following-up quotations, enquiries or other promises quickly enough.
2 Making unrealistic promises to customers.
3 Over-estimating their own ability to get a sale, and under-estimating the competitors' ability.
4 Exaggerating the probability, size and profitability of future orders.
5 Under-estimating a customer's potential.
6 Over-selling a customer, so that the customer buys more than is needed now.

The first two factors are ones where there is no excuse. A good salesperson knows what is possible, and then deals with customers on that basis. The next two are more difficult. They stem from the necessary optimism and self-confidence required by a salesperson. In compiling sales forecasts from the estimates of sales forces, a usual precaution is to reduce such predictions by a little to allow for excess claims. The final two factors, under-estimating potential and over-selling, are major errors. It is difficult to identify when under-estimating happens, but it obviously represents a lost opportunity. It is cheaper to get increased business from existing customers than from new customers, and hence the full potential of existing customers must be considered. The role of identifying problems by asking questions could be re-named identifying opportunities. For a salesperson every problem is a potential opportunity. But over-selling is perhaps a worse mistake. In the continuous contact between supplier and customer, this represents an abuse. It will not help the building of trust so necessary in a good relationship.

Control, motivation and sales management

This section covers the two conflicting roles involved in managing a sales force: controlling activities while encouraging salespeople to do a better job.

Control ratios

The decision to use a sales force to communicate with customers is an expensive one. Even a small sales team can cost several million pounds every year. Therefore the expenditure should be treated as an investment, in just the same way as an investment in other communication media, or an investment in plant or equipment. There are alternative ways of reaching customers, but if the sales force is the way chosen, the sales performance must be controlled.

An investment needs to be monitored to ensure it is giving an adequate return, in this case the return will be measured in terms of sales made. However, there is no way of guaranteeing sales, and, in many organisations, salespeople do over estimate the probability of getting future orders. Unfortunately, when these orders are not forthcoming, it is often too late for the manager to take action to generate the required level of business. While sales orders are obviously required as an output, the measurement of sales level as the control is only one way to gauge selling success. In fact, sales' levels are a resultant effect of the total selling operation. For instance, there should be a mixture of sales calls that produce the desired results, and some that do not. To assume all sales calls will produce orders is a mistake. Therefore it is important to measure elements of selling which can be considered the *cause* rather than the *effect* of sales performance.

In this context there are three key control ratios which could indicate how the business is developing. These are:

1 Call effectiveness.
2 Strike rate.
3 Prospecting success.

Call effectiveness measures the average return from a successful sales visit. It can be average sales revenue per order, or profit per order. Since the cost of a call is not very different (whether the order received is large or small), this measure can be used to show if too many small, perhaps unprofitable, calls are being made.

Of course, it is also important to maintain the level of successful calls. **Strike rate** measures the ratio of orders received to calls made, or sometimes orders received to quotations issued. It measures the productive level of the salesperson.

The third key measure involves new business, **prospecting success,** which obviously comes from new customers/prospects. If the customer group is not being renewed, there is a problem when an existing customer ceases to order. The measure can be expressed as numbers of new customers (who order for the first time) as a proportion of all prospect calls (where no order has yet been received). This measure reflects the difficulty in converting prospects into customers. It sometimes includes a measure of total calls as well.

These three ratios need to be linked to the total **call rate** to give a good measure of the effectiveness of individual salespeople. There are other ratios suggested in sales textbooks, but the controls covering how many calls a salesperson makes and how successful are they, on average, in each call, actually get closer to the cause of sales performance than the output of sales revenue.

Motivation

The management function is widely researched and many theories of motivation have been suggested. Motivation is particularly important with a sales force because of the scattered locations which could be involved, and the individual natures of most salespeople. This book is not the place to discuss the theories of human resource management (HRM) and psychology but a few relevant points can be made. Salespeople often work alone - regular, scheduled sales meetings, bringing people together, say once a month, can motivate individuals by group recognition and support. Salespeople tend to have a strong driving force. 'Stick-and-carrot' techniques do not work well in this situation. Money is not a universal motivator although it is very important. Research quoted in Lancaster and Jobber showed, 'self-satisfaction from doing a good job' as the top non-monetary factor in separate surveys of industrial and consumer salespeople. However, there was one major difference between these two groups, industrial salespeople rated 'satisfy customer needs' second, and consumer salespeople ranked it sixth. Figure 20.4 shows a basic motivational model.

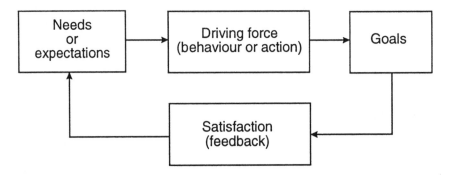

Fig 20.4 Basic motivational model (Source: L.J Mullins, *Management and Organisational Behaviour,* Pitman, 1989)

Sales management

As with motivation, there is little to separate sales management from general management. Stafford and Grant suggested the following format for successful sales management, but the same list could come from any management text book and not refer to sales management at all.

1	Planning	The setting of objectives for the team.
2	Organisation	The strategy for achieving the objectives.
3	Recruitment	Selecting the right people to staff the sales organisation.
4	Training	Developing the skills required to get the job done.
5	Motivation	Getting the best result from the team.
6	Control	Ensuring the results conform to the plan.
7	Monitor	Setting up a 'feed-back system'.

Lancaster and Jobber emphasised recruitment and selection, motivation and training, and organisation and compensation as the three issues of management of a sales force.

The size of a sales force

The sales force is an expensive resource, but the cost is not the prime consideration in determining size. The questions must be: What is appropriate for the task to be tackled? Three techniques are described by Lancaster and Jobber. These are:

1 The workload approach.
2 The productivity approach.
3 The 'vaguely right' approach.

The **workload approach** recognises that there is only so much work any individual can tackle. If it is possible to calculate the number of customers, and frequency of calls, then this can be related to the workload and hence a size of sales force. But this may not be appropriate to develop new customers. The **productivity approach** looks at sales potential and costs to work out when the marginal return matches costs. The **'vaguely right'** is much more scientific than it sounds but beyond the scope of this book.

Often sales forces are well established, which makes it difficult to increase or reduce the numbers employed. However, this really is short-sighted as the marketing environment could well be changing and the task required could differ over time. It does take time to train new salespeople, but this is happening all the time as salespeople are mobile in their careers. In any company up to 10 per cent of the sales force could leave every year. Hence, the level of investment in the sales force needs to be continually reviewed, and modifications can be accommodated as part of regular staff turnover.

The organisation of a sales force

The effectiveness of a sales force will be related to both the individual skills of the salespeople and the organisation chosen. For instance it would be difficult to continually change sales territories if it is accepted that a key role of selling is to build good relationships with customers. Historically, field sales forces have been subdivided into geographical territories. Sometimes division goes even further to have salespeople specialising with a small group of products, or a particular type of customer.

Geographical territories

Dividing the sales force into geographical territories allows a salesperson to become responsible for a certain geographical region. The territories should be organised in a way which makes the possible workload as similar as possible in each territory. The size of the territory should be such that little time is wasted in excessive travelling and all customers should be called upon frequently. This is known as 'the frequency of call rate'. A key advantage of a territorial design is continuity. Customers can get to know and trust the salesperson and administration can be kept simple.

Division by product

When the sales force is divided by product specialty, some salespeople are responsible for one group of products while others are responsible for different products. The main advantage of this method of sales force organisation is that the salespeople can concentrate on developing better product knowledge. A disadvantage is that costs may be duplicated if customers buy more than one of the firm's products, because this would entail a visit by more than one salesperson.

Division by type of outlet

By using this type of organisation of a sales force, a supplier hopes to take advantage of the different skills that may be required when servicing different industries. This is quite common in the industrial sector where engineering firms may make components which can be used in several large industries. The salesperson will then try to become an expert in selling to one particular type of industry, by building up knowledge about the needs of that industry.

There is no universally 'right' answer to sales force organisation. There can be 'intensive' coverage and 'selective' coverage in sales just as in channels of distribution (Chapter 15). Life insurance salespeople could claim to be part of both the communications mix and distribution. A large national life insurance company could use 'intensive' coverage even if it meant occasional conflicts when two salespeople contact the same prospect. Such conflicts would be inappropriate for a supplier of specialist machinery to industry; and it would be inefficient for a small bakery offering home delivery and using van salespeople. Here 'selective' representation is the most relevant. But for one multi-product company, organisation by products and customers meant some customers received multiple visits from sales representatives from the same company.

Example

At one time a survey by Cadbury Schweppes showed a single wholesaler received visits from Cadbury Confectionery, Cadbury Foods (Marvel, Smash, Biscuits), Typhoo Tea, Chivers-Hartley Jam and marmalade, Cadbury - Typhoo Catering Foods, Schweppes drinks, Jeyes disinfectants and Kenco coffee. Some of these calls were every week, some every month, but with eight separate representatives involved, then eight different relationships were being established. This situation has now changed as Cadbury Schweppes have sold several of these subsidiaries, but at the time the distribution of four of the companies was handled by a single delivery operation. Often this meant four separate deliveries, each week, to the same customer. Clearly a costly operation.

This example shows how sales organisation links to distribution for physical goods. In fact the whole marketing mix is inter-related, so any decision on a sales force or its organisation must be part of a total integrated marketing plan and not taken solely for sales convenience.

Future trends in selling

When thinking of salespeople, there is a general image of company car, lunch allowance, stopping at good hotels, in fact a good life. But in practice, the car doubles as an office, the lunch is often a rushed sandwich between calls and hotels are just boring. But selling can be a good life for those who enjoy meeting people. The problem is that much time is spent doing administration, driving, waiting, and sorting out problems caused elsewhere in your organisation. Three trends need to be considered to conclude this section on selling.

1 Can new technology be used to make salespeople more effective in their profession?
2 Are there situations where direct personal selling is no longer cost-effective, and what happens in this case?
3 Are there changes in the structure of industries that mean the sales role must be redefined?

Selling is about meeting people, establishing relationships and communication. This cannot be replaced by modern technology but it can be helped by such developments. The aim is to improve effectiveness. For instance, car phones can keep a salesperson in contact from his office (car). Entering orders into a portable computer is faster than writing an order. The orders can be down loaded automatically via telephone lines and the order directly input into the delivery schedule with minimal delay. Word processors can produce standard quotations twice as fast. Direct marketing databases can store much more information than a hand-written record card, and the information in the database can be analysed to help a salesperson target a customer more precisely.

So many uses are being made of modern technology to improve preparation and the following up of sales calls. Even during the call a salesperson would show a video or use a small printer to print a personalised quotation. But there is a point when the use of such devises will get in the way of the personal contact and if this is the case they must be rejected.

A direct call by a salesperson could be replaced by a telephone call. This could save 90 per cent of the cost of the call. The loss of contact might not be critical, although there is evidence of both a reduction in sales received and more especially of information required for the future. Sometimes a successful hybrid system can be used, combining fewer sales visits with regular telesales contact. Another development mentioned earlier is direct computer-to-computer re-ordering links between customer and supplier. These can again be supplemented with infrequent direct sales contact.

In some organisations and in some industries, suppliers have decided the cost of sales staff is greater than the benefits. These are areas where the supplier lets customers choose for themselves. In the past this has happened with self-service retail stores replacing traditional service, self-service petrol-stations, cash and carry wholesalers replacing delivered wholesalers, and direct (mail order) insurance companies challenging traditional insurance brokers. The sensible rule is to continually re-assess the investment in a sales force against the benefits received. Remember the alternatives available to reach and communicate with potential customers.

In some industries it is the customers and their needs that are changing. Not many years ago sales forces for major food manufacturers had several hundred people, each calling on a number of outlets. Now buying is centralised and a team approach is used with perhaps a senior sales account manager meeting a buying director, then account managers liaising with regional managers who control a number of stores, and finally, maybe a part-time merchandiser visiting an individual outlet. In this situation there is a need to ensure excellent team work. Good communications between the various members of the sales team and an appropriate contact with the customer are essential.

The major sales force may not be used, but the *senior account manager* could have a role to negotiate sales. The *account manager* might ensure orders are placed and to influence deliveries either direct to stores or to the retailer's central warehouse. The *merchandiser* is not a salesperson but efforts to improve product displays can ensure the product sells through the intermediary on to the eventual consumer. This type of multi-level contact can build very strong relationships, each at a relevant level. It is an example of assessing the task and answering the question, 'What is appropriate for the task?' The answer should cover all elements of marketing, but there is no reason that it must require a direct sales organisation.

Conclusion

This chapter has demonstrated the key role of personal selling as one way of reaching customers. While most selling activities are more immediate, or short term, then marketing the skills of understanding customer needs are equally necessary. There are many levels to building personal relationships with customers and a successful salesperson will understand all of these.

Selling is not just the actual customer contact, it includes a great deal of preparation and follow up. In these activities sales and marketing are closely related, and the people concerned need to work together.

Marketing managers have been described as representing the environment within the company as well as projecting the organisation out into its environment. To do this involves meeting customers. Salespeople are doing this all the time and can be a key part of such information channels. However, marketers must not leave it all to the salesforce who have a key task of getting the sales required now to keep the company in business. In many companies the marketing or product managers will plan to accompany a sales visit or attend a sales meeting at least once a month. But more than this, marketing must ensure the sales force are always informed of decisions from inside the company that could affect the sales actions.

Questions

1 What is the difference between a salesperson involved in 'prospecting' and a salesperson concentrating on account maintenance? Do you think these involve different skills.

2 Suggest some simple ways a salesperson can build a strong relationship with all customers even if that salesperson regularly contacts 500 such customers.

3 Why is preparation so important in the selling process?

4 How should a salesperson deal with 'objections' raised by customers during a sales presentation?

References

Blake, R and Mouton, J, *Grid for Sales Excellence*, McGraw-Hill, 1970.
Christopher, M, Payne, A and Ballantyne, D, *Relationship Marketing*, Heinemann, 1991.
Fenton, J, 'Sell sell sell', Sales leaflet.
Lancaster, G and Jobber, D, *Sales Techniques and Management*, 2nd Edn., Pitman Publishing, 1990.
McCall, J B and Warrington, J B, *Marketing by Agreement*, Wiley, 1984.

Miller, Arthur, *Death of a Salesman* 1949.

Mullins, L J, *Management and Organisational Behaviour*, 2nd Edn., Pitman Publishing, 1989.

Power, C and Driscoll, L, 'Smart selling' *Business Week*, 3 August 1992.

Stafford, J and Grant, C, *Effective Sales Management*, Heinemann, 1986.

Case study: personal selling
The Cincinnati Toolmaster

For many years the Cincinnati Milling Machine Company was the largest machine tool manufacturer in the world and enjoyed an unrivalled reputation for its range of products, their quality, design refinement and technical innovation. It was well run by members of the founding family, had a strong engineering and research base and efficient manufacturing in good premises located at three sites in the USA, two in England and one in Holland and one in France.

The company had an extensive market development department which recognised in good time that there was a trend within the machine tool market towards smaller machines manufactured in high volume. A new plant was developed primarily to manufacture products for this market. Among these was the Toolmaster milling machine. This was a well-made product but was considered expensive in comparison with the Bridgeport Turret milling machine against which it had been designed to be a direct competitor.

In spite of much marketing and sales effort the Toolmaster did not compete effectively with the Bridgeport and was eventually phased out. Bridgeport had meanwhile signed an agreement with Adcock and Shipway Ltd an established milling machine manufacturer in the UK and this ultimately led to a new factory being built specifically to manufacture Bridgeports for the European market. This was a successful venture and Cincinnati Milling decided to follow Bridgeport's example.

By this time the Bridgeport was considered somewhat old-fashioned especially in France and West Germany, so Cincinnati Milling designed an all-new version of the Toolmaster. It was designed for the European market to a specification drawn up as a result of thorough market research. Facilities were provided at the plant in France to manufacture the machine in volume both for the European and American markets. It was then introduced as a modern, good-looking machine which performed well. Much attention was given to marketing the machine effectively with regard to both promotion and selling effort.

In the UK, the main target market considered is Europe. This included developing a special sales force to concentrate exclusively on selling the new machine and a limited number of similar products. However, the new Toolmaster did not successfully compete with the Bridgeport and within a few years production ceased and the facility in France was closed. Meanwhile the Bridgeport continued to compete successfully with more than twenty similar products many of which were made in Taiwan, so inevitably had a significant price advantage.

Why had the Toolmaster been so unsuccessful in comparison with the Bridgeport? At the time it seemed that this had been due to a combination of the following: both of which were valid.

First, the Bridgeport was the original – when it was introduced it was a new product. It was very well made and its production employed some patented processes which made it a particularly nice machine to use. This was important since unlike most machine tools, many users owned their machines. In its basic form the Bridgeport was not expensive. A basic version of the Toolmaster had not been offered as in this form the price would not have been profitable.

There was, however, another more fundamental difference between the two organisations. This was in the way they marketed their products. The Bridgeport approach was to generate sales leads by advertising and direct mail and use a closely supervised sales force to convert this interest into sales. Their salespeople were generally ex-apprentices with practical machining experience, but little formal education. They carried order pads, wrote up orders for their customers and visited a large number of customers each day. Record keeping was focused on maintaining an extensive, up-to-date mailing list which included a large number of self-employed individuals. Product catalogues were basic but very detailed with regard to the availability of accessories and extra equipment. Formal proposals were only prepared when required by the customer otherwise a comprehensive price list was mailed.

Cincinnati had a very well-trained sales force. Many were graduates. All had spent at least two years as field service engineers and a similar period as engineering estimators. They had a very large product range to cover and were required to prepare detailed quotations for every prospect, follow these up and ensure that every customer order contained all of the technical information necessary for the order to be implemented. Average daily call rate was as a result, less than half that of a Bridgeport salesperson. Catalogues were high quality and focused on product and company image. Advertising generally featured high technology equipment rather than basic equipment like Toolmasters. Direct mail was focused on individuals employed by major companies.

This fundamentally different approach to the market reflects the very different market sector focus of the two companies.

Like many successful organisations the reasons for success were not properly understood. The Cincinnati Milling management assumed that because they were able to sell expensive high quality machines in comparatively large numbers they had the necessary marketing expertise to sell low value equipment as well. This was clearly not the case and an analysis of the companies who were their customers and the people they employed as sales engineers should have made this all too clear. Instead, the analysis was focused almost exclusively on the product. The tragedy is that the strategy of moving into the high volume sector of the market was correct, but by the time Cincinnati Milling had adapted to this market their pre-eminent position in the world market had been lost.

What could have been done to make the Toolmaster more successful?

There is a sequel to this story. In time Bridgeport found that to maintain their market position they needed to extend their product range. This resulted in the introduction of a range of high-value equipment, some of which was manufactured under licence and some imported. Like the existing Bridgeport products this equipment was competitively priced and of a high quality. However, these new products were much less successful than had been expected and resulted in the company becoming as susceptible to the economic situation as other machine tool companies.

It is tempting to assume this outcome was inevitable, but it was not. What could have been done to improve the likelihood of success with these new products?

21

MARKETING PLANNING AND CONTROL

Introduction

To be effective marketing has to provide a means by which an organisation can focus its resources to meet customer needs efficiently. First and foremost, this involves the efficient implementation of specific marketing functions such as promotion, product development, distribution and so on. Second, it involves the allocation of investment resources such as those required for new product development and promotion. Third, it involves the co-ordination of marketing with the other functions of the organisation. The marketing planning process has evolved to provide a framework for all three of these activities. For small organisations this is a straightforward process involving well established stages and, if required, the production of a document, 'The Marketing Plan'. Often this is can be used as the basis for negotiations with organisations such as banks which can provide start-up finance for a new venture or additional finance for expansion.

In many large organisations marketing planning has become an established formal procedure and part of the strategic planning process. In this context it is generally necessary to co-ordinate the marketing of a range of sometimes diverse products and this inevitably makes the process both more complicated and potentially more beneficial. Also, in many large organisations it has been found that the process itself has improved the level of co-operation and involvement of the managers involved.

The marketing planning process

It is a fundamental precept of planning there has to be an objective. Often the analogy of the journey is used to make the point that a route can only be planned if the starting point and the destination are known. This, however, overlooks the real purpose of planning and that is to improve the effectiveness with which a task is carried out. Using the journey analogy it could be in terms of reducing the time taken to reach the destination. But, to be anything other than an unjustified assumption, objectives must be stated. The situation tends to be more complicated in the social or business context since many, apparently sensible, objectives are not fixed, like a point on a map for example, but instead are moving targets, such as being market leader. Even recognising the basic objective of business is to increase the asset value of the owners at a rate commensurate with the risk involved. It is often difficult to formulate useful objectives even for business organisations and is inevitably difficult for other types of organisation.

One approach which has been adopted by many large organisations is to set overall objectives in a mission statement. This sets out how that organisation intends to fulfil its main business objectives while recognising the legitimate interests of other stakeholders such as customers, employees, suppliers and the communities in which the organisation operates. While a mission statement tends to be a general statement, objectives for a small business need to be specific to that business. For instance, a butcher intending to open a shop in a village where there are already two butchers is likely to be more successful if his objective is framed to emphasise how his shop will differ from his two competitors' shops. If one of these is centrally located and serves the community in general and the other is on a main road and serves more passing trade, then there could well be an opening for a specialist butcher which has premises away from the main centre, has lower overheads and thus can specialise in providing only the highest quality meat at slightly higher prices. The business objective would be to become the preferred supplier to the local community and beyond for meat purchased for special occasions.

To an extent the objective once set needs to be in the context of the skills and facilities available to the business. This involves recognising what these are in comparison to the competition. This is comparatively easy where the business is small but increasingly difficult as organisations become larger. The process is, however, the same and has become known as the business audit.

The marketing audit

Central to any business audit is the marketing audit which has two components. The first is concerned with the external environment and should therefore focus on any changes, either current or expected, which are likely to affect the organisation or the markets it serves. For many businesses the economic climate is of vital importance, so needs to be assessed critically. The technical and regulatory environments that affect the organisation, its markets and competitors also need to be at least discussed.

The *external marketing audit* focuses on the uncontrollable environmental factors affecting the business. It should include information which shows the size of the market in terms of both value and volume, and the trends in these. The position of the organisation should be compared with that of each significant competitor. The characteristics of the market should be defined and compared in terms of the range of products offered, their prices, distribution and promotion. In addition, the audit provides an opportunity for information gathered by the marketing research function, relevant to any aspect of the business, to be presented and its relevance assessed.

Example

An example of a change which had direct marketing implications but which were ignored by a very significant number of organisations was the need to charge VAT. In most of these organisations the preparation of invoices was an accounting function and the need to collect VAT considered a part of this. This resulted in many decisions which affected the way prices were presented being taken without considering the effect on customers. As a result many companies either disturbed cherished customer relationships or found that, having quoted VAT inclusive prices, they lost business because their prices were then higher than those of competitors who were quoting prices excluding VAT.

The *internal marketing audit* involves establishing the performance of the organisation and comparing this with previous periods to establish short- and long-term trends. The analysis needs to be sufficiently detailed to show differences by product and geographical area, with regard to sales, costs (manufacture, distribution and promotion) and profits. In addition, the current situation with regard to the marketing organisation, personnel, product development and marketing research should be reviewed. This latter part of the internal audit will need to be addressed even in marketing plans relating to a new business, since it will show the steps taken to organise these functions.

Whether produced by professionals working in a marketing research department or a person drawing up a marketing plan to obtain the finance needed to become self employed, the external and internal audits should be sufficiently thorough to show clearly how they relate to the business environment and, when appropriate, the direction of its current progress.

Marketing analysis

The audit process inevitably produces a great deal of data and information. To use this it is necessary to select those items which are likely to affect specifically the performance of an organisation or a competitor from those which either will affect both equally or have little effect. By treating the internal audit data separately from the external data allows the significant data to be classified under four headings:

- **Strengths**: These are the internal factors which are likely to enhance performance such as having a well-trained sales force, efficient production and high-quality products.
- **Weaknesses**: These are the internal factors which are likely to inhibit performance such as excessive capacity (high fixed costs), obsolete designs and long delivery schedules.
- **Opportunities**: These are the external factors which favour the organisation such as effective distributors, compliance with legislation, presence in growing market segments, security of supply of critical components or competitors being reorganised.
- **Threats**: These are the external factors which are likely to be to the organisation's disadvantage, such as strengthening currency making imported competition less expensive and exports more expensive, recently introduced competitive products, an ageing workforce and skill shortages.

The selection of data in this way is known as a **SWOT** analysis as these are the initial letters of the classifications used. Its purpose is to provide a framework within which the selected information can be compared, the strengths can be developed to match the specific opportunities identified and those weaknesses for which there is a corresponding threat addressed.

Objectives, strategies and assumptions

From the SWOT analysis it should be possible to draw up marketing objectives which are not in conflict with the corporate objectives as might be set out in the mission statement. To be useful a marketing objective needs to have two components. The first is to specify what is to be achieved. This has to be realistic in both the light of present circumstances and past performance. The second is to state the time by which the objective is to be achieved. The objective needs to be stated in absolute terms. It is not sufficient to specify it in terms of a market share or previous growth. This is essential since otherwise there can be no comparison between actual performance and the objective set month by month or week by week. If the objective is found for some reason to be unrealistic, it should be amended as otherwise it will have no value as a goal.

The next stage is to specify how the stated objectives are to be achieved in general rather than specific terms. This is an important step since it provides the structure within which the detailed steps involved can be selected and implemented. It is also a basically simple step in that, as was pointed out by Igor Ansoff, there are essentially only four strategies which lead to growth. These can be summarised in the well-known Ansoff Matrix (*see* Fig 12.13) or stated as below:

1 Increasing sales of existing products in existing markets. This could be done by increasing the amount used on each occasion or the occasions used. The promotion of breakfast cereal as an 'anytime-snack' is an example of the second of these approaches.

2 Introducing the existing product to new markets. Although exporting is the usual example given for this strategy, it can be more subtle as when baby shampoo was promoted as a frequent-use shampoo.

3 Introducing a new product to existing markets. This could be a substitute product providing it would be used in larger quantities such as in the case of frequent-use shampoos. More often it is a product which is used by the same market segment. The introduction of fabric softeners and special stain removers by the laundry detergent manufacturers is an example of this.

4 The fourth strategy identified by Ansoff is the introduction of a new product into new markets. This is generally considered to be a high-risk strategy although where the new product uses existing production technology, the risk may not be that significant. An example of this strategy would be the introduction of lawn mowers by Black and Decker Limited.

It is likely that this will be an iterative, rather than a sequential process since the selection of a strategy is likely to affect the perception of the objectives and, as a result, these will be amended thereby requiring the strategy to be reconsidered. The process will be further complicated by the need to impose assumptions on both the objectives and strategy. These may involve estimations relating to data which is not available, the continuation or reversal of present trends, the timing of anticipated events and so on. The assumptions are often summarised as a forecast, which can then be used to develop a provisional budget. The budget can then be used as the basis for subsequent stages of the planning process.

It is essential that the assumptions upon which such a forecast is based are clearly stated since it will allow the forecast to be amended as the assumptions respond to any changes in the situation upon which they were based. The logic of this can easily be lost once the forecast has been buried within a carefully constructed budget and the outcome subjected to a variance analysis. While it is fundamental to the use of marketing budgets (we will return to it in the section on control), the impact resulting from having to revise assumptions can be minimised by the planning process.

Marketing programmes

With clearly defined objectives, a strategy for achieving these objectives selected and with a set of clearly defined assumptions, the next stage of the marketing planning process is the development of programmes. The purpose of programmes is to specify the actions, responsibility, resources and schedule needed to achieve the stated objectives via the selected strategy. The simplest approach to programme development is to use the components of the marketing mix as a framework. This ensures all essential tasks are covered and properly co-ordinated. It also ensures that the programmes are focused on the market segments which have been specified by the objectives and strategy statements.

By using this approach, it will be necessary to have separate programmes for each of the marketing-mix elements. Depending upon the strategy these may be extensive or simple. For instance, where the strategy involves new products the programmes will be significantly more involved than if only minor product changes are considered necessary. Generally the introduction of new products will also necessitate a co-ordinated programme of promotion. This, as a result, might be considered as a single programme and separate from the general promotion programme. Often the complexity of the promotion programme will justify having a separate programme for each of the four elements of the promotion mix. Accordingly, there would be an advertising programme, a public relations programme, a sales promotion programme and a programme concerned with the personnel selling aspects of promotion.

In addition to the programmes that can be directly related to the principal objectives there are likely to be some which address specific issues raised in the internal or external audit. The example of the introduction of VAT would justify having an individual programme since it affected the organisation's approach to pricing and invoicing, its terms and conditions of sale and would involve expenditure for printing revised quotation, invoice and conditions of sale documentation.

Once the programmes have been detailed the total resources required for their implementation can be determined. Inevitably this will exceed the resources allocated in the budget developed from the initial objectives, strategy and assumptions. The iterative process involved in reconciling the cost of the required programmes with the available resources provides the opportunity to optimise these two factors. In doing so it is necessary to estimate the impact on the objective of each programme. The effect of both increasing and reducing the expenditure should be considered. For instance, if on the basis of existing data the most likely effect of reducing advertising expenditure is to make the situation worse, because of the corresponding reduction in sales revenue, an increase could have the opposite effect. Clearly this could increase the business risk unacceptably. As part of the reconciliation process, the effect that changing the assumptions would have should also be investigated so that the final plan has less risk and more potential of achieving the agreed objectives than any of the alternatives.

In carrying out this process it is inevitable that the underlying assumptions will have been fully evaluated and some innovative approaches considered. Usually the final plan will deviate only to a limited extent from the approach followed previously. The planning process should however ensure that a radical plan could be adopted if justified. Volvo provides a example of a company which responded appropriately to changing market conditions even though this required a significant revision of existing plans. By the early 1980s it had been expected that without a replacement for the ageing 240 series vehicle, the Volvo market share would be severely affected. A new vehicle was designed and the investment in a new production facility completed when it became clear that demand for the existing vehicle had revived. It was decided therefore to postpone the launch of the new vehicle in spite of the investment made. As a result, the 700 series vehicles were not launched for another two years with a corresponding extension to the expected life cycle of this model range.

Marketing control

In most organisations survival depends upon positive cash flow which in turn depends upon the level of new business in the form of orders received. Accordingly, the level of new business is generally considered a critical measure of performance. Unfortunately, it tends to be somewhat volatile. It is subject to seasonal variations, changes in the economic climate and is affected by much talked about factors such as confidence. Because of such external factors it is often difficult to attribute sales changes to sales force activity alone.

It is tempting, therefore, to simply compare the figure week by week or month by month with the figure shown on the budget, and providing there is no negative variance, to assume all is well. There are two serious and related problems with this approach. First, there is an underlying assumption that the budgeted figure, having been agreed or accepted, should be seen as a benchmark against which actual performance can be measured. In manufacturing businesses this is often seen as realistic since production rates are seen to be also dependent upon assumptions being made. These however involve the reliability of the plant and equipment used, operator training, freedom from strikes and so on. Generally, deviations from an anticipated level of reliability can be traced back to a faulty repair or an incorrectly carried out maintenance procedure. The improvement in reliability depends upon these problems being identified and rectified. The marketing budget is very different, since the forecast is based on many more arbitrary factors. To consider it as a benchmark is akin to suggesting that the weather is unreliable because it is not as forecasted.

The second problem is that opportunities will be missed unless performance, as measured by new business, is judged in terms of the current situation rather than with the assumptions used to develop the forecast and budget. For instance, if the new business is more than forecast and production is limited, profit can be increased by either reducing expenditure on advertising, for example, or by increasing prices. These are, however, short-term approaches. More often sales being above budget is an indication that the market is expanding more quickly than expected. This is serious since if nothing is done to match this expansion market share will be lost. Many well-established companies have fallen into this trap. They have consistently exceeded their pessimistically set budgets while at the same time loosing market share to competitors. This has two equally important implications. The first is that while production efficiency can be simply measured by output, new business cannot be used in the same way to measure marketing efficiency, unless it can be established that the assumptions, upon which the agreed budget was based, and the individual marketing programmes remain valid. There were periods when this may have been expected but they were a long time age. The modern experience is that situations can change rapidly and assumptions can become invalid just as quickly. The second implication is that to avoid these problems it is necessary to develop systems by which new business can be analysed in detail. The primary objective of the systems should be to discriminate between performance which can be attributed to factors external to the organisation and those which can be attributed to the implementation of the organisation's marketing programmes.

The implementation of marketing planning

Within an organisation the marketing planning process requires individuals who have a sound understanding of the principles of marketing. In particular, this has to be demonstrated by the commitment of senior management. Without this understanding the benefits of planning process are perceived in terms of reducing uncertainty rather than as it should be, of increasing the ability of the organisation to respond to uncertainty.

As should be evident from the preceding section on control, the marketing plan should be at the centre of the performance measurement process. It should also provide the starting point whenever there is a need to respond to changing external or internal circumstances which could affect the organisation, its customers, or the relationship between these.

When economic and technical situations are stable marketing planning might easily become a annual task. In the turbulent economic and technical environment in which organisations must now compete it has to be a continuing process. It should be stressed, however, that this does not mean that programmes are changed month by month. If the planning has been done effectively most, if not all, programmes will remain valid in spite of the assumptions upon which they were based. However, changing circumstances should be identified and analysed early enough to accommodate any needed modifications to the overall plan.

Conclusion

Marketing planning is the means by which well-organised companies bring together their marketing activities into a concerted action plan, ready for the market. A logical sequence will usually be followed in marketing planning, commencing with information gathering and analysis, combined with a marketing audit exercise involving issues and influences both within and outside the company. From the audit stage will be developed the marketing objectives to be addressed, while these in turn will largely direct the strategies to follow within the plan. Key assumptions made during the planning exercise need to be made explicit, as these will have some bearing on the flexibility and scope of the plan itself. Finally, no marketing plan will be complete without some provision for implementation, supporting organisation and control.

Questions

1 Taking any of the case studies in the text, develop a SWOT analysis to identify the major internal and external issues to be addressed.

2 What kinds of **market** information would be necessary for marketing planning, and how might it be obtained?

3 Compare and contrast the marketing plan for an established product with that for a new product.

4 Consider the view that companies will derive as much benefit from the **planning exercise** as from the marketing plan itself.

Reference

McDonald, M H B, *Marketing plans – and how to use them*, 2nd Edn, Heinemann, 1989

22

ORGANISING FOR MARKETING

Introduction

As the nature and role of marketing will vary among companies, so too will the resources involved and the approach adopted to marketing organisation. Exerting a particular influence on the way marketing is organised will be company policy on organisational issues such as centralisation, formalisation and management reporting, while a fundamental if general factor will be the level of market orientation shown by the company. While production-oriented companies are still to be found in large numbers in some sectors, writers such as Doyle have noted the prevalence of financially-driven management, and the strategic risks that may attend it. Marketing management and organisation will be affected by both the strategic requirements of the external environment, and by a host of internal issues such as organisational culture, values and attitudes, management style, the company's own development pattern, ownership history and the like. Even within the same market, faced with similar problems, two similarly-sized companies may therefore adopt totally different approaches to organising and resourcing their marketing function.

It should be stressed that the organisation chart itself can rarely be taken as an indicator of how serious or successful a company is in its marketing; market-leader companies such as Body Shop have built their success through entrepreneurial leadership rather than formal marketing appointments. Simply stated, a large marketing department bristling with specialists is not a sufficient nor, for some, a necessary condition for success. The organisation-wide imperative of the marketing message requires teamwork handling of customer issues *across* the company, so that functional specialisation without integration will be doomed to failure.

This necessary sharing and division of the marketing task may at least partly explain the differences companies show is where within their structure they locate marketing, or sub-functions of it, such as distribution or public relations. Of course, dispersal may carry the risks of fragmentation, or, worse, may thwart the development of marketing in any recognisable form within the company. As part of a continuing research initiative concerning corporate marketing activity, Piercy found within a cross-industry sample that no more than 25 per cent of reporting companies claimed to have an integrated full-service marketing function, with the majority of companies having non-integrated provision in the form of either sales orientation, strategy servicing, or a limited 'staff' advisory role. Problems commonly reported in the non-integrated provision ranged from under-resourcing, weak implementation and interfunctional conflict, to short-termism and a generally lower involvement of marketing in strategy.

Strategy matters play an important part in discussions of organisation, since on the one hand good strategy implementation depends on organisation, while on the other hand strategy formulation should be free of structural 'tramlines' - structure should follow strategy, not vice versa. In the sections that follow a brief examination will be made of the different approaches companies use in organising for marketing.

Organisational structures

Organisational structures without marketing

In many cases these will represent a less mature organisational form that pre-dates the emergence and use of marketing proper. Commonly associated with traditional companies in stable markets, or with production-dominated organisations, this structure will likely follow a four-way functional division between Production, Finance, Personnel and Sales departments, each with a separate chain of command, ultimately reporting to board level. Within such an organisation those activities that might otherwise be undertaken by a marketing department, are likely to be subsumed within the four functional 'pillars' of the structure, e.g. market feedback through the Sales department, forecasting and commercial analysis through financial planning, or through a nominated director. Though *some* market-related tasks are covered, it is unlikely that co-ordinated marketing will be performed to the standards achieved by, for example, marketing-led competitors. Of course, such an organisational approach may also be encountered within small developing companies, where an enterprising founder and informal workings may make for success, even in the face of resource constraints.

In other circumstances, though more exceptionally, it may be that a well-established company has prospered without separately formalising the marketing activities that it does undertake, often to a high standard. It would therefore be inappropriate to style such a high-performing company as ineffective or lacking in market orientation.

The functional marketing structure

Where marketing first takes organisational 'roots' in a company, it is most likely to be formally structured as a separate function. While it will represent a smaller department to start with, departmental status itself may come only after some intermediate phase of sales support, or a growing assortment of sub-activities 'lodging' within various other departments. A common intermediate step will be the creation of a marketing section or sub-department in parallel to the Sales department. Such an arrangement is likely to be sub-optimal, since it is unlikely to deliver integrated marketing, and may result in rivalry, rather than co-operation, between Sales and Marketing - indeed, cases where a long-established Sales department hinders or thwarts the development of marketing are not unknown.

The emergence and integration of marketing into one functional section or department is likely to come about as the level and complexity of previously dispersed activities increases, and as these new activities demand a co-ordination beyond the scope of previous organisational arrangements. The increase in marketing activities that prompts such a new structure will usually in turn be attributable to external changes such as increased competition or marketing maturity, or internal factors such as increasing promotional activity or a need for more market research or marketing planning support. A typical functionally-organised marketing department is illustrated in Fig 22.1. Essentially, the structure consists of an 'umbrella' organisation that embraces both the sales function and the more recent marketing activities such as market research, sales promotion and advertising. Significantly, in the example shown, marketing has achieved representation at board level through the installation of a Marketing Director, though it should be stressed that such strategy-level participation is unfortunately by no means universal. Often it is a Sales and Marketing Director.

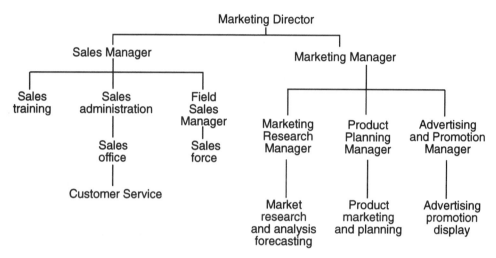

Fig 22.1 Functional marketing organisation

The major benefits of such a structure are that roles and reporting relationships are clearly defined, along conventional hierarchical lines, while specialisation is allowed without undue duplication or ambiguity. Activities requiring more horizontal integration can be accommodated by adding co-ordinator staff, e.g. new product development might demand such liaison, between market research and product planning, and through other departments such as R&D and Manufacturing. On the other hand, difficulties may arise if the organisation grows into a top-heavy hierarchy of specialists with strictly functional interests. Furthermore, frictions and inefficiencies may arise if increasing product and market diversification were to make heavily competing claims on the core specialisms. Such a structure is therefore more appropriate to everyday marketing support of a relatively narrow product range, or within more stable market settings.

Product-based organisation

Originally adopted en masse in the 1950s and 1960s by international fmcg (fast-moving consumer goods) companies, this structure has since spread to other sectors such as industrial manufacturing, and more recently financial services. Essentially, a *product* marketing focus is introduced through the appointment of product (or brand) managers, responsible for the commercial health of some assigned product(s) or brand(s). Though often seen as a 'mini general manager' for product marketing, the typical product manager will be of relatively junior status with little line authority over specialists either in marketing or elsewhere, so that effective working will rest heavily on persuasion and diplomacy, and hopefully the gradual assumption of 'expert power' through demonstrated successes. Figure 22.2 depicts a typical product management organisation.

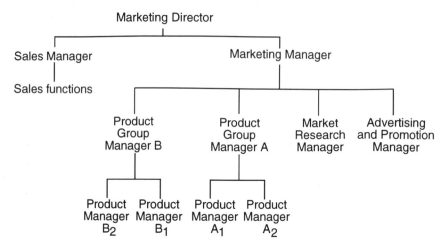

Note: The terms *product manager* and *brand manager* are virtually interchangeable, although strictly speaking a brand manager is responsible for a specific *brand*. Predictably, industrial companies tend not to designate brand managers, though the designation product manager is in more general use.

Fig 22.2　Product management structure

As shown Fig 22.2, product managers will often be organised in groups, under the responsibility of respective Product Group Managers, who are effectively marketing sub-managers at the level of a group of related products. The product manager is above all a liaison post, achieving for a specified product the necessary co-ordination of support from marketing specialists (e.g. market research, advertising) and other functions alike. Product managers will usually be accountable for the financial and commercial health of their products, for product marketing planning and strategy, and for co-ordinating any necessary product development or modification activity.

Product management has a number of advantages as an organisational format. Certainly it guarantees a focus and specialisation of management expertise at the product/brand level, so that all the major products in the range get the benefit of a full-time 'champion' dedicated solely to their well-being. In a multi-product setting, product management therefore ensures a level of management attention that would not be feasible under a functionally-based structure. As the product manager position entails extensive company-wide co-ordination duties, it also offers an excellent training ground for management; a fact that is often recognised in the recruitment policies of major companies.

Product management has a number of potential drawbacks, however, and it is probably true to say that companies are nowadays more critical and pragmatic in their attitude to this structure. Problems can arise in terms of reporting relationships and decision-making authority, while the 'healthy rivalry' shown among product managers may develop into unproductive competition and conflict. Some companies have re-thought their organisations because of the over-emphasis on product expertise, at the expense of functional experience, or even market focus. Again, product managers may become preoccupied with existing products, to the detriment of new product development: to remedy this, some companies have introduced a hybrid position, the *new product manager*. In some markets, too, competitive conditions have demanded a change in orientation away from product strategy towards more operational issues, for example within trade marketing. Finally, it has been the experience of some companies that a product management system becomes increasingly costly and top-heavy, as new products are added and as original product appointments grow into 'teams' through assistant managers, brand assistant positions and the like.

Market-based structures

The basic rationale for a market-based organisation is the need to give marketing attention to specific parts (e.g. groups, sub-markets, segments) of the market. A popular version of this approach is the geographic division, where distinct regions or districts, or indeed countries or country blocs, are handled separately, perhaps in separate locations – industrial companies, for example, may have regional office bases that double as mini-headquarters, housing administration, sales, spares and service, marketing and show-room facilities. Where a product or service is actually provided at the local level, throughout the market, such regionalised organisation may be used for *all* functions, including marketing, e.g. utilities, retail chains, banking, franchise organisations. In some of these cases, a regional organisation may exist alongside a central or corporate support organisation, even for specialist functions such as marketing.

Where companies offer the same product to different customer groups, trades or industries, there may be a need to organise their marketing around these groupings,

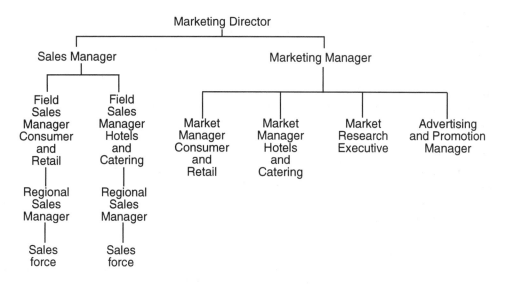

Fig 22.3 Market-based organisation

through the installation of *market managers*, or perhaps industry marketing groups or sections. Figure 22.3 illustrates a market-based organisation for a hypothetical manufacturer of cooking utensils. Not untypically, the example shown is a hybrid structure, where functions such as market research are 'shared' by both market sectors. The sales function, though, has a regional or territory structure, commonly adopted in selling, whatever headquarters structure the company uses for its marketing base.

The major advantage of a market-based structure is the specific focus it puts on customer requirements within different market sectors, and the flexibility and speed of response this affords. The major drawbacks of the structure centre on the resourcing issues of extra management layers, and the possible difficulties of co-ordination and communication associated with this. It may be worth noting that, while in principle the market-based structure is consistent with customer orientation, its practical value has been vindicated in research by Lynch, Hooley and Shepherd who found it to be a characteristic of a number of performance-centred British companies.

Composite or matrix structures

Having examined a number of common organisational approaches to marketing, it should be emphasised that in reality organisation structures will rarely take a simple or 'pure' form, while certainly there is little merit in 'design elegance' for its own sake. In an effort to 'get organised' for new problems, to experiment for improvement, and to combine the advantages of different structures, many companies have adopted composite or matrix organisations.

A *matrix organisation* is a grid-like structure along two (or more) dimensions, typically a dual combination of functions with certain business areas known as programmes or missions. The structure is commonly applied to meet the complex marketing requirements of a diversity in both products and markets, where a vigorous combination of functional, market and product expertise is required. As illustrated in Fig 22.4, the

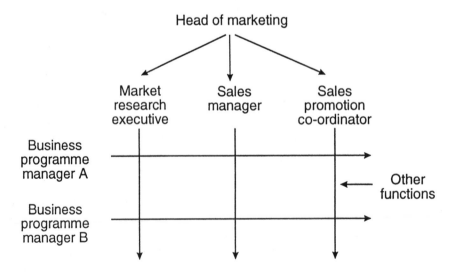

Fig 22.4 A matrix organisation

necessary co-ordination within the organisation will be achieved by designated programme (or project) managers drawing as necessary on the expertise of specialists in marketing and other departments. In managerial terms, the programme team members involved have two formal reporting relationships, one to the programme manager and one to their own department head.

Different companies are likely to produce their own variations on the basic theme. For example, Du Pont, the US producer of synthetic fibres such as nylon and acetate, organises around a product/market overlay system, where product managers work together with market managers, thus achieving for the company the advantages of both market and product expertise and experience. Other companies have adopted more modified versions of matrix structures, limited to perhaps strictly defined business units, or to particular activities such as new product development.

Note: the organisational aspects of new product development have already been covered in Chapter 13.

A number of managerial benefits have been claimed for the matrix form of organisation. Certainly it promises greater co-ordination in settings that demand functional interdependence and busy information and communications flows, while the instituting of dual reporting allows more devolved decision-making and thus faster and more flexible programming. Against these arguments, though, the experience of some companies confirms that matrix structures are no panacea, since they can create new problems in terms of resource costs, political arguments and other types of interdepartmental conflict.

Other organisational formats

Without attempting an exhaustive classification, the following organisational variants are worthy of brief mention.

- **Key account** organisation, a variation on market-based structuring, is common in consumer goods companies. Where major customers dominate a company's income, as with supermarket groups in the food sector, these are designated as key accounts or house accounts and given special marketing support through key account managers or groups. As such business will depend critically on negotiations and regular contacts with the customer's headquarters buying office, key account structures tend to be sales-dominated, and any associated marketing support sales-initiated.

- **Divisionalisation** may take a number of forms, usually involving formal corporate restructuring, and even financial re-structuring and devolution. **Divisions** may be based on broad product groups, geographical demarcation, or vertical divisions such as manufacturing-trading. Though usually employed for higher level strategic reasons, divisionalisation will have a direct effect on marketing organisation. Often, separate divisions will operate their own marketing functions, though dependence on some centralised corporate advisory or planning support is not uncommon.

- **Strategic Business Units (SBUs)** are identifiable business areas within a company (usually product-market combinations) that are handled as separate profit centres. The treatment may be largely financial and strategic, though marketing and other functions are likely to be organised to service the SBUs. This format is therefore effectively a type of matrix organisation.

- **Group marketing**: as with corporate marketing support within a divisionalised structure, a group of associated companies may draw on a common head office marketing service, with or without their own function at subsidiary level. In overseas markets, where local subsidiaries may have to be established as legal entities, local sales and service operations may be supplemented by marketing support at parent company level, although larger subsidiaries in major markets may warrant their own marketing departments staffed by country nationals.

Conflict and co-operation between marketing and other functions

It is obvious that the effectiveness of any individual function, and ultimately the whole company, will depend on co-operation among the specialist staff themselves *and* with their counterparts in other functions across the company. This is perhaps more necessary still for a function such as marketing, which by its nature tends to be more intrusive and integrative. Indeed, a rough indicator of marketing orientation could be the extent of effective inter-disciplinary working *on behalf of the customer*.

In reality, many issues and influences may stand in the way of this ideal. As marketing is founded on a potent and purposeful philosophy, so other functions can claim their own professional standards and orientations, which may be at least partly at odds with a 'textbook' marketing approach. Table 22.1 illustrates a number of issues that might present conflict or contention between marketing and other functions.

Table 22.1
Potential conflicts between marketing and other functions

Function	Conflict source
Engineering	Marketers may request more customised components, while Engineering prefer more standardisation.
R&D	Marketers may show interest in applied research and development work, or become frustrated with laboratory 'over-runs' in time or budget. R&D specialists may emphasise basic or 'pure' research.
Purchasing	Purchasing specialists may make decisions on component specifications, cost, purchase volumes and delivery times at variance with the preferences of (product) marketing specialists, or occasionally with no consultation.
Manufacturing	Manufacturing may insist on 'metric' accuracy in sales forecasting for planning purposes - regarded by marketers as unrealistic. Differences on issues such as production lead times, model or component changes, order scheduling, fabrication methods, etc.
Finance/Accounting	Potential differences over prices and pricing methods, cost allocation, profitability targets, credit control, marketing budgets.

Many of these frictions will represent differences in attitude within different functions, and the apparently contrary aims to which they feel commitment. For example, the manufacturing-marketing relationship, examined in operational conflict terms by writers such as Shapiro, appears to owe some of its difficulties to the inner versus outer orientations that might be ascribed, as a generalisation albeit, to manufacturing versus marketing. The following anecdote, by the well-known designer Kenneth Grange, provides a telling insight into the deep-seated hostility that can surface within the marketing-production relationship:

> One of my abiding memories is of a boardroom in a large company where the capital costs needed for a new product were under examination. On that day I sat among the product team; design, development and production men, their various interests represented by a brilliant, hard-pressed chief engineer.
>
> In the way those conversations go, a focus had been made on some detail; I think it was the value of prototype tooling. The fireworks started when the advertising director joined in. I then realised how deep was the contempt in which that urbane, witty and elegant man was held by my friend the production man. It seemed to me to point to a schism as serious as the management versus workforce, unions versus CBI that bedevils many industries
>
> (Kenneth Grange, *Management in Industry*, October 1983)

Inter-departmental conflicts of another sort, and certainly grievances, can be attributed to issues of 'ownership' or territory - *where* within the organisation certain functions should be located, and under whose authority. Within the broad marketing area, sub-functions such as public relations, customer service, packaging, and distribution, can often be the centre of ongoing 'border skirmishes' between marketing and other functional claimants. Certainly in some companies, the distribution area has recently witnessed such territorial rivalry, as it has merged with materials management to become an enhanced and independent logistics function.

Organisation structures should be robust enough to cope with such tensions, and to accommodate them at the everyday level through management control and co-ordination mechanisms, and ultimately through adaptation and evolution. In common with other functions, the marketing organisation should facilitate interfunctional co-ordination, and even conflict resolution, through the following mechanisms:

- explicit, rather than vague, organisational responsibilities and relationships;
- adequate support systems in key areas such as planning and information processing (information systems);
- inter-disciplinary liaison, planning, problem-solving and decision-making mechanisms such as meetings, committees, reports and audits;
- staffing solutions through liaison and co-ordination posts, joint undertakings through venture groups or task force activity, and a wider role for training and staff development.

Implicit in the above is the understanding that good *internal communications* will be a major source of improvement in interdepartmental relations, and general company effectiveness.

Some commentators have in recent years isolated the communications field, and related behavioural influences, as a key element of good management, *within* the company as well as outside. It is perhaps paradoxical that companies that spend literally millions on *outside* communications through their advertising agencies, will sometimes baulk at the thought of serious expenditures within the field of *internal* communications. A lesson for marketers here is that, as communicators they, of all people, should be sensitive to the *communications process* involved in their interactions with other functions. In particular, marketers should *promote* their plans and activities to ensure greater co-ordination and effectiveness - or, to follow the advice of Nigel Piercy, they should practise *internal marketing*.

Internal marketing

As outlined by its major British proponent, Nigel Piercy, internal marketing is nothing more nor less than the employment of marketing activities and approaches *within* the organisation, in order to gain support and necessary co-operation from other functions, key decision-makers and general management, and all those contributing to the effective execution of marketing strategies. The emphasis given by Piercy is primarily on internal marketing in order to ensure success of a company's general marketing programme, though it is possible to see a wider role for internal marketing as an aid to *any* functional programme. Piercy argues that, both at the everyday level of marketing implementation, and to the end of a gradual 'culture change' towards customer orientation, internal marketing has a contribution to make. He coins the general purpose term *Strategic Internal Marketing* (SIM) to encompass all such endeavours. It is particularly instructive, and more appropriate, for marketers to follow an extract of this author's rationale for strategic internal marketing:

> The silly thing is that it seems that the reality in many organizations is there is an explicit assumption that marketing plans and strategies will 'sell' themselves to those in the company whose support and commitment are vital. When made explicit in this way, this is just as naive as making similar assumptions that, if they are good enough, our products will 'sell themselves' to external customers.
>
> We have frequently been surprised that those same executives who have been trained and developed to cope with behavioural problems - like 'irrational' behaviour by consumers and buyers, or the problems of managing power and conflict in the distribution channel, the need to communicate to buyers through a mix of communications vehicles and media, and trying to outguess competitors – have taken so long to arrive at the conclusion that these same issues have to be coped with *inside* the company.
>
> The paradox is that we dismiss the 'better mousetrap' syndrome for our external markets, but adopt exactly this approach in expecting managers and operatives, whose support we need, to make a 'beaten path' to the marketing planner's office.

Piercy's advice is that, within the company, marketers should recognise the *internal marketplace* for their products and programmes, and respond to it by developing an *internal marketing programme* to support their programmes for the external marketplace. The internal marketing programme itself, therefore, should be produced alongside the primary external programme, and might mirror the external plan in its structure - internal target groups, intelligence and information sources, internal 'product' features and benefits, promotional mechanisms, internal marketing objectives and strategies. For a more detailed outline of the process, the reader is referred to the author's original and persuasive exposition (*see also* p147 and Fig 11.6).

Conclusion

Marketing, no less than any other business function, needs to be managed, controlled, and appropriately resourced. The organisation structure adopted for the marketing function will need to reflect and serve these managerial processes. Needless to say, it will also need to facilitate the effective execution of those marketing strategies required by the company's competitive position, and the general demands of the marketplace. As companies will vary in terms of resource strengths, market position, and general policies on matters of management and planning, the approach taken to organising marketing will vary somewhat in practice.

Of perhaps equal importance will be the internal, social and political aspects of the company as an organisation, and the related need for internal marketing.

Suffice to say, marketers need to be aware of the dynamic and behavioural interactions that beset them *within* the organisation. As noted in numerous research studies, the *'people'* dimensions of the *informal organisation* may well become more significant than the line geometry of the formal organisation chart.

Questions

1 'The key ingredients of success are surely strategy and execution. Organisation changes amount to little more than rearranging the furniture.' Comment.

2 Argue the commercial case for a closer working relationship between Marketing and the following specialisms:
- purchasing;
- accounting;
- design;
- credit control.

3 Consider the implications for Marketing organisations of continuing growth in a company's overseas business.

4 Write a diary page account of the typical working day of a consumer goods product manager, indicating the variety of tasks undertaken and the interactions achieved with other functional specialists.

References

Doyle, P, 'Marketing and the British chief executive', *Journal of Marketing Management*, Vol. 3, No. 2, 1987.

Grange, K, (Designer) *Management in Industry*, October 1983.

Lynch, J E, Hooley, G J and Shepherd, J, *The Effectiveness of British Marketing*, University of Bradford Management Centre, 1988.

Piercy, N, 'The role and function of the Chief Marketing Executive and the Marketing Department', *Journal of Marketing Management*, Vol. 1, No. 3, 1986, 265-290.

Piercy, N, *Market-led Strategic Change: Making Marketing Happen in Your Organisation*, Harper Collins Publishers (Chapter 10).

Shapiro, Benson P, 'Can marketing and manufacturing coexist?', *Harvard Business Review*, Vol. 55, September/October 1977.

23

CONSUMERISM, SOCIAL RESPONSIBILITY, ETHICS AND MARKETING

Introduction

This chapter looks at the way marketing is affected by consumerism, social responsibility of organisations and issues of ethical behaviour from both marketers and their companies. There is no general definition of these topics which would be acceptable in all countries. The relevance of them and their effect will depend upon such issues as affluence, education and culture. This book can do no more than raise the issues for further attention by all who work in organisations.

However, all readers of this book are consumers. If you have not suffered yourself, then it is almost certain that you can find friends who have been subjected to unacceptable service and poor goods. The normal reaction is to 'vote with your feet' and, if possible, go to another supplier the next time. You will already understand that good Marketers recognise this and try to keep their customers happy by making acceptable offerings. There is nevertheless a need to consider three further dimensions in the practice of marketing. These are in addition to consumer satisfaction, but could also be involved in that satisfaction. They are the issues of

- **Consumerism**: Organised group pressure but not necessarily from your consumers, consumerism is aimed at protecting consumers from all organisations with which there is an exchange relationship, as well as influencing organisational behaviour to the benefit of the consumer groups.
- **Corporate social responsibility**: The 'duty' of a firm to conduct its activities in the interest of society as a whole. It also encompasses the choice an organisation will take about the extent of such behaviour.
- **Ethics**: involve decisions of individual moral principles taken by people working for any organisation. It is the study of what is 'Right' in any activity, and is of course influenced by collective values present in an organisation.

There is an obvious starting point for marketing and general behaviour which is the need to *obey the law*. However, even this is not always easy as legislation varies between countries, and what is acceptable in one situation is illegal in another. Going further and linking legal constraints to consumer sovereignty is not enough. Questions are raised about marketing techniques themselves. It is often suggested that these techniques artificially stimulate consumption so people buy, and continue to buy, products that are either unwanted, worth little or both. Marketing has to justify itself against these charges of encouraging materialism and the waste of scarce resources as portrayed by Vance Packard in his 1960 book, *The Waste Makers*.

So we have three separate but inter-related subjects: consumerism is a result of group pressure; corporate social responsibility is the way an organisation chooses to react irrespective of such pressures; and ethics are issues about what is 'right' for individual workers.

Consumerism

There is no single, agreed definition of consumerism. It can be said to include any organised group activity aimed at influencing organisational behaviour. Perhaps the catalyst for the modern consumer movement was Ralph Nader with his book on automobile safety, *Unsafe at Any Price*.

In any exchange the individual has little power. Consumerism is one response to redress the balance. The movement has grown in this century into a powerful force; no longer do members of the public sit back and accept that everything produced, and promoted by companies, is acceptable - they probably never did. They now communicate with organisations with powerful collective voices.

Advertising used by organisations to promote product benefits to the target consumer is still a strong persuader, especially if the product relates to the consumer's wants and needs. But there is a desire from consumers to receive more than this, and this desire is sometimes encompassed in what is described as the *Societal Marketing Concept*. This is where suppliers, in addition to trying to satisfy the needs and wants of consumers, at least maintain, if not improve, the well-being of society as a whole. Consumers have 'rights' which are important for all marketers to appreciate. In recent months the UK government has encouraged the development of a citizen's charter which includes a 'patient's charter' for the National Health Service, a 'passenger's charter' for rail travellers, and various other customer-focused initiatives.

The real awakening of consumerism was in the USA. Before Nader's book, President Kennedy highlighted the obligation an organisation owes to its customers in his 'Consumer Bill of Rights'. This encompassed four main areas that should be basic rights for all consumers:

1 The right to safety.
2 The right to be informed.
3 The right to choose.
4 The right to be heard.

The idea of rights can be traced back to the 'inalienable rights' included in the US Declaration of Independence by Thomas Jefferson. The marketing profession of today must be aware of these rights and combine them where possible in any marketing plans for products and services. They form a good framework for considerations.

The right to safety

When a purchase is made the consumer has the right to expect that it is safe to use. The product should be able to perform as promised and should not have false or misleading guarantees. This 'right ' is in fact a minefield for the marketing profession. Products which were at one time regarded as safe for use or consumption, have subsequently been found by modern research not to be so. There was a time when cigarettes were regarded as not being harmful to health, sugar in foods was not highlighted in television advertising as being bad for teeth, and the public were advised to 'go to work on an egg' – in retrospect, was it safe to do so? Other examples are to be found in the medical field such as the Thalidomide drug which caused deformity to children born to mothers who took this prescribed drug.

Legislation which highlights 'product liability' has been introduced in several countries. This has forced suppliers to consider their responsibility. But should companies go further in a positive rather than a negative way? It could be said that this right will be closely linked to legislation and it is obvious that marketers who fail to protect consumers do so at their peril.

The right to be informed

The right to be informed has far reaching consequences: it encompasses false or misleading advertising, insufficient information about ingredients in products, insufficient information on product use and operating instructions, and information which is deceptive about pricing or credit terms. But this adopts a negative approach. Avoiding trouble is not sufficient. Any marketer should take advantage of every opportunity to communicate with consumers and to inform them about the benefits and features of the product offered. It should be no protection in claiming that consumers fail to read instructions. Marketers must ensure fully effective communications between consumer and supplier. But this 'right' determines that customers should be given adequate information in order to implement the next right – the right to choose.

The right to choose

The consumer has the right to choose and, of course, marketing does try to influence that choice. But, in most western markets competition is encouraged and products should not confuse consumers. As an example, it has been suggested that to make this right easier to attain, packaging should be changed so that similar products from different firms are packaged in exactly the same quantities, or at least use both metric and imperial weights/ measures and so make value comparisons easier for the customer. In fact, Sainsbury provide this comparative information on shelf tickets, but Tesco do not. The unanswered question remains: Do consumers use this information in making choices, or do they use other criteria?

The right to be heard

The right of free speech is present in all western countries. However do organisations listen to consumers? In a well-focused marketing organisation such feedback should be encouraged, and it should be treated as a key input for the future. This right allows consumers to express their views after a purchase, especially if it is not satisfactory. When anything goes wrong with a purchase the customer should expect that any complaint should be fairly and speedily dealt with.

Consumerism, while awakening the public to this right, has not had total success. There are always complaints which are not dealt with quickly or to the customers satisfaction.

Can the marketing world help rectify this by focusing more attention on how companies should treat customers?

Pressure groups

Consumerism is now seen as the coming together of pressure groups to represent the rights of buyers to the sellers. It is, in fact, a feeding back of consumer views to the marketers and therefore should be encouraged, but only as far as the aims of both sides are positive. Six distinct types of pressure groups can be identified.

1 Government-encouraged groups to monitor the behaviour of legalised monopolies. e.g. OFWAT, OFTEL, etc.
2 Independent groups campaigning for a change of product such as the Campaign for Real Ale (CAMRA).
3 Groups, including some charities, campaigning for legal restrictions to protect society. ASH (Action on Smoking and Health) and ROSPA (Royal Society for the Prevention of Accidents) are good examples.
4 Groups coming together after a tragedy to influence future operating practices of organisations. Lockerbie, Herald of Free Enterprise, Hillsborough and Bradford are examples.
5 Commercial pressure groups. The Consumer's Association, Egon Ronay, and *What Car?* magazine are such enterprises.
6 Media watchdogs such as Esther Rantzen with the 'That's Life' programme.

Some of these groups focus on trying to influence government, others directly on to organisations, and of course some try to influence both parties, with the object of changing how companies act. In category 3 it is easy to sympathise with the aims of ASH if you are a non-smoker. The activities of ASH, such as the promoting of a national Non-Smoking Day, are clearly good ways of marketing the aims of that pressure group.

Pressure groups such as those campaigning against meat companies, the Animal Liberation Front in the UK is one example, are actually targeting the wrong area when they engage in illegal acts to impede the activities of commercial firms. Decisions of law are made by governments, and all companies have rights to trade within the law.

Consumerism and marketing

All consumer groups affect the marketing environment in which organisations operate. In addition, it should be realised that individual pressure groups are each 'marketing' their ideas, but this is not considered here. Pressure groups can be considered as one way of receiving feedback from consumers. By working with such groups marketers can gain increased influence, and this can be reflected in additional exposure as the pressure groups can generate positive PR for co-operative suppliers. Where it is an area of individual consumer taste, such as beer, the Campaign for Real Ale successfully encouraged suppliers to meet demands.

So marketers need to work with organised consumer groups and understand the power of such groups in reflecting consumer attitudes and in shaping demand. The consumers of today can vote with their spending power. There is a growing realisation that this is happening. Companies that recognise this and comply with such expectations, hold a strong marketing advantage over their unaware competitors. In 1991 *The Times* reported:

Stop drinking Nescafé for the sake of babies in Brazil, the General Synod told us this week. But as far as the Church of England's legislators are concerned, we may continue to enjoy Rowntrees' sweets, Findus fish fingers and Crosse & Blackwell soup – and our babies may continue to sup breast milk substitutes.

Yet these are also products of the Nestlé group, which, campaigners claim, promotes bottle feeding in third world countries, encouraging mothers to give up breast feeding, and increasing the risk of disease. Nestlé says that it is acting in accordance with a World Health Organisation code of 1981; the campaigners retort that it is breaching rules added to the code in 1986.

'We chose not to target baby milk, because it seemed inappropriate to boycott a product that some child might genuinely need,' says Patti Rundall, the national co-ordinator of Baby Milk Action, the pressure group that inspired the motion passed by the synod. 'Nescafé is Nestlé's highest profile brand, and the company can well afford to lose some of its market share without its affecting jobs.'

Campaigners do not necessarily measure effectiveness only in terms of policies reversed and products withdrawn. 'There is little doubt that numerically more boycotts fail than succeed,' the magazine 'The Ethical Consumer' said last year, adding: 'Even an 'unsuccessful' boycott can be a useful campaigning tool.'

However, when the Avon cosmetics group announced in June 1989 that it was giving up animal-testing, a spokesman admitted that consumer boycotts had influenced the decision. A similar animal testing campaign against Boots, the chemist, has been less successful. The campaign is directed at Boots shops, but its targets include drug-testing by Boots Pharmaceuticals.

(George Hill, 'Those we have loved to hate', *The Times* 19 July 1991)

Social responsibility

Social responsibility is not defined in Michael Baker's dictionary of marketing terms, but he does give a definition for a social responsibility audit:

> An evaluation or assessment of the policies and practices of an organisation to establish how and to what extent it is behaving in a socially responsible manner, e.g. in terms of employment practices, relationships with its local community, environmental protection etc.

From this it can be seen that corporate social responsibility covers issues of interest to marketing as well as other business functions. However, anything that affects the way an organisation interacts with its stakeholders could be seen as a marketing issues.

Marketing has been defined in this book in terms of a satisfying exchange process between supplier and customer. The first part of this chapter shows that consumer groups often demand more from organisations by organised pressure. It is perhaps appropriate that organisations attempt to achieve what Gordon Wills referred to when he said that efficiency and worth of marketing must be judged by what they do for society as a whole. An American Chief Executive Officer described this by saying: 'A new dimension must be observed – a new 'bottom line' for business really is 'social approval'. Without this economic victory would be pyrrhic indeed.'

Sutherland and Gross in their book, *Marketing in Action*, try to relate this new dimension to marketing in a definition of the boundaries of social marketing.

Social Marketing takes account of the consumer's need for wider satisfaction beyond just product satisfaction. In other words, consumers place a value on their quality of life as well as the quality of their possessions. In its wider context, social Marketing refers to the study of markets and marketing in general within the social system as a whole.

This is not a tight definition perhaps because the boundaries of social marketing have yet to be agreed. However social marketing can be seen as a direct reaction to consumerism. The question is whether it is enough to just react to consumerism or whether an organisation should go further in its relationship with its environment.

The Independent newspaper reported (on 14 July 1991) in an article by Matthew Fearnley:

Marketing: A green and caring image will help corporations promote their products in the Nineties
Companies find it pays to have a conscience

The Body Shop is so well known for its unusual business methods that its latest scheme – the handing over of nearly half of its 40 UK shops to managers and staff in a five-year plan called Partnership – would not ordinarily attract much interest.

But Anita Roddick's company is not alone in this kind of venture.

Peterborough-based Thomas Cook is funding the building of a local hospital; Butlins is offering day visits for under-privileged children; and earlier this month Cadbury raised about £500,000 for young sufferers of cerebral palsy with its 'Strollerthon', which attracted 12,000 walkers. Kentucky Fried Chicken is operating with the Tidy Britain Group to remove litter and educate people on how to improve the environment, and ICI, is turning redundant sites into nature reserves.

'During the Eighties value was placed on wealth creation. But now people judge companies by their effect on things like local communities,' says ICI spokesman Bob Mitchell.

Two factors are accelerating the switch to corporate responsibility. First, according to work carried out by both the Henley Centre and Mori, there is a massive swing away from the attitudes of the Eighties. Greed is no longer good; ethics are in.

Secondly, products are becoming increasingly similar. Wally Olins of the design group Wolf Olins explains: 'It's increasingly the case that only those companies as effective as the best in their industry will survive, which means products are getting closer and closer together. The only way to differentiate between them is emotionally rather than rationally.'

This debate often revolves around questions of cost and benefit with many authors rejecting actions that do not offer an immediate benefit to the organisation. One interesting counter to this is the glass company Pilkington. Two issues stand out in the paper by Tom Sorell. One is that in the 1950s the company succeeded in developing a new advanced manufacturing process - float glass. The development had been very expensive but instead of capitalising on the competitive advantages of the new process, Pilkington's licensed it to competitors. Lord Pilkington said,

A great deal was said about ethics: that it was not our job to deliberately deny any existing glass competitor the opportunity of living in competition with us. I don't think we were short-sighted or rapacious... There was a great deal of investment worldwide in plate, and people needed to have time to write off this plant or convert over. The alternative was chaotic disruption of a great industry.

Of course the company received over £400 million in royalties over the next 20 years, but it is unclear if the decision was really the best commercially. However, when Pilkington came to take over its largest competitor for car safety glass and to merge with the dominant Triplex company the Monopolies Commission declared it was 'satisfied that Pilkington is conscious of its responsibility, as a monopolist, to the public interest. This sense of responsibility may be associated to some extent with the long-established dominance of the Pilkington family within the business. There would, we think, have to be some quite unforeseen change... before Pilkington would deliberately set out to exploit its position of strength at the expense of the public interest'.

So Pilkington exercised its market position in a responsible way. In 1986-7 a hostile takeover bid for Pilkington was launched by the BTR conglomerate. This is the second issue where Pilkingtons used its latent good-will as a 'responsible' company, in this case to defeat the bid. The chairman's report the following year stated:

> Our ability to demonstrate that it was possible to achieve world leadership in an industry, while maintaining that important balance between the interests of the shareholders, employees, and the wider community, was a powerful and convincing defence. Throughout the bid we were able to rely on the wholehearted support of our employees. This support gathered momentum and widened to all of the communities in which we work, to the media, and to all three political parties. I cannot recall a similar bid where such universal support was generated by a target company.

The Pilkington case involves issues of overall policy but does give an example of two unexpected paybacks from a history of benevolent action in its industry and within its home community in St Helens, Lancashire.

Consumers are now able to buy publications which 'inform the public about the social, environmental and ethical policies of companies' such as *Shopping for a Better World*, published by Kogan Page. More and more firms are introducing policies which will show them to be socially responsible.

Britain has been in the throes of an environmental awakening during the last decade. Environmentalism and subsequent consumer actions have developed as society has changed, the degree of social responsibility expected from firms also dramatically increased. The marketing response to two of these issues will be covered in the next section.

Social responsibility and marketing

Earlier in this chapter we explained how some consumers having become aware of the marketing concept now expect more than products and services which satisfy their needs and wants. They look for the added bonus of the Societal Marketing Concept where the well being of society is also catered for. The situation has now arisen where it has become impossible in some industries to produce what customers want, without an accompanying high cost in environmental terms.

(a) The ozone layer

The damage which has occurred to the ozone layer is of concern to all mankind as future consequences of this would appear to be far reaching. The immediate effect that this known damage has had, is that the public have become very much aware of what causes damage to the ozone layer. One of the major factors is that the emission of chlorofluorocarbons (CFCs) throughout the years has built up to dangerous levels creating the thinning of the ozone layer. Although this could be caused by CFCs released several years ago, it is only now the problem has become apparent. One of the effects of this thinning is that many more people will be in danger of contracting skin cancer, the ozone layer formerly having offered some protection from the harmful ultra-violet rays of the sun.

Manufacturers of suntan oil and moisturisers have found that they have more business as people become aware that they must protect their skin from harmful ultra-violet rays. Women who formerly used pure moisturising lotion are now asking for moisturising lotion with a sun protection factor. Suntan lotion now is produced with varying protection factors. This is a major change from the times when the lotion was perhaps just olive or coconut oil.

Chlorofluorocarbons are chemical compounds which have been used in aerosols and packaging materials, and are still used in refrigeration and air-conditioning plants. The fact is, that products using these potentially harmful chemical compounds are still bought by the general public. Industries see this as being active demand - many would question if the consumers actually have a real choice.

Some socially responsible companies have voluntarily tried to eradicate the use they make of CFCs; other companies have been forced by consumer pressure to do so. Over the last few years most aerosols have been changed. Manufacturers have abandoned the use of CFCs and are actively using this fact as a selling point in their advertising campaigns. The diversity of products which can be purchased in an aerosol is vast, ranging from hairspray to furniture polish. Imagine the effect that this has had upon the marketing world.

Another aspect of the ozone-layer problem, is that packaging of goods uses up the raw material, wood, which is used for paper production. As there is a tremendous demand for paper the forests of the world are being depleted. Forests absorb carbon dioxide and emit oxygen which reduces harmful effects in the upper atmosphere. Although the majority of the general public do not want to return to the days when many products were not packaged, they expect companies to act in a socially responsible manner with regard to the type and amount of packaging used. Giant steps have been taken in the last few years, some firms even using their packaging policies as a selling point. Procter & Gamble have taken this one step further. Published on their Pampers nappies is the following information: 'Pulp: Made with care for the environment. The traditional chlorine bleaching process is not used. Pampers pulp is purified with an oxidation process. With smaller bags Pampers saves raw materials and energy: less packaging, less waste and fewer lorries for transport.'

There will undoubtably be more changes which will affect marketing in future years, brought about because of the knowledge of the damage being done to the ozone layer. How well the marketing world will keep abreast of these changes is yet to be seen. It is becoming increasingly clear that the power held both by consumers and socially responsible companies, to bring about changes of benefit to the environment is a very important factor indeed.

(b) Animal welfare

Some companies have used the fact that they are against animal testing in their marketing campaigns. One such company is The Body Shop, where leaflets explaining its policies are freely available to customers, an extract from one such leaflet states:

> The Body Shop never has and never will test ingredients or final products on animals or authorise such tests on its behalf. We adhere to BUAV'S five-year rule – every six months, our suppliers and manufacturers must sign a declaration stating that they are not testing our ingredients on animals and have not done so within the last five years. This dynamic policy is proving successful in changing the practices of suppliers and manufacturers who used to test on animals.

The Body Shop has tried to raise public awareness on the issue of animal testing and to this end has worked closely with the British Union for the Abolition of Vivisection.

Not only has the general public's attitude towards the testing of products and substances on animals changed, but also their attitude towards the killing of animals for their fur. Many businesses which dealt with the sale of fur coats no longer exist, the demand for such coats having almost disappeared in Britain. This is not the case in all European countries; in Scandinavia many people, both male and female, wear fur to combat the cold winters. For marketing purposes, it is most unlikely that interest will be revived in Britain for fur, such is the strength of public opinion against cruelty to animals. This has extended also to the trade in ivory and crocodile skin, etc.

Social responsibility towards animal welfare has developed to such an extent that companies such as ICI and Unilever carry out in-house research to try to find alternatives to testing products and substances on animals.

Ethics

Ethics involve issues of human behaviour and human judgement applied in everyday situations. Kenneth Andrews in his US article 'Ethics in Practice' started by saying:

> As the 1990s overtake us, public interest in ethics is at a historic high. While the press calls attention to blatant derelictions on Wall Street, in the defense industry, and in the Pentagon, and to questionable activities in the White House, in the attorney general's office, and in Congress, observers wonder whether our society is sicker than usual. Probably not. The standards applied to corporate behaviour have risen over time, and that has raised the average rectitude of businesspersons and politicians both. It has been a long time since we could say with Mark Twain that we have the best Senate money can buy or agree with muckrakers like Upton Sinclair that our large companies are the fiefdoms of robber barons. But illegal and unethical behaviour persists, even as efforts to expose it often succeed in making its rewards short-lived.

Why is business ethics a problem that snares not just a few mature criminals or crooks in the making but a host of apparently good people who lead exemplary private lives while concealing information about dangerous products or systematically falsifying costs? Observation suggests that the problem of corporate ethics has three aspects: the development of the executive as a moral person; the influence of the corporation as a moral environment; and the actions needed to map a high road to economic and ethical performance – and to mount guardrails to keep corporate wayfarers on track.

One problem in business, especially consumer markets, is that customers are often not technical professionals. They do not have the skills to fully assess the products they are offered except in a general way of judging the fitness of that product for the purpose for which it was purchased. But does the average consumer know how much water can be 'added' to a frozen chicken? The Trading Standards officers do, but is it appropriate for employees or their companies to ensure the maximum levels or is this just good business practice?

In another industry how expert is an individual in assessing different life assurance policies? There is again a regulator, LAUTRO in the UK, but even with safeguards and periods after purchase when decisions can be changed, there are still opportunities for policies which pay the highest commission to be recommended more strongly than others.

When selling a house there is a legal restraint of 'Caveat Emptor' – let the buyer beware. The ethical question for the seller is whether to just answer questions as asked or to volunteer information that might make a sale less likely. With regards choices made by individual executives to justify questionable conduct, Saul Gellerman suggests four 'rationalisations':

1 The activity is not 'really' illegal or immoral.
2 The activity is in the individual's, or the corporation's, best interest.
3 It will never be found out.
4 Because it helps the company, the company will condone it.

The decisions reflected here are all taken by individuals, but as suggested by Andrews, the influence of the corporate as a m*oral environment* can put pressure on managers to act in a particular way. Andrews suggests that while an individual's initial values will come from family and school, most of the influence on ethical behaviour related to business 'will occur in the organisations in which people spend their lives'. And since many decisions are not clear cut, it is the corporate influences which can determine the behaviour. However the authors of this book suggest to all marketers that they consider any decision carefully. Ted Tulefa in his book, *'Beyond the Bottom Line'*, asked the question, 'Can the good guys finish first? His conclusion is one of hope that:

> the corporate villains will fall by the wayside, leaving the finish line to those businesses that play the game hard, but fairly. As democracy and competition both increase, earning the public's goodwill will become less and less an ancillary preoccupation, and move ever more forcefully to the forefront of Manager's attention'.

Ethical marketing concept

Companies, in order to have the success they desire, must not only be able to sell a product or service, they need to be seen to adhere to high standards, both in the service offered and ethically. It appears that it may be the right time to move a stage higher than the Societal Marketing Concept, and introduce an Ethical Marketing Concept.

Everyone has their own standards of ethical behaviour, their own moral standards. In the last decade these moral standards may have changed, circumstances alter, but the basic beliefs people have are hard to influence. A sense of what is fair permeates into industry, and employees are the vehicle for this. There are exceptions to this fair play, and it is on these unfair issues that the ethical concept will have to try to attack. Employees may not be accurate when filing in expense claims and in most cases the inaccuracies will not be to the benefit of the company. Gifts to purchase managers from companies seeking a contract may be far in excess of a bottle of whisky at Christmas. Contracts are won from a foreign company only after the submission of a very tightly worded tender – the real money to be made on the variations the client is sure to ask for later when the work is well underway. Are these all examples of unethical behaviour?

Other issues regarding the actual marketing of products also raise questions as to ethical standards. As an example: should a marketing manager suggest a bold flash on the front of his company's food product reading 'No added colours' and rely on consumers not reading the ingredients panel to see that while this claim is true there are many added flavourings?

There are other practices which cannot be published, not illegal in themselves but certainly ones which are aimed at gaining business and not operating in a way that is fair to customers. An ethical code of conduct is much needed in order to introduce practices which are acceptable and agreed throughout industry. An Ethical Marketing Concept would be a marvellous goal to achieve, but will it be possible given that in the wider arena of the European Community the blend of cultures may be such that what is good for one country may not be good for another?

Conclusion

This chapter has considered the wider implications for marketing within the field of consumerism, social responsibility and ethics. Certainly since the 1960s, the consumerism movement has gathered pace, making an imprint on corporate behaviour in general, and marketing in particular. Most categories of products on sale in western markets are now the subject of, and at least partly the result of, consumerist interest in quality, performance, value and related issues.

Social responsibility is a much wider field, encompassing arguably all activities, practices and policies through which a commercial organisation affects society at large and its interests. Ethics, a related field, touches on the morality of behaviour of individuals and groups that are party to decisions made within an organisation.

While it is difficult to pass judgement on the multitude of 'grey' areas within corporate decision-making and behaviour, it can be clearly demonstrated that there is now a society-wide concern for responsible corporate behaviour and moral standards in business decisions. Marketers, no less than other business specialists, need to embrace these challenges as a facet of their own professionalism.

Questions

1 Consider the view that consumerism would not have developed in the first place if marketers had been doing their job properly.

2 Obtain a copy of the mission statement of any organisation of your choice, and consider the extent to which it addressed the issues raised within this chapter.

3 What conflicts of morality and acceptable corporate behaviour might face a company operating across a spread of international markets?

4 Mention has been made of NHS Patient's Charter and the Passenger's Charter of British Rail. Working on your own experience as a student, what issues might be addressed within a proposed Student Charter?

References

Andrews, K, 'Ethics in practice', *Harvard Business Review*, September/October 1989.

Baker, M, *Dictionary of Marketing and Advertising*, 2nd Edn., Macmillan, 1990.

Fearnley, M, 'Companies find it pays to have a conscience', *Independent on Sunday*, 14 July 1991.

Gellerman, S, 'Why 'good' managers make bad ethical choices', *Harvard Business Review*, July/August 1986.

Hill, G, 'Those we have loved to hate', *The Times*, 19 July 1991.

Packard, V, *The Waste Makers*, Penguin, 1960.

Quinn, J B, 'Pilkington Brothers Plc case study' in H Mintzberg and J B Quinn, *The Strategy Process*, Prentice Hall, 1991.

Sorrel. T, in Bowman and Asch, *Readings in Strategic Management*, Macmillan, 1987.

Sutherland, J and Gross, N, *Marketing in Action*, Pitman Publishing, 1991.

Tuleja, T, *Beyond the Bottom Line*, Penguin, 1987.

Wills, G, 'Marketings social dilemmas', *European Journal of Marketing*, Vol. 8 No.1, 1976.

24

MARKETING IN ACTION

Introduction

This chapter is designed to look at marketing in particular situations. A large number of ideas and techniques have been discussed. Obviously not all are equally relevant in every application. To give some indication of the emphasis in several different contexts, the authors have drawn on their varying experience to look briefly at five areas.

- Consumer product marketing.
- Industrial marketing.
- Services marketing.
- International marketing.
- Non-business marketing.

Consumer marketing

The first serious development of marketing techniques was in the consumer markets of the USA. Companies such as Procter & Gamble became the 'universities' of marketing where people learnt the elements of the marketing mix and devised plans to win market share. As these marketers moved to other companies and other industries they took with them the skills of product development, and the ability to create unique selling propositions and effective promotions. These skills have been modified in other industries, but the emphasis on the marketing mix still remains in fast-moving consumer goods (fmcg) markets. The major objective in such markets is to build brand loyalty, as the products are typically low-value regular purchases such as food, drink, confectionery, household and health-care items, magazines, stationery and many others.

It was in one of these markets that Coca-Cola devised the tests of Acceptability, Affordability and Availability. This test is used in a wider context in this book, but for fmcg products the aim is to maximise all of the As with the widest group of potential consumers. Information is continuously sought on product performance. This information comes in two basic forms, comparative data on market share and related issues from retailer and consumer panels, and acceptance/awareness data from tracking studies. It is feedback that discovers even small variations in performance and highlights trends which could require attention. These markets value the long-term investment to build brand names such as Mars, Kit Kat, Persil, Coke, Marlboro. Typically, main media are used and quite large advertising budgets (advertising/sales ratios can reach 10 per cent). An interesting study by *Grocer Magazine* (28 March 1992) looked at the share of certain grocery markets taken by retailers' own brands and found it was least in markets where manufacturers' brands spent most on advertising (*see* Table 24.1).

Table 24.1
1990 estimates of grocery market shares

Market advertising/sales ratio (%)		Own-label share (%)
Toothpaste	12	5
Pet Food	5.1	7
Tea	3.7	16
Yoghurt	1.9	42
Flour	0	50

Advertising is no guarantee of success and many years of investment are necessary to develop strong brands. However, fmcg marketing does involve large promotional budgets and a great deal of attention to communicating with the millions of customers for any product. Contact with these customers is, of necessity, non-personal and so sophisticated marketing research is used to obtain feedback.

Consumer durables

Unlike fmcg, consumer durables are less frequently purchased. But one of the differences between consumer and industrial markets is the large number of potential individual customers. In order to reach such customers communication is again vital.

Durables could be washing machines or cars or video recorders or classic clothing. As discussed in Chapter 12, most consumer durables would fall into one of two categories: shopping goods or speciality goods. If the former, then the marketing task is determined by the consumer and the need for useful comparative information. The usefulness will come from providing facts about the benefits that are valued by the customers and are the ones used to make decisions. An example of durable marketing can be seen by considering how car companies communicate with their customers. At one level you will see evocative advertisements for Ford or Volvo creating a glamour and a general position for the manufacturers, using television and other mass media. This is complemented by press advertisements giving other details and often the financial deals. Direct mail communication or sales promotion competitions are used to encourage customers to visit showrooms for the particular marque. Once in the showroom the actual cars are supported by technical information in brochures and from the direct sales staff.

This sequence shows a range of different techniques used to bring a potential customer ever closer to the point of purchase by integrated programmes of communication. Sometimes information is given in a direct way to compare one model with another and influence the comparisons of product suitability prior to actually seeing the product.

The emphasis on information can be seen with many 'shopping' products. There is also an emphasis on after-sales service. This is due to the period of time between the purchase and the need to replace the durable. When the time comes for replacement the experience with the product will be very important in a customer's decision process. It was once said: 'The quality of a product is remembered long after the price is forgotten'. With durables it is certainly true that their performance is remembered rather than the purchase details. Therefore a consumer who has enjoyed excellent service from a product will remember that when the time comes for a replacement. The issue is a very personal one as exemplified by the differing experiences of two of the authors regarding cars.

> One of the authors has a Vauxhall Cavalier, which was a former company car. It has already covered over 230,000 miles with few problems. However, it is nearing time for replacement and this person is convinced that a Vauxhall should be the next purchase.
>
> Another has a Vauxhall Astra which has proved unreliable at times and recently required a new engine. He has had a poorer experience so is not so keen on this make next time round.

In the cases above the importance of the channel of distribution is highlighted as it is the local distributor who gives the majority of after-sales service and can build a strong position for the future.

It must be remembered that durables are not only infrequent purchases, but they are also likely to involve substantial money. Issues of affordability are relevant, but perhaps value is a more important measure. Consumers do not necessarily buy the cheapest car or washing machine, but they buy the one that offers the features that they require. The features offered with a durable product will vary enormously. There is likely to be much more variety than for a non-durable product. These features form what we have called the 'total product', or some authors call the 'augmented product'. Some of these features are important only at the point of purchase, such as free road fund licence or a full tank of petrol for a car, or free fitting for a carpet or washing machine. These are really promotional additions sometimes described as the 'bells and whistles'. Other features are more substantive for the future, such as a sunroof in a car or special economy programme with a washing machine, or freeze-frame facility on a video recorder.

All features cost money to provide and not all features are valued by purchasers. Marketers responsible for consumer durables have to decide about such features in a diverse market place. The ability of Toyota Motors to produce customised cars, with personally chosen features, while producing volume cars, is one way marketing and production can combine to make a very attractive offering to customers.

Industrial marketing

In earlier chapters distinctions have been made between products which are purchased for use by individuals, such as a can of Coca-Cola, and products which are purchased by organisations. The point was further made that many of the products purchased by organisations are, like toilet tissue, the same as those purchased by consumers. Furthermore, most products purchased by consumers have in their turn been purchased by wholesale and retail organisations before reaching the final consumer.

Industrial marketing involves those products which are used by organisations in the course of their business. Accordingly it involves three different types of products. First, there is the capital equipment required in all types of organisation whether engaged in manufacturing or providing a service. Second, there are products which either as raw materials or finished components are used as part of the manufacturing process, and third, there are those products which are used in the manufacturing process, but do not become part of the final product.

Thus the supply of the empty cans and bottles used by Coca-Cola to package their product, the sugar and other ingredients used to manufacture the syrup, the compressed carbon dioxide gas used to carbonate the drink and the material in which the cans and bottles are subsequently packed are all examples of industrial products. Likewise, so are the filter equipment used to process the water used in the drink, the detergent used each day to clean the machinery, the machinery used to fill and print the cans and bottles, the conveyors used to transport the packed cans to the dispatch area and the lorries used to deliver the product.

Like consumer marketing, organisational marketing involves optimising what is being offered to a potential buyer in terms of the product itself, the price of the product, the availability of the product and the method by which the potential customer is made aware of the product. Organisations differ from consumers in a number of important ways. In particular there are fewer transactions and the value of each is generally much higher. There are also similarities, especially, as with consumer marketing, the importance of understanding the need that the potential customer wants the product to fulfil.

These needs depend upon a number of factors. In particular, the reason that an industrial product is being purchased. Many factors depend upon this. For instance, the expertise within an organisation develops as a result of experience. This means that the routine purchases, particularly those which affect the final product, will be monitored very carefully. As a result, it is likely that there will be a very good understanding of the relative values of the products offered by different suppliers. As a result of this knowledge it is quite likely that the preferred choice will not be the cheapest. For less frequent purchases or those not directly concerned with the product being manufactured, it is likely that there will be less understanding of value and as a result a tendency to consider price and specification as the main buying criteria.

It is the recognition that the buying criteria are likely to vary from organisation to organisation that is the key to successful industrial marketing. It is of course market segmentation. Very often this segmentation involves not simply changing the product but changing the level of service provided by the organisation. Even suppliers of raw materials have found that by applying this approach not only can they increase their share of the market but can at the same time improve their profitability. What is required is the recognition that different types of customers are willing to accept different levels of service, and then finding a method by which this knowledge can be applied. This may involve setting up a separate division which specialises in supplying a specific segment of the market. Organisations adopting this approach usually have to overcome two problems. The first is that providing a different level of service often is against the culture of the organisation and strongly resisted by the staff. This is best overcome by ensuring that the staff can see the advantages that the organisation will offer its customers. A second problem can be associated with this in that the old organisation is likely to compete with the new organisation, thereby putting at risk many of the potential advantages of the approach.

Where industrial products are ancillary to the production, such as might be the case with computers or delivery vehicles it is quite likely that an organisation will buy on the reputation of the supplier rather than the suitability of the product. Hence the well-known adage, 'No one ever got fired for buying IBM!' It is for this reason that the creation of a brand within an industrial market can be so important. This involves, as it does in the consumer market, a single-minded approach to promotion. Also, like some sectors of the consumer market, it is necessary to create this brand awareness within a small specific market sector. Generally it is possible by using the technical press, not only for advertising but also for promoting the brand through consistent editorial coverage. This requires, for most companies operating in industrial markets, senior management commitment to public relations.

Service marketing

This book has emphasised marketing techniques irrespective of whether they are applied to tangible products or services. The difference between products and services is irrelevant from a general viewpoint but there are some aspects of services that must be understood when involved in service marketing. At one level a service is a total product without a core.

Services can be offered to consumer markets, industrial markets, international markets, or be given in non-business situations. Therefore services can be seen as a subset of the marketing described in any of the other sections in this chapter. First and foremost, it is important to decide if the service could be described as a service product or a product service.

The term *service product* refers to a service which is a self-standing offering and therefore fits the view taken in this book of a service which can be considered under the general heading of *product*. Examples of *service products* could be

- a plumber mending a broken pipe;
- an accountant auditing company accounts;
- a doctor visiting a sick patient;
- a taxi journey.

Kotler defines a service as: 'any act or performance that one party can offer to another that is essentially intangible and does not result in the ownership of anything. Its production may or may not be tied to a physical product'. This definition emphasises two key elements of a service.

1 Its intangibility.
2 Its lack of ownership.

There are three other distinctive features which must be considered.

3 Inseparability – the fact that production of a service is inseparable from delivery.
4 Perishability – services cannot be stored or kept in a warehouse. Spare seats on airplanes or cancelled appointments with your doctor represent capacity lost

forever if not 'consumed' when available. Promotion and pricing is sometimes used to overcome this factor

5 Variability – because each delivery is unique there is no standardisation of output. The production and delivery depend on the two parties involved and different needs and wants of the consumer directly matched by different skills of the provider.

Product services are also subject to the five distinctive factors above. However, because product services are attached directly to a product and are one of the added-value elements offered to augment that product, there is a feeling that some form of ownership could be present. Kotler describes product services as: 'Tangible goods with accompanying services'. He goes on to describe 'the offer which consists of a tangible good accompanied by one or more service to enhance its consumer appeal'. Kotler also refers back to Levitt's observation that:

> the more technologically sophisticated the generic product (e.g. cars or computers), the more dependent are its sales on the quality and availability of its accompanying customer services (e.g. display rooms, delivery, repairs and maintenance, application aids, operator training, installation advice, warranty fulfilment). In this sense, General Motors is probably more service intensive than manufacturing intensive. Without its service, its sales would shrivel.

The example given earlier related to two of the authors who both have a General Motors car. They have varying experiences hence, the variability of services received. The issue with product services is that the product is the key element, car or computer described by Levitt, and the service is an added element to increase the attractiveness of the offer. The marketing emphasis in this case is then on the product and not the accompanying service. With a 'service product' it is the service that dominates, although in this case a tangible product could be offered to enhance the service. This could be a meal supplied on an airflight or a prescription written by a doctor, or a guarantee from a builder.

Much has been written about the difficulties of considering services as part of the traditional 4P-framework of marketing. Booms and Bitner suggested a further three Ps for services:

*   People;
*   Process;
*   Physical evidence.

These factors were mentioned in Chapter 11. All can, in fact, apply to products as well. It is not the 4Ps or 7Ps that are important but a good offer, and a good promotion of that offer. Rod Sheaff's book, *Marketing for Health Services*, differentiated between operational factors – including delivery, leadership and internal communications, resourcing and service design – and promotional aspects of a health provider. However, it is appropriate to reconsider the three issues of people, process and physical evidence.

People are involved in all relationships. An advertisement for Marriott Hotels can put the service element provided by people in this sector into perspective.

> There were no taxis and no chance of catching my plane until the Marriott receptionist took a personal interest in the matter. Without hesitation she made an executive decision. If she couldn't order a car in time to get me to the airport, she'd take me in her own. It was no stretch limo but thanks to her I made the flight. I believe, at Marriott, they call it Empowerment. It means that the staff see their roles as being

more than just a duty. They're really sensitive to guests' needs and assume responsibility for attending to them. I needed to catch that plane and they ensured I did. It's been the same whenever I've stayed at a Marriott and the new UK hotels will be no different, I'm sure.

Sometimes, however, the service providers are not very well-paid people, such as those who offer services in McDonald's, or serve in a hotel or a bank. This is where the existence of good internal marketing becomes important. An article by Schlesinger and Heskett entitled 'Service driven – service company', suggests that over 70 per cent of service sector workers are in dead-end jobs. The problem of motivating such staff is obvious. The authors suggest a new look at delivery, but only if acceptable to the customers. They say:

> Companies cannot design new standards of service by following old routines. In many service industries, one or two leading companies have realized this and begun to do business in a radically different way that represents a 180-degree turnabout from the old industrial paradigm. Its consequences are apparent to everyone – customers, employees, managers, and competitors.
>
> At the heart of this new approach to service are the needs and expectations of *customers*, as the *customers* themselves, not the operating system and its constraints, define them (new routines).

Process is the actual interaction at the time of the relationship. Physical evidence can range from a ticket for a train journey to the layout and decor in your retail bank. The marketing of services must, therefore, concentrate on the actual delivery as much as on the other aspects of marketing.

International marketing

How 'international' is the company's perspective of marketing?

Most business enterprises start life in the service of markets that are basically local or at most national in character. That this should be so is not difficult to understand. In all countries, whatever the state of economic development, there will be a ready 'home-grown' market for the community's basic and everyday requirements. With economic and technological advances, new opportunities will appear, to supply markets that are no longer confined to the potential of the home country. Indeed, strategically, it is nowadays a difficult if trite truism that 'the world is becoming a smaller place' as changes in technology, communications, economic alignments and political geography make for an internationalisation and convergence of markets. Such a 'globalisation' process is affecting marketing no less than other functions such as manufacturing, logistics or finance, or business in general.

International marketing by stages

Companies involved in international business will tend to have different objectives, different orientations and different approaches to the market. While a gradation or scale of activity may not be clearly apparent, there will be a contrast to be seen in the roles and postures adopted by organisations in their dealings with overseas markets. At the one end of the spectrum will be the firm that scrambles around for overseas sales as a temporary stop-gap measure, to keep its machinery running or to export surplus or redundant stock. Such blow-hot-blow-cold courtships are not untypical of the attentions shown in foreign markets by the periodic exporter.

In another category entirely will be the company that plans to cultivate and exploit international opportunities to the mutual benefit of itself and its stakeholders. With a clearer view of some long-term future and a proven record of flexible marketing, such a 'global' company will identify as readily with the international market as with its country of origin.

Most companies actively engaged in international marketing will fit somewhere between these two examples, and research indicates that company internationalisation is a stage-wise process of experimentation, experience and development. Table 24.2 presents a view of some different guises of international marketing, from export (sales) activity to the full-blown global marketing that is associated with the larger 'transnational' corporations.

Table 24.2
Variants on international marketing

Activity	Characteristics
1 Exporting/export sales	Sales-led push into export markets, often dominated by short-term objectives.
2 Export marketing	Export sales and distribution, supported by HO directed marketing support.
3 International marketing operations	A marketing-led approach to international business, co-ordinated from company HQ. Some overseas supply, i.e. no longer wholly exports.
4 Multinational marketing	Wherever viable, market-based marketing and operations, i.e. multi-market approaches tailored to local conditions.
5 Global marketing	Marketing on a worldwide scale, strategically co-ordinated to exploit global markets or customer groups.

It should be stressed that the variants of international marketing depicted in Table 24.2 are somewhat generalised stereotypes, and that they do not represent the international development path taken by all companies. In recent years certainly, competing theories have emerged in terms of the commercial wisdom or appropriateness of different strategies, and the interested student would be well advised to consult the specialist literature for a more detailed exposition.

Decisions within international marketing

On deciding to enter the international marketplace for the first time, or possibly considering adding new overseas markets, a company would do well to adopt a purposeful strategic approach, based on informed decisions. The major decision areas involved are outlined in Fig 24.1.

> **1** Whether to market internationally?
>
> **2** Which market(s) to enter?
>
> **3** How to enter selected markets?
>
> **4** Marketing activities and strategy
>
> **5** Organisation and management control

Fig 24.1 Key decisions in international marketing

1   Whether to market internationally

This represents a critical decision, since it has major strategic implications. Many strategy-based arguments could be ranged in favour of international marketing. Aside from the profit opportunities that do exist in *selected* markets, companies might be influenced by the need to strategically diversify their market base, to exploit a growing internationalisation in their prime market, or to capitalise on the overseas potential of new products or technologies. A classical marketing strategy might involve following key customers abroad – the stay-with-the-market strategy typified by leading international consultants, advertising agencies, insurance companies and other service-based organisations. More defensive strategies might involve efforts to counter seasonality or instability in the home market, or to justify capacity increases or seek scale economies.

Whatever strategic rationale a company may have for looking abroad, it would need to weigh up the 'downside' of the argument, the risks involved. In spite of accelerating globalisation, the business environment in many overseas markets will still be risky and unfamiliar in terms of economic and competitive conditions, legal factors, government policy and controls, and social and cultural influences on the marketplace. Table 24.3 illustrates some of the more common difficulties and risks that await the unwary entrant to the international arena.

Table 24.3
Difficulties and Risks in the International Marketplace

- Credit Risk

- Cash flow problems
- Bureaucracy

- Exchange rate fluctuations, currency upheavals
- Language & communications problems

- Controls on profit repatriation
- Cultural resistance

- Taxation problems
- Alien business culture

- Non-tariff barriers

- Political problems

- Legal traumas

While many of these difficulties can be minimised by careful research and good management, they nevertheless represent real potential pitfalls, even for the company seasoned in international business.

2 Which markets to enter?

No less than mainstream marketing itself, international marketing will likely be more successful through careful targeting within selected markets. Especially in the early days of internationalisation, a company would be better to restrict its attentions, *and resources*, to at most a few promising markets, and to treat these as a learning and trialling ground for hopefully more ambitious steps later.

Mindful of the risks inherent in overseas ventures, many companies will seek earlier custom, likely through export sales, in those few markets that may have produced interest, enquiries or unsolicited orders in the recent past, or perhaps where they have contacts for other purposes, such as sourcing. Often there will be a tendency to approach markets that are 'psychologically' nearer, perhaps through language, cultural or even geographical proximity, e.g. German companies may relate more readily to Austria or Switzerland, Swedish companies to other Scandinavian markets.

Such intuitive reasoning may well prove useful guidance to a company, but there may be a case for adopting a more rigorous and deliberate set of market selection criteria in order to objectively assess overseas opportunities in relation to company resources and capabilities. At its most basic there is a role for detailed SWOT analysis approaches, while developments from this would lead to detailed research into market and competitor environments, albeit within a research budget constraint limited to a few selected 'shortlist' markets. Certainly within chosen target markets key entry and operating decisions will be better informed through market research efforts, perhaps involving a mix of secondary information sources and market-based primary research activities.

3 How to enter selected markets?

Exactly *how* a company enters and supplies a foreign market has major influences on the extent to which it capitalises on market potential, and on the strategic control it allows itself over market development.

Usually the early phases of internationalisation will lead the company into limited resource commitments, often facilitated by using *indirect* channels of market entry, which offer advantages of both risk - and knowledge sharing. Such indirect channels will involve the use of third parties, or intermediaries, that may be based either in the exporter's market or the overseas territory. A variety of such intermediary entry routes, and more direct servicing channels are presented in Table 24.4.

In principle, a company might 'travel far' in export markets through trading on its own doorstep with export merchants in its home market, specialist 'export houses' perhaps specialising in certain trades or geographical markets, or with buying offices of overseas interests (e.g. department stores) based in the 'home' market. More commonly, companies will select and appoint foreign-based intermediaries such as agents or distributors, thereby at least achieving a closer representation at the market level. For practical purposes, it is worth pointing out that agents act 'on behalf' of the exporter (or legal 'principal'), while distributors buy and sell on their own behalf within the overseas market.

More direct representation in the overseas market will be achieved usually only by taking higher investments and risk. Obviously, the establishment of an overseas-based

Table 24.4
Market entry and servicing channels

Indirect	Direct
• Home-based export agents, traders, and buying offices	• Export sales, H.O. Sales personnel

• Overseas-based:-
  - Agents
  - Distributors
	• Overseas-based sales staff

	• Full-scale manufacturing and marketing overseas

	• Joint ventures:-
	  - assembly, manufacture, full-scale j.v.
	  - licensing/franchising

sales force, sales subsidiary or full-scale, full-service overseas subsidiary, would involve major investments that would only be justified by major market opportunities, likely verified by a successful record through lower-risk trading channels such as agency or distributor operations. Within the overseas market, risk-sharing and investment-paring may be served by collaborative approaches such as licensing, franchising, or other joint venture arrangements.

4   Marketing activities and strategy

The marketing mix to be devised for an overseas market, and the strategy underlying it, will depend on a number of factors ranging from company resources, and general marketing policies, to local market conditions and chosen entry/servicing channel arrangements. Given the diversity to be met in overseas markets in terms of cultural and social influences on purchasing, legal and trade constraints on marketing practices, and differing competitive scenarios, the design and implementation of an appropriate marketing mix is by no means a straightforward matter. Even in simple 4-P terms the marketing mix appropriate to one market may be totally unsuccessful in another. Some companies will seek to fine-tune their marketing programmes to local conditions, perhaps guided by research findings that indicate the scope for segmentation or differentiation strategies; while other companies will express a policy commitment to more standardised marketing across perhaps a wide spread of overseas markets. Still other companies will have little choice, in the early days at least, but to follow the advice of their local agents or to make nominal provision for marketing through offering discounts or other support incentives to their local distributors.

The exact make-up of the marketing mix may have to change, in whole or in part, according to market circumstances and company policy preferences. Interestingly as distribution arrangements will be 'given' for any one time within any market, so too may be the basic logistics/supply arrangements, and the implications these hold for costings and price strategy. Not surprisingly, therefore, companies will often adapt their marketing mix along the apparently more discretionary dimensions of product and promotion/communications. These two dimensions will of course constitute a major element of the 'offer mix' in the market since they concern at once the product *and* how it is presented and communicated to the market.

Changes to the physical product may be required in many markets, for predictable reasons such as use circumstances, physical conditions (even climate, transit distances, etc.), and differences in industry standards, product and safety regulations and the like. Other product changes, more arguably, may be made for reasons of perceptual differences among target buyers, taste preferences, aesthetic and styling preferences and the like.

Within the communications mix, perceptual, cultural and linguistic differences may make for sometimes radical departures from the company's domestic advertising and promotion strategies and tactics. Indeed, it could be claimed that it is in the area of intangibles such as culture and social influences that companies will most often risk costly mistakes in overseas markets.

5 Organisation and management control

At least in principle, the distances, time differences and communications problems in international marketing call for perhaps *better* organisation and management control mechanisms than elsewhere within a company's business. However, experience suggests that many companies give less care to managing overseas business than the attentions they give to their domestic markets. Not surprisingly, many failures in overseas marketing could be ascribed to a lack of management control, poor organisation or faulted strategy.

To be successful in international marketing, a company should, from the outset, invest time, effort and resources into a strategic, planned approach, supported by dedicated staffing and organisational arrangements and effective information and communications systems. Without such commitment, even speculative 'export' sales will be consigned to at best marginal activity, at worst costly misadventures.

Non-business marketing

Just as marketing offers business organisations opportunities to be more successful so it has been realised that these same techniques could be applied with as great a benefit in non business activities. This includes government organisations, providers of services such as the National Health Service, charities, and special interest groups such as political parties. While it is not unusual for many of these organisations to be referred to as non-profit making organisations, this has the disadvantage of denying them the expectation that through prudent management their income might exceed their costs, thereby yielding a surplus which can be invested in improved facilities or services.

It is not after all the pursuit of such a surplus which is the principal characteristic which separates business from other types of organisation. The real difference is that the fundamental objective of a business is to increase the asset value of the owners at a rate which is commensurate with the risk involved. Even when businesses try to accommodate the interests of a wide range of stakeholders, this fundamental objective helps to focus the overall activity, since failure to meet this objective will ultimately lead to the organisation being disbanded or taken over.

One of the major benefits of applying marketing principles in the non-business context is that they provide effective alternatives to the financial surplus for measuring organisational performance. Examples of these can be seen in the various charters which have been implemented by the government in order to improve the accountability of organisations such as British Rail and the National Health Service.

Another benefit of applying marketing principles in the non-business context is that it allows the often complicated transactions involved to be properly analysed. An example of where the failure to do this prevented an organisation from responding quickly enough to changing circumstances can be seen with regard to the Blood Transfusion Service. For many years this organisation depended to a significant extent upon the co-operation of the many manufacturing companies which regularly provided facilities for blood donor sessions. It provided the basis for ensuring both constancy of supply and the efficiency of the collection service. During the 1980s many of the companies which provided these facilities reduced the size of their work force to such an extent that they no longer justified having their own blood donor sessions. The Blood Transfusion Service responded by expanding the number of local sessions they ran, only to find it was increasingly difficult to attract sufficient donors. What had not been appreciated was the actual cost incurred by the donor when giving blood. Time was a cost which had previously been 'paid' by the companies, who had not only provided the Blood Transfusion Service with the facilities it needed for the donor session, but had also allowed their employees to attend during working hours. It was not until the real cost to the donor was appreciated, and steps taken to minimise this by providing appointments and better information, that it was possible for the Service to bring demand and supply back into balance.

Another common problem faced by non-business organisations is that of multiple publics. Just as business organisations have a number of stakeholders such as customers and employees, so non-business organisations often have in addition to staff and clients, donors and volunteers. The exchanges involved between each of these groups and the organisation is likely to differ both with the frequency and degree of the commitment. As a result, the organisation has to be especially careful to ensure that any changes made to improve the effectiveness of one of these groups is acceptable to the others as well as to the public in general. This is one area where a lack of basic understanding of marketing has resulted in some very worthwhile charities losing support by applying marketing theory to improve the effectiveness of the staff, without taking proper account of the impact this can have on the other groups upon which the organisation has to depend.

Conclusion

This final chapter has tried to give a flavour of the richness of marketing in many different types of organisations. It will be realised that the basic concept of an *offer* that is *acceptable*, *affordable* and *available* applies in all cases. It then needs to be *promoted* in the most appropriate way. It is not a question of placing advertisements all over the place, but deciding a target market and finding an effective way of reaching it.

The elements of the so called marketing mix are important but the emphasis changes for different products/services and different situations. Understanding the exchange relationship is the key to marketing in all situations, and then resources and programmes can be devised to maximise the return.

Questions

1 'Companies do not make purchases; they establish relationships' (Charles S Goodman). Discuss the validity of this observation on industrial marketing.

2 Consider the potential value in adopting marketing techniques within a public sector organisation such as a public library.

3 'In service organisations, people come first.' Discuss this assertion in terms of the marketing concept.

4 What practical advice would you give to a small manufacturing company intent on entering the export market?

References

Boom, B and Bitner, M J, 'Marketing strategies and organisation structures for service firms', in D Cowell, *The Marketing of Services*, Heinemann, 1984.

Drucker, P, 'The new productivity challenge', *Harvard Business Review*, November/December, 1991.

Kotler, P, *Marketing Management*, 7th Edn., Prentice-Hall, 1991.

Levitt, T, 'Production line approach to service' *Harvard Business Review*, September/October, 1972.

Schlesinger, L A and Heskett, J L, 'Service driven - service company, *Harvard Business Review*, September/October, 1991.

Sheaff, R, *Marketing for Health Services*, Open University Press, 1991.

APPENDIX I
GLOSSARY OF MARKETING TERMS

Above the line - A term applying to main media expenditure and its traditional accounting treatment. Now used for all costs of traditional media.

Acceptability - A test of a product offering from a customer viewpoint.

ACORN (A classification of Residential Neighbourhood) – a so called, geodemographic database of residential locality types. Commercially available from CACI.

Ad hoc research - research which is conducted first hand on a one-off basis, for a particular research project.

Adoption - Rate at which people accept and become users of a product. Often associated with the diffusion of innovation curve.

Advertisement - A message from a person or an organisation to potential customers containing a specific message and in paid for media space. Sometimes shortened by practitioners to 'ad' and by the general public to 'advert'.

Advertiser - A client placing 'paid for' advertising.

Advertising - An element of the marketing mix involving the use of paid media.

Advertising agency - An organisation which specialises in all forms of communication on behalf of clients.

Advertising campaign - A planned approach to communication over a defined period of time.

Advertising media - Communication channels such as radio, television, newspapers, magazines and posters.

Advertorial - An advertisement written in an editorial style to attempt to give more credibility to the message.

Affordability - A test of the value or price of an offering from a customer viewpoint.

Agent - An individual or company acting in a sales capacity on behalf of a principal. An agent does not take ownership or handle the goods.

AIDA - (Attention, Interest, Desire, Action) A mnemonic used in advertising. First used by Strong in 1924. One of the hierarchy models.

Availability - A test of the convenience of an offering from a customer viewpoint.

Awareness - A measure of the proportion of a target audience who have heard of a particular product or service. Can be measured on a 'prompted' or 'unprompted' basis.

Below the line - Expenditure on promotional activities which traditionally reduces revenues or involves non-commission media.

BRAD (British Rate and Data) - The accepted tariff book of advertising in the UK.

Brand - An article identified by a name, symbol, trade mark of characteristic which differentiates it from competitive offerings.

Break-even point - Point at which the costs of production equal the revenue from selling.

Budget - The amount of money allocated to performing a particular task.

Buyer behaviour - The way in which customers act, and the steps taken in the purchase decision process.

Communication mix - *See* promotional mix.

Competitive advantage - An element within a product offering that is particularly attractive to customers, and not offered by competitors.

Consumer - The final user of a product or a service.

Consumer Goods - products which are targeted at individuals in the general population, rather than at organisations.

Consumerism - A movement which aims to change the actions of organisations in favour of particular groups.

Consumer panel - A research method using a group of consumers who continuously report on their purchases over an extended period of time (see panels).

Continuous research - Research that is conducted regularly over an extended period of time, used to monitor trends in the marketplace.

Controllable factors - *See* the marketing mix).

Convenience sample - As the name implies a research sampling technique using the most practical or convenient selection method to provide the necessary respondents.

Copy - The written or broadcast words used in an advertisement.

Cost per thousand (CPT) - Used in advertising as a measure of cost per thousand people viewing or reading the advertisement.

Cost plus pricing - A pricing approach where an agreed percentage is added to the costs of a product.

Coverage - The percentage of a selected target audience that have an opportunity to see a particular advertisement.

Customer - In marketing it is generally anyone buying a product or service.

DAGMAR - (Defining Advertising Goals for Measured Advertising Results) – An acronym for one of the hierarchy of effects models of advertising.

Decider - Used in studying industrial buying as the person who makes the purchase decision, usually in a formal capacity.

Delphi method - A forecasting technique using the opinions of a panel of experts to develop qualitative forecasts.

Demographic - Information relating to broad population statistics, such as age, sex, income, education level or marital status.

Depth interviews - A research technique involving detailed discussions with individual respondents to explore in detail issues such as motivation, beliefs, etc.

Derived demand - The demand for a component or intermediate product dependent on the sale of the final good or service.

Desk research - Research which uses existing sources of information, usually called secondary data.

Differentiated - A separation of a total product from competitors. Can be a marketing mix unique to one supplier.

Differentiated marketing - A marketing strategy which is making different offerings to each segment of a market.

Diffusion - The rate at which new products move through various adoption categories.

Direct mail - A form of below-the-line advertising where personalised letters are sent directly from the advertiser to potential customers.

Direct marketing - An approach offering products without intermediaries where the supplier sells directly to customers.

Distribution channels - Routes through which products go from the supplier to the consumer.

Distributor - A person or organisation who distributes goods. Distributors take ownership from suppliers and are responsible for collecting payments.

Diversification - A process of introducing new products into new markets unrelated to an organisation's current customers.

Elasticity - Sensitivity of customer demand to changes in price.

Exclusive distribution - A policy of organisations to restrict availability of products to a limited number of outlets.

Experiment - A research approach which evaluates alternatives to identify the optimum mix.

Exploratory research - A pilot marketing research used to review a problem in general forms before committing larger expenditure to the study.

Fast-moving consumer goods (fmcg) - Regularly purchased products, usually of low value.

Field research - Research which is conducted externally in a market, not using existing published sources.

Fieldwork - The activity of gathering information in the marketplace.

Focus group - A research technique where groups of consumers are brought together to discuss their views and attitudes to a specific topic. Produces quantitative data.

Franchising - A contractual relationship between a seller and an outlet which uses the sellers format, product and name.

Global brands - Goods which can have universal appeal and are marketed in many countries with little modification to product or image.

Gross profit margin - The difference between direct cost and selling price.

Group discussion - *See* focus group.

Hierarchy of needs - A model of consumer behaviour suggested by A. Maslow.

Image - The perceptions of a product, brand, or company by customers and consumers.

Industrial goods - Products which are required by industrial organisations.

Intensive distribution - A policy of organisations to maximise the availability of products.

Intermediary - A general name for a person who acts as a link in the flow of goods from a supplier to a final consumer.

Life cycle - *See* product life cycle.

Likert scales - Market research scale which use statements for respondents to indicate agreement or disagreement.

Loyalty (also brand loyalty) - The extent to which customers repurchase a particular product or brand.

Macroenvironment - The general external business environment in which a firm functions.

Market development - A strategy of an organisation to increase sales by offering their existing product in new markets. Used by I. Ansoff in his famous matrix.

Market leader - The organisation which has the greatest share of sales in a given market.

Market penetration - A strategy of an organisation to increase sales by offering more of their existing products in their existing markets. Used by I. Ansoff in his famous matrix.

Market research - General research of external factors relating to an organisation's marketplace.

Market segmentation - The identifying of specific market segments in a marketplace then developing different marketing offerings which will be attractive to each segment.

Market share - The relative sales of a product in relation to the overall market sales. Can be measured in either sales value or sales volume.

Marketing audit - A systematic appraisal of the strengths and weaknesses of a company in relation to its marketplace, and the evaluation of the opportunities and threats in that market.

Marketing concept - The underlying philosophy that companies should be customer-oriented and that all an organisation's staff should work together to achieve this focus.

Marketing environment - The social, economical, legal, political, cultural, competitive and technological factors which affect an organisation and its marketing decision. *See* PEST.

Marketing Information System - Information which is relevant to the company's marketing operations, including marketing research, intelligence and market analysis. Often contained on computer databases.

Marketing mix - The controllable elements of the marketing function, originally containing 12 factors but sometimes reduced to the 4Ps of product, price, place and promotion.

Marketing orientation -The focus of an organisation on both customers and competitors to develop a relevant marketing offering.

Marketing planning - The systematic process of analysing the environment and a company's resources. Then developing objectives and suitable strategies and action plans to meet those objectives. Also the feedback and control of such actions.

Market research - The collection of marketing information which may influence marketing decisions. It is an aid to decision-making but not a substitute for it.

Marketing strategy - The long-term direction of an organisation relating to marketing actions and the interaction of controllable variables.

Mark-up - A cost plus pricing technique.

MEAL (Media Expenditure Analysis Limited) - A firm that collects and publishes information on major UK media use and cost by companies.

Media - Channels of communication such as television, radio, newspapers, etc.

Media owners - The controllers of media who try to encourage the use of their channel and often provide comprehensive data about readers and viewers.

Multi-stage sampling - A market research technique often used in political sampling where several random samples are used to give a convenient sample, say one street in one political ward in one constituency.

New product development - The process of identifying, developing and evaluating new offerings.

Niche - A small discrete segment of a market which can be targeted with a distinct marketing strategy.

Non-price competition - Other benefits such as warranties or additional features or merchandising which can give an offering a competitive advantage.

Objective - In planning, a target to be achieved.

Objective and task method - A method of establishing a promotional budget. It is based on the task to be achieved rather than money available. Good in theory but difficult in practice.

Observation (research) - A research approach which involves studying customers reactions and behaviour without any artificial stimulates.

Offer mix - The mix of product, price and availability offered to a customer. Not including communication of that offer.

Omnibus survey - A regular questionnaire-based field research survey with a large sample. Organisations can commission one or more questions to be asked, the survey includes questions from a number of different companies.

OTS (opportunity to see) - The average number of viewing occasions for a particular advertisement.

Panels - (consumer panels) - Groups of consumers who regularly monitor buying or usage information often through keeping diary records.

Pareto Effect - The 80/20 rule. The largest proportion of sale, value or profit will often come from a small proportion of customers.

Perception from psychology - The way a product or event or stimuli is received and evaluated by a customer. The importance lies in the attempt to understand how people interpret messages.

Personal interview - A research method where the researcher meets the respondent to carry out a survey.

Personal selling - An element of the promotional mix, where a supplier uses representatives to visit customers.

PEST analysis (sometimes STEP) - Elements of the macro, external environment, political/legal, economic, social/cultural and technological.

Place - an element of the 4 Ps of the marketing mix. *See* distribution.

Point-of-sale - Usually in retail, the area where a retailer's customer buys a product supplied by that retailer.

Positioning, also product positioning - The establishing of factors valued by consumers in purchase decisions. Then the matching of product features to those factors.

Postal survey - A research method which communicates with a respondent using a postal questionnaire.

Primary data - Original data obtained from field research.

Product development - A strategy of an organisation to increase sales by creating new products for existing markets used by I. Ansoff in his famous matrix (*see also* new product development).

Product life cycle - The different stages through which a product develops over time. It covers development, birth (or introduction), growth, maturity and decline. The stage a product has reached in its life cycle will affect the marketing mix decisions which should be taken.

Product line - A number of related products offered by a supplier, which often cover the needs of several different segments.

Product management - The function responsible for the tactical and strategic planning of a company's existing and new products.

Product mix - The total range of products or servicecs that an organisation offers.

Production orientation - The focus of an organisation on to product quality and production capability. This differs from marketing orientation.

Promotion - An element of the 4 Ps of the marketing mix, it covers the ways in which an organisation communicates with its market.

Promotional mix - The elements of promotion enabling an organisation to communicate with its market. These include advertising, personal selling, sales promotion and publicity.

Prospecting - The selling technique involved with identifying new customers.

Psychographics - A base for segmentation derived from attitudes and behavioural variables.

Publicity - An element of the promotional mix. *See* Public Relations.

Public relations - A deliberate, planned and sustained effort to establish and maintain positive understanding between an organisation and its publics.

Pull strategy - A marketing strategy in which the manufacturer promotes directly to the final customers, and hopes that they will demand the product from intermediaries. The product is then 'pulled' through the distribution channels by customer demand.

Push strategy - A marketing strategy in which the manufacturer promotes to the intermediaries, who in turn promote to their customers. The product is therefore 'pushed' through the distribution channels by manufacturer and distributor effort.

Qualitative research - Research which produces numerical data, often from large samples. This is sometimes called hard data.

Questionnaire - A prepared set of questions used to obtain information from a respondent.

Quota sample - A sampling method where those questioned have to match a defined proportion on a number of attributes, e.g. sex, age, occupation.

Random sample - A sampling method where everyone has an equal chance of being included.

Rate card - The published cost of advertising media.

Recall - *See also* awareness

Research brief - A structured document given to a research agency including background to the organisation, objectives of the research, limitations and aiming.

Respondent - A person interviewed or contacted in a market research survey.

Retail audit - The research undertaken in retail outlets involving checking invoices, delivery notes and sales records to determine the precise volume of goods sold. Results are often syndicated to several suppliers.

Sales call - A visit made by a sales representative to a potential customer.

Sales orientation - The focus of an organisation on to customers with the aim of achieving short-term sales.

Sales promotion - An element of the promotional mix. Techniques and incentives used to increase short-term sales.

Sampling frame - Information which is available from existing published sources.

Segment - A grouping of customers who have common characteristics or features.

Shopping good - Products which are considered purchases such as many consumer durables.

Skimming - A pricing strategy where an organisation sells at a high price initially to maximise short-term profit margins.

Societal marketing - Marketing which attempts to improve social benefit.

Socio-economic groups classification - A grouping of the population according to the occupation of the head of the household: A, B, C1, C2, D, E.

Speciality good - Consumer goods for which customers are prepared or make an effort to acquire.

Sponsorship - An element usually considered part of the promotional mix where money is linked to an event or a participant in an event.

Strategy - An overall, long-term direction or approach which a company aims to follow, derived from the Greek words meaning to lead an army.

Stimulus - A 'trigger' that starts a purchasing process.

SWOT analysis - SWOT is an acronym for strengths and weaknesses, opportunities and threats. The SW refer to internal resources of an organisation. The OT to the macroenvironment.

Syndicated research - Research conducted on behalf of more than one organisation. Such as: consumer panels, retails audits and omnibus studies.

Tactics - The specific operational activities undertaken in support of an organisation's strategy.

Target market - The segment of a market at which an offer mix is directed.

Test marketing - The initial launching of a product into a limited area for a trial period to test its marketing mix prior to national sales.

Trade Press - Published journals aimed at industrial and commercial readers.

TVR (Television Ratings) - A measure of coverage representing 1 per cent of a potential television audience. Calculated by using panel research information.

Undifferentiated marketing - A common marketing strategy aimed at the total market without modifications for specific segments.

Unique Selling Proposition (USP) - A selling claim based on a distinctive product feature or unique element in the marketing mix.

Vertical marketing systems (VMS) - The integration of operators at different levels of a distribution chain to offer a co-ordinated package.

Wholesaler - An operation which buys products in bulk reselling them in smaller quantities to retailers.

Width (of a product line) - The variety and diversity of products offered in a product line.

APPENDIX II
THE USE OF SHORT CASE STUDIES FOR STUDYING MARKETING PRINCIPLES AND PRACTICE

Most cases describe actual business situations although in some cases fictitious names are used. Many are based on real-life management problems, although sometimes the facts are modified to highlight particular situations. But the problems described are very similar to those that are encountered daily by managers. There are many benefits from using cases.

1 Cases can cover a range of organisations and industries and thus provide a far greater range than you are likely to experience in day-to-day management.

2 They help to build knowledge of a number of specific situations by dealing intensively with problems in each case.

3 In addition, cases and case discussions provide a focal point for an exchange of the lessons of experience. In discussing case situations, it is easy, often unconsciously, to draw from your different accumulated experiences, rules-of-thumb, or simple observations of events. This is to be encouraged in these cases. The discussion of cases provides a way of re-assessing the lessons of experience, and gaining an increased measure of learning from them.

4 Cases also help to sharpen analytical skills. You need to work with both facts and figures to produce quantitative and qualitative evidence to support recommendations and decisions. These could be challenged both by your instructors and your colleagues. It is important that you learn to defend your arguments and to develop an ability to think and reason in a rigorous way.

5 Cases are obviously useful for developing sets of principles and concepts that can be applied in practice. Each case should be considered by itself. But out of each will come important concepts and approaches. Taken together, a series of cases should develop some key ideas that can then be applied in specific managerial situations.

6 Perhaps the most important skill to be gained from studying cases and case situations is learning to ask the right questions. This is a really critical business skill. 'Discussion questions' could be suggested by your instructor, but that does not preempt the task of identifying the key problems. You must always still ask yourself: 'What really are the problems here?' It is too easy to just re-arrange the facts and figures without defining the *real problems* in the case.

7 Perhaps the greatest pedagogical benefit derived from the case studies is that they generate a high degree of involvement in the learning process. You will tend to learn the most from those things in which you are most deeply involved. But it follows, too, there is little that can be learned from even the best cases without solid preparation.

There are, of course, major differences between cases and actual management. It is important to appreciate that:

- The 'facts' come in nearly written form. Managers in business rarely receive information in this way. Their knowledge usually comes through being *in situ* and via interactions with fellow managers, as well as memos, statistical reports, and even the external media.
- A case usually describes the situation at a single point in time. 'Real time' business problems are usually a continuing occurrence both in receipt and in implementation. It is not often that a manager can deal with one problem, put it away, then go on to the next 'case'.
- Any decision or recommendation made by students studying a case is just that - a recommendation. Students don't have the responsibility for implementing their decisions.
- A case is designed to fit a particular unit of study time. It will focus on certain categories of problems/marketings situation in order to explore them in more detail.

The marketing cases in this book are very short. They do not need great analysis. In fact they are really *case-based examples*. However, all will benefit from discussing the situations with other students. When studying them it might be helpful to follow the sequence below.

The first task is to read through quickly to put it into perspective. Initially the best preparation will come from working by yourself. Then, based on this, the next step is to decide whether the information is reliable. This will require a more thorough second reading leading to an assessment of what is good or bad practice from the facts given. The aim is to try to isolate the real key problems which are there to be solved, or the lessons to be learnt.

It is best that you note down the problems to be tackled and the relevant areas for analysis. For example, if the problems are 'Should we introduce Product X? To whom should it be sold? What should be our advertising strategy?', the areas for analysis might include:

- trends in the marketplace;
- break-even analysis;
- buyer behaviour;
- segmentation;
- competition; and
- communications needs.

The information in the case should be considered to see what links together. In particular it is necessary to see what helps the understanding of each area, and to draw some meaningful observations and conclusions. These may, in turn, provide the basis for answering the questions that have been suggested.

The purpose of individual preparation is to enhance the learning opportunities when discussing the case in class. The more familiar you are with the case facts and the more ideas you have about the case problems, the better prepared you will be to *take in, react to, and learn from* the ideas of others in a group discussion. Through interchanging ideas and constructive debate you will build analytical skills, develop judgement and gain conceptual understanding.

The next step is to present your arguments to other students and to listen to their views. This can be done in pairs, or in larger numbers, or in a seminar group. The purpose of the discussion of cases is to help to refine, adjust and fill out your own thinking. It is *not* to develop a consensus or a 'group' position. In fact it is not necessary, or even desirable that you agree at this stage.

In a seminar you will usually be allowed to take the case where you wish. This is where you fully explore the issues and problems which you have identified. The seminar group is for you to express, support and defend your conclusions and recommendations. Most learning comes from controversy and discussion. The effective use of cases as a learning vehicle depends heavily on participation. This will benefit both your own education and will benefit the learning of all other students as well. The more you contribute, the more you will get from it. It is therefore a responsibility of every student to get involved.

Discussion in class is also not only an effective way for you to think rigorously, but it allows you to develop skills in communicating, in 'thinking on your feet' and in responding to questions under pressure. Expressing your own views, and defending them, are all part of a distinctive experience.

However important it is to express your views, *listening* is even more important. It's easy to become so preoccupied with what we think that our minds become closed to the thoughts of other participants in the discussion. In class, as well as in business, it is just as important to be open-minded and to be willing to shift positions when good arguments are presented.

The role of a seminar leader is to lead the discussion into a consideration of other areas that you may have missed, or even to require you to make a decision. At the end it is likely the discussions will be summarised to draw out the useful lessons and observations that come from class discussion comments, but please remember that there is no *right* answer in cases. The measure of your individual progress in any one case discussion is not based so much on your own after-class assessment of whether your ideas were 'right'. *Instead it is more useful to ask: 'How much did I take away from the discussion that I didn't know when I came in?'*

APPENDIX III
SOURCES OF SECONDARY DATA

Government statistics

- CSO Guide to Official Statistics, HMSO London.
- Government Statistics: a brief guide to sources
  (free from Central Statistical Office)
- Business Monitors: industry data (free from CSO)
- CSO Annual Abstract of Statistics – Annual UK figures over 10-year periods showing trends. More detailed and current data appear in
  - Monthly Digest of Statistics
  - Economic Trends (monthly)
  - Financial Statistics
  - British Business
  - Transport Statistics (annual), National Travel Survey
  - Family Income & Expenditure Survey (annual)
    (Office of Population Census and Surveys)
  - Social Trends
  - United Kingdom Balance of Payments
  - United Kingdom National Accounts

Abstracts and indexes

Abstracts contain short summaries of published articles. Indexes present listings of articles and information sources.

- **Anbar management publications.** Anbar appears in five separate editions, eight times per year:
  1 Accounting and data processing abstracts
  2 Management services and production abstracts
  3 Marketing and distribution abstracts
  4 Personnel and training
  5 Top management abstracts
- Business Periodicals Index (monthly): mostly U.S. coverage, some UK journal sources, good on financial and business matters.
- Economics titles/abstracts (fortnightly) - scope covers economics, business, trade, markets
- Research Index: 2-week intervals, quarterly volumes; academic, management periodical and business press sources (company and industry sections).

- SCIMP (Selective Co-operative Index of Management Periodicals), consortium production between thirteen European Business Schools Broad coverage of business, management and market reporting and sources, strong European coverage.
- Times Index (including Sunday Times and supplements)
- Financial Times Index – monthly, in 3 sections: companies, subject, people.
- British Humanities Index – broader academic, current social and political sources.
- Marketing Surveys Index – published in association with Chartered Institute of Marketing.
- Contents Pages in Management (publ. Manchester Business School)
- McCarthy Information Services: company and subject indexes, card data summaries.

Directories, guides, yearbooks

- Kompass Register of British Industry and Commerce, published in 3 sections company information; product information; financial data.
- Key Business Enterprises (Dun and Bradsteet) – top 20 000 British companies profiled.
- Kelly's Business Directory – over 80 000 companies listed by sector and location.
- ASLIB Directory of Information Sources in the UK.
- Advertisers Annual
- Croner's Reference Books for Business
- BSI Buyers' Guide - British Standards information sources.
- Directory of British Associations
- Directory of Directors
- European Directory
- Europa Yearbook
- Europa Publications Ltd
- Sell's Directory of Products & Services
- Stock Exchange Official Yearbook
- Trade Associations and Professional Bodies of the UK
- UN Statistical Yearbook
- Who Owns Whom
- Willings Press Guide
- Europe's 15 000 Largest
- Major Companies of Europe 1989-90
- ICC Directory of UK Stockbroker Reports
- Times 1000

Useful addresses

Association of British Directory Publishers
17 Kingsway
LONDON WC2B 6UN

British Direct Marketing Assoc.
Grosvenor Gardens House
Grosvenor Gardens
LONDON SW1W 0BS

British Export Houses Assoc.
16 Dartmouth Street
LONDON SW1H 9BL

British Institute of Management
Management House
Parker Street
LONDON WC2B 5PT

British Overseas Trade Board
Dept of Trade & Industry
1 Victoria Street
LONDON SW1H 0ET

British Standards Institution
2 Park Street
LONDON W1A 2BS

British Statistics Office
Cardiff Road
Newport
GWENT NP9 1XG

Central Office of Information
Hercules Road
LONDON SE1 7DU

Chartered Institute of Marketing
Moor Hall
Cookham
Maidenhead
BERKS SL6 9QH

Companies Registration Office
Companies House
Crown Way
Maindy
Cardiff CF4 3UZ

Confederation of British Industry
Centre Point
103 New Oxford Street
LONDON WC1A 1DU

Current British Directories
CBD Research Ltd
154 High Street
Beckenham
KENT BR3 1EA

Dept of Trade and Industry
Ashdown House
123 Victoria Street
LONDON SW1E 6RB

Institute of Export
64 Clifton Street
LONDON EC2A 4HB

International Chamber of Commerce
Centre Point
103 New Oxford Street
LONDON WC1A 1QB

INDEX